The Palestinian Peasant Economy under the Mandate

HARVARD MIDDLE EASTERN MONOGRAPHS

XXXVII

The Palestinian Peasant Economy under the Mandate

A Story of Colonial Bungling

Amos Nadan

DISTRIBUTED FOR THE
CENTER FOR MIDDLE EASTERN STUDIES
OF HARVARD UNIVERSITY BY
HARVARD UNIVERSITY PRESS
CAMBRIDGE, MASSACHUSETTS
LONDON, ENGLAND

The photo of a fallāḥ plowing in a field was taken by Zev Vilnay in 1930 next to the El Midya village in Ramle Sub District (photo number 631, Zev Vilnay's collection, Yad Izhak Ben-Zvi, Jerusalem).

ISBN 0-932885-31-4
Library of Congress Catalog Number 2005931376
Printed in the United States of America

Contents

List of Tables

List of Figures

List of Maps and Documents

Acknowledgments

This book is based on my Ph.D. thesis on *The Arab Rural Economy in Mandate Palestine, 1921–1947: Peasants under Colonial Rule* (2002) written at the Department of Economic History of the London School of Economics and Political Science (LSE). I am grateful to my two dedicated supervisors, both from the LSE—Gareth Austin and Kirsten Schulze—for their intellect, open-mindedness, broad knowledge, and personal kindness. They are, indeed, superb supervisors.

I am indebted to the Department of Economic History for being a home for me over a period of four years and for its generous financial assistance. I also wish to thank Ian Karten, the AVI fellowship, and the Anglo-Jewish Association for their generous financial support during my Ph.D. studies, as well as the School of History and the Department of Middle Eastern and African History at Tel Aviv University for the joint postdoctoral fellowship they granted me in 2002 and for a subsequent postdoctoral Young Truman fellowship at the Harry S. Truman Research Institute for the Advancement of Peace at the Hebrew University of Jerusalem.

I appreciated the assistance of many librarians and archivists in Britain and Israel. The Barclays Archives in Manchester deserve special recognition for their excellent facilities and for the help of their archivists, Jessie Campbell and Josephine Horner, in the search for relevant documents.

I would like to thank my interviewees, who added another important dimension to this study, for their hospitality and time. Mohammed Mar'i from Mashhad deserves special thanks for his helpfulness in introducing me to interviewees and providing access to some private papers from the Mandate period.

This book is dedicated to my wife, Noga (in translation, Venus), for bringing so much light and love to my life. I also wish to thank our loving parents, Nehemia (of blessed memory) and Tirtza Levtzion and Eli and Margalit Nadan (may they live long).

Amos Nadan

Note on Transliteration

Words transliterated from Arabic follow the version used in the *International Journal of Middle East Studies;* however, *ta marbūtah* appears as *ah* (unlike the usual method in IJMES). Transliteration of Hebrew vowels is according to pronunciation (a, o, e, i, u), while the consonants follow the Arabic form (e.g., ש is the same as ش), apart from the following: ב = *v*, ו = 7, ג = *g*, פּ = *p*, צ = *z*. Some names that are often transliterated in different ways into English are given in the commonly used form (e.g. *Al Difa* newspaper and not *al-difā*ʻ).

Principal Currencies and Measurements

1 Palestinian pound (£P)	=	1 British pound (£) or 1,000 mils (thousandth of £P) Until 31 March 1928, the Egyptian pound (£E) was a legal tender in Palestine (and was about 2.5 percent higher than the British pound). In this book, all £E prices were converted to £P (including mils where applicable)
1 (metric) dunum/dunam	=	1,000 square meters or approximately $^1/_4$ acre Prior to 1928 the unit measure for rural land in Palestine was the Turkish dunum (0.9133 dunum). All Turkish dunums are converted here to metric dunums
1 meter	=	100 centimeters or approximately 39.4 inches
1 kilometer	=	1,000 meters or approximately 0.62 miles

1 kilogram	= Approximately 2.205 lbs (weight)
1 (metric) ton	= 1,000 kilograms

Introduction

For nearly four hundred years, the land of Palestine was a backwater of the Ottoman empire, characterized by villages and a traditional peasant economy. In 1917 and 1918, the country was conquered by the British army. At the end of World War I, the Treaty of Versailles marked the beginning of a new era in the Middle East, and under the Mandate form of government inspired by U.S. President Woodrow Wilson, which was intended to be an enlightened interim stage between colonial rule and future independence, Britain was awarded control of Palestine. In 1920, the British military administration was replaced by the civil administration of the new Mandatory government. Nearly three decades later, in 1948, British rule ended with Israel's declaration of independence, endorsed by the League of Nations.

In the 1880s, Jewish settlers began to immigrate, inspired by the Zionist dream and/or fleeing persecution, and by the time the country was conquered by British troops, their numbers were increasing. In 1917, the Balfour Declaration, which "favour[ed] the establishment of a National Home for the Jewish people,"[1] had opened the way for a massive influx of Jews into the country. This was to transform its ethnic[2] and economic structures from being part of a relatively large and unified Ottoman economy into a small economy with two subordinate economies, Arab and Jewish, which had limited interactions.[3] These changes gave rise to tensions and recurrent armed confrontations, in which both Arabs (especially from rural areas), Jews, and British troops took an active part (discussed below).

It was also a period of socioeconomic transition, especially during World War II, as Arab migrants moved from rural to urban centers, and their economic and social ties with extended families in the villages became more remote.[4] At the same time, there were growing inequalities within Arab society.[5] Inescapably, the story of the Arab rural economy in Mandate Palestine has to be studied within the multifaceted context of the economic and noneconomic factors influencing it.

THE LITERATURE: ACHIEVEMENTS AND GAPS

Studies of the history of the Arabs in Mandate Palestine cover various angles, particularly the national and political. Many refer only incidentally to economic aspects, and this applies to works written during the Mandate period[6] as well as since.[7] Economic research into the Arab economy is sparse, especially when the subject is the rural economy.

Still, some studies have made valuable contributions to our knowledge of the Arab rural economy. An early one is that of Sa'id Himadeh and his colleagues from the American University of Beirut, published in 1938. It deals with markets, natural resources, land tenure, agriculture, transportation, trade, and the banking and fiscal systems. This mainly descriptive account, however, stops in 1938, is based largely on certain government publications, and hence focuses on formal institutions and markets.[8] Another significant contribution was made by Moḥamad Yūnīs al-ḥusayni in his 1946 book on the socioeconomic development of the Arabs in Palestine. While most of his sources were government publications, he nevertheless provides important insights into the economy of the *fallāḥīn* (Arab agriculturists, the majority of whom were peasants; sing. *fallāḥ*) from his direct interaction with some *fallāḥīn* and Bedouins. This enabled him to discuss previously unexplored aspects of the village custom of inheritance, the *mushā'* (communal land) arrangements, and the beliefs regarding cycles of rain and rainless years.[9] These, together with books by Reverend C. T. Wilson and Elihu Grant (both semianthropological works about the *fallāḥīn* economy),[10] examine the *fallāḥīn* economy from within.

Since the Mandate, three studies have dealt with long-term trends in the Arab economy. Kenneth Stein's 1987 article on Palestine's rural economy was important in setting out the external factors that influenced its evolution up to 1939; among these were government policies, natural occurrences (such as plagues), and man-made events.[11] In contrast, the effect of Charles Kamen's book in 1991 was to widen the historiographic debate. As discussed below, it lacks firm evidence, often fails to use available material, and does not have even one source in Arabic.[12] Finally, Jacob Metzer and Oded Kaplan's work, also published in 1991, on the Arab and Jewish economies during the Mandate period, as well as the findings separately discussed by Metzer in *The Divided Economy of Mandatory Palestine* in 1998, added to the understanding of macroeconomic trends.[13] These are the most detailed studies in the area of macroeconomic characteristics and trends in the Arab rural sector. While Metzer and Kaplan claim an overall macroeconomic improvement per capita until 1939, the macro- and microeconomic analysis of Stein (although less detailed than Metzer and Kaplan's) implies stagnation. As discussed below, there is much uncertainty in Metzer and Kaplan's studies with regard to macroeconomic characteristics and trends. The present book proposes a different view altogether.

In several studies, Metzer demonstrates that the government of Palestine repeatedly transferred capital originating in the Jewish economy into the Arab sector.[14] How, then, did these transfers help to shape the Arab rural economy? This is another question that I seek to answer.

Other post-Mandate works on the Arab rural economy have tended to focus on specific aspects. Rachelle Taqqu studied internal migration by Arab villagers in the 1940s.[15] Ylana Miller looked at the interaction of formal rural associations and the *mukhtārs* (village heads) in cooperating with the government.[16] Ya'akov Firestone examined the practice of sharecropping and some changes in the institution of *mushā'* (elaborated below) in two Palestinian villages.[17] The work of the geographer-historian, Shukrī 'Araf, added to Firestone's study as he explored some aspects of land practices in Arab villages both in Mandate Palestine and Israel.[18] Rosa El-Eini published several articles in *Middle Eastern Studies* in 1997 to 1998 on banks and credit and on fiscal and agricultural policies.[19] Her research was the most detailed carried out at that time on British policies; however, it is concerned mainly with what the British intended to achieve and therefore leaves open many questions, notably in regard to the extent to which policies were implemented, as well as their effects. Finally, the anthropologist Rosemary Sayigh interviewed former *fallāḥīn* who found refuge in Beirut following the war of 1948. Her interviews give a nongovernmental perspective on *fallāḥīn* life, including economic activities.[20]

The case of the Arab economy in Palestine is rather unusual. It is the story of an economy with an ever-shrinking territory because of Jewish land purchase. The study of Arab ownership of lands and Jewish land purchase is therefore crucial for an understanding of the Arab rural economy. The most extensive work on this is Stein's *The Land Question in Palestine 1917–1939;*[21] significant studies since the mid-1990s are by Mohammad al-ḥizmāwī on land property in Palestine 1918 to 1948[22] and by Warwick Tyler on state lands in Mandate Palestine 1920 to 1948.[23]

An area of research that has developed more recently is into the socioeconomic aspects of the uprising. Stein compared the Arab Revolt of 1936 to 1939 with the Intifada that began in 1987.[24] Using Stein's and other materials, Issa Khalaf analyzed what he calls "the effect of the socioeconomic change on Arab social collapse" during the 1940s.[25] In an essay published in 2003, I examined the economic and social dimensions of the Arab Revolt, the Intifada of 1987, and the Al-Aqsa Intifada of 2000.[26] These studies, as well as other materials, are helpful in examining the effect of the Arab Revolt, in particular, and the violence, in general, on the *fallāḥīn* economy.

Assisted by these and other works, as well as official publications, unpublished materials, and a series of interviews, my aim is to answer the following questions: What was the structure of the Arab rural economy under the British Mandate? How much did it change during the period, and why? The British military regime, for which information is scarce, is excluded from the discussion, as is the period after the departure of the British from the country. Consequently, the years selected are those from 1921 to 1947 inclusive.

PRIMARY SOURCES

The government of Palestine did not consistently collect data on the economic conditions of Arabs in rural areas, yet from time to time it commissioned studies on particular aspects. The most intensive period of investigation followed the 1929 uprising, when the government sought to identify the rural roots of the unrest. Over the next two years, four commissions were appointed to investigate conditions in the Arab rural economy. They became known by the names of their chairmen: Johnson and Crosbie, Hope Simpson, French, and Strickland.[27] At that time, additional material was provided by the census of 1931.[28]

There was also a limited investigation in 1936 of the distribution of landholdings in 322 Arab villages. This gives a restricted view of Arab rural landholding at that time, as it included Jewish lands in many of the villages.[29] Another limited study was made in 1944, in which only five unnamed villages were studied. Its claim that "the villages selected fairly represented the typical cereal-growing Arab villages . . . throughout the country"[30] should be treated with skepticism. Indeed, not a single reason is offered in support of this. Finally, because the raw materials (such as the questionnaires) are not available for any of these studies,[31] the use of these inquiries for economic history research is limited.

The government often collected other statistics, such as estimates of crops and yields. These usually represented the whole country, without subdivisions between the Jewish settler community and the Arab community. It is doubtful that the government could have had precise information on crops and yields. In the Johnson-Crosbie report, for example, estimates from different government investigations of the same year were presented. The gap between the lowest and the highest estimates was huge. The highest figure for wheat production was 79 percent more than the lowest, 100 percent in the case of dura, 126 percent in the case of qatani (pulse), 139 percent in the case of barley, and no less than 333 percent in the case of sesame.[32] The controversy about yield figures goes beyond this, as the first comprehensive survey of cultivated land was not undertaken until 1935, for the purposes of the rural property tax.[33]

It should also be recognized that although it was the only sizable and in-depth investigation, covering 104 Arab villages, the Johnson-Crosbie report of 1930 could not provide a comprehensive view of income and expenditure on *fallāḥīn* farms. The investigators suspected that the villagers, hoping to get support from the government or at least to pay less tax, gave false information to appear poorer than they actually were. They therefore revised the declared information, and the extent of the revisions indicates their suspicions. They added 67.5 percent to the declared incomes and subtracted 26.6 percent from the declared expenditures (see Table I.1). The credibility of such extensive revisions is so questionable that the revised estimates may be as unreliable as the returns. Unfortunately, the original data from that inquiry, with more detailed information such as the completed questionnaires, was not deposited in the Israel State Archives, so that the official published report remains the only source. Hence, it seems that the Johnson-Crosbie report sheds hardly any light on income and expenditure in farms and villages, although it does provide other important data that are used elsewhere in the present study.

Statistics for the number of nomads are the least accurate. In

Table I.1 Gross Income and Expenditure of 104 Palestinian Villages, 1930 (according to the Johnson-Crosbie Report; all Palestine except Beersheba subdistrict)

Category	Declared in the Villages, £P	Report Estimates, £P	Disputed sum between Estimates to Declared, £P
A. Incomes			
Income from agriculture (cultivation and livestock breeding)	431,443	799,232	367,789
Other incomes (56% labor outside the village, 32% transport outside the village, 12% other)	113,438	113,438	0
Balance of incomes	544,881	912,670	367,789
B. Expenditures			
Cost of production (including expense of cultivation and livestock breeding, hiring labor, transport outside the village, and other village sources)	318,181	205,850	112,331
Subsistence from food produced in the village	400,254	358,122	42,132
Other requirements for living and clothing	400,254	168,528	231,726
Share of communal expenses	21,066	21,066	0
Taxes (for 1930)	81,449	81,449	0
Rent paid (only outside each village)	62,897	62,897	0
Interest on debt averaging £P27 per family at the rate of £ 8 annually per family	168,528	168,528	0
Balance of expenditure	1,452,629	1,066,440	386,189
C. Net Incomes			
Profits	−907,748	−153,770	753,978

Source: Government of Palestine, *Report of a Committee on the Economic Condition of Agriculturists* (Johnson-Crosbie), pp 2–27.

the 1922 census, their number was simply guessed. The 1931 census returns are the best for the Mandate period, but they were still far from accurate about the nomads, as they were based on a combination of counts and the opinions of those with close knowledge of each tribe. Returns from later years, when no census was taken, are even more doubtful because of lack of nomad cooperation.[34] Nevertheless, the proportion of nomads was small. The 1931 census suggests that they accounted for 7.2 percent of the total non-Jewish population (10 percent of the rural and nomadic non-Jewish population). In practice, however, it was smaller, since settled Bedouins who also cultivated lands (i.e., *fallāḥīn*) were counted as nomads.[35]

Nomad lands in the southern district were not surveyed accurately.[36] In addition, nomads refused information about their livestock, causing a continued gap in data.[37] Where segregation of agricultural data is possible, the nomads' share in the product should be borne in mind, as well as the doubtful accuracy of the statistics about them and their property.

Government and other sources are particularly deficient on the structure of the Arab export-oriented citrus farms. There is not a single known government investigation, nor is there extensive material on these farms from other sources, apart from regularly published data on exported crops. Consequently, this book does not deal directly with Arab citrus farms. Nevertheless, the citrus groves, which were located entirely in the narrow strip of the coastal plain, made up only a small minority of all farms. According to the survey of 1931, a mere 2 percent of all head-of-family Arab farmers were engaged in citrus farming as their main occupation. The total area of the Arab-owned citrus farms increased from around 90,000 dunums in 1930 to 123,000 dunums in 1945[38] (a rise of about 37 percent), indicating that citrus farming remained an unusual occupation for Arab farmers.[39] Because the picking of the citrus fruit created a peak in demand for temporary labor, citrus farms will figure in this study as an additional source of income for *fallāḥīn* outside their own farms. In addition, some of the sparse information about citrus farms (e.g., the wages paid) helps us to explore related issues.

Illiteracy rates were high in Arab rural society.[40] According to the 1931 census, about 21.3 percent of the Moslem rural population were literate, and according to the survey of five villages mentioned above, this stood at 29.1 percent by 1944. However, the definition of a literate person was very broad: a person who could "read out a few lines from a newspaper" and/or "all children attending school and having completed one year were treated as able to read and write."[41] Not surprisingly, there is not a single known memoir written by a *fallāḥ*. The operational implication for research is that it is necessary to find other kinds of written material that deal with interactions with *fallāḥīn*, such as court records,[42] as well as collecting oral evidence.

SOME THEORETICAL APPROACHES

Under Mandate Palestine, the Arab rural economy was primarily a peasant economy. The vast majority of Palestinian Arab agriculturists were peasants engaged in part-subsistence and part-surplus agriculture.[43] A common view during the Mandate period, held by British administrators and some Zionist writers, was that the *fallāḥīn* and their institutions were "irrational." The broader position was that the peasants' culture or mental habits were the source of a conservative inability to make economic-related judgments and to adapt to change; in less politically correct language, the *fallāḥīn* were too ignorant to manage their own farms wisely. Their supposed incompetence and lack of economic sense was thought to be highlighted by their failure to introduce certain improvements that were relatively common in the Jewish sector.

This presumption of irrationality was, I argue throughout, inappropriate to the specific case of the *fallāḥīn* economy, as well as to peasant economies in general. In reality, the differences between the two sectors in Palestine were related primarily to the comparatively lower availability of capital and lower cost of labor in the Arab sector. Further, the term *irrational* was used by its proponents as a substitute for *illogical* and not to signify poor maximization that might have occurred for other reasons, such as James Scott's safety-first approach.[44]

One might ask why such a misleading concept is important for this study. This paradigm greatly influenced British policies. Convinced that "the foremost need of the [Arab] agricultural industry is rationalisation,"[45] the British put a great deal of effort into "rationalizing" the *fallāḥīn* and their institutions, in a mode similar to that suggested by Karl Marx in his discussion of capitalist colonialism (see below).[46] A major impetus for such activity was the government's conclusion that Arab rural discontent in 1929 was to some extent the result of economic distress in rural areas; therefore, the government began to spend a considerable amount of money on rationalization projects aimed at improving the economic conditions of the *fallāḥīn*.

Mostly because of these innovations, the British claimed a great improvement in the *fallāḥīn* economy. Such an assessment is doubtful, particularly because of insufficient data to support it. For example, the British argued that their land reform had enabled substantial investment to be put into land, yet no investigation of patterns of investment before and after the reform was ever carried out. In the case of credit reform, the British also claimed significant success, since "the practice of borrowing from moneylenders is no longer followed by the majority,"[47] yet the same source admitted that "non-Arab bankers held that [Arab] indebtedness to moneylenders and merchants is now negligible; while Arab bankers thought it still to be considerable."[48] Thus, there is a need to investigate the extent to which the British succeeded in improving the economic conditions of the *fallāḥīn* and how much their (in my view, erroneous) perception of irrationality affected the outcome. Both lines of inquiry are undertaken in the present book.

Karl Marx, when discussing with the case of India but making general observations, argued that capitalist colonial penetration would force a country into a European-style development. This would occur because colonial rule would destroy native institutions "by breaking up the native communities, by uprooting the native industry, and by levelling all that was great and elevated in the native society."[49] At the same time, the ruling colonial power would change the infrastructure of the country by developing lines of communication (including transport, such as trains), or other projects such as irrigation.[50] These projects would bring about massive industrialization by "rapid improvement of instruments of production [and] by the immensely facilitated means of communication."[51] Marx predicted that in these countries the social relations of production would change from a non-European style of "primitive agriculture," which he called precapitalist, into a capitalist one. This process would come about not because of individual choices or motivation but as a consequence of government action.[52] On similar lines, it can be argued that the general approach of the British toward the *fallāḥīn* in the Mandate period fits such a paradigm. For reasons that seemed valid to them at the time, the British engaged in policies of eliminating indigenous institutions and creating Western-style ones instead, as envisaged by Marx.

A New Institutionalist (rational-choice) political economy may be defined as the extension of the economizing logic of market economics. It thus tries to explain the nonmarket institutions that inevitably surround market activity. In his theory of institutional change, Douglass North defines institutions as "the rules of the game in a society or, more formally, the humanly devised constraints that shape human interaction."[53] Consequently, "institutions structure incentives in human exchange, whether political, social or economic."[54] Institutions, he maintains, are path-dependent (shaped by past choices that constrain further ones). He tends to give greater weight to changes in economic outcome that are the result of institutional change than to changes of institutions due to economic incentives. This seems to be related to his tendency to view institutions as often obstructing better economic results.[55]

While North emphasizes the case of inefficient institutions

that are locked in a path-dependent mode and hence negatively influence economic performance, the theory of induced institutional innovation emphasizes the unlocked mode of institutions and the way in which economic factors change an institution so that it then works efficiently. It suggests that changes in the demand for institutional innovation are induced by changes in relative factor scarcities, reflecting informally, if not formally, shifts in relative resource endowments. For example, if a population increases, the value of land increases relative to that of labor, and as a result land-tenure systems are expected to change, informally if not formally. In this case, property rights in land become more sharply defined and more cheaply enforced.[56] The concept of *fallāḥīn* irrationality and the theories of Marx, of North, and of "induced institutional innovation" are discussed in several places in this study. Other theories are examined in the sections to which they are relevant.

RESEARCH STRATEGY, SOME MAIN ARGUMENTS, AND ETHICS

The approach taken is to combine qualitative and quantitative evidence and primary and secondary material in the three official languages used under the Mandate. Various archives provide government and nongovernment information at both macro and micro levels. The main government sources used were the Israel State Archives, the Public Records Office (London), and the Rhodes House Archive (Oxford). For example, materials collected in the Israel State Archives are from the Chief Officers' Collection, as well as from the collections of different departments and subdistricts and materials from the Supreme Moslem Council. They include strategies and policies and information about how these were implemented. Petitions and other correspondence from different villages and villagers provide more microeconomic insights, as do some registers of loans and lands. Important material was found in the Barclays Bank Archives in Manchester on the economic conditions of the *fallāḥīn* and the credit system in Palestine. Other sources consulted were the Central Zionist Archives in Jerusalem, the *Hagana* (pre-state Zionist militia) Archives in Tel Aviv, and the Palestine Exploration Fund Archives in London.

However many written materials are available, this kind of research cannot be successfully accomplished without oral accounts. I therefore interviewed a number of individuals who were part of Arab rural society before 1948 or who were involved in the Arab rural economy in the Mandate period. They were former *fallāḥīn,* merchants who usually operated as moneylenders, landowners of big and small estates, *mukhtār*s, and Jews who were directly or indirectly involved with the Arab rural economy.

My interviewees were not necessarily a representative sample of the populations they came from. They were among the fortunate people who lived to tell the tale. To achieve openness in interviews, I built up mutual confidence by being accompanied and introduced in most cases by a common friend or friends. Because of this procedure, most of the interviews were in the Galilee area, where I lived for a long period, yet the subjects covered were extensive.

No interview was similar to another. It was necessary to keep these to a reasonable length and to concentrate on specific areas, and interviewees had had different experiences and highlighted aspects that they wished to talk about (not all relating to this study). There was thus a sense of compromise in what was discussed.

From the beginning, the idea was not to conduct another survey but rather to hear the voices of the *fallāḥīn* and of others who tended not to write (as mentioned, fully literate *fallāḥīn* were rare) and to reduce the possibility of producing an account that suffered from a problem highlighted by Edward Said—that "the present crisis dramatises the disparity between texts and reality."[57] I therefore sought to learn directly from the interviewees about their perceptions, definitions, and judgments. To avoid preconceptions, I asked open-ended questions, such as "What were the options for *fallāḥīn* wishing to obtain loans?" and "What did *mushā'* mean?" Finally, interviews created an opportunity to hear—without fear, in today's changed political environment—about activities that were illegal under the British Mandate, especially the practice of high-interest moneylending.

Aided by new evidence, I argue that the study of the economic history of the *fallāḥīn* has been neglected and misunderstood and that the gaps in much of the existing literature are primarily a function of insufficient and inaccurate data, which have also led some scholars to rely too heavily on theoretical and political assumptions instead of on evidence.

Careful use of various kinds of data on net Arab agricultural product gives an approximate representation of the Arab sector at that time and demonstrates that the picture presented by Metzer and Kaplan of high and sustained growth during the years 1922 to 1939 is incorrect. Rather, the story is one of little or no growth, and when combined with the continued and fairly high demographic growth at that time, a pattern of ongoing deterioration per capita becomes apparent. This result is derived from a detailed reconsideration of Metzer and Kaplan's data, from the use of alternative direct data on output, and from indirect quantitative and qualitative data, most of which were not used in earlier studies.

The 1940s, however, were a different story. The government figures on net Arab agricultural product are much more accurate and reliable, showing that the narrative of high and sustained growth during this period can be supported. It is a case of growth that occurred chiefly because of the increase in relative prices of agricultural foodstuffs and not as a result of significant agricultural development. This was due to the changed security situation during World War II (the constraints on shipping and the development of Palestine into a large military base), which led to an increase in demand for agricultural foodstuffs. At the same time the income for *fallāḥīn* from farm and nonfarm employment increased significantly, especially through employment in the military. This brought about a decrease in *fallāḥīn* unemployment and underemployment and a concomitant increase in real wages for low-skilled laborers, who included the *fallāḥīn.*

The primary mission of the British in Palestine was to hold and administer the country. After the Disturbances of 1929, the Mandatory government believed that Arab rural-urban migration should be discouraged to reduce discontent. The main tool for achieving this was to improve economic conditions in the Arab villages. Thus, the government tried to help the *fallāḥīn* by reducing taxation and by supplying some agricultural services. But the misguided British paradigm of *fallāḥīn* irrationality drove the British to engage in inappropriate, Marxist-style reforms. The investigation of these is unique to the present study, and the findings show clearly that British interventions were in general characterized by high expenditures with very limited returns. If the government had spent more on agricultural services and especially on agricultural infrastructure (primarily, irrigation programs), then the investment in the *fallāḥīn* economy might have delivered significant prosperity. Other conclusions, especially on the structure of the *fallāḥīn* economy and the changes that occurred, are also presented.

The book is divided into three parts. Part 1 deals with the political setting during the Mandate period and its influence on the rural economy. Part 2 examines trends in the Arab rural economy and the patterns of investment, specialization, and produce in Arab agriculture that are the basis for discussing growth, income, and development in this sector. Part 3 is a micro-study of the *fallāḥīn* economy and of the ways in which it was affected by the various reforms and services introduced by the British.

Finally, in view of the continued tensions, those who study Mandate Palestine are usually categorized as pro-Arab, pro-Zionist, or pro-British or from the left/right/center, and so forth. I hope that readers will consider my analysis in the light of the actual evidence, as this is what guided me during the research, and not any political agenda. Indeed, the story of this study began with a dissertation for my master of science degree in economic history at the London School of Economics and Political

Science. At that time, based largely on colonial accounts, I had concluded that as a result of government transfer of funds from the Jewish economy to the Arab economy, the structure of the Arab rural economy had been enhanced and significant development had taken place, such as progressively higher income for *fallāḥīn* farms. But after examining much more material of various kinds, I have now reached the opposite conclusion.

NOTES

1. Government of Palestine, *A Survey of Palestine: Prepared in December 1945 and January 1946 for the Information of the Anglo-American Committee of Inquiry* (Jerusalem, 1946), p. 1.
2. About 93,000 Jews lived in the country in 1922, and about 554,000 in 1944, an increase from 11.4 to 32.6 percent of the total population. Government of Palestine, *A Survey of Palestine,* pp. 147–52, with the amendments suggested in Justin McCarthy, *The Population of Palestine: Population History and Statistics of the Late Ottoman Period and the Mandate* (New York, 1990), p. 35.
3. Jacob Metzer, *The Divided Economy of Mandatory Palestine* (Cambridge, 1998).
4. Moḥamad Yūnīs al-ḥusayni, *Al-tatwūr al-'ijtimā'ī fi filasṭīn al-'arabiyyah* (Jerusalem, 1946), pp. 170–74; Issa Khalaf, "The Effect of Socioeconomic Change on Arab Social Collapse in Mandate Palestine," *International Journal of Middle Eastern Studies,* no. 1 (1997), pp. 93–112.
5. As discussed below.
6. For example, Yūsif Haykal, *Al-qaḍīyah al-filasṭīniyah: taḥlīl wa-naqd* (Jaffa, 1937); David Horowitz and Rita Hindan, *Economic Survey of Palestine* (Tel Aviv, 1938). Although the latter book deals with the economic issues of Mandate Palestine, it lays emphasis on the Jewish economy and considers the Arab one only very briefly on pp. 203–14.
7. For example, Arieh Avneri, *The Claim of Dispossession: Jewish Land Settlement and the Arabs, 1878–1948* (Tel Aviv, 1980); Charles S. Kamen, *Little Common Ground: Arab Agriculture and Jewish Settlement in Palestine, 1920–1948* (Pittsburgh, 1991);

Walied Khalidi (ed.), *From Haven to Conquest: Readings in Zionism and the Palestine Problem until 1948* (Washington, DC, 1987).

8. Sa'id B. Himadeh (ed.), *Economic Organisation in Palestine* (Beirut, 1938).
9. Al-ḥusayni, *Al-tatwūr al-'ijtimā'ī fi filasṭīn al-'arabiyyah.*
10. Charles Thomas Wilson, *Peasant Life in the Holy Land* (London, 1906); Elihu Grant, *The People of Palestine* (Philadelphia, 1921, reprinted 1976).
11. Kenneth W. Stein, "Palestine's Rural Economy, 1917–1939," *Studies in Zionism,* 8, no. 1 (Spring 1987), pp. 25–49. See also his essay in Hebrew, "Hitpatḥuyot bakalkalah hakafrit ha'aravit be'erez yishrael (1917–1939) vemashma'uteyhen haḥevratiyot vehapolitiyot," *Qathedra,* 41 (October 1986), pp. 133–54.
12. Kamen, *Little Common Ground.*
13. Jacob Metzer and Oded Kaplan, *Mesheq yehudi 7e-mesheq 'aravi* (Jerusalem, 1991); Metzer, *The Divided Economy.*
14. Especially in his "Fiscal Incidence and Resource Transfer between Jews and Arabs in Mandatory Palestine," *Research in Economic History,* no. 7 (1982), pp. 87–132.
15. Rachelle Taqqu, "Internal Labor Migration and the Arab Village Community under the Mandate," Joel S. Migdal (ed.), *Palestinian Society and Politics* (Princeton, NJ, 1980), pp. 261–85.
16. The *mukhtār* was a village member appointed as the head of the village. In some villages there was more than one *mukhtār.* Ylana N. Miller, *Government and Society in Rural Palestine, 1920–1948* (Austin, TX, 1985).
17. Ya'akov Firestone, "Cash-Sharing Economics in Mandatory Palestine," *Middle Eastern Studies,* 11, no. 1 (1975), pp. 3–23 and no. 2. pp. 175–94; Ya'akov Firestone, "The Land-Equalizing *Mushā'* Village: A Reassessment," Gad G. Gilbar (ed.), *Ottoman Palestine, 1800–1914* (London, 1990). These papers are considered in the discussion on land tenure in Chapters 4 and 6.
18. Shukrī 'Araf, *Al-qaryah al-'arabiyyah al- filasṭīniyah: mabnī wa-'isti'imālāt 'arāḍī* (Tarshīḥā, 1996).
19. Rosa I. M. El-Eini, "Rural Indebtedness and Agricultural Credit Supplies in Palestine in the 1930s," *Middle Eastern Studies,* 33, no. 2 (1997), pp. 313–37; "Government Fiscal Policy in Mandatory Palestine," *Middle Eastern Studies,* 33, no. 3 (1997), pp. 570–96.

20. Rosemary Sayigh, *Palestinians: From Peasants to Revolutionaries* (London, 1979).
21. Kenneth W. Stein, *The Land Question in Palestine, 1917–1939* (London, 2nd ed., 1985).
22. Mohammad al-ḥizmāwī, *Milkiyah al-arāḍī fī filasṭīn 1918–1948* (Acre, 1998)
23. Warwick P. N. Tyler, *State Lands and Rural Development in Mandatory Palestine, 1920–1948* (Brighton, 2001).
24. Kenneth W. Stein, "The Intifada and the 1936–1939 Uprising: A Comparison," *Journal of Palestine Studies,* 19, no. 4, issue 76 (1990), pp. 65–85.
25. Khalaf, "The Effect of Socioeconomic Change," pp. 93–112.
26. Amos Nadan, "From the Arab Revolt to al-Aqsa Intifada: The Economic and Social Dimensions," Tamar Yegnes (ed.), *From Intifada to War: Milestones in the Palestinian National Experience,* in Hebrew (Tel Aviv, 2003), pp. 53–85.
27. Government of Palestine, *Report of a Committee on the Economic Condition of Agriculturists* (Johnson-Crosbie); Government of Palestine, *Report by Mr. C. F. Strickland of the Indian Civil Service on the Possibility of Introducing a System of Agricultural Cooperation in Palestine* (Jerusalem, 1930); Great Britain, Colonial Office, *Report on Immigration, Land Settlement* and *Development, by Sir John Hope Simpson* (London, 1930); Government of Palestine, Palestine Development Department, *Agricultural Development and Land Settlement in Palestine (First and Supplementary Reports), by Lewis French, Director of Development* (Jerusalem, 1931).
28. Government of Palestine, *Census of Palestine 1931: Report by E. Mills, Assistant Chief Secretary* (Alexandria, 1933), 2 vols.
29. Government of Palestine, *A Survey of Palestine,* Part III, "for official use only," p. 1197.
30. Government of Palestine, Department of Statistics, *Survey of Social and Economic Conditions in Arab Villages, 1944: Special Bulletin No. 21* (Jerusalem, 1948), p. 1.
31. These are not available in the Public Records Office (see lists at the PRO) or in the Israel State Archives (information from Mr. Gil'ad Livne, ISA)
32. Government of Palestine, *Report of a Committee on the Economic Condition of Agriculturists* (Johnson-Crosbie), p. 9.

33. Government of Palestine, Department of Statistics, *Village Statistics, 1937* (data collected in 1935: Jerusalem, 1937), p. 5.
34. Justin McCarthy, *The Population of Palestine,* pp. 28–32.
35. Government of Palestine, *Census of Palestine 1931* (1933), vol. 1, p. 4 and vol. 2, pp. 12, 18–19.
36. Government of Palestine, Department of Statistics, *Village Statistics, 1945* (Jerusalem, 1945).
37. Government of Palestine, Department of Statistics, "Enumeration of Livestock," *General Monthly Bulletin of Current Statistics,* August 1943, pp. 237–38. For another example of problems in counting, see Government of Palestine, Department of Statistics, *Statistical Abstract of Palestine, 1944–45* (Jerusalem, 1946), p. 235.
38. Government of Palestine, *A Survey of Palestine,* pp. 339, 724.
39. Government of Palestine, *Census of Palestine 1931* (1933), vol. 1, pp. 283–88 and vol. 2, pp. 289–92.
40. Government of Palestine, *A Survey of Palestine,* p. 639.
41. Government of Palestine, Department of Statistics, *Survey of Social and Economic Conditions in Arab Villages,* pp. 32–33.
42. Many cases from the Civil Courts of Mandate Palestine are available in different publications.
43. These will be discussed in depth in Chapter 4.
44. James C. Scott, *The Moral Economy of the Peasant: Rebellion and Subsistence in Southeast Asia* (London, 1976).
45. Government of Palestine, *Report of a Committee on the Economic Condition of Agriculturists in Palestine and the Fiscal Measures of Government in Relation Thereto, W. J. Johnson, R. E. H. Crosbie et al.* (Jerusalem, 1930), p. 41.
46. Karl Marx, "The Future Results of British Rule in India," *New York Daily Tribune,* 8 August 1853, reprinted in Shlomo Avineri, *Karl Marx on Colonialism and Modernization* (New York, 1969), pp. 132–39.
47. Government of Palestine, *A Survey of Palestine,* p. 367.
48. Ibid., p. 366.
49. Marx, "Future Results."
50. Ibid.
51. Excerpts from Marx's "Manifesto of the Communist Party" of 1848, as mentioned in Avineri, *Karl Marx,* p. 36.

52. Anthony Brewer, *Marxist Theories of Imperialism: A Critical Survey* (London, 1990), p. 11; Avineri, *Karl Marx*, pp. 1–5, 279, 470.
53. Douglass C. North, *Institutions, Institutional Change and Economic Performance* (Cambridge, 1990), p. 3.
54. Ibid., p. 3.
55. Ibid., especially pp. 92–104. See also Douglass C. North, "The New Institutional Economics and Third World Development," John Harriss, Janet Hunter, and Colin M. Lewis (eds.), *The New Institutional Economics and Third World Development* (London, 1995), pp. 17–26.
56. Vernon W. Ruttan and Yujiro Hayami, "Toward a Theory of Induced Institutional Innovation," *Journal of Development Studies,* 20, no. 4 (1984), pp. 203–23.
57. Edward Said, *Orientalism* (London, 1978), p. 109.

The Palestinian Peasant Economy under the Mandate

Part One

THE POLITICAL SETTING AND THE ARAB RURAL ECONOMY

· ONE ·

Politics and the Arab Rural Economy

On 2 November 1917, during the military conquest of the country later defined as Mandate Palestine, the British government, through its Foreign Secretary Arthur Balfour, undertook to support the creation of a Jewish national home in Palestine. By implication, this permitted mass Jewish migration into Palestine:

> His Majesty's Government view with favour the establishment of a National Home for the Jewish people and will use their best endeavours to facilitate the achievement of this object, it being clearly understood that nothing shall be done which may prejudice the civil and religious rights of existing non-Jewish communities in Palestine, or the rights and political status enjoyed by Jews in any other country.[1]

The Balfour Declaration was embedded in the confirmation of the Mandate by the League of Nations (Article 2). Nevertheless, from the early days of the British military administration, the declaration proved unacceptable to the Arabs living in Palestine, who saw it as a threat to their existence.[2] The political consequence of the Balfour Declaration was the development of an ethnonational segregation. The Zionist organizations were led by the Jewish Agency for Palestine, supporting implementation of the Balfour Declaration. The Arab leadership, especially the Supreme Moslem Council and the Arab Higher Committee, opposed the establishment of a Jewish national home and promoted a Palestinian Arab national home.

The way in which the different political aspirations of the British, the Jews, and the Arabs shaped the Arab rural economy is integral to understanding the events that shaped the development of that economy. This chapter therefore examines the three main politically oriented dimensions that had or were intended to have a significant impact on Arab economic life:

- The direct economic influence of Jews on the Arab rural economy (various forms of integration and disintegration are discussed in regard to the labor market, land purchase, and trade),
- The changing pattern of British policies toward the Arab rural economy, and
- The effects of ethnonational conflict on the Arab rural economy, both in the long and short terms.

THE DIRECT ECONOMIC INFLUENCE OF JEWS ON THE ARAB RURAL ECONOMY

The ethnonational segregation between the Jews, who were mainly settlers, and the Arabs, who were mainly indigenous, divided the economy into two quasi subeconomies—a comparatively richer Jewish economy and a poorer Arab one. A clear segregation between the two subeconomies existed in employment, production, and property ownership,[3] yet there was fairly open trade between them. In the following section, the influence of the direct interactions between the Jewish sector and the Arab rural sector is explored.

The Segmented Ethnonational Labor Market

In Mandate Palestine, there was a tendency to employ Arabs in Arab-owned assets and Jews in Jewish-owned ones.[4] Potentially, joint enterprises of Arabs and Jews would have provided jobs for both ethnic groups. In practical terms, however—probably because of mistrust—neither partnerships nor joint ownerships appear to have been common.[5] Consequently, apart from cases of employment by the government and by foreigners,[6] there was a clear ethnonational segmentation in the labor market.

This segregation was especially apparent in wage differences between Arabs and Jews. Jewish labor was much more expensive, in the same occupations, than Arab labor (where free competition exists, wages are expected to be the same).[7] In 1939, for example, the daily wage of low-skilled Arab laborers in Arab citrus plantations was 100 mils for males and 60 for females, whereas Jewish laborers in Jewish plantations received 190 and 165 mils, respectively.[8] This segregation also meant that levels of employment (and hence of unemployment) differed widely in the Jewish and Arab sectors.[9] Another aspect related to wage differentials was the development of labor-intensive agriculture in the Arab sector, unlike the comparatively capital-intensive Jewish agriculture.[10]

As much as segregation existed, however, it was not hermetic, and there were exceptions. The higher wages in the Jewish sector created a syndrome of little incentive for Jews to seek employment in the Arab sector. Some Arabs found employment in Jewish assets, yet even then, they were paid far less than Jews in the same occupation.[11]

One important influence on Arab employment in the Jewish sector (and one that determined the huge wage differential) was the organized Zionist political pressure to employ Jews rather than Arabs. Unlike the settlers of the First *'aliya* (influx of Jewish immigrants) of 1882, the settlers of the Second *'aliya* (1904–14) and later waves of immigrants had to give preference to employing Jews, a policy known in Hebrew as *'avoda 'ivrit* (literally, Jewish employment).[12] The Histadrut (the General Federation of Jewish Labor) developed a near monopoly on the supply of labor to the Jewish sector[13] and imposed effective constraints on the employment of Arabs in Jewish enterprises. Jewish farmers had to give priority to Jewish laborers and to pay them much more than Arab laborers, in line with Histadrut instructions,[14] otherwise the farmers would have felt slighted and would even have been intimidated and physically beaten.[15] The rationale behind the Histadrut's policy was to give Jews jobs and high wages to encourage further Jewish immigration.[16]

Tensions between Arabs and Jews were another influence on Arab employment in the Jewish sector. In the 1930s, these were such that only on very limited occasions was non-Jewish labor "imported" into the Jewish economy,[17] a trend that accelerated particularly during the Arab Revolt of 1936 to 1939.[18]

Not surprisingly, as can be seen in Figure 1.1, the estimated share of Arabs employed in the Jewish sector decreased from the beginning of the Mandate period until 1935 and dropped significantly following the revolt. Still, the steady expansion of the Jewish economy meant that the ratio of Arabs employed in the Jewish sector to the total Arab labor force increased up to 1935 (it later decreased).

The Influence of Jewish Land Purchase on Fallāḥīn Employment

Land was either in Jewish or Arab hand, and was not jointly owned by people from the two sectors.[19] This segregation was especially clear because the most important aim of Jewish land purchase was to establish ownership to enable settlement. The land was regarded by Zionist organizations—the main purchasers—as "Jewish national assets."[20]

Demographic growth in the Arab rural sector was faster than land development. This phenomenon also meant ever-increasing land scarcity in Arab villages (see Table 1.3). The combination of the tendency not to employ Arabs in Jewish enterprises and of intensive Jewish land purchase resulted in a further increase in land shortage and even in unemployment for *fallāḥīn* who previously occupied the purchased lands, as the following colonial documents from 1933 and 1945 indicate:

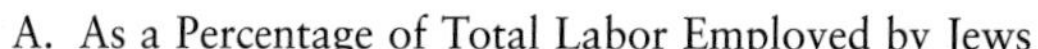
A. As a Percentage of Total Labor Employed by Jews

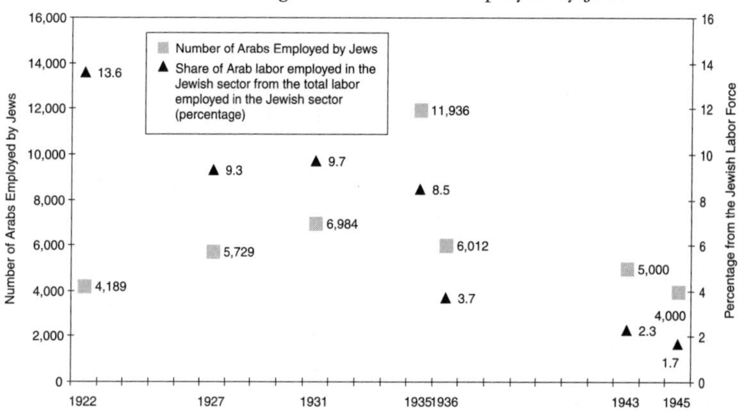

B. As a Percentage of Total Estimated Arab Labor

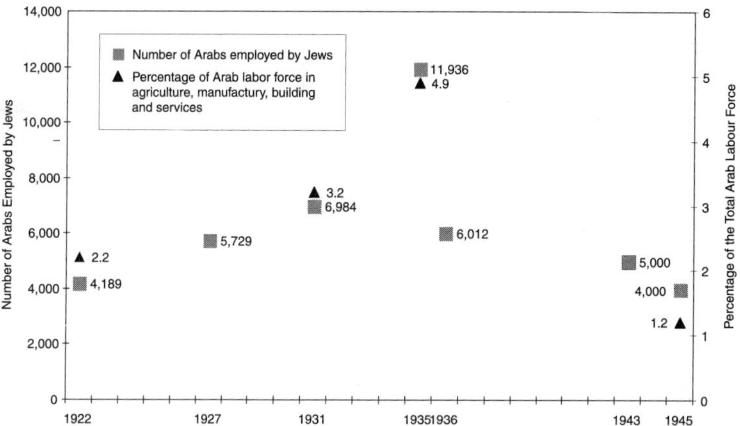

Figure 1.1 Arab Labor in Jewish Employment

Source: Metzer and Kaplan, *Mesheq yehudi 7e-mesheq 'aravi,* pp. 115–16, 149, 153.

Note: Data for the total Arab labor force in 1922 are for 1921.

> In former years when one Arab sold land to another, the landowner changed, but the tenants remained, and those who laboured on the land for a regular or seasonal wage still continued to earn that wage. To some extent this practice was, and is, maintained by some organisations such as the Palestine Jewish Colonisation Association. But the Zionist Policy is different. When the Jewish National Fund purchases land, not only the landlord is changed, but the tenants and all the wage-earning labourer class are compelled to move; for the Zionist policy is not only to acquire ownership, but also to ensure that all the work required on the land shall be carried out by Jews only. . . . The result is the growth of a body of "landless" Arabs, who may be divided into three classes: (a) Tenants; (b) Small owner-occupiers; (c) Labourers.[21] [1933]

> Many of the Arab vendors in the plains [where Jewish land purchase mainly occurred], have now no lands to cultivate—unless they go to the hills; many hill villages had "detached areas" in the plains which were purchased by the Jews, and the previous owners now swell the numbers of those eking out a living from the residue of the hill lands. Perhaps as a natural result, there has in the hills been a widespread attempt to cultivate the lands which were previously regarded as the grazing ground of the village, or which were public "forests" on the neighbouring mountain slope.[22] [1945]

According to some authors, however, the most significant effect of land purchase was not landlessness but more intensive agriculture as a result of investment (mainly in irrigation), with a consequent improvement of *fallāḥīn* farms. It is argued here that this claim is not well-founded.

Although restrictions on land purchase were almost ineffective until the 1940 Land Transfer Regulations,[23] any attempt to restrict sales was viewed by the Jewish Agency as a threat to the ultimate Zionist goal of establishing a national home. Not surprisingly, Jewish propaganda in favor of Jewish land purchase was widespread. According to the Jewish Agency, land sales to

Jews would stimulate the Arab rural economy and enable Arabs to intensify production on their farms, bringing more employment and prosperity to *fallāḥīn*.[24]

Charles Kamen asserts—without firm evidence—that the process outlined in this propaganda (or what he calls the "Arthur Ruppin proposal") actually occurred—namely, that Jewish land purchase significantly benefited the Arab rural economy.[25] According to Ruppin, if an Arab farmer sold part of his land to Jews, he would gain significantly in the long term because he would be able to install irrigation and plant more citrus fruits for export.[26] Thereby, Kamen argues, land purchase was a mechanism for developing *fallāḥīn* farms. He suggests that *fallāḥīn,* with an average plot of about 50 dunums, would sell plots of about 20 dunums and plant citrus trees on other parts of their land.[27]

But the chances of such transactions occurring were extremely low. The Jews did not usually buy small plots of around 20 dunums unless they were confident that they would be able to create a Jewish territorial zone.[28] Also, Kamen refers to irrigation, but the opportunities to irrigate lands away from the coastal plain were limited (as discussed in Chapter 2) and were not really taken up. Furthermore, a glance at aggregate changes in quality and quantity of non-Jewish lands between 1935 and 1945 in the subdistricts where Jewish land purchase was comparatively high (that is, a transfer of more than 4 percent of non-Jewish lands into Jewish hands; see Map 1.1. for areas in Jewish possession in 1944) similarly fails to support Kamen's view. Indeed, as can be seen in Figure 1.2, no cultivated lands of any type were added in the Beisan and Nazareth subdistricts. Although some improvements are perceptible in the Safad and Acre subdistricts, these were minor and insignificant when comparing the amount of land purchased. It should therefore be recognized that Kamen's assertion that Arab farms were improved as a consequence of Jewish land purchase does not reflect the main trend. Finally, as demonstrated in the following section,

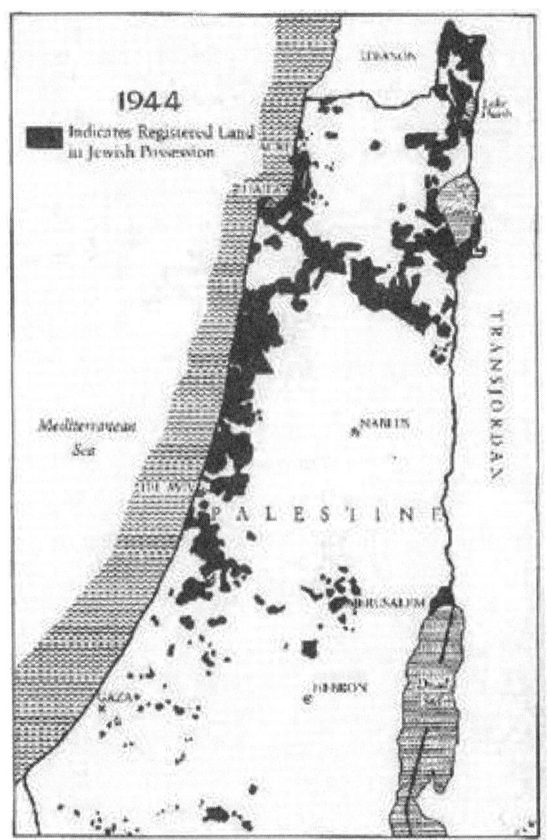

Map 1.1: Jewish Land Possession, 1944

Source: Stein, *The Land Question in Palestine,* p. 210. For a more detailed map, see ISA/Map Collection/Land in Jewish Possession as at 30 June 1947.

most lands were sold by nonowner-cultivator farmers. This, again, stands in opposition to Kamen's assumption of massive sales by *fallāḥīn* of parts of their farmland.

Given that Jews did not usually employ Arabs, especially on land that was purchased, that there was increasing unemployment in the Arab sector for low-skilled labor (at least until the 1940s),[29] and that land purchase was not compensated by major

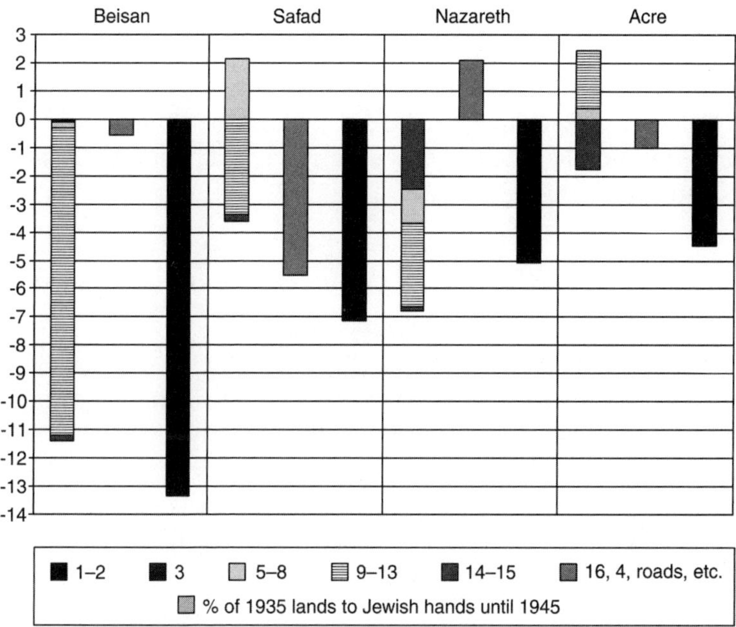

	1–2	3	5–8	9–13	14–15	16, 4, roads, etc.	Jewish Lands
Beisan	−0.07	−0.04	−0.22	−10.86	−0.22	−0.59	13.35
Safad	−0.01	0	2.14	−3.36	−0.28	−5.52	7.1
Nazareth	−2.48	0.01	−1.18	−2.99	−0.17	2.08	5.06
Acre	0	0	0.4	2.03	−1.78	−1.04	4.45

Figure 1.2: Changes in Arab Ownership of Land in Selected Subdistricts, 1935 to 1945 (percent)

Sources: Government of Palestine, Department of Statistics, *Village Statistics, 1937;* Government of Palestine, Department of Statistics, *Village Statistics, 1945.*

Note: Categories 1–3 and 5–15 represent cultivated lands. Generally speaking, the lower the category, the better the quality of land. The *Village Statistics* categories are discussed at length in Chapter 2.

investment in the land (in particular, there was no significant investment in labor-intensive cultivation, as is further discussed in chapter 2); it is clear that Jewish land purchase, combined with the Jewish employment policy, restricted the employment of *fallāḥīn* and therefore had a negative impact on the *fallāḥīn* economy.

The Influence of Land Sales on the Wealth of fallāḥīn and Other Arabs

The Jewish National Fund (JNF) and other Jewish financial sources offered large sums of money to Palestinian landowners to buy their land. Because of the political motivation for Jewish land purchase—the establishment of large territorial zones in Jewish hands to create a national home on this land—the prices offered were far above market value for agricultural land and therefore very tempting to some owners. But even though substantial sums were available for purchases, the Jewish budget was still finite. Not surprisingly, lower-priced land was more attractive.[30] In addition, there were two other significant determinants besides price: whether land settlement was conducted in villages with several landowners (as described in Chapter 6) and whether a landowner was able to sell a large territorial zone.[31]

In *The Land Question in Palestine 1917–1939,* Kenneth W. Stein shows that Arab vendors were usually landowners who were not owner-cultivators. Many of them owned large estates and lived out of the country. Others were Palestinian notables, among whom were politicians. Some *fallāḥīn* also sold land, but this practice was far less significant.[32] The Jewish Agency's statistics support Stein's argument. They seem to imply that the poorest *fallāḥīn,* the tenants,[33] were employed on the lands that were most commonly sold (the data are for both cultivated and uncultivated lands). According to these statistics, between 1890 and 1936 (the period prior to the Land Transfer Regulations of 1940 when the majority of Jewish-owned lands were purchased from Arabs) most lands for which information is available were purchased from owners living outside Palestine (53.6 percent) and from noncultivators (24.6 percent), and only 9.4 percent of vendors were owner-cultivator *fallāḥīn* (13.4 percent were "others") (Table 1.1). This (combined with the finding of the Johnson and Crosbie investigation of 1930 that 66 percent of cultivators who were family heads and lived in the investigated 104 villages possessed land, although no statistics on land ownership are provided)[34] seems to suggest that the very large proportion of non-*fallāḥīn* sellers was due not to the large amount of land in their ownership but rather to their (unlike the *fallāḥīn*) far higher tendency to sell their land. Hence, as far as the *fallāḥīn* are concerned, the most significant effect of land purchase was unemployment (as observed earlier) and not the formation of wealthier *fallāḥīn*.

When faced with evidence that many sellers were also politicians who were known to be Palestinian nationalists, Stein postulates that they might have been unaware of the correlation between land sales and Jewish national development.[35] But politicians were deeply involved in the prevention of land sales to Jews, both officially and unofficially. For example, the financial bank of the Arab Higher Committee *(bank al-'ummah al-'arabiyyah)* deliberately bought land from Arabs in difficulties in the hope of preventing Jewish land purchase.[36] The Arab National Fund (*ṣandūq al-'ummah al-'arabiyyah,* also known as Umma Fund), a political organization, was active mainly in trying to prevent land transfer from Arabs to Jews.[37] There is evidence suggesting that agents from the Arab Higher Committee were sent to intimidate and assault those who were suspected of wishing to sell land to Jews.[38] Instead, it seems to be a case of the free-rider syndrome—a conflict between the private interests of an individual and those of the collective of which he is a part. Selling one's own land at a tempting price could always be seen by certain politicians as more important than the collective need to prevent such sales. Here, Mancur Olson's *The Logic of Collective Action*—whenever an individual acts for a collective, he sees his own interest[39]—is also relevant.

Table 1.1 Characteristic of Sellers of Land to Jews

	From Owners Living Abroad	From Owner Living in Palestine	From Arab Peasants *(fallāḥīn)*	From Others	No Information Available about the Transaction	Total
Jewish land purchase 1890–1936, in dunums	358,974	167,802	64,201	91,001	549,868	1,231,846
Proportion of the land for which information is available	52.60%	24.60%	9.40%	13.40%	—	

Source: Gertz and Gurevich, *Habityashvut haḥakla'it ha'ivrit beerez ishrael;* (1938), p. 39.

Still, Stein believes that "perhaps for more than any other reason Arabs sold land to the Jews during the Mandate for economic reasons."[40] This seems to be much more relevant. If price was tempting enough, more Arabs would sell. For example, an intelligence report from 1935 mentions a meeting between the Grand Mufti (the head of the Supreme Moslem Council) and the seminomadic *fallāḥīn* in the Beisan area. At the meeting the Mufti asked the *fallāḥīn,* "if the Jews should offer £P10 per dunum, would somebody sell?" The answer of the *fallāḥīn* was that nobody would sell. But when the Mufti increased the price to £P100, the response was that at such a price "there will be people who would sell."[41] If high enough incentives existed, sellers would be found.

Could it be that the reason for the much lower tendency of peasants to sell lands, compared to other noncultivators, is primarily related to different economic incentives and not, for instance, to varying degrees of nationalism? I propose a tentative hypothesis is that this was the case but that more comprehensive research is needed. It was mentioned above, in regard to the purchasing policy of the Jewish institutions, that the preference was to buy up large estates. From the outset, Jewish land purchase concentrated on large estates, and when the availability of these estates diminished as a result of Jewish land purchase, especially during the 1930s, the Jews targeted owners of smaller estates.[42] It is likely, therefore, that at least in earlier times, Jews tended to offer more per dunum for large estates than for small ones. The breakdown of land ownership in the hands of *fallāḥīn* indicates that they usually did not have large estates (the pattern was rather that every landowner *fallāḥ* owned small pieces of land). Indeed, the Johnson and Crosbie report suggests that only 25 percent of owner-cultivator *fallāḥīn* households had more than two faddāns of land (roughly nine dunums) in their possession.[43] In addition, even after the British "land settlement," some *fallāḥīn* did not own a single consolidated plot, and their land was split up into several small plots.[44] On the whole, it seems that *fallāḥīn* lands were less attractive for Jewish land purchase, which could have given rise to a situation where comparatively higher prices were offered to bigger landlords.

Furthermore, it is possible that to make bids to owner-cultivators attractive, there was a need to offer them a relatively higher price per dunum, even when dealing with the same quality and quantity of land, than the attractive offers already being made to noncultivator landlords. In other words, the "reservation price" (the minimum at which a person would sell) was lower in the case of noncultivator owners. As long as their land was cultivated, the big and/or absentee landlords had to pay money to middlemen (in subletting, for example), whereas such transaction costs were not borne by an owner-cultivator. In addition, while the former would calculate his returns primarily in terms of money because his produce was regularly sold, the latter calculated his returns both in money and kind (these issues are discussed in detail in Chapter 4). This meant that if an owner-cultivator sold, he had to face the (transaction) cost of buying food, rather than producing it himself. In addition, as is discussed in more detail below, the labor market did not always prosper, and such an owner-cultivator could face unemployment, unlike the landlord for whom land was only a partial source of income.

It may be concluded that the sellers were mainly non-*fallāḥīn,* probably for deep-seated economic reasons. While these sellers gained, the poorest *fallāḥīn,* the tenants, were the losers. They lost their jobs in times of increasing unemployment (certainly until the prosperity of the 1940s, discussed in more detail below). Hence, at the micro level, land purchase brought an economic deterioration for peasants—especially those who were tenants.

A Note on Land Purchase and National Accounts

National income accounts, such as those for Palestine, are "current" and not "capital" accounts (in the case of the rural economy, the measure is of essentially of outputs; note that Metzer and Kaplan's study excluded discussion of land purchase). This should be remembered when examining the case of the Arab economy in Mandate Palestine, since it is an example of a nation selling its capital. It is especially important to bear this in mind for the Arab rural economy. A sale of, say, five dunums to buy a cow from Beirut would appear in the national accounts as a contribution to economic growth. But this sale was only a transfer of funds from the capital account to the current account.

Knowing that about 53 percent of the sellers (see Table 1.1) were owners living abroad, it is likely (although this needs further research) that much of the money from sales was not reinvested in the Arab economy. Not only were many of the landlords absentee (and major landlords, such as Sursock, appeared to close their businesses in Palestine after land sales), but instances of violence against those who sold lands to Jews[45] caused some vendors to leave the country, either permanently or for a few years.[46] Hence, much of the money from sales to Jews might have flowed out of the country.

In a more regular situation, the influence of such a flow would be seen in the long term, yet in the specific case of Mandate Palestine, where data are available for a few years that cannot be compared with other data (see the discussion in Chapter 3), long-term changes are barely visible. The extent of land purchase was considerable. Estimates by the Jewish Agency suggest that between 1920 and 1936 about £3,403,119 (in current prices) was paid for land purchase (Table 1.2). At roughly the same time (1922–36), Metzer and Kaplan argue that a significant increase in net national product (NNP) took place in the Arab sector of about £P4,918,000 (in current prices).[47]

The Influence of Arab-Jewish Nonland Trade on the Arab Rural Economy

Although the Arab population increased significantly during the Mandate, the Jewish population rose much faster, especially because of immigration. It is estimated that about 52 percent of

Table 1.2 Estimated Cost of Land Purchased by Jews, 1920 to 1936

A. Recorded Land Purchase

Price in £P Paid Per Dunum		Area in Dunum Purchased within Each Category			
Price per Dunum	*Median*	*1920–22*	*1923–27*	*1928–32*	*1933–36*
0.100–0.500	0.3	0	0	0	0
0.501–1.000	0.7505	0	0	0	0
1.001–2.000	1.5005	8,230	6,480	640	28,140
2.001–3.000	2.5005	29,770	94,890	5,330	4,160
3.001–4.000	3.5005	32,240	90,260	42,580	6,980
4.001–5.000	4.5005	0	3,490	11,850	32,120
5.001–7.500	6.2505	31,090	11,710	24,890	0
7.501–10.000	8.7505	960	2,370	1,470	760
10.001–15.000	12.5005	1,670	690	3,500	50
15.001–20.000	17.5005	0	330	1,610	2,730
20.001 and more	(calculated as 24)	450	0	0	4,920
Average price per dunum in £P		4.1	3.2	4.9	4.9

B. Estimated Share of Recorded Sales of the Total Jewish Land Purchase

	1920–22	*1923–27*	*1928–32*	*1933–36*
Percent	74.8	68.2	64.3	35.7

C. Estimated Total Spending on Land Purchase in £P

	1920–22	1923–27	1928–32	1933–36	Total 1920–36
Recorded	434,049.5	686,990	457,036	394,747.5	1,972,823
Unrecorded	146,230.5	320,327	253,751	710,987.5	1,431,296
Total	580,280	1,007,317	710,787	110,5735	3,404,119

Source: Compiled from Granovsky, *Land Policy in Palestine,* p. 38.
Note: Since no exact figure exists for each sale, the midpoint was taken as the price for each category of prices.

Table 1.3 Estimated Rural and Urban Settled Populations in Palestine

	Rural Population: Non-Jews	Percent of Moslems	Urban Population: Non-Jews	Percent of Moslems	Rural Population: Jews	Urban Population: Jews	Percent of Jews in Palestine's Population
1922 (census)	514,614	94.9	209,079	71.9	16,901	76,444	11.4
1923	523,695	94.9	214,091	72	18,896	80,982	11.9
1924	532,940	94.9	219,226	72.1	21,127	85,791	12.4
1925	542,347	94.9	224,486	72.2	23,621	90,885	12.9
1926	551,919	94.9	229,872	72.2	26,410	96,281	13.5
1927	561,662	94.9	235,388	72.3	29,528	101,998	14.1
1928	571,577	94.9	241,039	72.4	33,014	108,054	14.7
1929	581,668	94.9	246,826	72.5	36,912	114,470	15.4
1930	591,936	94.9	252,753	72.5	41,270	121,266	16.1
1931 (census)	602,387	94.8	258,824	72.6	46,143	128,467	16.8
1932	611,595	94.8	268,165	72.7	50,206	140,603	17.8
1933	620,946	94.8	277,847	72.7	54,627	153,886	18.8
1934	630,442	94.8	287,877	72.8	59,437	168,424	19.8
1935	640,084	94.7	298,271	72.8	64,671	184,335	20.9
1936	649,876	94.7	309,041	72.9	70,365	201,749	22.1
1937	659,819	94.7	320,203	72.9	76,561	220,808	23.2

1938	669,917	94.7	331,767	73	83,303	241,668	24.4
1939	680,170	94.6	343,750	73	90,638	264,499	25.7
1940	690,582	94.6	356,167	73.1	98,620	289,486	27
1941	701,155	94.6	369,034	73.1	10,7304	316,834	28.3
1942	711,893	94.5	382,367	73.2	116,753	346,766	29.7
1943	722,796	94.5	396,183	73.2	127,033	379,525	31.1
1944 (government estimates)	733,869	94.5	410,500	73.3	138,220	415,380	32.6
1945	745,112	94.5	425,333	73.3	150,391	454,621	34
1946	756,531	94.4	440,705	73.3	163,633	497,569	35.5
1947	768,127	94.4	456,633	73.4	178,042	544,575	37.1
Average annual population growth 1922–31	1.77		2.40		11.80	5.94	
Average annual population growth 1931–44	1.53		3.61		8.81	9.45	

Sources: Government of Palestine, *A Survey of Palestine,* pp. 147–52; Government of Palestine, *Census of Palestine 1931,* 0. 1; Justin McCarthy, *The Population of Palestine,* p. 35.

Notes: Data for 1922 were amended according to McCarthy's adjustments. This means an addition of 8.2 percent to the Muslim data provided by the government, an addition of 11.4 percent to the Jewish, 3.9 percent to the Christians, and a subtraction of 10.5 percent from "Others." This was done because of inaccuracies in the census of 1922. Data for 1922 and 1931 are based on censuses, while those for 1944 are based on estimates and are therefore probably less accurate. "His Majesty's Forces" are also included in the figures. Presumably, this mostly influenced the data on Christians. Nomads are excluded from these data. In 1931 the number of nomads was estimated as 57,265 (all Muslims). Estimates for years where census/estimates are not available (i.e., all years except 1922, 1931, and 1944) were constructed by using the average annual population growth for a particular period as a proxy for growth in each year.

overall demographic growth in Palestine from 1922 to 1944 was caused by the increase in Jewish population. This climbed from about 11.4 percent of the total population to 32.6 percent (Table 1.3). The level at which the Jewish sector consumed Arab produce could therefore have had a considerable effect on Arab rural incomes.

On its own, the Jewish economy was not self-sufficient in food production. The Jewish central marketing cooperative, Tnuva, was obliged to market Jewish commodities primarily to "Jewish markets," but it used to purchase Arab commodities in cases of shortage.[48] In addition, direct trade, not via Tnuva, was common. Arabs "exported" their agricultural products to the rapidly growing Jewish markets. Indeed, in spite of the tension between Arabs and Jews, trade in agricultural products remained significant. Although Arab leaders tried to stop trade with the Jews during the Arab Revolt of 1936 to 1939, especially during the six-month Arab Strike of 1936 (which brought a certain decrease in trade at that time),[49] even then many Arabs marketed their crops to Jews.[50] Where vegetables were cultivated especially during the 1940s, many Arab merchants with trucks started coming to the villages to collect produce for the Jewish markets.[51] In addition, there were numerous cases of Arabs marketing their crops directly to Jewish consumers,[52] and many Jews chose to shop in the Arab markets, where the prices of various products were cheaper. This was common in the mixed Arab-Jewish cities of Haifa and Acre.[53]

Even the pessimistic estimates of the Jewish Agency for the years 1934 to 1939 suggest a high integration between Jewish and Arab sectors, although this diminished during the Arab Revolt of 1936 to 1939. According to these estimates, the Arabs supplied about 61 percent of Jewish consumption from local vegetable produce in the two years before the revolt and 26 percent during it.[54] This was while the share of Arabs in aggregate output may be estimated at 88 percent.[55] These data (especially for the nonrevolt period) show close interaction; especially when the same source advises that the data are for vegetables supplied to the Jewish urban market, but "exclusive of supplies to Jews with oriental food habits who are consumers in Arab markets."[56] Such "oriental habits," as well as direct purchase from *fallāḥīn* who came to sell their own produce to Jewish consumers, suggest a picture of almost open trade.

The government of Palestine collected data on prices in the "Jewish markets" and in the "Arab markets." The prices in the Jewish markets were higher than in the Arab ones. An obvious factor is the extra cost paid for transactions via Tnuva. In addition, as Deborah Berenstein points out, the Tnuva prices were higher because of the need to compensate for higher wages in the Jewish sector.[57] Finally, not all products were the same. The Arab tomato, which in many cases was unirrigated, was known to be smaller than the irrigated Jewish one.[58] Such differences in products could lead to variations in prices. Even with these constraints and when unmediated purchases from Arabs to Jews are not recorded, the prices in both Jewish and Arab "markets" (i.e., from Jewish and Arab businesses) showed fairly similar trends. This, too, indicates a high level of integration.

A comparison between the prices for agricultural products available both in Jewish and Arab markets (nonpasteurized milk, local flour "extra," live hens, local eggs, onions, and tomatoes) supports these suggestions. Even so, an explanation on data quality should be given. In 1939, the Mandatory government started to publish monthly figures of some staples, some of which were also combined in their cost of living calculations. These included data from September 1938. In addition, they distinguished between Arab and Jewish markets. However, from November 1940 the data are less accurate. This is because of the government's imposition of price controls on the markets and subsidies on some products.[59] Indeed, during that period a significant black market developed in opposition to price controls:

> dissatisfaction generally arose from a widely held opinion that the cost-of-living index did not truly represent the position, owing to the non-availability of some of the commodities on which it based and black-market operations in others.[60]

Hence, data from November 1940 onward cannot show all the trends in the market, and for the purposes of this study, data for the months August to October 1940 have not been used either because some of the weightings changed (such as measurements for "Palestine market" instead of "Arab market"). This gives a restricted period of coverage—in one case, 23 months—although the use of monthly intervals and different products allows the observations to be adequate. Because the gap between different prices in real currencies creates a large disparity, all the prices were normalized to the index of Arab prices for each commodity. On average, prices in the Jewish markets were higher by 21 percent. Plotting the data for the whole period (Figure 1.3a) suggests that even though a correlation exists (i.e., there is some tendency for the different marked points to cluster around an imaginary straight line), it is not statistically significant (the return for the coefficient of determination, R^2, is only 0.26; more details on the meaning of this coefficient are provided in chapter 3). On the other hand, when the period of the Arab Revolt of 1936 to 1939 is taken out (Figure 1.3b), the shape of the picture changes to quite a high correlation ($R^2 = 0.61$), considering that Tnuva purchased Arab commodities only in cases of shortage in

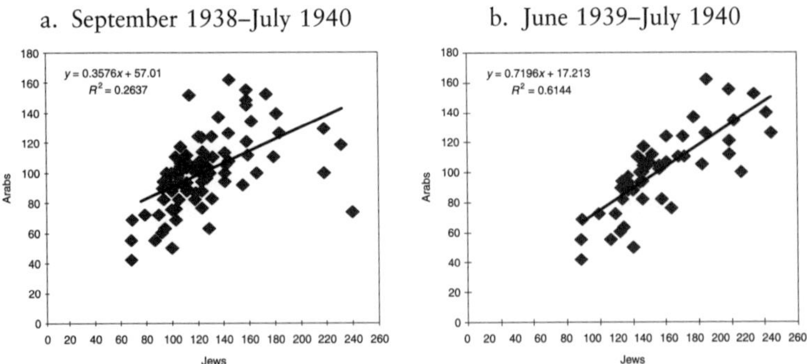

Figure 1.3 Retail Prices of Arab versus Jewish Commodities

Source: Complied from Government of Palestine, Department of Statistics, *General Monthly Bulletin of Current Statistics* (various years, Jerusalem).

Jewish agriculture and bearing in mind the transaction costs paid to Tnuva and the effect of the Histadrut's wage policy on prices.

It should be noted that the integration of the Arab and Jewish markets kept agricultural prices in the former higher than if such integration had not taken place. The growth in population increased agricultural demand in the country to a point where local production of foodstuffs was insufficient. It became necessary to import food, and import controls were placed on crops following the Disturbances of 1929, as a measure to assist the *fallāḥīn* (these measures are discussed in more detail below). Such a restriction had not existed in the late Ottoman period.[61] Even so, controls were limited because of the multiple effects that such a policy might have had on other sectors and on other poor people and because of trade agreements with other countries.[62] In addition to import duties, the transport costs and payments to mediators—who tended to proliferate when importing was involved—put the local agricultural sector (both Arab and Jewish) in a better position than that of the economies exporting to Palestine.

Overall, unlike the land purchases (combined with the Jewish labor policy), whose impact on the Arab rural economy and probably on the Arab economy in general was negative, the impact of the foodstuffs trade between Arabs and Jews benefited the Arab economy, in particular the Arab rural economy. These two forms of direct integration were not the only ways in which the Jewish sector influenced the Arab rural economy. Meanwhile, the government attempted to play the role of mediator between the two.

THE CHANGING PATTERN OF BRITISH POLICIES TOWARD THE ARAB RURAL ECONOMY

The increasing tension between Arabs and Jews in Palestine created a syndrome of the Mandate government constantly attempting to keep the country calm, in the hope that this would ease the burden of administration. The British wanted to create a stable situation between Arabs and Jews and tried to satisfy both sides—in retrospect, an impossible task. Jewish immigration, a cardinal issue in the establishment of a Jewish national home, was permitted by the British but was restricted in response to Arab resistance, a policy that commenced with the Immigration Ordinance of 1920 after the attacks on Jews that year. It was reinforced by the White Papers of 1930 and 1939, following the Disturbances of 1929 and the Arab Revolt of 1936 to 1939, which were the most significant Arab uprisings; the two weeks of disturbances were in effect a premature uprising before the longer-lasting revolt. At the same time, Jewish land purchase was regulated in various ways, mainly in the hope of solving the problem of landless Arabs.[63]

It was not the case that the creation of a Jewish national home alongside or instead of an Arab-Palestinian one was a prime objective of the British. When, for example, during World War II, British leaders discussed the "main strategic interests of the British Commonwealth and Empire" with regard to Palestine,[64] the issue of national homes or even the protection of the populations did not emerge. Rather, the interests outlined were

> (a) Control of sea and air communications from Europe through the Mediterranean to India, the Far East and Southern Africa.
> (b) Security of our [British] sources of oil and their supply lines [the oil pipeline from Iraq].
> (c) A secure base for our Imperial Reserve.[65]

It was particularly the British attempts to keep the country calm that pushed the Mandatory government to implement pro-*fallāḥīn* economic policies following the Disturbances of 1929, in the belief that the discontent had, to a large extent, emerged for socioeconomic reasons. The fear of further discontent in the postrevolt period prompted the idea—and consequent decision—to create a large military base in Palestine during World War II, a development that increased the prices of agricultural foodstuffs, as well as the job opportunities for *fallāḥīn* outside their farms (discussed in more detail below).

The Start of Pro-*fallāḥīn* Economic Policies

Following the Arab Disturbances of 1929, the British government in London sent an inquiry chaired by Walter Shaw to study the situation. In March 1930, this committee presented its report, which concluded that tensions between the Jews and the Arabs were the result of Jewish immigration and land purchase.[66]

To calm the country, the British decided to reduce the level of both Jewish immigration and land purchase. The Shaw Committee's recommendation was endorsed by the reports of two further government inquiries, known by the names of their chairs, Hope Simpson and Lewis French.[67] Blocking land purchase in a situation where Jews tended not to employ Arabs meant improving the economic conditions of the *fallāḥīn*. On the other hand, reducing immigration slowed down local demand for foodstuffs and thus limited the earnings of the *fallāḥīn* (it also had an influence on capital importation).

The attempt to reduce land purchase, as already mentioned, was not really successful until 1940. The immigration policy, however, was partly successful, although some illegal immigration continued.[68] But these were not the only new policies following the disturbances. The British concluded that the *fallāḥīn*, especially the poorest ones and the landless former *fallāḥīn*, had the greatest potential to rebel:

> The *fellah* [*fallāḥ*] is usually heavily in debt, improvident and unfitted to urban life. Political exploitation, which is active in Palestine, tends to create in the "landless" class a feeling of disaffection and unrest. Sir Arthur Wauchope is definitely of the opinion that this constitutes a potential danger, which should be arrested without delay, if serious consequences are to be averted.
>
> The attention of the late Government was drawn to this problem by the Report of the Shaw Commission on the disturbances of

1929 (Cmd. 3530, March 1930) and by the report of Sir John Hope Simpson (Cmd. 3692, October 1930).[69]

Thus, in addition to immigration and land purchase policies, the government believed that to reduce discontent and discourage urban migration, it was necessary to improve economic conditions in the Arab villages.[70] The main ways of doing this were suggested in the Johnson-Crosbie and Strickland reports, published in 1930.[71] The policies planned by the government to help the *fallāḥīn* were to reduce taxation, accelerate land registration and reforms, intervene in the credit market and provide security for loans to *fallāḥīn*, offer some grants to Arabs, and take action to stimulate productivity in the Arab villages. These interventions are assessed in depth in Part 3, except for taxation, which is discussed below. These measures were in addition to the import controls placed on crops following the Disturbances of 1929, which were intended to protect the *fallāḥīn*.[72]

The Continual Reduction in Taxation

Agricultural taxes had a long history in the region. In the late Ottoman period, *mukhtār*s collected taxes for the government but also extracted much money for themselves, supported in these activities by the Ottoman irregular forces. The tithe paid at that time was estimated to be between 20 percent and 50 percent of the gross yield.[73] In addition, the Ottoman irregular forces were harmful to the population. They were undisciplined, underpaid, and ill fed and forced the *fallāḥīn* to feed both them and their animals. Occasionally, they even assaulted and robbed their unprotected hosts.[74]

At the beginning of the Mandate period, the main direct taxes[75] levied on agriculture were (from the most to the least important) on crops (the tithe), on animals (the animal tax), and on immovable property (the house and land tax, also known as *werko*), all of which were inherited from the Ottoman period.

During the early years of the Mandate, the British introduced only those changes that they considered necessary for honest and efficient administration. They continued to levy the tithe at a rate of 12.5 percent of gross income (the Ottomans, to meet their own pressing needs, had added a special impost of 2.5 percent to the standard 10 percent). The British levied in cash but only after collecting information about the payment that the *fallāḥ* would receive for his produce.[76]

In 1925, the tithe was brought back to 10 percent of the gross income of the farm. To give both government and cultivator greater certainty about the amount to be paid each year, the Commuted Tithe Ordinance of 1927 determined the tithe payable by villages as the average of the annual amount paid in the previous three or four years.[77] However, crop prices were lower in 1928 and 1929 than in the average of the years before, so for that year farmers had to pay much more than 10 percent.[78]

Nevertheless, the reduction of taxes following the Disturbances of 1929 was substantial. Between 1930 and 1935, large amounts of tax were remitted for the *fallāḥīn* because of poor yields.[79] In 1934, for example, about half of the total tithe due was remitted.[80]

In 1935, both the tithe and the house and land taxes were replaced by a single tax, the rural property tax. The new tax applied to all Palestine, apart from the Beersheba subdistrict (certainly until 1945, when it was first surveyed).[81] The rural property tax brought a significant official reduction in taxation from 1935. The basic calculation was 10 percent on supposed *low estimated net* income,[82] and in areas where the rural property tax was levied, the house and land tax was no longer imposed.[83] In addition, with the new tax there was no levy on low quality lands (although some modifications took place; see Table 2.2).

Furthermore, the high inflation from 1935 to 1945, especially during the 1940s,[84] significantly reduced the burden of this tax, since no comparable amendment of the sums was made (see Table 2.2). When dealing with payments, it is also important to note that during the Arab Revolt of 1936 to 1939 many *fallāḥīn* did not pay taxes.[85] Hence, the overall picture in regard to land taxation for the *fallāḥīn* was a gradual reduction during the Mandate period, with the most significant shift resulting from the British change in attitude following the Disturbances of 1929.

The animal tax, however, continued throughout the Mandate period and followed a different trend. The nominal price remained the same during 1922 to 1944 (150 mils per cattle, buffalo, or camel; 50 mils for goat or sheep; 100 for swine), but it changed in 1945 (600 mils per cattle, buffalo, or camel; 200 to 400 mils for goat, when the sliding scale was made according to number owned; 200 mils for a sheep; and 400 for a swine).[88] In constant prices, this meant a notable increase from 1928 to 1930, stable prices in the 1930s, a significant fall up to 1944, and the highest levy in 1945 (Figure 1.4).

Data provided by Metzer for the years 1927 and 1936 and data that are available in the *Survey of Palestine* for 1945 enable certain comparisons between these benchmark years. Still, the comparisons lack data on the *werko* tax, paid mainly in the case of 1927 (in areas where property tax was imposed, neither *werko* nor tithe was levied), causing underestimation of the

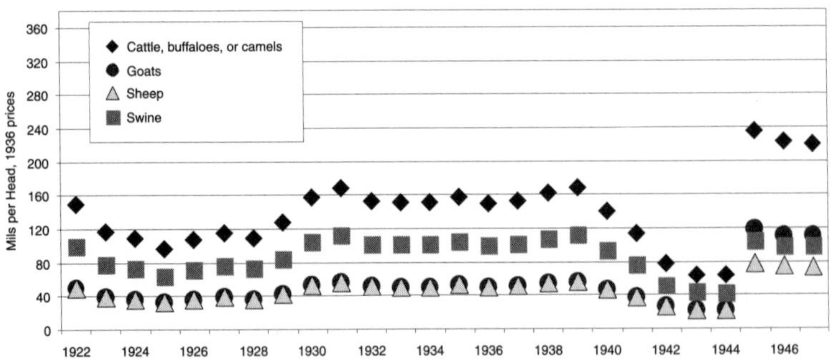

Figure 1.4 Animal Tax: Per Animal Head

Source: Government of Palestine, *A Survey of Palestine,* p. 543.

Note: The price for goats in 1945 is the middle price: the scale was between 200 and 400 mils, according to the number of goats in possession.

figure for that year. Also, the returns for 1945 are after the change in animal tax rates. This means that it is not representative of preceding years. To give a rough idea of the change, both the returns from the animal tax, and the assessed share that had to be paid according to pre-1945 rates, are presented in Figure 1.5.

Taking into account the returns in Figure 1.5 and previous comments about misrepresentation of animal tax for 1945, it seems that the overall trend can be described as a gradual reduction in the total taxes paid by the Arab rural sector throughout the years 1922 to 1944. The most significant change, as mentioned, came as a result of the different British attitude after the Disturbances of 1929. However, these trends changed for the years 1945 to 1947, when a higher animal tax was levied, although it did not return to the levels of the 1920s.

Combining the returns from Figure 1.5 with those of the demographic growth (Figure 1.6) shows that the decrease of taxes per capita was even more significant that the total decrease.

Government Resource Allocation: From Jews and Other Arabs

The reason that the government could afford to follow such a sympathetic tax policy toward the Arab rural economy can be found in the tax revenue it received from other branches of the economy. The outcome, as the government statistician expressed in 1944, was that "the burden of taxation on agriculture is extremely light."[87] This, especially in regard to Arab taxes, is clearly seen in Figures 1.7 and 1.8. In any case, it should be recognized that rural taxation was low throughout the Mandate period.

This was only part of the story, however. Metzer also tracked the incidence of economic services provided by the government (separate from services like health and education, discussed under human development), and his study supports the government's change of policy from another viewpoint: total spending

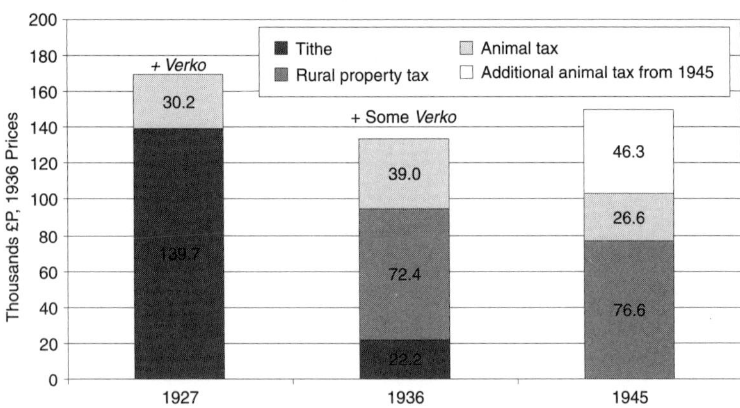

Figure 1.5 Arab Rural Direct Taxes

Sources: Metzer, "Fiscal Incidence," pp. 95, 106; Government of Palestine, *A Survey of Palestine,* pp. 577–78. For price index, Metzer, *The Divided Economy,* p. 241.

Notes: Werko returns for the rural areas were not found. As explained, the earlier the year, the more *werko* had to be paid. Tithe and *werko* returns for the Beersheba subdistrict seem to be included in rural property tax returns for 1945. "Additional animal tax from 1945" together with "animal tax" is the total return for animal tax for 1945. The segregation between the two was calculated by using the data mentioned in Figure 2.11 (on livestock in Arab ownership, 1930 and 1943) to calculate yearly annual growth of the different animals in Arab possession from 1930 to 1943 and using this to create estimated returns in livestock ownership for 1936 and the supposed returns for 1945. This was done with cattle, buffaloes, goats, sheep, and camels (there were no exact figures for swine, but these seemed to be hardly ever raised by Moslems and Jews). The total value for animal tax was then calculated for 1936 and 1945 by multiplying the returns for each kind of livestock (camels, goats, etc.) in the tax according to 1936 prices. This meant that although there was a relative increase in livestock ownership in the Arab rural sector, there was a decrease in the total sum that had to be paid in 1936 prices by 31.7 percent. Since the returns are before remissions, the returns for animal tax for 1936 minus 31.7 percent were regarded as the returns for "animal tax" in 1945. The subtraction of these from the real returns gives the "additional annual tax for 1945."

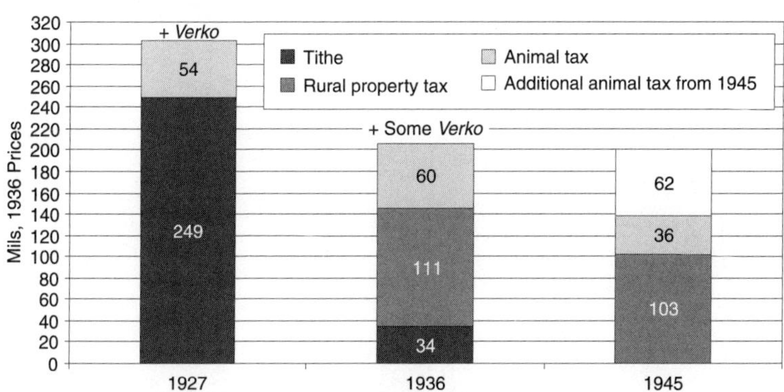

Figure 1.6 Arab Rural Direct Taxes per Capita Rural Inhabitants
Sources: See sources for Figure 1.5 and Table 1.3.

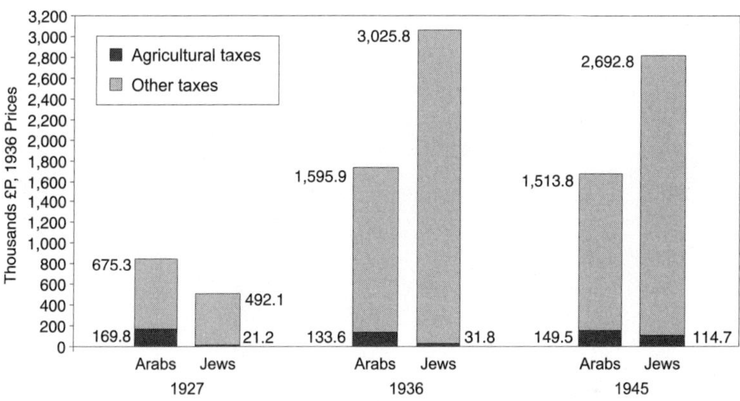

Figure 1.7 Taxes Paid to the Mandatory Government
Sources: Metzer, "Fiscal Incidence," pp. 95, 106; Government of Palestine, *A Survey of Palestine*, pp. 577–78.

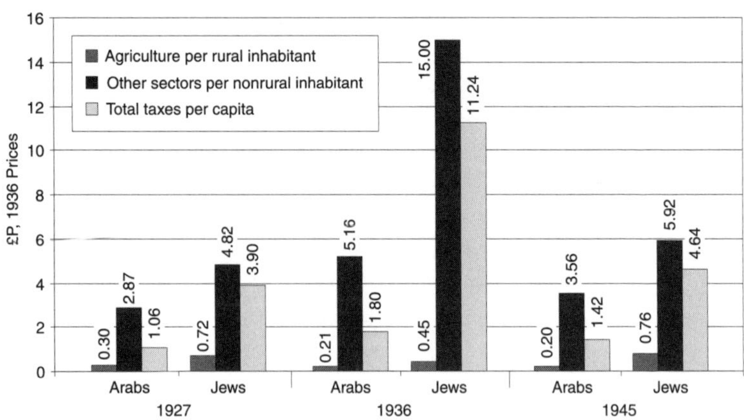

Figure 1.8 Taxes Paid by Different Branches of the Economy per Capita

Sources: See sources for Figures 1.7 and Table 1.3.

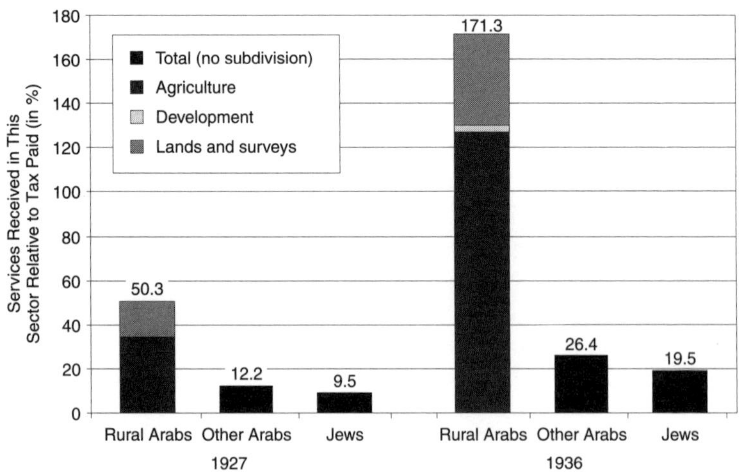

Figure 1.9 Services Received from the Government Relative to Taxes Paid

Source: Metzer, "Fiscal Incidence," pp. 87–132.

on Arab rural services increased markedly from 1927 to 1936. This can be seen in Figure 1.9 (note that the expenditure on agriculture, from selected departments, represents only part of the total).

Overall, although there was some fluctuation, especially the rise in taxes in 1928 and 1929, taxation on the Arab rural sector gradually deceased during the Mandate period. This is true until 1944 because the animal tax increased in 1945. A significant change in level of taxes occurred following the Disturbances of 1929, which also led to higher government spending on Arab agriculture.

The new policies extended the phenomenon of the government's reallocation of savings originating in the Jewish sector (especially) and in the nonagricultural Arab sector, into the Arab rural sector. The government also mediated a spillover of technology from the Jewish to the Arab sector (see Chapter 7). The question of how productive this expenditure was is discussed in Part 3.

THE EFFECTS OF ETHNONATIONAL CONFLICT ON THE ARAB RURAL ECONOMY

We have already seen that more violence led to less employment of Arabs in Jewish assets, although such employment was always limited, and that the British desire to keep the country peaceful led to the introduction of pro-*fallāḥīn* policies, especially after the Disturbances of 1929. Here, ethnonational conflict led to a reduction in taxation, which positively influenced the Arab rural economy, and also led to heavy expenditures, with varying results. Essentially, the overall returns were insignificant for the majority of the *fallāḥīn,* especially the poorer ones (see Part 3). Still, the general picture is that the disturbances acted as a modest impetus to the economy of the *fallāḥīn.*

The story of the Arab Revolt of 1936 to 1939 was different. As is discussed below, during the actual years of the revolt, its overall effect on the *fallāḥīn* economy was negative, athough some individual *fallāḥīn* gained from this uprising. In the long run, however, the consequences were strongly positive.

The Short-Term Effect of the Arab Revolt of 1936 to 1939 on the Arab Rural Economy[88]

In the Arab Revolt of 1936 to 1939, the economic losses of the majority of the *fallāḥīn* far exceeded their gains. This seems to be agreed both by *fallāḥīn* and other observers.[89] It is true that in the revolt the majority of the *fallāḥīn* did not pay taxes (and did not repay them later).[90] However, in place of government taxes *fallāḥīn* had to pay "taxes" or "fines" to the rebels or make "contributions" to them.[91] They were obliged to do this to survive. In Kafar ʻAma, for example, *fallāḥīn* were beaten and their *mukhtār* was killed after they refused to pay the £P50 demanded.[92] Armed bands kidnapped people for "investigations" and later released them in exchange for ransom.[93] These roving militias stole animals and other goods from villagers; in the village of ʻArabe, for example, about 800 head of cattle were stolen by an Arab band. Since the ʻArabah's cattle was sold by the armed bands in the nearby area at 25 percent less than the real market price, meat prices dropped for a couple of months.[94]

The *fallāḥīn* also faced marketing problems. Not only did the bands' capture and disposal of agricultural products occasionally cause a fall in prices, but the interaction with the Jewish economy differed from more peaceful times, bringing a decline in Jewish access to Arab markets and vice versa. At the same time, the purchasing power of the urban Arab diminished.[95]

The *fallāḥīn* also suffered a reduction in income from employment outside the farm, except for those who had participated in the revolt. During the general strike, many of them could not find work in the towns.[96] Employment in Jewish assets, already at a very low level, was reduced even more because of the hostility.[97] Finally, those who found jobs had to face a different problem—the bands used to "collect their wages for the revolt."[98]

The British military punished villages as a way of bringing pressure to bear on them to denounce the rebels. In Kafar Burka, for example, British soldiers crushed many oil jars on the roads, dipped blankets from the houses in the oil, and smothered hens. Elsewhere, as in 'Ajun, the *fallāḥīn* had to pay fines in kind for rebel actions carried out near their village. Similar examples are known from the villages of Qula, Umm al-Fahem, Sindi'ani, Sakhnin, Zir'in,[99] Mashhad, and Tur'an. In the last two, the army also forced the villagers to walk barefoot on the thorny leafs of *ṣabbār* (a variety of cactus).[100]

Assistance from the government was even less. The agricultural station in Majdal, for example, had been "looted and damaged by bandits during 1938."[101] Other payments to villages found their way into the hands of the Arab bands, as a *faṣīl* (subband) commander indicated: "I have in my possession £P25 which has been drawn from the Government for the village."[102] Finally, the limited opportunities to get bank loans became even less, and Barclays Bank changed its policy toward loans (see Chapter 5).

Those who gained materially from the Arab Revolt of 1936 to 1939 were the participants in the bands. They benefited from their wages and their share in the collections (including contributions, seizures, robberies, and thefts). Some of them, especially band leaders, were enriched by these activities. The revolt was also used as a cover for criminal behavior quite unrelated to the collective national action. In spite of their high profile, the proportion of band members in the population at the height of the revolt was no more (and possibly much less) than 5 percent of male rural inhabitants.[103] There were other ways of gaining. Some people did not have to repay the Jewish moneylenders (see Chapter 5) who had been killed. At certain times during the revolt, many Jewish farmers did not go to their fields, after a decision to save life and not property. *Fallāḥīn* took advantage of this by stealing agricultural equipment and crops and letting their herds graze on Jewish lands.[104]

In the short term, then, the Arab Revolt of 1936 to 1939 had a negative economic impact on most of the *fallāḥīn,* although some benefited from it.

The Long-Term Effect of the Arab Revolt of 1936 to 1939 on the Arab Rural Economy

While the Disturbances of 1929 led to governmental assistance for the *fallāḥīn,* the Arab Revolt of 1936 to 1939 aroused considerable anxiety about security matters. It was during the revolt that the British reached the conclusion that if a strong army was not maintained in Palestine, the prospects of controlling the country and the region would not be high. In 1938, this view was expressed in the minutes of the Colonial Defence Committee:

> The political situation in Palestine and Transjordan is unsettled, but these countries are under British administration, and under war conditions we ought to be able to take more drastic action to put down disturbances than is politically possible in peace. . . . It is clear that if we were to lose control over either Iraq or Palestine, when we were at war with Italy, this would involve us in grave disadvantages and might seriously compromise our military position in the Middle East. . . . The primary task for the garrison of Palestine should be the security of the following communications:—
> (a) The road from the Transjordan frontier to Haifa.
> (b) The road and railway from Haifa to Egypt.
> This will entail the protection of the Jaffa-Jerusalem area. . . . The possibility of war being the opportunity for rebellion in Palestine will depend on the strength of the forces which we have in the country . . . whatever their feelings about the proposed Partition, the Jews will be unlikely to take violent actions against us.[105]

The massive flow of military funds to Palestine made the British feel that the situation was more likely to be kept under control:

> With 2½ million p.a. being spent on internal security plus large bodies of British and Australians in Palestine, internal troubles are not likely to arise among Arabs.[106]

While the desire to have a strong army in the country was influenced by fear of more Arab resistance, the result was the development of Palestine into a large British military base. This, as is discussed later, had significant economic outcomes that favored the Arab economy: many low-skilled Arab laborers of rural origin found part- and full-time employment, wages rose, and the presence of the military increased the demand for local crops, bringing further rises in foodstuff prices. Hence, in spite of the short-term decline during the revolt, the long-term trend was one of marked improvement for the *fallāḥīn* economy. The prosperity of the 1940s, therefore, cannot be studied in isolation from the ethnonational conflict in Palestine. The British fear of continued insurrections and their political and military interest in keeping control of the country brought an indirect transfer into it of colonial resources originating outside Palestine.

CONCLUSION

This chapter began by discussing the direct economic influence of Palestine's Jewish community on the Arab rural economy. It was argued that Jewish land purchase, driven by the *'avoda 'ivrit* policy, had a detrimental effect on the Arab rural economy. On the other hand, the impact of the foodstuffs trade between Arabs and Jews benefited the Arab rural economy. While there are problems in measuring the overall direct influence, it is impossible to assess the indirect influence—for example, whether the Disturbances of 1929 and the Arab Revolt of 1936 to 1939, which had an overall positive long-term influence on the Arab rural economy, would have occurred without a growing Jewish presence in Palestine. It is evident that the debate about overall trends resulting from different political aspirations needs to be undertaken on a wider level than Arab-Jewish interaction, especially in regard to the complex Arab-Jewish-British triangle.

The primary mission of the British in Palestine was to hold and administer the country. Following the Disturbances of

1929, the Mandate government believed that there was need to discourage Arab urban migration to reduce discontent. The main tool for this was the improvement of economic conditions in the Arab villages. The policies devised to help the *fallāḥīn* were to reduce taxation, to accelerate land registration and reform, to intervene in the credit market, and to supply agricultural services. While reduction of taxation was positive as far as the *fallāḥīn* were concerned, different reforms had different impacts. These are discussed in Part 3.

It was violence, again, that drove the British to change their policies in Palestine. Their desire to have a strong army in the country was influenced by a fear of continued Arab resistance; the result was the use of Palestine as a large British military base. As discussed below, this had significant economic outcomes favoring the Arab rural economy in terms of employment, income, and output.

The only sphere in which violence caused an economic decline was Arab employment in Jewish assets. But not only was such employment already small; the violence also reduced the level of land purchase, which meant less of a decline in agrojobs, due to the combined effects of land purchase and the *'avoda 'ivrit* policy.

In the long run, therefore, the uprisings led to an improvement in the Arab rural economy, with the British playing the role of mediator, channeling funds into that subeconomy from the Jewish sector and the nonagricultural Arab sector. The Arab Revolt of 1936 to 1939 brought another, unforeseen advantage—the input of colonial resources originating outside Palestine. One cannot escape the conclusion that for the duration of British rule over Palestine, violence served to benefit the economy of the *fallāḥīn*.

The short-term effect of the revolt was, however, negative for the *fallāḥīn* economy. Armed bands, as well as British "contraviolence" harmed the *fallāḥīn*. They also faced marketing problems, alongside the more rapid loss of employment in Jewish assets (here, the relatively short interruption of the disturbances seemed not to be significant).

Some *fallāḥīn,* however, benefited from the revolt. Likewise, a few *fallāḥīn* gained from Jewish land purchase (i.e., from one of the very causes of the uprisings—yet the sellers were usually non-*fallāḥīn*). Still, these benefits were small-scale and should not distort the overall picture of the *fallāḥīn* economy. If anything, they reflect an increasing inequality within *fallāḥīn* society.

NOTES

1. Government of Palestine, *A Survey of Palestine: Prepared in December 1945 and January 1946 for the Information of the Anglo-American Committee of Inquiry* (Jerusalem, 1946), p. 1. This policy, approved by the British Cabinet on 31 October 1917, was expressed by the Foreign Secretary in a letter to Lord Rothschild on 2 November 1917.
2. For the evolution of the policies, see broadly ibid., pp. 1–85.
3. Jacob Metzer, *The Divided Economy of Mandatory Palestine* (Cambridge, 1998).
4. As discussed below.
5. I am not aware of any comprehensive data on partnerships. However, from cases brought to the courts dealing with partnerships, a clear division between Arab and Jewish partnerships can be identified. See, for example, *Current Law Report, The Law Report of Palestine, Collection of Judgements of the Courts of Palestine,* and other law collections for the Mandate period, available in the Law Library, the Hebrew University of Jerusalem. In addition, in none of my interviews was any interaction mentioned between the sectors apart from trade and employment.
6. Government of Palestine, *A Survey of Palestine,* p. 767; Alon Kadish, "Ovdey maḥanot hazava kemiqre boḥan be-ḥeqer ha-ḥevra ha-falesṭinit" (forthcoming); Tamir Goren, *'meḥorban lehit' osheshut: korot ha-'uḥlusiyah ha'aravit beḥaifa, 1947–1950* (M. Phil. thesis, University of Haifa, 1993).
7. See the many examples in government publications: Government of Palestine, Office of Statistics, *Wage Rate Statistics Bulletins/ Real*

Wage Statistics Bulletin/ Employment and Pay-Rolls Bulletin (Jerusalem, various dates); Government of Palestine, Department of Statistics, *General Monthly Bulletin of Current Statistics* (Jerusalem, various dates); Government of Palestine, Department of Statistics, *Statistical Abstract of Palestine* (Jerusalem, various years).

8. Government of Palestine, *A Survey of Palestine,* p. 737
9. See Chapter 4.
10. See Chapter 3.
11. Zvi Sussman, "The Determination of Wages for Unskilled Labour in the Advanced Sector of the Dual Economy of Mandatory Palestine," *Economic Development and Cultural Change,* 22, no. 1 (1993), pp. 95–113.
12. Gad G. Gilbar, *Kalkalat hamizraḥ hatikhon ba'et haḥadasha* (Tel Aviv, 1990), pp. 195–96. See also Jewish Agency for Palestine, "The Palestinian Arabs under the British Mandate," *Palestine Papers,* no. 4, (London, 1930).
13. Deborah S. Berenstein, *Constructing Boundaries: Jewish and Arab Workers in Mandatory Palestine* (New York, 2000), pp. 1–80 (especially p. 44).
14. Sussman, "The Determination of Wages," p. 99.
15. Yuval Elizur, *Loḥama kalkalit: me'ah shnot 'imut kalkali byn yehudim le'aravim* (Jerusalem, 1997), pp. 80–83.
16. Sussman, "The Determination of Wages," pp. 95–113.
17. Ibid.
18. Berenstein, *Constructing Boundaries,* pp. 87–88; Interview with 'Amiram Argaman from Kibuz ḥamadiya (Mr. Argaman, b. 1928), grew up in the Jewish settlement of 'Atlit and studied in Haifa; he had very close connections with Arabs who lived in villages adjacent to 'Atlit) (29 August 2000); Interview with Yosef Barzilay from 'Afula (Mr. Barzilay, b. 1906, immigrated from Holland in 1927; he was one of the founders of the settlement Kvozat Shiler, later secretary of Nes Ziyona, and afterward mayor of 'Afula) (20 August 2000).
19. Jews rarely had shares in Arab *mushā,'* as discussed in Chapter 6. See also ISA/Map Collection/Land in Jewish Possession as at 30.6.1947.
20. Kenneth W. Stein, *The Land Question in Palestine, 1917–1939* (London, 2nd ed., 1985).
21. PRO/CO/733/290/8, February 1933, Secret, Cabinet, "Policy in

Palestine: Memorandum by the Secretary of State for the Colonies," p. 1.

22. ISA/(RG2)//L/88/45, 31 August 1945, a letter from the acting director of the Department of Lands Settlement to the chief secretary.
23. For the years until 1939, see broadly Stein, *The Land Question.* For the 1940s, see the discussion and data in Government of Palestine, *A Survey of Palestine,* pp. 260–71.
24. Jewish Agency for Palestine, *Land Settlement, Urban Development and Immigration: Memorandum Submitted to Sir John Hope Simpson, C.I.E., Special Commissioner of His Majesty's Government, July 1930* (London, 1930), pp. 33–35.
25. Charles S. Kamen, *Little Common Ground: Arab Agriculture and Jewish Settlement in Palestine, 1920–1948* (Pittsburgh, 1991).
26. Jewish Agency for Palestine, *Land Settlement, Urban Development and Immigration,* pp. 33–35.
27. Kamen, *Little Common Ground,* pp. 173–93.
28. See broadly Stein, *The Land Question.* For a detailed map of Jewish lands in 1947, see ISA/Map Collection/ Palestine: Land in Jewish Possession, 1947. For detailed documents about Jewish land purchase, see CZA/S25/3368.
29. See Chapter 3.
30. Stein, *The Land Question.* Stein mentions this point many times in his book. See his index for "Jewish Land Purchase Limited by Capital Shortage," and the example on p. 37.
31. Stein, *The Land Question,* pp. 3–79; Gabriel Baer, *Mavo layaḥasim ha' agrariyim bamizraḥ hatikhon, 1800–1970* (Jerusalem, 1971), pp. 53–58, 178; Yossi Katz, *Beḥazit haqarqa': qeren kayemet leyisrael beterem hamedina* (Jerusalem, 2001), pp. 38, 97, 166.
32. See broadly Stein, *The Land Question.*
33. For further information on tenancy, see Chapter 4.
34. Government of Palestine, *Report of a Committee on the Economic Condition of Agriculturists in Palestine and the Fiscal Measures of Government in Relation thereto, W. J. Johnson, R. E. H. Crosbie et al.* (Jerusalem, 1930), p. 21.
35. Stein, *The Land Question,* pp. 65–70.
36. Yehoshua Porath, *Mehamehumot lameridah: hatnu'a ha'aravit hapalestinit, 1929–1939* (Tel Aviv, 1978), pp. 122–28.

37. *ṢSandūq al-'ummah al-'arabiyyah, taqrīr majlis al-aidārah al-mukarrim 'ila al-jam'iyyah al-'umūmiyyah al-'ādiyyah lil-'ai'ādah sanah 1945* (Jerusalem, 1946); Arab Bank, *Twenty-five Years of Service to the Arab Economy, 1930–1955* (Amman, 1956), p. 44.
38. See ISA/(RG2)/BOX326/653, 15.5.1947, Ṣudki al-Tabariyy's letter to the Arab Higher Committee.
39. Mancur Olson, *The Logic of Collective Action* (London, 1971); Mancur Olson, "The Varieties of Eurosclerosis: The Rise and the Decline of Nations since 1982," *Jean Monnet Chair Papers* 32 (1995), pp. 1–37.
40. Stein, *The Land Question,* p. 69.
41. CZA/S25/10191, February 1935, Reports by A. H. Ha-Cohen for 1934–35, 2nd Report, p. 13.
42. See broadly Stein, *The Land Question;* Katz, *Beḥazit haqarqa'.*
43. Government of Palestine, *Report of a Committee on the Economic Condition of Agriculturists* (Johnson-Crosbie), p. 21. For the approximation of an average *faddān,* see Roger Owen, *The Middle East in the World Economy, 1800–1914* (London, 2nd ed., 1993), p. xiii.
44. As discussed in Chapter 6.
45. See, for example, ISA/(RG2)/BOX326/653, 15.5.1947, Ṣudki al-Tabariyy's letter to the Arab Higher Committee.
46. During the Arab revolt of 1936–39, many Arab leaders fled the country. Abboushi argues that those who fled did not sell lands. But some names of fleeing notables can be found in Stein's list of Arab politicians and notables involved in land transfer. Wasfi F. Abboushi, "The Road to Rebellion: Arab Palestine in the 1930s," *Journal of Palestine Studies,* 6, no. 3, issue 23 (1977), pp. 41–43; Stein, *The Land Question,* appendix.
47. Jacob Metzer and Oded Kaplan, *Mesheq yehudi 7e-mesheq 'aravi beerez ishrael: tozar ta'asuqa ṣezmiḥah betqufat hamandat* (Jerusalem, 1991), pp. 28, 38, 139.
48. Interview with Meir Frank, (Mr. Frank from 'Afula was manager from 1940–47 of the dairies of the Jewish Tnuva marketing and producing cooperative next to 'Afula) (29 August 1998). Also Interview with Shraga Punq from Kibbutz Kfar Ha-makabi (Mr. Punq was an agriculture guide and a manager of vegetable production of his settlement during the years 1938–48) (28 August 1998).

49. Berenstein, *Constructing Boundaries,* pp. 68–70; interview with Yosef Barzilay; interview with ʻAmiram Argaman; Jewish Agency for Palestine, Economic Research Institute, *Jewish Agriculture in Palestine: A Progressive Factor in Middle East Economy, by Dr. Ludwig Samuel* (Jerusalem, 1946), pp. 50–51; Yehoshua Lurie, *ʻAko ʻir haḥumut* (Tel Aviv, 2000), pp. 410–24.
50. Yoval Arnon-Ohana, *Falaḥiym ba-mered ha-ʻaravi be-'erez yishrael 1936–1939* (Tel Aviv, 1978), p. 61.
51. Interview with Meir Frank; interview with Shraga Punq; interview with Al-ʻOthmān Sālim Maṣrāwa (Mr. Maṣrāwa, b. 1918, worked as a *fallāḥ* on his family farm until his village, Safuriyya (north), was destroyed in the 1948 war) (30 August 1998).
52. Interview with Meir Frank; interview with Shraga Punq; interview with Al-ʻOthmān Sālim Maṣrāwa; interview with Yosef Barzilay; interview with ʻAmiram Argaman.
53. Lurie, *ʻAko ʻir haḥumut,* p. 99; interview with ʻAmiram Argaman; interview with Mohammad Aḥmad Abū Aḥmad (Abū Riaḍ) from Nazareth, (Abū Riaḍ, b. 1918, was a butcher and merchant of animals and meat during the Mandate period).
54. Jewish Agency for Palestine, Economic Research Institute, *Jewish Agriculture in Palestine,* pp. 50–51.
55. Calculated from data available for 1936, 1943, and 1944. For 1936 and 1943: Government of Palestine, Department of Statistics, *Statistical Abstract of Palestine 1944–45,* pp. 223, 226, and Government of Palestine, *A Survey of Palestine,* p. 320 (for all Palestine); State of Israel, Central Bureau of Statistics, "Jewish Agricultural Production by Branches (1936/37, 1943/44, 1947/48)," *Statistical Bulletin of Israel,* 1, no. 1, July 1949, p. 34 (for the Jewish share). For 1944: *Survey of Palestine,* pp. 325–26. The Arab share was calculated as the figures for all Palestine less the Jewish share.
56. Jewish Agency for Palestine, Economic Research Institute, *Jewish Agriculture in Palestine,* p. 50.
57. Berenstein, *Constructing Boundaries,* pp. 43–44.
58. E.g., Interview with Ya'ir Rooder from Kiryat ḥayim (Mr. Rooder (b. 1939) remembered the busy trade between Arabs and Jews; Jews used to buy in the Arab markets as well as directly from *fallaḥīn* that came to sell in Jewish settlements) (21 December 2000).

59. Government of Palestine, Office of Statistics, *General Monthly Bulletin of Current Statistics* (Jerusalem, various years); Government of Palestine, Department of Statistics, *Statistical Abstract of Palestine, 1944–45.*
60. Government of Palestine, *A Survey of Palestine,* p. 745.
61. Husni Sawwaf, "International Trade," Sa'id B. Himadeh (ed.), *Economic Organization of Palestine* (Beirut, 1938), pp. 387–89; Government of Palestine, *A Survey of Palestine,* p. 450.
62. Nacum T. Gross, "Hamediniyut hakalkalit shel memshelet erez ishrael betkofat hamandat," in his (ed.), *lo 'al haroach levada* (Jerusalem, 1999), pp. 181–85.
63. See broadly Government of Palestine, *A Survey of Palestine,* pp. 1–85.
64. PRO/CO/731/88/21, 25 July 1944, top secret, "War Cabinet, Post Hostilities Planning Staff, British Strategic Requirements in Eastern Mediterranean and Middle East."
65. Ibid.
66. PRO/CO/733/182/9, 17 January 1930, confidential report from Chancellor, High Commissioner of Palestine, to Lord Passfield, P.C., His Majesty's Principal Secretary of State for the Colonies, p. 26.
67. Great Britain, Colonial Office, *Report on Immigration, Land Settlement* and *Development, by Sir John Hope Simpson* (London, 1930); Government of Palestine, Palestine Development Department, *Agricultural Development and Land Settlement in Palestine (Lewis French).*
68. Government of Palestine, *A Survey of Palestine,* pp. 23–102.
69. PRO/CO/733/290/8, February 1933, Cabinet, Secret, Policy in Palestine: Memorandum by the Secretary of State for Colonies, p. 1.
70. Ibid. See also Rosa I. M. El-Eini, "Government Fiscal Policy in Mandatory Palestine," *Middle Eastern Studies,* 33, no. 3 (1997), pp. 570–96.
71. Government of Palestine, *Report of a Committee on the Economic Condition of Agriculturists* (Johnson-Crosbie); Government of Palestine, *Report by Mr. C. F. Strickland of the Indian Civil Service on the Possibility of Introducing a System of Agricultural Co-operation in Palestine* (Jerusalem, 1930).

72. Husni Sawwaf, "International Trade," pp. 387–89; Government of Palestine, *A Survey of Palestine,* p. 450; Gross, "Hamediniyut hakalkalit," pp. 184–85.
73. Fred M. Gottheil, "Money and Product Flows in Mid-Nineteenth-Century Palestine: The Physiocratic Model Applied," David Kushner (ed.), *Palestine in the Late Ottoman Period: Political, Social and Economic Transformation* (Jerusalem, 1986), pp. 220–21; Moshe Ma'oz, *Ottoman Reforms in Syria and Palestine, 1840–1861* (Oxford, 1968), pp. 56–59.
74. Ibid., pp. 56–57; interview with Abū 'Abdallah from Mashhad (Abū 'Abdallah, b. 1921, was the *mukhtār*'s son in the Mandate period and later became the *mukhtār* of his village) (6 April 1999 and 17 August 1999).
75. Other taxes and payments were not regular, such as taxes on Land Settlement (see chapter 6) and payments to courts.
76. Government of Palestine, *A Survey of Palestine,* pp. 246–47; Sarah Graham-Brown "The Political Economy of the Jabal Nablus, 1920–48," Roger Owen (ed.), *Studies in the Economic and Social History of Palestine in the Nineteenth and Twentieth Centuries* (Oxford, 1982), pp. 96, 157, 166; M. F. Abcarius, "Fiscal System," Himadeh (ed.), *Economic Organization in Palestine* (Beirut, 1938), p. 516.
77. Government of Palestine, *A Survey of Palestine,* pp. 246–47; Graham-Brown, "The Political Economy of the Jabal Nablus," pp. 96, 157, 166; Abcarius, "Fiscal System," p. 516.
78. Great Britain, Colonial Office, *Report on Immigration* (Hope Simpson), p. 174. See also Graham-Brown, "The Political Economy of the Jabal Nablus," pp. 96, 157, 166; Ze'ev Avrahamoviz and Izḥaq Guelfat, *Hamesheq ha-'aravi* (Tel Aviv, 1944), p. 41.
79. Stein, *The Land Question,* p. 18.
80. Government of Palestine, *A Survey of Palestine,* pp. 247, 250–54. See, for example, ISA/(RG7)/BOX627/AG/1/2, "Remissions: Rural Property Tax."
81. Government of Palestine, Department of Statistics, *Village Statistics, 1945* (Jerusalem, 1945). E.g., for Beersheba subdistrict returns: Government of Palestine, *A Survey of Palestine,* p. 254.
82. Government of Palestine, *A Survey of Palestine,* pp. 247, 250–54.
83. Avrahamoviz and Guelfat, *Hamesheq ha-'aravi,* pp. 41–42.

84. Metzer, *The Divided Economy,* p. 241.
85. E.g., Arnon-Ohana, *Falaḥiym,* p. 31; Abboushi, "The Road," p. 43; interview with Jamāl 'Ilyās Khuri from Meghar (Mr. Khuri, b. 1905, was a *fallāḥ* and later a policeman during the Mandate period) (23 August 1999).
86. Government of Palestine, *A Survey of Palestine,* p. 543.
87. Government of Palestine, Department of Statistics, *National Income of Palestine 1944, P. J. Loftus, Government Statistician* (Jerusalem, 1946), p. 29.
88. This subsection is a summary of some of the main findings in chapter 9 of my Ph.D. thesis.
89. The vast majority of my interviewees, *fallāḥīn* and others, seemed to agree on this issue. CZA/S25/22834, 21 April 1939, a letter from A. Sason to Ben Gurion "operations among the Arabs"; BR/11/317, September 1936, a report on bad and doubtful debts; BR/11/356, March 1939, attachment of notes from 1938 for a report on bad and doubtful debts.
90. E.g., Arnon-Ohana, *Falaḥiym,* p. 31; Abboushi, "The Road," p. 43; interview with Jamāl 'Ilyās Khuri.
91. Many examples were given earlier. See also Ted Swedenberg, "The Role of the Palestinian Peasantry in the Great Revolt (1936–9)," Ilan Pappe (ed.), *The Israel/Palestine Question* (London, 1999), pp. 154–55; Ṣubḥī Yāsin, *Al-thawra al-'arabiyyah al-kubra' fī filiṣtin 1936–1939* (Cairo, 1967). p. 66. Various examples can be seen in CZA/S25/22541, Attil Documents.
92. Arnon-Ohana, *Falaḥiym,* p. 61.
93. CZA/S25/3028, undated, Intelligence report, "Review on the Saghar Arabs of Beit She'an Valley."
94. Arnon-Ohana, *Falaḥiym,* p. 148.
95. CZA/S25/22039, April 1937, Intelligence from the (Jewish) Arab Bureau, "The Occurrences among the Arabs," (translated).
96. Arnon-Ohana, *Falaḥiym,* p. 36.
97. See chapter 3.
98. See undated letter about such collection in CZA/S25/22541, Attil Documents.
99. Arnon-Ohana, *Falaḥiym,* pp. 65–66.
100. Interview with Slīmān 'Adawī from Tur'an (Mr. 'Adawī, b. 1926–28, was a *fallāḥ* in the Mandate period and an agriculture adviser in Israel; he worked with some who had been agriculture

advisers in the Mandate period) (5 April 1999); interview with Abū 'Abdallah.

101. ISA/(RG7)/BOX629/AG/8, letter from Acting Director of Agriculture and Fisheries to Director of Public Works, 29 May 1939.
102. CZA/S25/22541, Attil Documents
103. More about this will be published in a journal article.
104. Arnon-Ohana, *Falaḥiym,* pp. 27–28.
105. PRO/CAB/16/182, February 1938, secret, "Committee of Imperial Defence: Mediterranean, Middle East and North-East Africa."
106. PRO/CO/732/86/28, 12 September 1940, "Situation in Palestine: visit by Colonel Newcombe to Iraq" (a report by Colonel Newcombe [the Colonial Office's investigator to the Middle East in 1940]).

Part Two

TRENDS IN THE ARAB RURAL ECONOMY

· TWO ·

Investment, Specialization, and Produce in Arab Agriculture

It is widely acknowledged that investment is vital for economic growth. This approach is taken in old structural-change growth theories, such as Rostow's and Lewis's, where massive investment is a key factor; in the subsequent approach of Solow, especially in the case of developing economies; and in "new growth theories," where the emphasis is on investment in physical capital (including better technologies) and in human capital, in addition to the so-called endogenous and exogenous factors.[1] This chapter focuses on investment in agriculture, specifically irrigation and land.

Three other areas covered are farming specialization, agricultural produce (crops and livestock), and the relative prices of agricultural commodities. All are fundamental to the comprehensive discussion of economic growth and development that is undertaken in this and the following chapter.

THE LACK OF INVESTMENT IN IRRIGATION

The climate of hot summers and wet winters that was typical of Mandate Palestine is transitional between Mediterranean and desert types and varied throughout the country. The four main regions—the coastal plain, the hill country, the inland plains, and the desert—differed from one another in amount of precipitation (although all had more in the north) and in type of land. This divergence and further variations within each region meant an uneven suitability for cultivation, both in terms of output per land unit and susceptibility to hazards, such as flooding in the plains[2] (Maps 2.1, 2.2, and 2.3).

Most of the land on the coastal plain—the strip between Haifa and Gaza—permitted the growing of a variety of field and tree crops, including citrus where irrigation was available. The hill country (the brown areas on Map 2.1) contained rocky outcrops as well as much land suitable for cultivation; grains, legumes, and tree crops could be easily grown, whereas vegetables were usually produced on the better land of the hill villages. On the inland plains (the green areas on Map 2.1, excluding the coastal plain), the climate and soil were similar to that of the surrounding hills. The land was less stony but more susceptible to temporary floods in certain areas, where the permanent swamps, although gradually drained during the Mandate period, prevented cropping in some places. In the deserts (the colorless areas on Map 2.1), the lack of precipitation limited cropping to those areas next to water resources, although some enclaves permitted the growing of unirrigated barley.[3]

The shortage of water restricted the amount of land capable of cultivation and also was a significant determinant of agricultural output on cultivated land.[4] The precipitation in the wet season—usually rain, between October and April—was a main source of water for agriculture. It was, naturally, free; but on land where it was the only water source, the risk from crop failure was higher than on irrigated land because the amount of precipitation and the intervals between rainy and dry days greatly affected crop output.[5] A low-yield year had also multiyear effects, as Moḥamad Yūnīs Al-Ḥusayni noted in the case of seminomadic *fallāḥīn* in the northern Negev. On average, a very low-yield season occurred every four years. Following this, many lands were left fallow, since not enough seed remained for sowing. Still, it should be recognized that although

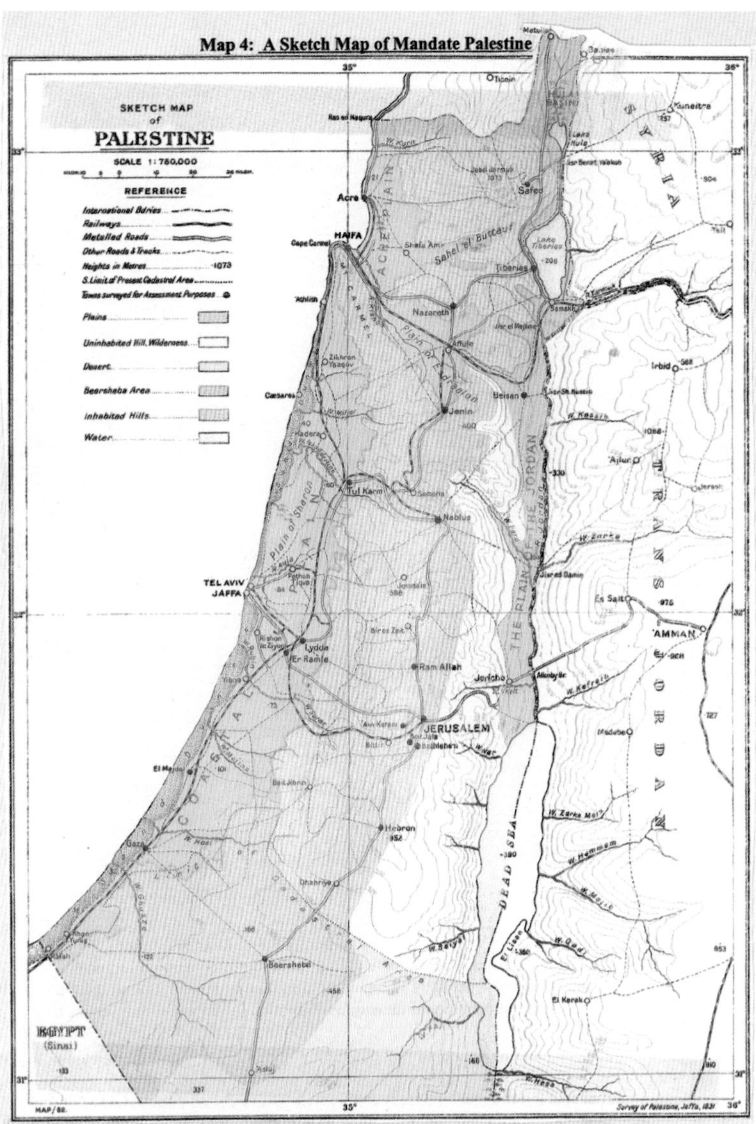

Map 2.1 A Sketch Map of Mandate Palestine, 1931

Source: Government of Palestine, Palestine Development Department, *Agricultural Development and Land Settlement (Lewis French)* (1931).

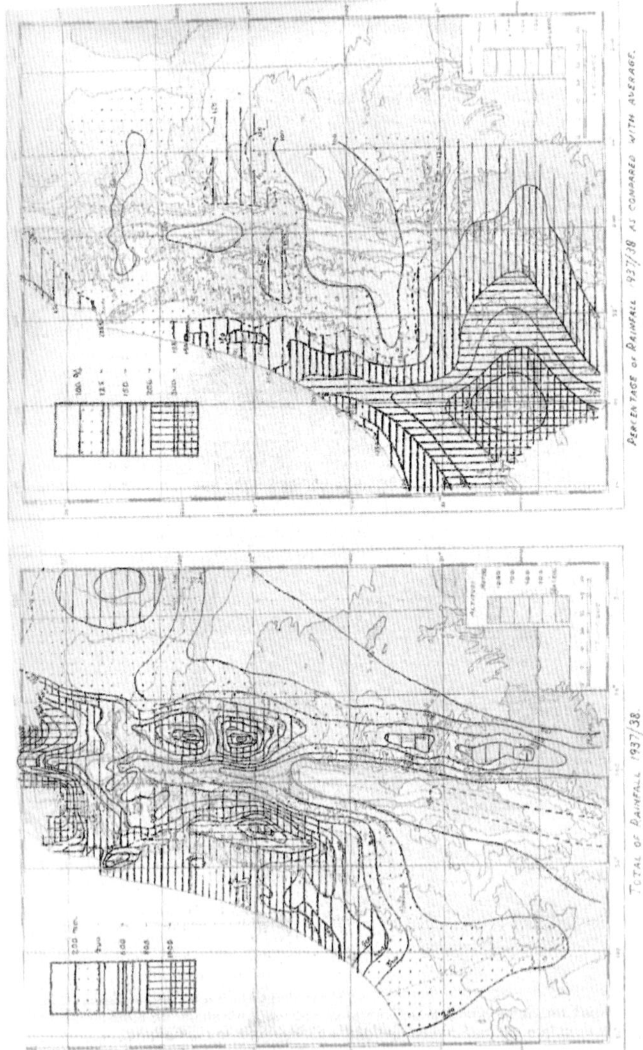

Map 2.2 Rainfall Map of Mandate Palestine, 1938
Source: Government of Palestine, *Blue Book 1938* (Jerusalem, 1939), p. 392.

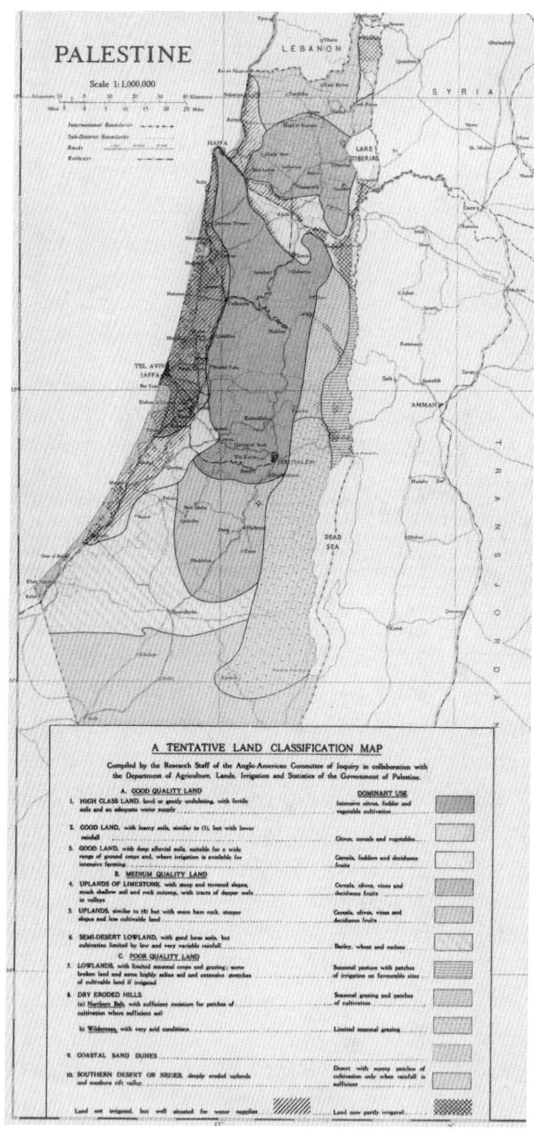

Map 2.3 Dominant Use of Lands, Quality of Lands, and Irrigated Lands, 1945

Source: ISA, Mandatory Maps Collection, map number 297.

Note: Although some details are missing from this map, such as villages with significant irrigation systems, it gives a comprehensive picture of differences between areas under the Mandate.

four years was the average figure, the amount of precipitation could never be predicted. Even Al-Ḥusayni mentioned two successive years of crop failure due to water shortage in the 1940s, causing a considerable reduction in the area under cultivation.[6]

Advantages of Irrigation

Humanly developed sources of water tended to reduce risks. Not only was the likelihood of crop failure from insufficient precipitation reduced significantly on irrigated plots, but irrigation enabled a wider range of crops to be grown. This allowed farmers to respond more adequately to market demand. In addition, the conversion of an unirrigated plot to an irrigated one more than doubled the output per land unit. On unirrigated land, it was possible to grow only a single crop in a year, either a summer or a winter one, because for summer crops the land had to lie fallow in the winter to preserve the water in the ground until seeding time. On irrigated land, however, it was possible to have two crops, and the yield was also much higher.[7] Indeed, government data for the agricultural year 1944 to 1945 suggest that even the production of vegetables (generally, summer crops) in the Arab sector was higher by a ratio of 2.2:1 on irrigated lands than on unirrigated.[8] Conditions that year do not seem to have been unusually favorable to irrigation (there was no drought, for instance),[9] and this ratio might have been common.[10] As early as 1930, the government argued that there was a shortage of "cultivable" land,[11] and many lands in arid areas were defined as "uncultivable" because of lack of water,[12] but the installation of irrigation systems in arid areas was able to transform uncultivated lands into cultivated ones. The need for Arab rural workers to find part-time employment outside the farms reflected seasonal fluctuations in the Arab rural economy,[13] and the potential to grow more than one crop a year on irrigated land would have created higher year-round demand for labor. Hence, more irrigated land could have contributed to the *fallāḥīn* economy.

Irrigation on Arab Lands

In spite of the known advantages of irrigation, most of the Arab-cultivated areas in Palestine remained unirrigated throughout the Mandate period. This is particularly surprising because water for irrigation was free in the rural areas; the government did not impose any restrictions, such as pumping fees, on these "commons."[14] By regional division, as can be seen from Table 2.1 and Map 2.3, the plains were distinctive for availability of irrigation. By ethnic division, there was a correlation between areas of more Jewish farming and areas of higher irrigation. While this does not of itself prove a greater Jewish share in the water, further analysis, using information about Arab and Jewish shares in different crops, leads to the conclusion that Jewish agriculture was, indeed, much more dependent on irrigation than that of the Arabs. Ultimately, this was the result of possessing land in areas that were more suitable for irrigation. In addition, capital and cheap credit were more readily available to Jews.[15]

In 1947, although the government estimated that the average annual amount of water from springs, rivers, and wadis was 1,700,000,000 cubic meters, only around 12 percent of this was used.[16] While the proportion of irrigation was much lower in Arab than in Jewish agriculture, the reasons that more water was not used for irrigation will be discussed with special reference to the Arab sector—the focus of this study—with the Jewish sector compared where relevant.

Were Irrigation Systems Backward?

Humanly developed sources of water for irrigation required investment. In the Arab rural sector, two categories of water supply were generally used for irrigation, both representing low investment. One was the use of open water resources available next to the fields. To use this required comparatively modest investment, and it is therefore referred to as "easily accessed water."

Table 2.1 Schedule of Cultivated and Irrigated Lands in Palestine, 1947

A. Data

	Cultivated Land (dunums)	Irrigated Land (dunums)	Ethnic Composition
Regional Division			
The coastal plain	2,400,000	310,000	Arab and Jews
Acre plain	320,000	20,000	Arab and Jews
Huleh (the inland plains)	240,000	40,000	Arab and Jews
Esdraelon and Upper Bireh (the inland plains)	450,000	20,000	Mainly Jews
Hittin and Himma lands (largely a plain with some hill-country characteristics)	40,000	3,000	Arab and Jews
Valley of Jezreel (the inland plains)	160,000	5,000	Mainly Jews
Shel el Battauf (the inland plains)	65,000	—	Arabs
Shal el Arrabe (the inland plains)	30,000	—	Arabs
Marj as Sanur (a plain in the hill country)	20,000	—	Arabs
Central Jordan Valley: Migdal, Samakh, Bishatiwa, etc. (the area next to the Lake of Tiberias, and the Jordan Valley)	70,000	7,000	Arabs and Jews
Beisan plain (the area next to the northern part of the Jordan Valley)	180,000	70,000	Mainly Jews
Lower Jordan Valley, including Wadi Fari'a (the area next to the southern part of the Jordan Valley)	225,000	15,000	Arabs
The hills and small plains within the hilly area (the hill country)	2,500,000 to 3,500,000	10,000	Arabs
Beersheba subdistrict (the wilderness)	"Several millions"	1,000	Mainly Arabs

B. Summary

	Cultivated Land (dunums)	Irrigated Land (dunums)	Irrigated Lands (percent)
Regional Division			
The coastal and Acre plains	2,720,000	330,000	12.1
The inland plains (excluding Acre plain)	945,000	65,000	6.9
Beisan and around the Jordan Valley and the Sea of Galilee	475,000	92,000	19.4
The hills*	3,020,000	10,000	0.3
Hittin and Himma lands	40,000	3,000	7.5
Beersheba subdistrict (the wilderness)	"Several millions"	1,000	Almost none
Ethnic Division			
Mainly Jews	630,000	90,000	14.3
Arab and Jews	3,070,000	380,000	12.4
Mainly Arabs	"Several millions"	1,000	Almost none
Arabs*	3,340,000	25,000	0.7

Sources: Government of Palestine, *Memorandum on the Water Resources*, p. 31. For the ethnic segregation, see ISA, Map Collection, Palestine: Land in Jewish Possession, 1947. For less detail, see Map 1.1.

Notes: It is not possible to segregate the data in the *Memorandum* into exact figures for Arabs and Jews. The source overestimated the area under cultivation. To avoid changing the intentions of the report, it is not corrected in this table. A more accurate account of cultivated land is provided later in this chapter.

* Taking the hill country as 3,000,000 dunums (average of the estimates).

As can be seen in Map 2.3, apart from the coastal plain and the plains of Acre and Esdraelon, irrigation took place primarily in areas adjacent to open water resources. Here the water was available in easily accessed form and required a low level of capital investment. This was also the case in areas adjacent to the Jordan River and its lakes (Hula and Tiberias; the Dead Sea is too salty for irrigation), the 'Auja (Yarkon) River, and a few other springs supplying water that was used for irrigation throughout the year. In addition, the gathering of wadi stormwater (water that flowed downhill for short periods after heavy rain) in cisterns and in winter ponds that appeared in the wet season made irrigation possible. This was organized by individuals without government assistance, certainly until 1942.[17] In this form of irrigation, the cheapest methods were used in the Arab sector,[18] as the irrigation officer of Palestine, Dawson Shepherd, suggested in his report for 1929:

> There is a striking evidence of backwardness in irrigation practices and the uneconomical use of water in the area lying along the eastern slopes of the Judean Hills, stretching down to the Jordan canyon from the Dead Sea to Beisan. The use of water in the field cannot be called irrigation except perhaps in places where attention is paid to vegetable culture. . . . [On other occasions] the water is allowed to flow over the land with almost or no attempt at direction. It is not uncommon to see deep channels worn in the ground by too rapid flow. Advantage is taken of naturally level patches and the flow of the water reaching these very often covers a larger area than that under crop. There is seldom any attempt made to secure an equal depth of water over a field with the result that as great an area receives too much water as too little. It is a difficult thing to prove but, on observation, one is forced to the conclusion that little more than 20% of the water originating from the springs does useful work. . . . The quantity of water in the Hill Country is not as large as in the Jordan district and difficulties connected with the conveyance of it to crops are greater. The water is consequently put to more valuable use and much closer attention is paid to its distribution. There is waste in distribution but field practice is reasonably good.[19]

In Grant Elihu's *The People of Palestine,* which is based on research on the Arab farmers in the hill country up to 1921, a similar description appears:

> The gardens of 'Artas, near Solomon's Poll, of 'Ayn Karim, of Silwan and of Jenin might with encouragement be matched hundreds of times . . . by pools and cisterns, conduits and irrigation, the peasant farmers could make garden spots where now to the eye of a stranger all looks hopeless.[20]

The second category of water supply was nearby underground water. To utilize this required comparatively more investment than "easily accessed water," and it is therefore termed here "less easily accessed water." This mode of obtaining water was frequently observed on the coastal plain—unlike other areas in Palestine—both at the beginning of the twentieth century and in later years:

> In the maritime plain, especially in the orange-gardens in the neighbourhood of Jaffa, irrigation is carried on from large wells, 60 to 100 feet [about 18 to 30 meters] in depth, from which water is pumped by means of an endless chain of earthenware jars or wooden buckets, passing over a wooden wheel, and dipping into the water at the bottom . . . another means of irrigation from shallow wells, pool, and rivers, is the *Shaduf* [a kind of wooden swing with a bucket connected to one side], which is but rarely seen in Palestine.[21] (Wilson, 1906)

> There is an urgent need for action along the Coastal Plain. The fear of general lowering of the water table, following the extremely rapid development of orange cultivation, has been freely expressed and has apparent foundation in the fact that some wells have had to be deepened, with consequent renewal of capital expenditure and additional revenue expenditure on irrigation.[22] (Shepherd, 1929)

> With the exception of those three areas [around Tel Aviv and Haifa and between Lydda and Rehovoth] in which the lowering of the water table has given cause for concern, there is, generally speaking, room for a considerable increase in pumping from the

underground reservoirs of the country.[23] (Government Memorandum, 1947)

It is not surprising that irrigation with underground water was much more frequent in the coastal plain than elsewhere. In the plain, most underground water could be found at shallow depths of 20 to 40 meters,[24] unlike the rest of Palestine. When the government investigated the availability of underground water, it found it hard to trace in areas such as the Jordan Valley and Hebron and between Gaza and Beersheba. Moreover, when water was located, it was mostly too saline for irrigation.[25] When a generous amount of water was accidentally discovered in a few government surveys, it was in the Jewish settlements on the Plain of Esdraelon.[26]

The disparity between the relatively high proportion of irrigated land in the coastal plain and the low proportion in the rest of the country is either because underground water did not exist or was not found or because accessing it demanded higher investment than on the coastal plain. This runs against Kamen's assertion that irrigation in Arab farms developed because of capital received by Arabs from Jewish land purchases. Without these funds, he maintains, Arabs would not have been able to construct irrigation systems.[27] Instead, as mentioned, many of these lands were already irrigated at the beginning of the Mandate period.

In cases where water was available, however, why were the irrigation methods so simple, such as those described by Shepherd? While Arab irrigation was sometimes perceived as backward, with practices unchanged over thousands of years,[28] irrigation in the Jewish sector was often referred to as different. Some observers asked why traditional modes of irrigation continued to be used in Palestine when new inventions could be seen on the farms of Jewish settlers.[29] One reason is that investment in capital-intensive projects for irrigation was less likely to occur while labor in the Arab economy was significantly cheaper than in the Jewish economy.[30] It was therefore far less expensive to irrigate by labor-intensive projects. Another reason is lack of capital. The installation of modern irrigation systems was simply too costly for many *fallāḥīn*. It is hard to determine the exact costs of installing irrigation, especially because of different needs in different areas and the lack of extensive and accurate data. Nevertheless, an account submitted by the high commissioner for Palestine in 1934 about the cost of installing an irrigation system in the Ain Arud agricultural and horticultural station (Hebron subdistrict) may give some clues. Its assessment was that £P410 was required for creating and irrigating 50 dunums in the first year. This was without pipes, in the Arab mode (£P300 for the creation of a well and the purchase of a pump and engine, £P80 for the creation of a cistern, and £P30 for maintaining the pump engine for a year). By comparison, the monthly salary of a gardener was £P6, a donkey was valued at £P10, and a mule at £P40.[31] Hence, it seems that the high cost of irrigation and the lack of capital[32] and credit[33] for Arab farmers were additional barriers to the development of existing irrigation systems on Arab lands.

However, when in the 1940s income from agriculture increased simultaneously with higher labor costs in the Arab sector,[34] motor pumps became more common in the Arab sector. Apart from this, irrigation consisted of reaching nearby water sources (both easily and less easily accessed, such as wells, cisterns, and streams) and using narrow open canals to the plots and between the beds (i.e., without the use of pipes, so that these canals had to be constantly maintained).[35]

Another aspect that influenced the development of irrigation was sheer lack of information. *Fallāḥīn* did not search for water in areas where they did not have information that it was available.[36] Indeed, it was irrational to dig without information (unlike in the coastal plain and the Plain of Esdraelon), as the chances of finding water were too low. Even with the information that the Zionists had about water sources in the Plain of Esdraelon (where their activity might be described as motivated more by nationalist reasons, "to conquer the land," *kibūsh ha-*

qarqa', than by economic necessity), only 34 out of 70 bores found any water in 1938.[37] Moreover, that level of success would have been lower if the Zionist organizations had not had equipment for deep boring, which enabled them to locate water previously beyond the range of ordinary digging.[38]

At the end of the Mandate period, then, most Arab lands were unirrigated. Geographical factors were not the sole determinant of this. The availability or not of capital (and credit) for Arab landowners who wished to engage in irrigation projects combined with a lack of information about underground water influenced the development of irrigation by individuals. In addition, the irrigation systems used in the Arab sector were simple, both because of capital constraints and the labor-intensive nature of the economy. Indeed, when in the 1940s labor expanded and capital became more abundant, some transfer into capital-intensive irrigation was noted. Labor and capital were not the only factors, however, because the government itself played a significant role in irrigation development.

Government Constraints on Irrigation

Irrigation with easily accessed water could have developed further if certain institutional constraints had not existed. Under the official *Mejelle* law, inherited from the Ottomans, the government owned all the water. This law dealt with upper-ground water, the main source of free water. The practice was otherwise, however, since the government did nothing to enforce its right until 1944 and not much after that.[39] Consequently, the custom that the landlord who had water on a plot of land also owned it was the de facto law. In these circumstances, the owner of a plot without accessible water could not use water for irrigation or else had to pay the "owner" for it. This is fully explained in *A Survey of Palestine:*

> However favourable the principles of the *Mejelle* may be to good irrigation procedure, there is in Palestine no legislation to apply the principles in administrative practice. During the seventy years

> which have passed since the *Mejelle* was compiled, many private users of public water supplies have come to believe that their title to the share they use is that of absolute ownership of water, completely independent of the land; and even some of the tenants of admittedly Government land have for some years been applying the Muslim law of inheritance to the water rights they claim, and have been selling, leasing and pledging astronomical fractions. In some cases a right which must be imaginary has changed hands. Those having the means, financial or otherwise, are able to acquire appropriate water at the expense of less influential cultivators.[40]

The government believed that it had to control the supply of water for irrigation, had to increase the amount to farmers, and had the right to introduce some charges for water use.[41] But it took no significant positive action, apart from some attempts to trace underground water. In fact, it hindered the development of irrigation, as it left unclear the situation in regard to property rights over water. Thus, private investment in irrigation did not secure long-term possession because the government could claim ownership of both water and project. The situation would have been better if the government had acted according to its convictions or, alternatively, had made sure that the informal institution of water ownership was replaced by the use of water as common property free to everyone for agricultural use (some practical restrictions would have been needed, of course). Paradoxically, even legislation affirming the de facto informal ownership would probably have encouraged long-term private investment, since property rights would have been secured, and this would have moved the rural economy forward.[42]

In 1929, Dawson Shepherd stressed the importance of government action in developing irrigation systems:

> [The] irrigation service should be in a position to advise on the development of springs and wells. Development in the hills will follow the construction of reservoirs to impound the winter floods and the digging of new wells by the cultivators themselves. For the latter purpose the services of an agricultural bank would be essen-

> tial, for there must be a very appreciable supply of subterranean water at present untapped owing to the lack of capital.[43]

But the government was indecisive. According to a committee that it appointed in 1940 to prepare a general development program, "too little had been done in the past in the matter of irrigation."[44] These conditions were virtually unchanged throughout the Mandate period. Very few loans were given by the government for irrigation,[45] those were only of small sums, and a limited attempt was made in the Negev to trace underground water and to collect upper-ground water, resulting in two additional local wells.[46] Some plans were outlined to extract more water from available sources, as well as from distant areas. The latter involved large projects, such as the diversion of the Liddani and Banyas Rivers into a lined high-level canal into the Battauf to irrigate the Plain of Esdraelon and the Battauf areas. These plans remained on paper.[47]

The Failure to Benefit from Irrigation

The geography of Palestine inevitably meant that different crops suited different parts of the country and resulted in varying levels of output per land unit. Citrus flourished on the coastal and Acre plains, and olives did better in the hill country. Lack of rain inhibited productivity in some areas and determined their suitability for certain crops, especially in the arid district of Beersheba, where barley had to be the main crop. Apart from regional differences, there were also intravillage differences in types of land and crop suitability.

In principle, the expansion of irrigation could have brought significant benefits to the Arab economy. It would have reduced the risk of crop failure, allowed a wider range of crops, multiplied yields, transformed arid lands into cultivated ones, and reduced seasonal unemployment. But irrigation systems did not become extensively used in the Mandate period and especially not in the Arab rural sector. Water was not available in many places, or its presence was not known. Where it was available, only small-scale projects demanding comparatively little capital could be developed by individuals. In such cases, simple irrigation systems were usually installed in the Arab sector, both because of capital constraints and the labor-intensiveness of the economy. Long-distance projects could not have been realized by the Arab private sector. A major change could occur only if the government created long-distance projects that served as agricultural infrastructure.

The government did not remain entirely passive. It announced its ownership of all the water in Palestine. It also pledged that the prevailing custom—that landlords who had water on their lands owned it—would be abolished. But by its subsequent inaction, the government left unclear the status of property rights over water. In practice, this meant that private investment in irrigation did not secure long-term possession because the government could claim ownership both of water and project. Consequently, only inexpensive projects were set up. The situation would have been better if the government had imposed its right to sell water or else legalized the informal institution of water ownership. It could also, with additional legislation and enforcement, have secured the access of "non-water owner" farmers to water resources. All in all, these various factors produced a situation where investment in Arab irrigation was insignificant.

QUESTIONING INVESTMENT IN LAND

Apart from irrigation, there were two other possibilities for land development: improvements in the quantity and quality of land. These are analyzed mainly at the macro level, so that micro-level changes (such as the effects of investment on a single farm or the decline occurring in another) are not included. Instead, an aggregate picture is presented of the Arab rural economy as a whole.

Kamen argues that significant agricultural development occurred in the Arab sector during the Mandate period:

> Substantial changes occurred [in Palestine] both in total area devoted to different crops and in their yields. . . . The relative share of subsistence agriculture in the economy of the Arab cultivators declined during the Mandate, as a greater proportion of the total agricultural product, whether measured by quantity or value, was derived from the intensive form of cultivation rather than from dry cereal farming. Most cultivators, however, continued to depend on grain crops. Intensive agriculture was irrigated, and its product was destined for the market. The major crop was citrus for export. . . . The other major market crop was vegetables, grown primarily for local consumption. No systematic information is available regarding the organisation of Arab citrus and vegetable production.[48]

But these "substantial changes" in Arab cropping did not occur. Continuity and in some respects decline rather than substantial changes better describe the trends. Kamen's basic error is that his data for the expansion of the area under cultivation in the Arab sector frequently combine figures for the whole of Palestine (i.e., they combine Jewish and Arab agriculture; the agriculture of "others" was negligible).[49] Similarly, he does not always use statistics from the return related to land use. Instead, he frequently uses the return for changes of yield over the years as a proxy for structural change in the agricultural footing. By so doing, he ignores "natural factors" such as rains and plagues, which were the main cause of variation in yields. In addition, he ignores changes in measurements. The statistics of yield return are often inadequate, especially for the 1920s and 1930s, when it was also common that the underestimation of crop returns was successively greater for earlier years (see Chapter 3). As a result, Kamen's description of changes in the Arab sector is more guesswork than analysis.

Two other micro-oriented arguments that Kamen puts forward are, first, that citrus and vegetable growers cultivated irrigated lands to produce for market but that other *fallāḥīn* continued to depend on subsistence dry-cereal farming and, second, that subsistence agriculture declined. But in 1945, about 55 percent of the vegetables produced on Arab lands were unirrigated.[50] In addition, this impression conveyed by Kamen of subsistence-farming, cereal-growing Arab peasants, versus market-integrated Arab farmers, is not well founded, and even Kamen admits he lacks "systematic information . . . regarding the organisation of Arab citrus and vegetable production." In fact (as is explored in Chapter 4), vegetables and fruit were grown by many ordinary, so-called subsistence *fallāḥīn,* who used to produce and consume these so-called cash crops in the same way as they did with wheat and other "subsistence crops." Where edible crops (the vast majority of crops in Palestine) were concerned, they were used in the peasant mode of consumption and marketing known as "part subsistence, part surplus."

Measuring Land Quality and Quantity in Palestine

Systematic data about the Arab land that was devoted to different crops and about the agricultural qualities of such land do not exist for all the Mandate period. The quality of data is better for the 1930s and 1940s. At that time, the Department of Statistics collected some statistics about different villages in *Village Note Books*. They recorded the different agricultural uses and quality of lands and some outputs.[51] The reason for collecting such records was the decision to change the old tax system (a tithe of the total yield) to a tax according to quantity and quality of land—regardless of yield (in practice, this also meant a reduction in taxation; see Chapter 1):

> The Rural Property Tax [was] a tax per dunum at varying rates on categories arranged according to the estimated productivity of the soil, and in some relation to the net annual yield. Generally, the rates of tax per dunum approximate to 10 per cent of low estimated net annual value of the several categories of land. The last three categories were originally exempted from the payment of the tax on the ground of their low net annual yield.[52]

For the purposes of rural property-tax administration, all the village lands of Palestine, except for the Beersheba subdistrict where the tithe was retained, were surveyed in 1935 and 1945. The outcome of these surveys, with their more comprehensive data, was collated in *Village Statistics.*[53] At the time of the surveys, the Department of Agriculture held the best information on village lands and could therefore update its aggregated statistics for all of Palestine. This seems to be why, after the 1945 survey, the department concluded that it had to revise the figures it had previously collected about all the areas under wheat and barley in 1945 by about 50 percent—from 2,954,000 dunums to 4,500,000.[54] It is therefore likely that a comparison of the data from these two benchmark years can show an improvement or deterioration in land quality, as well as an increase or decrease in village lands.

The data on villages provide information about the number of dunums according to different categories of lands for each village in Palestine. Sixteen categories of land are shown in Table 2.2. Categories 1 to 3 and 5 to 15 are of cultivated lands. Category 4 is of land that is built on or reserved for the erection of buildings and that does not relate to agriculture. Category 16 is broadly defined as "uncultivable" land and included "forest planted, indigenous and uncultivable land . . . roads, railways, rivers and lakes." Some of this had the potential to be transformed into cultivated land (for example, when an area of "indigenous land" was reclassified as Category 14), and as we shall see, this was not uncommon.

In regard to ethnic segregation, the *Village Statistics, 1935* provides information about "Jewish" lands, "non-Jewish" lands, and "roads, railways, rivers and lakes." The 1945 report keeps the same separation but makes an additional subdivision of the "non-Jewish" sector into "Arabs," "Others," and "Public." To be able to compare returns from the two sets (1935 and 1945), those for "non-Jews" are compared. However, it should be recognized that the "non-Jews" group was comprised mainly of Arabs. The divisions of 1945 show that Arabs dominated the ownership of "non-Jewish" cultivated lands (Arabs 94.1 percent, public lands 4.6 percent, and others 1.3 percent) and also the "uncultivable" lands (Category 16), yet less significantly, since a larger proportion of these were registered as public lands (Arabs 80.6 percent, public 18.2 percent, and others 1.2 percent). The public ownership definition did not mean that all these lands were blocked from Arab rural use. Indeed, villagers had grazing rights in most of the public forest reserves near villages (no rights were given to nonvillagers).[55] Overall, "non-Jewish" lands were predominantly under Arab control.

A comparison of the data for 1935 and 1945 shows that the total cultivated land (both Jewish and non-Jewish) had increased by 2 percent between 1935 and 1945 (Table 2.3). This refers to all Palestine except for the Beersheba subdistrict. At the same time, nonagricultural land for human use had significantly increased (built-on areas by 62.3 percent and roads and so on by 21.6 percent). On the other hand, there was a decrease in "uncultivable" land by 4.4 percent and in total land by 0.14 percent (apart from the shift into "cultivable," and it is possible that some village land was transferred to urban municipalities between 1935 and 1945).[56]

The transformation of about 2 percent of the so-called forest-planted and indigenous and uncultivable land into cultivated land, especially since such lands were usually referenced as "uncultivable," spells out the ambiguity of the uncultivability concept. In relation to the *Village Statistics,* this means that lands under category 16 were not necessarily uncultivable but rather that this category represents *uncultivated* land.[57] This can also be seen in a British report describing the changing of "uncultivable" lands into cultivation when land became scarcer:

> There has in the hills been a widespread attempt [by Arabs] to cultivate the lands which were previously regarded as the grazing ground of the village, or which were public "forests" on the neighbouring mountain slope.[58]

A key to this ambiguity is the definition of "uncultivable" land. In practice, one interpretation defined land as intrinsically uncultivable, while the other could argue for cultivability via

Table 2.2 Village Statistics, Categories of Lands

Category	Description	Basic Tax per Dunum or Part Thereof (in mils)	
		1935	1945
1	Citrus (excluding Acre subdistrict)	825	400
2	Citrus (Acre subdistrict) (lower taxes as an incentive)	410	40
3	Bananas	560	560
4	Village built on area or land reserved thereof and any area that in the opinion of the official valuer is revised for the erection of buildings	160	160
5	First-grade irrigated land and first-grade fruit plantation (hereafter other than citrus and bananas)	40	40
6	Second-grade irrigated land and second-grade fruit plantation	35	35
7	Third-grade irrigated land and third-grade fruit plantation	30	30
8	First-grade ground crop land and fourth-grade irrigated land and fourth-grade fruit plantation	25	25
9	Second-grade ground crop land and fifth-grade irrigated land and fifth-grade fruit plantation	20	20
10	Third-grade ground crop land and sixth-grade irrigated land and sixth-grade fruit plantation	18	18

11	Fourth-grade ground crop land and seventh-grade irrigated land and seventh-grade fruit plantation	15	15
12	Fifth-grade ground crop land and eighth-grade irrigated land and eight-grade fruit plantation	12	12
13	Sixth-grade ground crop land and ninth-grade irrigated land and ninth-grade fruit plantation	8	8
14	Seventh-grade ground crop land and tenth-grade irrigated land and tenth-grade fruit plantation	NIL	4
15	Eighth-grade ground crop land	NIL	2
16	Forest-planted and indigenous and uncultivable (read "uncultivated"; see discussion) land	NIL	NIL

Source: Government of Palestine, Department of Statistics, *Village Statistics, 1945;* Government of Palestine, *A Survey of Palestine,* pp. 251–52.

Table 2.3 Overview of Changes according to the Village Statistics, 1935 to 1945 (all Palestine excluding Beersheba subdistrict)

		Category 16 (dunums)			
	Cultivated Land: Categories 1–3 & 5–15 (dunums)	Forest Planted, Indigenous, and Uncultivable Land	Roads, Railways, Rivers, and Lakes	Build on and Urban Areas (dunums)	Total (dunums)
Non-Jews, 1935	6,113,413	6,166,353	—	103,241	12,383,007
Non-Jews, 1945	6,093,944	5,940,277	—	121,956	12,156,177
Change, dunums	−19,469	−226,076	—	18,715	−226,830
Change, percent	−0.4	−3.7	—	+18.1	−1.8
Jews, 1935	943,770	252,541	—	43,544	1,239,855
Jews, 1945	1,106,771	198,560	—	116,314	1,421,645
Change, dunums	163,001	−53,981	—	72,770	181,790
Change, percent	+17.2	−21.4	—	+167.1	+14.7
Palestine excluding Beersheba, 1935	7,057,183	6,418,894	115,979	146,785	13,738,841
Palestine excluding Beersheba, 1945	7,200,715	6,138,837	141,139	238,270	13,718,961
Change, dunums	143,532	−280,057	25,160	91,485	−19,880
Change, percent	+2	−4.4	+21.6	+62.3	−0.14

Sources: Government of Palestine, Department of Statistics, *Village Statistics, 1937;* Government of Palestine, Department of Statistics, *Village Statistics, 1945.*

further investment, such as building terraces. In fact, the cultivable/uncultivable definitions became somewhat politicized in the Mandate period, and there were many disputes about what could be cultivated and what could not. The origin of the "cultivability" approach was in the investigations of 1930, where the British decided to limit land transfer from Arabs to Jews by ruling that Jews could not buy land from Arabs except when sufficient cultivable land per Arab farmer would remain.[59] Disputes about cultivability existed not only among Jews, Arabs, and British officials but also among officials themselves. When, for example, in 1931 the Director of Surveys estimated the cultivable lands in Palestine at 8,044,000 dunums, the Commissioner of Lands assessed it as higher by about 53 percent, at 12,333,000 dunums.[60] Perhaps surprisingly, while the government estimated the cultivable lands in Beersheba subdistrict as about 2,000,000 dunums,[61] Moḥamad Yūnīs Al- Ḥusayni's figure was higher by 45 percent (totaling 2,900,000 dunums).[62]

This debate about what could have been cultivated was not the only one. There was a lesser debate about what had to be regarded as cultivated land. When comparing the statistics of the Department of Agriculture with those of the *Village Statistics*, an apparent paradox emerges, in that the figures on cultivated lands vary between the two sets (Table 2.4). At first glance, this is surprising, since, as mentioned, there was a tendency in the Department of Agriculture to update the agricultural statistics following the surveys for the rural property tax. The reasons for this may be different suppositions about the nonsurveyed lands of the Beersheba subdistrict and slightly different weighting methods. For example, low-quality lands that were partly cultivated were named "patch cultivation" by land surveyors:[63] one method could count the area between the patches, while the other could exclude it. Nevertheless, as can be seen in Table 2.4, the data from the survey (excluding the Beersheba subdistrict) and that from the estimations (including the Beersheba subdistrict) suggest that the cultivated land in Palestine increased slightly from 1935 to 1945 (by 2 percent excluding the Beer-

Table 2.4 Village Land in Palestine, in Dunums

	Department of Statistics Figures on Cultivated Land			Department of Agriculture Figures on Cultivated Land
	Excluding the Beersheba Subdistrict	Beersheba Subdistrict	All Palestine	All Palestine
Total, 1935–36	7,057,183	Unknown	Unknown	7,587,600
Total, 1945	7,200,715	2,000,000 (estimate)	9,200,715	7,600,500
Change	+2.03%	—	—	+0.17%

Sources: Government of Palestine, Department of Statistics, *Village Statistics, 1937;* Government of Palestine, Department of Statistics, *Village Statistics, 1945;* Government of Palestine, *A Survey of Palestine,* pp. 320–39; Government of Palestine, Department of Agriculture and Fisheries, *Annual Report for the Year 1945–46,* pp. 7, 15, 33.

Notes: Statistics for cultivated lands of the Department of Agriculture in 1935 are for 1936, since no comprehensive statistics were found for 1935. Those for 1945 were adjusted according to the official estimate that areas under wheat and barley were 4,500,000 dunums and not as previously given (2,954,000).

sheba subdistrict and by 0.2 percent inclusive). Hence, while in both statistics cultivability meant, in practice, land under cultivation, there was still a minor debate about the extent of land that this involved. To get a more accurate picture, statistics on land under cultivation are used both from *Village Statistics* and the Department of Agriculture.

The Deterioration in the "Non-Jewish" (Primarily Arab) Sector[64]

Unlike the picture for all Palestine, there was a decrease in cultivated lands in "non-Jewish" ownership by 0.4 percent. There was also a decrease by 3.7 percent in the uncultivated Arab lands and an increase in built-on areas (as seen in Table 2.3; *Village Statistics* returns, excluding Beersheba). Yet as is discussed below, other government estimates argued for a greater decrease in cultivated Arab lands (by 1.7 percent; see Table 2.5).

The main source for the decrease was the transfer of lands into Jewish hands[65] (see Chapter 1 for the impact of this on the Arab rural economy). It should be mentioned, however, that this decrease is mainly attributed to the years 1935 to 1940, since Jewish land purchase was restricted in most areas outside the Beersheba subdistrict following the Land Transfer Regulation in February 1940 (Figure 2.1).[66] Overall, the statistics of land purchase for the period 1935 to 1945 seem to represent a lower effect than in previous years. Even in that period, the transfer of "uncultivable lands" into cultivation did not fill the gap (see Table 2.3). Therefore, the quantity of cultivated land in Arab hands declined during the years 1935 to 1945. This was true for uncultivated land as well.

The *Village Statistics* data also help to assess the agricultural quality of Arab lands because the statistics from the two surveys provide information in their 16 categories about the number of dunums in the villages, and in general, the lower the category of cultivated land, the higher the agricultural development. This is especially clear for categories 5 to 16. Categories 1 and 2 (citrus)

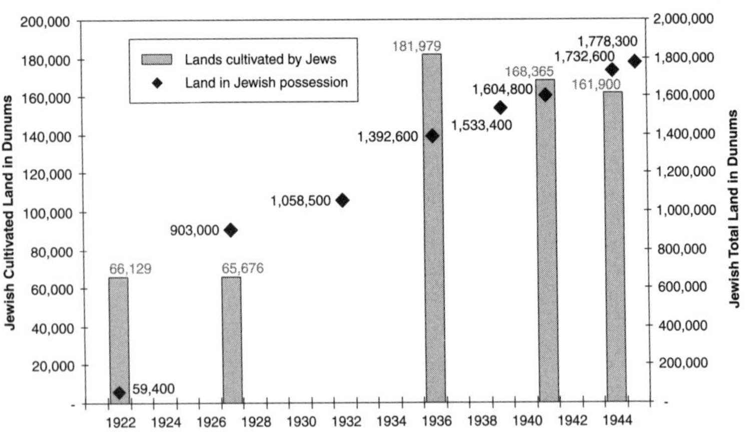

Figure 2.1 Lands in Jewish Possession and Cultivated Jewish Lands

Sources: Aaron Gertz (ed.), *Statistical Handbook of Jewish Palestine* (Jerusalem: Jewish Agency for Palestine, Department of Statistics, 1947), p. 140; Aaron Gertz and David Gurevich *Hityashvut ḥakla'it 'ivrit beerez ishrael: sqira klalit 7esikumey mi fqadim* (Jerusalem, 1947), statistical annexes.

reflected a highly intensive, irrigated crop (see Table 2.2). During World War II citrus trees were uprooted and the land converted to irrigated vegetables,[67] however, so a change from category 1 or 2 to 5 does not automatically mean that the land was underdeveloped. Any change in category 4 from one period to the next does not indicate a change in investment on agriculture. Not all categories are distinguished in the *Village Statistics:* categories 1 to 2, 5 to 8, 9 to 13, and 14 to 15 are combined. Hence, a change in the quality of land from, say, 10 to 9 cannot be seen, but a change from 9 to 8 can.

A comparison of changes from 1935 to 1945 is presented in Figure 2.2. It shows that there were no significant changes in the quality of Arab agricultural land, although some improvement seemed to occur. The most significant figures are the increase in categories 5 to 8 and the decrease in categories 9 to 13. In other trends, more land remained in categories 14 to 15, while less land stayed in citrus and bananas.

The minor improvement that took place in the quality of Arab

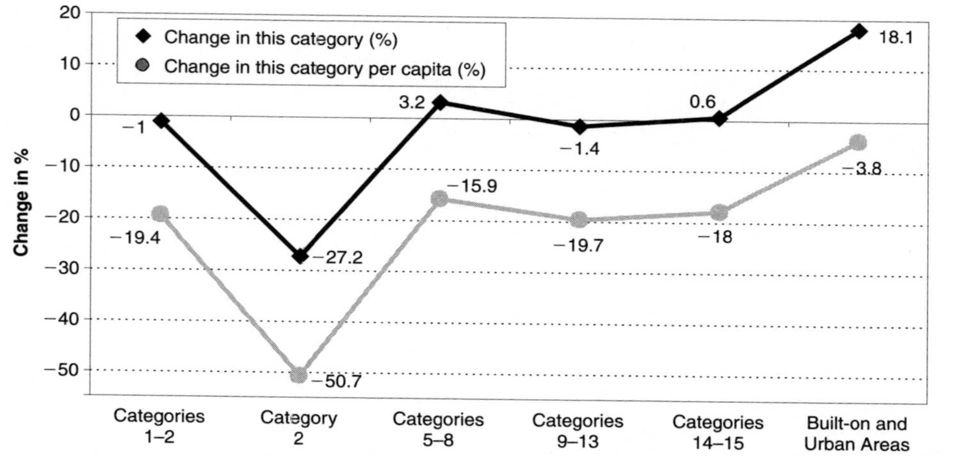

Non-Jewish Lands	Categories 1–2	Category 3	Categories 5–8	Categories 9–13	Categories 14–15	Built Areas	Popluation
In 1935 (dunums)	143,160	3,847	1,076,383	3,994,199	895,824	103,241	941,247
In 1945 (dunums)	141,720	2,802	1,111,168	3,936,711	901,543	121,956	1,155,860
Change (dunums)	−1,440	−1,045	+34,785	−57,488	+5,719	+18,715	+214,613

Figure 2.2 Change in Quality and Quantity of "Non-Jewish" Land, 1935 to 1945
Sources: Government of Palestine, Department of Statistics, *Village Statistics, 1937;* ibid., *1945,* Table 1.3.

land between 1935 to 1945 represents a minor investment in land. To this should be added the lack of significant investment in irrigation and the small reduction of total land in Arab possession. These, when aggregated, seem to suggest a period of stagnation and low investment (in micro terms). But when the data are combined with the rapid demographic growth in the non-Jewish sector, a clearer picture of deterioration per capita Arab rural inhabitant emerges, both in the quality and quantity of land (see Figure 2.2). In none of the categories was there an improvement per capita. The growth in population was faster than land development between 1935 and 1945.

What about the preceding years—1922 to 1935? It is clear that irrigation did not improve much during this period. It is also clear that Jewish land purchase and Arab rural demographic growth reduced the ratio of land to Arab rural inhabitants. No comprehensive data are available for other forms of development, such as investment in terraces or tree planting. Still, unlike the 1920s and 1930s, income from agriculture increased during the 1940s (see below). This encouraged investment, and more capital was available for investment at that time because of the increase in total real income. On the other hand, the 1940s were also a period of greater employment of villagers outside their villages, and as they found supplementary employment, labor-intensive work, such as building of terraces, was less likely to occur. While it is hard to reach a definitive conclusion, the facts available might imply a weaker pattern of investment prior to 1935. To sum up, the evidence from this and the previous section suggests that investment in land and irrigation (aggregately speaking) rarely occurred on Arab-owned land during the Mandate period and, per Arab rural inhabitant, continually deteriorated.

CROPS SPECIALIZATION AND OUTPUT

Understanding the nature of farming specialization in the Arab sector gives a closer picture of the structure of and changes in

Arab agricultural produce, draws attention to the response to market incentives, highlights important differences between net and gross income in different periods, and explains the production trends for different crops. These topics are the basis of a large part of the discussion in this book

Specialization on Arab Farms

The statistics of the Department of Agriculture, combined with those of the Jewish Agency, provide details of Arab cultivation. The Department of Agriculture published data about crop specialization in Palestine for various years beginning in 1936.[68] At that time, they had relatively accurate data, especially after the surveys of 1935 and 1945 for the rural property tax. In parallel, the Jewish Agency conducted several surveys of Jewish cultivation in Palestine. The deduction of "Jewish" from the "all Palestine" returns permits a rough analysis of Arab cultivated lands for the years 1936, 1942, and 1945. The figures should be viewed as approximate, especially since the data for the Jewish sector are for the preceding year in the cases of 1942 and 1945 (i.e., for 1941 and 1944).[69] In addition, the findings for 1941 to 1942 are from the in-between surveys (i.e., between 1935 and 1945) and should bc regarded as less accurate and probably underestimated.[70] The results, after subtraction of the Jewish share, are presented in part A of Table 2.5, and part B gives statistics on the Arab share in cultivation available from the *Survey of Palestine.*

There are some differences between the statistics of parts A and B in Table 2.5. These might relate to different estimations of cultivated lands in Palestine or possibly just a mistake regarding the sources for B, since the statistics contradict some of the returns presented three pages earlier from the same source.[71] Still, there are some clear results about the pattern of crop growing that can be derived from the two sets. Grains and legumes, predominantly wheat and barley,[72] were the most prevalent crops on Arab lands (about 80 to 85 percent of total cultivated land),

Table 2.5 Arab Cultivated Lands in Palestine (approximate figures)

A. Subtraction of Jewish Land from Total Land

	1936	1941–42	1944–45			1936–45
	Dunums	Percent	Dunums	Dunums	Percent	Change in Dunums
Grains and legumes	6,283,632	84.9	(5,556,600)	5,793,627	79.6	−490,005
Other field crops	296,736	4.0	(291,061)	406,851	5.6	+110,115
Vegetables (including melons)	137,556	1.8	(200,474)	246,022	3.4	+108,466
Olives and almonds	523,096	7.1	(624,926)	631,700	8.7	+108,604
Citrus	101,140	1.4	(148,579)	146,000	2.0	+44,860
Other plantations	62,488	0.8	(27,030)	53,500	0.7	−8,988
Total	7,404,648	100.0	(6,848,670)	7,277,700	100.0	−126,948
Index of total cultivation	100			98.3		

B. Government Data for 1945

	Grains and Legumes	Vegeta-bles	Melons and Watermelons	Fodder	Olives	Other Plantation	Citrus
Dunums	5,621,859*	239,733	120,304	23,970	592,546	355,709	122,958
Percentages	79.4	3.5	1.7	0.3	8.4	5	1.7

* The figures of the total land under wheat and barley were adjusted; the ratio between Arabs and Jews was kept the same for calculating the Arab additional fraction. See the explanation in the text for difference between parts A and B and for changes in grains and legumes, as well as for other field crops in part A.

Sources: Gertz and Gurevich (1938), statistical annexes 20–21; Gertz and Gurevich (1947), statistical annexes; Aaron Gertz, *Habityashvut ha7hakla'it ha'ivrit beerez ishrael: sefer yad statisti le7haklaut* (Jerusalem, 1945), pp. 70–71; Gertz, *Statistical Handbook*, pp. 162–63; Government of Palestine, *A Survey of Palestine*, pp. 323, 326, 339.

followed by olives at about 7 to 8 percent (the statistics for olives and almonds in section A represented mainly olives).[73] Vegetables accounted for about 2 to 3.5 percent (note that in part A melons and watermelons are included in vegetables, unlike part B), and citrus about 1.5 to 2 percent.

In regard to the changes that occurred between 1936 and 1945, the comparison (based on part A)[74] indicates that Arab cultivated lands decreased by 1.7 percent between these years (representing a higher change than the 0.4 percent suggested by the *Village Statistics;* see Table 2.3). It shows that although most of the tilled land remained under grain and legumes, there was a decrease in the total land under such crops, probably from 88.9 to 85.2 percent.[75] This change, with a slight reduction in "other plantation" is not insignificant because it permitted more vegetable cropping and more planting of olives and citrus. Still, it is important to note that not all trends are evident here. Not only did total cultivated land decrease between the two benchmark years; there was also, as we have seen, a combination of Jewish land purchase causing a decrease in land availability and a transfer of "uncultivable" lands into cultivation. Thus, the overall changes were not always changes on the same land plots.

Comparison of Gross Income from Crops

How can the changes outlined above be explained? It seems that variations in prices and gross income provide a partial explanation—especially because gross returns do not necessarily reflect net returns and the problem of segregation in the returns for Arab and Jewish sectors is also a factor. Since the transfer was mainly from grains and legumes to other crops, the comparison of returns for different crops relative to grains and legumes can be helpful. It is important to note that the figures used are based on *Village Note Books* returns for the post-1934 period (the highest data quality for the Mandate period). In Figure 2.3, chart A compares gross income per dunum of certain crops to that of grains and legumes (no information about yields per unit

A. Index of Gross Income per Dunum in Comparison to Wheat

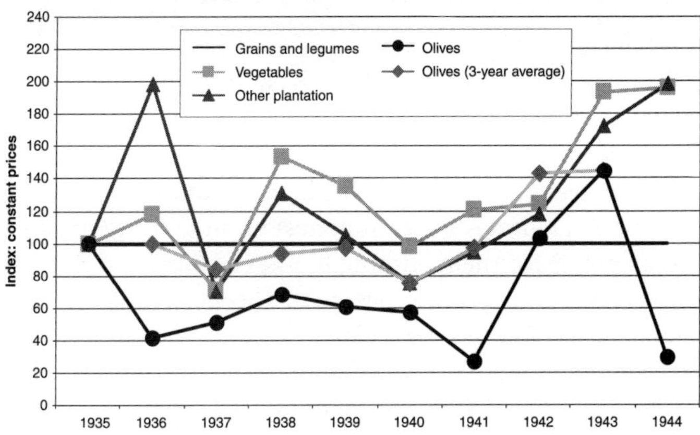

B. Index of Wholesale Prices of Certain Crops in Comparison to Wheat

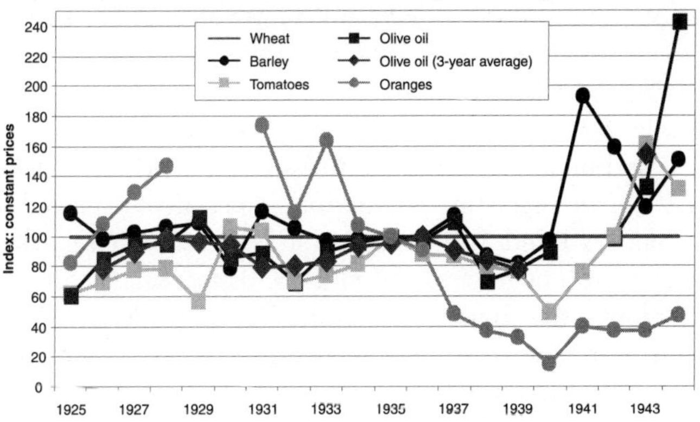

Figure 2.3 Gross Income and Prices for Certain Crops, in Constant Prices

Source: Government of Palestine, Department of Statistics, *Statistical Abstract of Palestine* (various years).

Notes: The price index of each commodity was divided by the annual figure of wheat according to the index of constant prices (taking 1935 as a base year) and multiplied by 100. For Figure 2.4B, the data were calculated from the tables in the Department of Statistics source dealing with "area, production, and value of principal crops," which are available for the years 1935 to 1944. During the 1940s, price controls were imposed. The comparison in chart B from 1942 onward is less accurate, since wheat and barley prices represent the subsidized prices (SP). Chart A seems to give a fairly sound comparison for the 1940s because controlled and uncontrolled prices are combined. Prices are in constant prices, which have been deflated according to Metzer's index for the Arab sector in Metzer, *The Divided Economy,* p. 241.

area is available before 1935), and chart B presents evidence about the prices of certain commodities between 1925 and 1944, thus offering a longer-term perspective. While data for chart B are available only for certain crops (and not aggregated as in chart A), wheat—the commonest grain and legume crop—stands as proxy for them, although not, of course, an exact substitute; the same with tomatoes, which were the most common vegetable crop, and oranges, which were the commonest citrus fruit.[76] Finally, prices of olive oil stand as proxy for prices of olives (there are no comprehensive data for fruit prices).

It can be seen that in spite of some fluctuations, the relative gross income from vegetables (and to a lesser extent the relative prices of tomatoes) increased significantly during the years 1935 to 1944. This reflects a relative increase in vegetable output per land unit (see below) and the stronger local market demand for vegetables[77] from Jewish immigrants, from the British Army (which had many units in Palestine during World War II), and from the growing Arab population, especially in urban areas (see Chapters 1 and 3).[78] Yet it should be noticed that market incentives were not high in the mid-1930s, especially for unirrigated crops—the majority of which were grown by Arabs—since at that time there was an overproduction of unirrigated vegetables in the summer months.[79] Hence, as far as vegetables are concerned, it is likely that market incentives had an important influence on bringing more lands under cultivation. Because the most noticeable relative change in prices occurred in the 1940s and because the activities increasing output per land unit of vegetables were at their height during the 1930s and 1940s (especially during wartime),[80] the most significant change in crop specialization seems to have occurred after the mid-1930s and not before. In this connection, it is worth mentioning that the qualitative descriptions of agriculture in the 1920s and 1930s indicate that grain was a major crop, with secondary cultivation of fruits and vegetables.[81]

The yield from olives, with regard to the species grown in Mandate Palestine, tends to vary greatly between years, and a low-yield year usually followed a high-yield year and vice versa (a phenomenon that was only partly related to rainfall).[82] To get a clearer picture while following the overall olive trend, in addition to the original returns, returns according to the three-year average method are presented in both charts (e.g., the return for "olive oil (3-year average)" for 1940 is an average of the years 1939, 1940, and 1941). This method leaves some years out of the comparison, especially the border years (no average was presented if information was missing for any three successive years). The picture that emerges is one of considerable relative improvement in income from olives during the 1940s. Even here, it is likely that market incentives influenced the transfer of more lands into olive growing. The fact that the most marked change occurred in the 1940s, combined with the qualitative returns referred to above, might imply that planting was less significant pre-1935.

In the case of citrus, some changes occurred between 1936 and 1945 that cannot be seen in Figure 2.3. Citrus production steadily increased from the beginning of the Mandate period up to 1939 in response to market demand. But later some citrus groves were even uprooted because of constraints on exporting by sea while German submarines operated in the Mediterranean.[83] This gave some boost to vegetable cropping, as the Department of Agriculture reported:

> Uprooting of groves continued. About 6,000 dunums were uprooted during the year, these uprooted areas being in most instances used for the production of vegetables."[84]

It is interesting to note that although the comparative decline in citrus prices began in 1933 (see Figure 2.3), the level of investment seems to have been unchanged, presumably because of the long-term nature of tree-crop investment (Figure 2.4). Similarly, in spite of the wartime fall in prices, many lands remained under citrus in the hope of better days. The inability to export the fruit at that time, especially during the agricultural years 1940 to 1941 and 1941 to 1942, caused losses in that the cultivation of

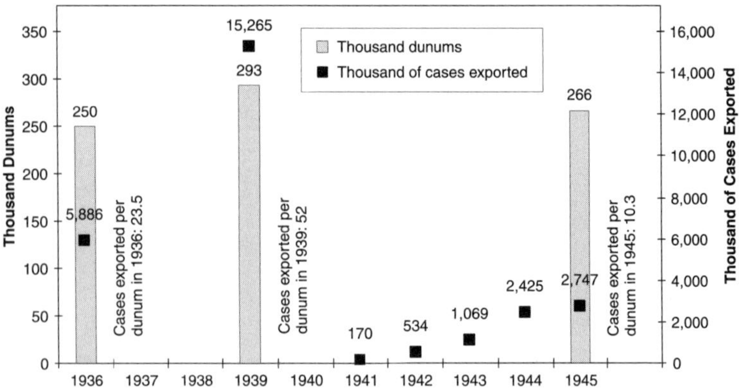

Figure 2.4 Citrus in Palestine: Area Cultivated and Cases Exported, 1936 to 1945

Source: Government of Palestine, *A Survey of Palestine,* pp. 336–37, 355.

many groves was neglected and crops were left to rot on the tree. Some remedy was found by feeding fruit to livestock or burying it as manure,[85] but a number of orchards were uprooted.[86]

Finally, Figure 2.3 shows that the relative price of barley increased. Clearly, it would have delivered better returns than the average for grains and legumes. This gives an insight—obscured by the aggregate picture—into why the shift away from grains and legumes was not faster. Most important, in spite of the limitations, it seems that the change in crop specialization in Palestine was heavily dependent on market incentives, and the incentives for modification were especially high in the 1940s. Yet if this was the case, why was the changeover so small?

Why Not a Larger Shift to Vegetables?

We have already noted that the shift in the relative prices of vegetables and fruits occurred during wartime. A rapid response to the new demand for food could be achieved by moving to vegetable cropping. Unlike additional planting of fruits, there was no need to wait until trees reached maturity before a marketable crop was produced. Also, bearing in mind that the war was the major determinant of this movement in relative prices (the build-up of troops in Palestine and the constraints on sea trade because of German submarines) and that it could end at any time, it is probable that there was a preference to move toward vegetable cropping because of its greater flexibility. Why, then, was this not larger in the Arab sector?

Vegetables, however, require relatively more water—and higher-quality land—than grains and legumes,[87] so that not all grain and legume lands could be transferred to vegetable cultivation. This is closely connected to the known low investment in irrigation. Even so, vegetables could be grown on unirrigated lands, and in the Arab sector 55 percent of vegetable lands were unirrigated in the agricultural year 1944 to 1945.[88]

Still, it seems that much more land could have been turned over to vegetables on an unirrigated basis, but the incentives for this were not always high. One reason is that prices tended to fall when unirrigated vegetables went to market, and because vegetables were nearly all ready at a particular time, they tended to flood the market, leading to cheaper prices. One might also argue that the low response to increased vegetable cropping was an outcome of the peasant mode of agriculture (part surplus, part subsistence), but this does not seem to be the case, particularly because vegetables are edible crops and were used for both subsistence and marketing. They also had a long shelf life and were carefully conserved by the peasants for consumption throughout the year (see Chapter 4).

At the same time, vegetables demand significantly higher investment than grains. Their cultivation was far more intensive and demanded much more labor (which varied according to type of vegetable). In 1938, when the government advised on vegetable cropping in Palestine, it suggested paying close attention to the "labour capability of the farmer."[89] It was only during the prosperity of the 1940s that both the relative prices of vegetables and the opportunities and wages for low-skilled Arab laborers increased significantly (see Chapters 1 and 3). This meant that inputs for vegetable cropping were also much higher in the 1940s, which emphasizes the necessity for any discussion on incentives for transformation to deal with net rather than gross income.

Implications for Net Agricultural Output Figures

Although no comprehensive data on net returns were available for use in the present study, it has been noted that vegetables and plantations required greater long-term investment (because of no fruits for several years from planting of trees and a preference for irrigation of vegetables), as well as short-term investment (labor and fertilizers—discussed below). This conclusion is especially important for the discussion of net agricultural product in Chapter 3.

Metzer and Kaplan's calculations of net output were based on changes in total agricultural output and did not take into account specific crops or even branches of crops.[90] Rather, they use a restricted calculation of net output as a fraction of gross output (their net outcome for the years 1922 to 1939 varied only between 63.7 and 74.2 percent of the gross).[91] This tendency, in light of transfer into vegetable cropping, could lead to increasingly overvalued net returns compared with earlier calculations.

The distortion caused by this method of calculation was not insignificant, since even a small change in vegetable and fruit production translated into a significant change in gross income. For the Jewish sector, data for estimated agricultural output are available for the years 1937 and 1945. The subtraction of these from the available data for "all Palestine" gives the "Arab share," presented in Figure 2.5. It is important to note that these returns are a very rough approximation and that 1945 was during the prosperity, when relative prices of agricultural product increased, especially for prices of fruits and vegetables. Still, the modest change in crop specialization meant a substantial increase in value of gross agricultural output. While gross output

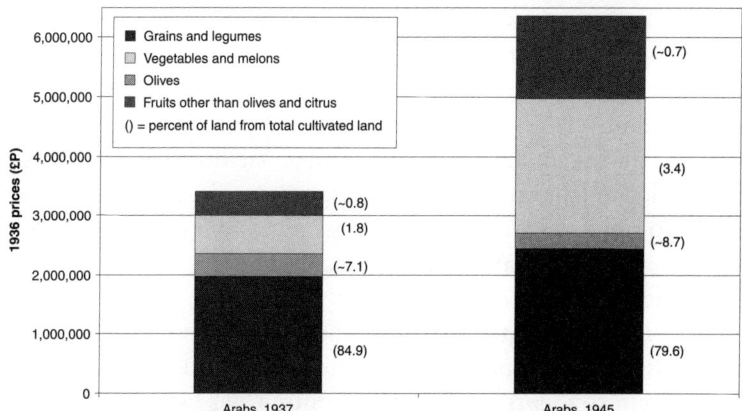

Figure 2.5 Rough Approximation of Gross Income from Main Branches of Arab Agriculture (excluding Citrus)

Sources: Government of Palestine, Department of Statistics, *Statistical Abstract of Palestine* (1939), p. 41, and (1944–45), p. 226; Gertz, *Statistical Handbook of Jewish Palestine,* p. 166.

Note: The returns should be viewed as rough estimates.

(in money terms) of Arab grains and legumes was higher in 1945 by about 24 percent, the total agricultural output was higher by 87 percent (65.7 percent "per capita rural inhabitant"[92]). This was largely the result of the returns in fruits and vegetables. However, in full calculations of net returns, the outcome of total agricultural output would appear far less dramatic than the immediate picture given by the gross returns in Figure 2.5.

Bearing in mind the significant differences between gross and net returns, I now make a final assessment of outputs from cultivation.

Did Output per Land Unit Increase?

While neither land quality nor irrigation showed substantial improvement, other inputs were possible where there was more intensive use of labor in cultivation, more capital, and new techniques. Such inputs included the use of high-yield varieties (HYVs) of seeds, better manure, deeper ploughing, better weeding, and the use of pesticides, all of which can increase the output per unit (yield per dunum).[93]

Nevertheless, much caution is needed. Yields per dunum were highly dependent on natural factors, such as the amount of precipitation, the intervals between rainy and rainless days, climatic variation in each year, different plagues, attacks by insects, and life cycles (as far as olives are concerned). Because of the many variations and the lack of comprehensive data about each factor,[94] it would be imprudent to create an equation that combines all of them to identify a "normal" output per land unit.

Long-term returns can give a rough idea of overall trends, but there are several constraints. The weighting systems were different for the years 1922 to 1928 (based on tithe returns), 1929 to 1934 (based on some field inquiries in villages and discussions of results from these inquiries with the *mukhtār*s; this was the period when some data were collected in the *Village Note Book*s and yet the tax on produce remained), and 1935 to 1945 (field inquiries in villages, discussions with the *mukhtār*s, and a tax now on land, not yield). This also meant that in the later years, there was less underestimation (the lower the taxes on produce, the less incentive there was for reporting low returns). In addition, the data before 1935 predate the rural property tax survey and are therefore less accurate. A comparison can thus be done within each group but not between them, and some comparison problems exist in the 1929 to 1934 period.[95] In addition, within the periods, a change in output per dunum may be surmised only if a significant change occurred within subgroups (e.g., 1935 to 1940 versus 1941 to 1945); otherwise, no meaningful conclusions can be reached.

There is a need to deal with each crop separately, since each has a different yield (wheat produces a different yield per dunum in terms of weight than, say, tomatoes). While data on yield per dunum are available mostly for the years 1935 onward,[96] the comparison here will concentrate on 1935 to 1945. Finally,

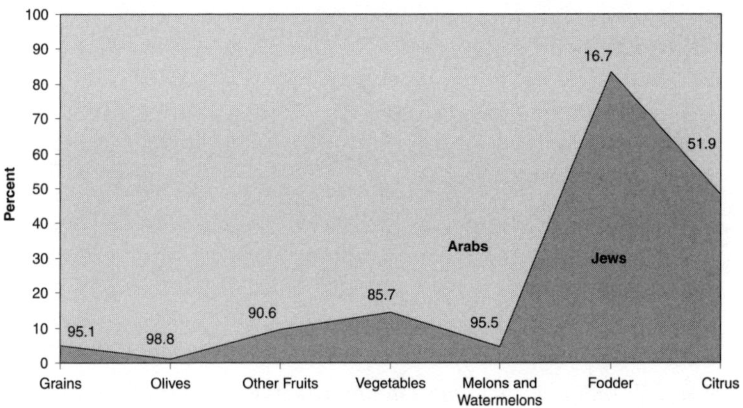

Figure 2.6 Arab and Jewish Shares in the Farming of Distinct Crops, 1945

Sources: Government of Palestine, *A Survey of Palestine,* pp. 323, 339; Government of Palestine. Department of Agriculture and Fisheries, *Annual Report for the Year 1945–46,* pp. 7, 33.

Note: Grains data for 1945 were modified by keeping the percentages as in the first source and using the total grains as updated in the second.

since the data are available for all Palestine (Arabs and Jews), the Arab share in total land shown in Figure 2.6 should be carefully noted.

Generally speaking, Arabs dominated the growing of grains and melons and to a lesser extent fruit trees and vegetables. Fodder was predominantly in Jewish hands, and citrus was equally divided between the two sectors.[97] To what extent, then, can one speak about continuity or change in output per land unit in the produce that was predominantly Arab?

Figures 2.7 to 2.9 show no obvious trends in output per land unit in grains and fruit trees. This is not the case for vegetables and melons, where significant increases in output per land unit can be seen (compare pre-1937 returns with those from 1937). Here supportive evidence is available from 1931 (probably early surveys) that reinforces the picture emerging from examining 1935 to 1945. This increase in the output of vegetables seems to

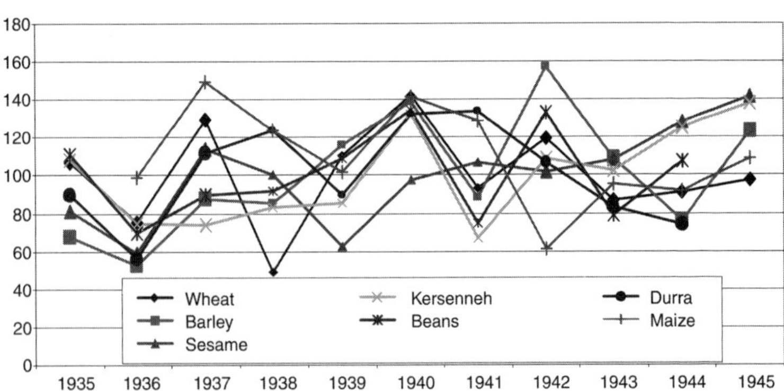

Figure 2.7 Index of Yield per Dunum (Average = 100), Grains and Legumes

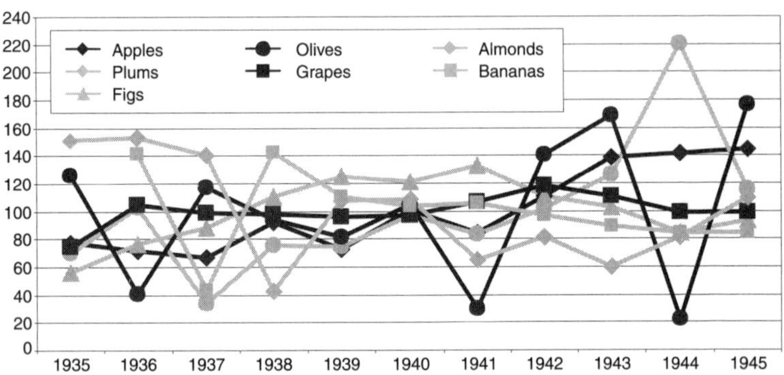

Figure 2.8 Index of Yield per Dunum (Average = 100), Tree Fruits

be closely related to the activity of the Department of Agriculture (see Chapter 7). Still, since most of the Department's activity was during the 1930s and 1940s,[98] this could imply that no such increase in output per land unit occurred in the 1920s.

The conclusion has to be drawn that crop specialization in the Arab sector did not change significantly during the Mandate period. This is not to deny that modest changes took place, and indeed they did, probably mostly from the mid-1930s until the end of the period. The main reasons for this lack of significant

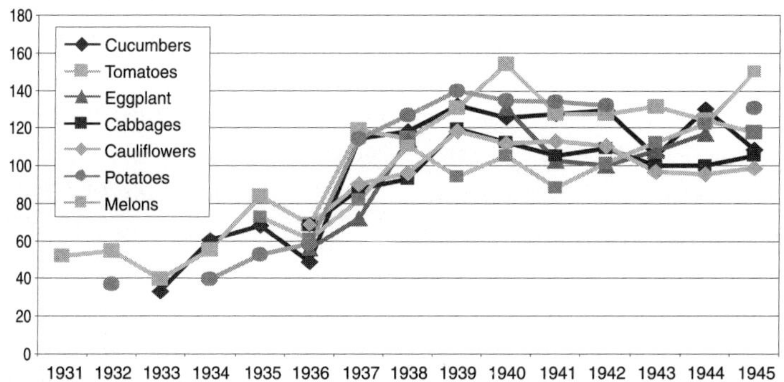

Figure 2.9 Index of Yield per Dunum (Average = 100), Vegetables and Melons

Sources for Figures 2.7 to 2.9: Government of Palestine, Department of Statistics, *Statistical Abstract of Palestine* (various years); Government of Palestine, Department of Agriculture, *Annual Reports* (various years); Government of Palestine, *A Survey of Palestine,* pp. 320–27.

change seem to be the lack of irrigation and the consequently reduced market incentive for change. In addition, the need to discuss net incomes adequately for the understanding of trends, as well as for a fruitful discussion of net agricultural output, has become apparent. Finally, in regard to Arab agriculture, the only significant change noted in output per dunum was in vegetable cropping. This increase was related to the Department of Agriculture's activity, which is discussed in Chapter 7.

LIVESTOCK SPECIALIZATION AND OUTPUT

The following discussion of the patterns of product specialization in livestock breeding and the changes in it includes an inquiry into the accuracy of the statistics. This information leads to a more precise analysis of the Arab share in livestock.

Livestock: Aggregate Statistics

Before 1930, the data cannot be regarded as more than unsupported estimates. Indeed, the first census of livestock was held only in July 1930.[99] A comparison of pre-1930 data with data from 1930 also calls into question the reliability of the figures, as can be seen in Figure 2.10 (note especially the extreme case of buffaloes). The overall picture for livestock ownership in Palestine for the 1920s is therefore obscure.

Even after the first census in 1930, the data remained far from accurate. That enumeration, like all others taken in the Mandate period (1932, 1934, 1937, 1943) was based on declarations by *mukhtārs*. These were not very accurate. *Mukhtārs* (and the *fallāḥīn* even more so) tended to underreport what they owned because the animal tax was paid per head (excluding poultry).[100] This is indicated by the following quotations from the annual reports of the Department of Agriculture:

> It was decided in connection with the World Agricultural Census, to complete in 1930 a census of livestock. . . . Livestock census forms were distributed in June through the agency of the District Administration, to all Mukhtars, with instructions to complete

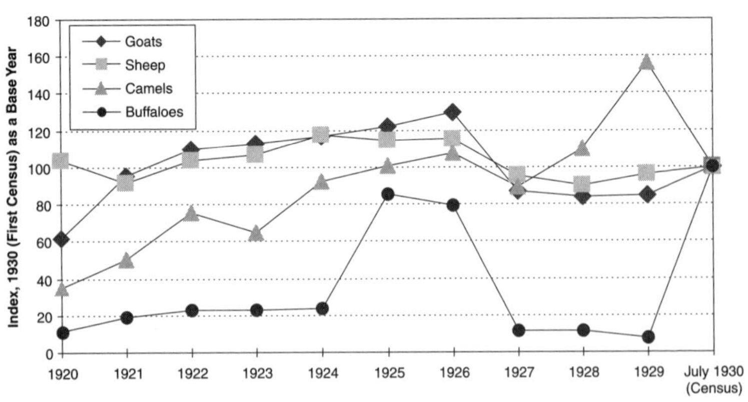

Figure 2.10 Index of Pre-1930 Government Estimates of Livestock (February)

Source: Government of Palestine, Department of Statistics, *Statistical Abstract 1936,* p. 33.

Note: The animals selected for the comparison are those for which numbers are available for most of the period. They were owned mainly by Arabs.

> during July, as accurately as possible, and return them to District Officers. As no livestock census was taken previously, stock owners were very suspicious and considered the census as a preliminary to imposition of additional taxation. Every endeavour was made, however, by the District Officers to calm their fears and the value of a livestock census fully explained to them. It is considered, however, that the figures rendered fail to reflect the total numbers of animals in the country. This particularly applies to cattle and poultry, as such animals are not subject to taxation. [The case for cattle seems to be a mistake; see Figure 1.4.] The tribes of Beersheba and a few tribes located in the Jericho Sub-District, however, refused to give any information. Estimated figures in respect of Beersheba Sub-District have therefore been provided by the District Officer.[101]

In spite of official efforts, it seems that censuses did not succeed in producing accurate results:

> Enumeration forms were distributed by the District Administrative Officers to all Mukhtars with instructions to complete them as accurately as possible and return them before the end of August [1932]. . . . It is considered, however, that there are more animals in the country than the statement shows, as owners are very reluctant to give any information as to their possessions and usually state that they have a smaller number of animals than they actually possess owing to fear of additional taxation.[102]

Notwithstanding these shortcomings, livestock censuses present the best data, and there is no reason to believe that the tendency to underreporting changed between the different censuses. The first census in 1930 is therefore compared with the last one in 1943.

It is worth mentioning that the use of these two benchmark years does not disguise any trend emerging from the intermediate data for 1932, 1934, and 1937, since these, in principal, show the same trends as the two benchmarks.[103] The returns are presented in Figures 2.11 and 2.12.

The data for Palestine as a whole indicate a significant increase in livestock rearing between 1930 and 1943. The most

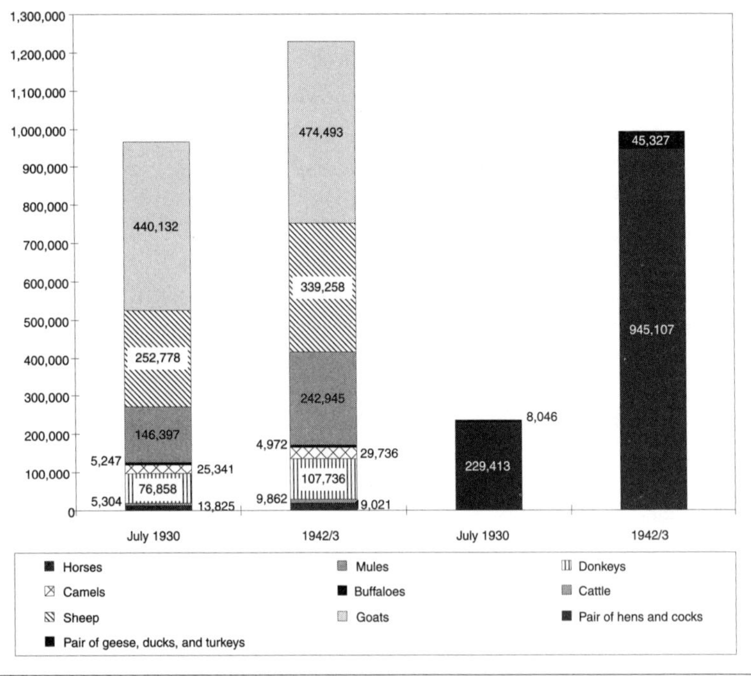

	Horses	Mules	Donkeys	Camels	Buffaloes
In Arab Title, 1943	88.7%	74.3%	97.8%	100%	100%

	Cattle	Goat	Sheep	Hens and Cocks	Geese, Ducks and Turkeys
In Arab Title, 1943	88.3%	97.7%	94.4%	64.6%	18.1%

Figure 2.11 Livestock in Palestine According to Censuses, 1930 and 1943

Source: Government of Palestine, Department of Statistics, *Statistical Abstract of Palestine 1944–45,* p. 235.

Notes: Data for "hens and cocks" and "geese, ducks, and turkeys" for 1930 are for 1932 (note that these are presented in pairs). About 50 camels were in Jewish possession in 1942 and were included in donkeys. Cattle suffered frequent epidemic diseases during 1926 to 1936, causing great losses (Stein, *The Land Question,* pp. 143, 145). For the 1932, 1934, and 1937 agricultural censuses, there are separate data for "poultry" and "laying hens and cocks" (the latter is part of the former). Since in 1943 the data are only for "laying hens and cocks," however, the comparison here is between data of this category (Government of Palestine, Department of Statistics, *Statistical Abstract of Palestine 1944–45,* p. 235; ibid., *1936,* p. 33; ibid., *1943,* p. 86. While the figures for 1930 are for "all Palestine," those for 1943 are only for Arabs and Jews. Hence the gap between these censuses could even have been slightly higher because the first census excluded animals belonging to "others," including the British forces.

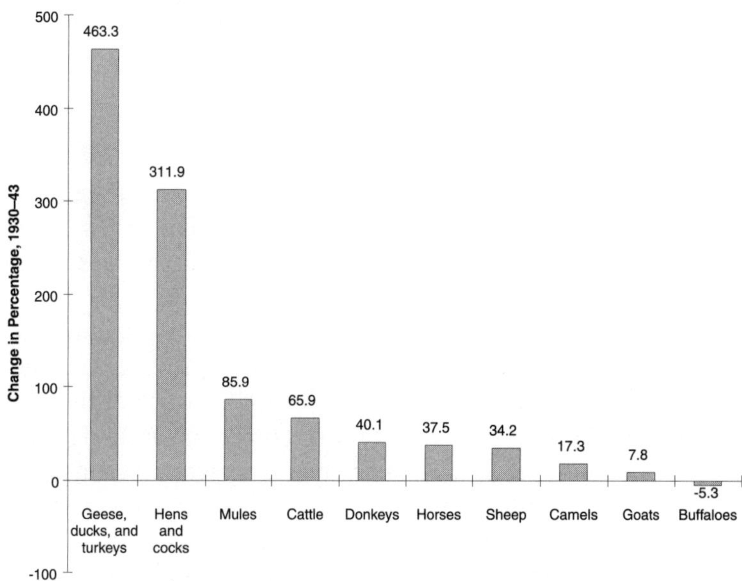

Figure 2.12 Change in Percentages in Livestock in Palestine According to Censuses, 1930 to 1943
Source and notes: See Figure 2.10.

noticeable change can be seen on the left side of Figure 2.12—the increase in bird rearing. Other animals increased significantly as well. Figure 2.11 shows that the main types of four-legged livestock were goats, sheep, cattle, and donkeys, while chickens led the poultry section; geese, ducks, and turkey were much less important.

Beginning in 1931, the government of Palestine provided hatching eggs and birds free to Arabs or at nominal prices.[104] This (as is discussed in Chapter 7) had a significant influence on the growth in poultry. In addition, the government provided veterinary services, which indirectly assisted the rearing of animals. It is possible that much of the total increase, apart from poultry, was related to a natural increase in animal breeding. In the case of meat, the rising demand was not met solely by the country's stock but also caused massive importation of animals for slaughter (Table 2.6).[105]

Livestock in the Arab Sector

Taking these data for Palestine as a whole, the share of the Arab rural sector in the change can now be assessed. The data separation is not perfect, yet an idea of the main trends can be seen in Figure 2.11.

As Figure 2.11 shows, in 1943 the buffaloes, camels, donkeys, and goats were predominantly held by Arabs. Since there was no known change in the composition of Jewish livestock during the 1930s and 1940s, a crude adaptation is made for our purposes, while data about the four types of animal are treated as in Arab ownership. For cattle, hens and cocks, and sheep, data exist for livestock in Jewish ownership for the years 1927 and 1936.[106] The average number between the two years stands as a proxy for Jewish ownership in 1930; these were subtracted from the data for all Palestine in that year to arrive at the Arab share. With no supplementary evidence about horses, mules, and birds other than hens and cocks, these are left out of the comparison. Yet as Figure 2.11 indicates, neither horses nor mules were the most important of the riding and working animals of the Arab economy in 1943, nor were "other birds" central to Arab poultry rearing. The trends shown in Figures 2.13 and 2.14 give a rough idea of the main trends in animal rearing in the Arab sector.

Figures 2.13 and 2.14 show that the most significant increase between 1930 and 1943 in Arab livestock ownership was in hens and cocks (457 percent; 356.2 percent per capita), and there was a more modest but still significant increase in the number of cattle (62.3 percent; 32.9 percent per capita), donkeys (40.2 percent, 14.8 percent per capita), and sheep (30.2 percent, 6.6 percent per capita). For camels and goats, there was an increase in total number, but at the same time there was a decrease

Table 2.6 Slaughtered Animals from Imports and from Local Supply

	1930	1931	1937	1938	1945
Cattle slaughtered	20,706	23,419	53,590	55,044	69,857
Cattle imported for slaughter	6,581	8,155	27,101	28,130	27,887
Imported out of total slaughtered	31.7%	34.8%	50.5%	51.1%	39.9%
Goats slaughtered	79,918	60,734	100,338	67,251	76,945
Goats imported for slaughter	19,927	22,496	85,812	40,461	37,767
Imported out of total slaughtered	24.9%	37%	85.5%	60.1%	49%
Sheep and lambs slaughtered	149,254	187,728	219,929	184,425	206,301
Sheep and lambs imported for slaughter	76,672	110,100	237,838	100,837	133,773
Imported out of total slaughtered	51.3%	58.6%	108.1%	54.6%	64.8%

Source: Government of Palestine, *A Survey of Palestine,* pp. 821–22.

Notes: The figures should be regarded with suspicion, as they cover only about 80 percent of the slaughter places of the Jews and about 38 percent of those of the Arabs; also, some slaughtered meat was imported.

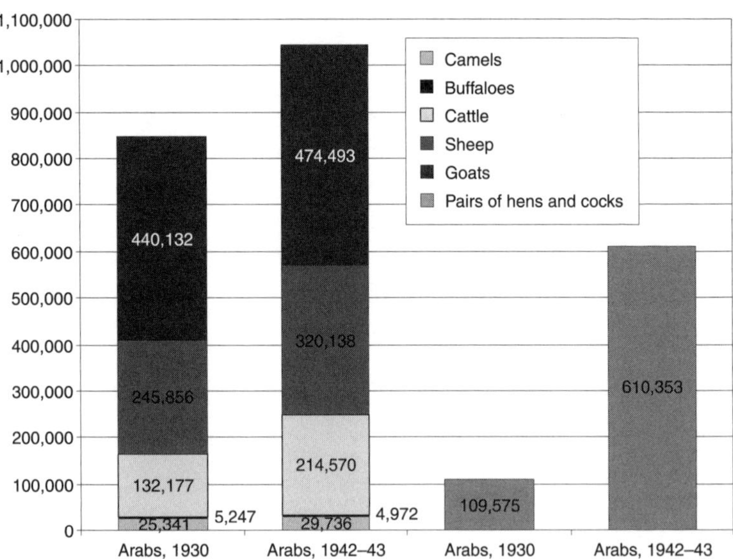

Figure 2.13 Rough Estimate of Livestock in Arab Ownership, 1930 and 1943

Sources: Government of Palestine, Department of Statistics, *Statistical Abstract of Palestine 1944–45,* p. 235; Gertz, *Statistical Handbook,* pp. 164–65.

Notes: For calculation methods and the precautions to be taken while reading this data, see the preceding discussion.

in per capita availability of these livestock. Finally, buffaloes showed a decrease both in total and per capita numbers.

The earlier discussion of crop values dealt with prices of crops in Palestine. Data for livestock prices under the Mandate are scarce, and those selected for the price analysis of livestock are therefore the average for each of the main types of animal and are taken from custom reports on imports for 1930 and 1943. By definition, these prices were not necessarily similar to those inside the country and might have been higher, since there seemed to be a tendency to import better brands. There was, for example, a preference for importing *bayrūtī* (literally, "from Beirut") cattle, which were considered to have a high resistance to

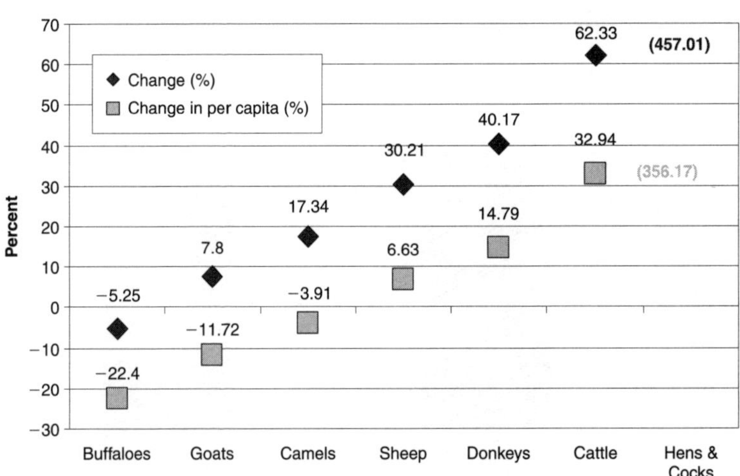

Figure 2.14 Rough Estimate of Change in Total Livestock in Arab Ownership and Livestock per Capita Rural Inhabitants, 1930 and 1943

Sources: In addition to those for Figure 2.13, Government of Palestine, *A Survey of Palestine,* p. 150, Table 1.3.

disease. But they appear to have been more expensive. One of my interviewees said that because of the cost, only "rich" *fallāḥīn* could have bought *bayrūtī* cattle, while the others had native *(baladī)* cattle.[107]

In terms of value, Figures 2.15 and 2.16 indicate that between 1930 and 1943 there was an annual growth in the value of livestock in Arab ownership of about 2.2 percent (with a total increase of 33 percent). This implies that the increase in value of livestock in the Arab sector was slightly less than that in the more capital-intensive Jewish sector.[108] However, when dealing with per capita returns, it becomes clear that the population growth was higher than the increase in livestock value, since that value decreased by 7.6 percent between 1930 and 1943.

It has been mentioned that although the aggregate data on "Arab agriculture" primarily comprises returns for the economy

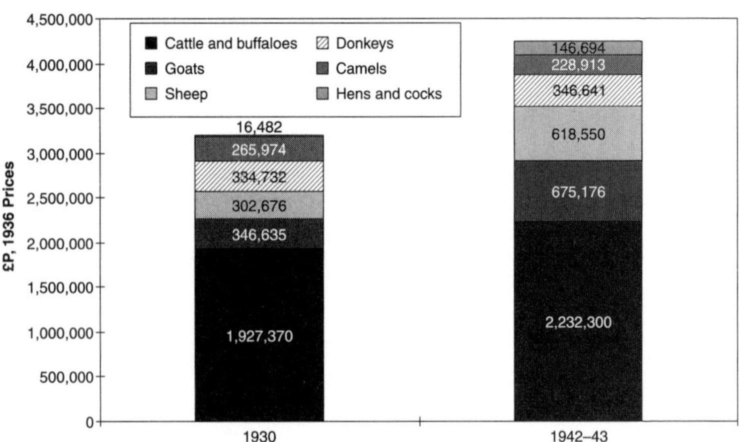

Figure 2.15 Rough Estimate of Livestock Value in Arab Ownership, 1930 and 1943

Sources: For prices: Government of Palestine, Department of Customs, Excise, and Trade, *Statistics of Imports, Exports, and Shipping for the Year Ended 31st December 1930,* pp. 179–80, 295; Government of Palestine, *Statistics of Foreign Trade for the Years Ended 31st December, 1942 and 1943: Compiled and Published by the Department of Statistics in Collaboration with the Department of Customs, Excise and Trade,* pp. 6–7, 67. For livestock: see Figure 2.13.

associated with the *fallāḥīn,* it also includes other returns for other Arabs. This is especially relevant for livestock, since some urban dwellers owned various animals,[109] and the Bedouin also raised animals.[110] Moreover, livestock breeding was not the main occupation of the *fallāḥīn.* It is therefore relevant to discuss their livestock in more detail.

Fallāḥīn livestock was usually part of the farm and was raised by the *fallāḥ*'s family. In the villages of Dehi, Tur'an, and Mashhad in Galilee, each *fallāḥ*'s farm customarily had one or two goats, two to four sheep, a few hens, and occasionally a donkey and a cow or bull.[111] There were, of course, *fallāḥīn* who had more than others, yet it is clear that the changes in their livestock ownership are, to some extent, supportive evidence for changes in wealth. This was noted by observers such as Charles

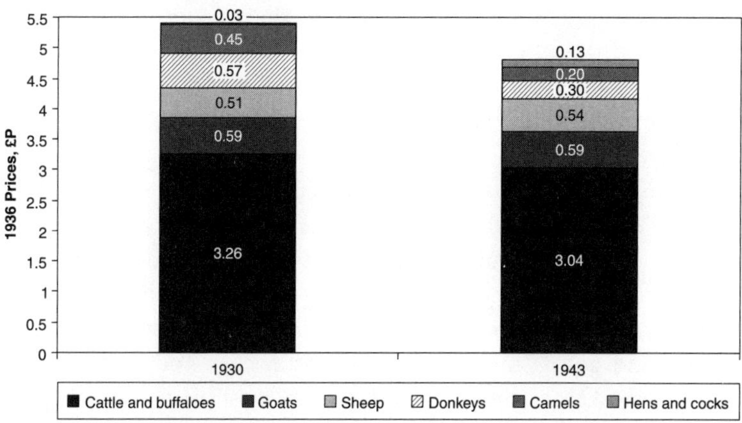

Figure 2.16 Value of Livestock in Arab Ownership per Capita Rural Inhabitants, 1930 and 1943 (estimate)
Source: Figures 2.14 and 2.15; Table 3.1.

Thomas Wilson ("the cultivation of the soil being, with cattle rearing and sheep keeping, the chief source of wealth")[112] and E. Grant ("the rearing of sheep, goats and cattle is the vocation of the villagers")[113] as well as Abū ʻAbdallah, a former *mukhtār,* who told me that "everybody had his own livestock. The rich had more, and the poor had less."[114]

Since the data do not distinguish between urban, rural, and nomad populations, can these subdivisions in the Arab sector be identified? Urban share, by its nature, seemed to be small. Yet what about the division between animals raised by *fallāḥīn* and by Bedouin? Unlike the *fallāḥīn,* livestock breeding was the main occupation of the Bedouin.[115] *Fallāḥīn* did not wander with their flocks all year round and therefore reared their animals on winter grazing and commonly had to add dry food in the summer.[116] Consequently, there was also a difference in type of livestock breeding. At that time, Bedouin did not keep cattle and chickens like the *fallāḥīn.* The government estimated in 1930 that 87 percent of camels, 68 percent of sheep, and 43 percent of goats were raised in the "Beersheba nomadic areas." On the other hand, it suggested that less than 6 percent of cattle were raised there.[117] Remembering the proportion of cattle and chickens in the increases in number of head and in value, it can be assumed that the *fallāḥīn* had a significant share in the increase in livestock.

To sum up, the most significant increase between 1930 and 1943 in Arab livestock ownership was in hens and cocks. There was a more modest but still significant increase in the number of cattle. These improvements were noted mainly in the *fallāḥīn*'s villages. Although there was a total increase in the number of camels and goats (these were both in *fallāḥīn* and Bedouin areas), there was at the same time a decrease in the per capita availability of these livestock (buffaloes show a decrease in both measurements). In terms of the value of livestock in Arab ownership, between 1930 and 1943 there was a total increase of about 33 percent, but when population growth is combined with these figures, a per capita rural inhabitant decrease of 7.6 percent is shown.

THE EFFECT OF URBAN-RURAL BARTER TERMS OF TRADE

One influence on *fallāḥīn* income (and thus on net output) was the terms of trade between agricultural and nonagricultural products. A comparison of "agricultural" and "nonagricultural" prices gives some indication of the purchasing power of the *fallāḥīn*. If the relative price of "nonagricultural," "urban" commodities (i.e., commodities that the *fallāḥīn* purchased and did not produce) against rural prices increased, then the purchasing power of the *fallāḥīn* was likely to decrease, and vice versa. A limited way of identifying some changes is to convert current prices of agricultural commodities into constant ones. This enables a comparison to be made between agricultural commodities and the average price of all commodities (that is, "agricultural" and "nonagricultural"), although because of the overlap only substantial changes can be noticed. Still, such a comparison is useful, since the changes were substantial.

The prices of products available for this comparison are limited, especially because of the need to maintain the same definition of a product (e.g., "mutton" and not "kosher mutton") and to have full time-series of prices (some prices are not available for all years). Nevertheless, the returns are for significant agricultural commodities: wheat, barley, mutton, eggs, chick peas, tomatoes, and onions. All prices were deflated to the same base year, 1925 (Figure 2.17).

As can be seen in Figure 2.17, the relative prices of agricultural commodities varied throughout the 1921 to 1944 period. However, the average returns seem to suggest that from 1925 to 1932 relative prices were fairly stable. They then became lower (with some increase during the Arab Revolt of 1936 to 1939, which might be ascribed to increased transaction costs and thus prices, as is described in Chapter 1). The prosperity years, however, brought a significant change in relative prices. While in 1940 the average return on the index was 88, it stood at no less than 164 in 1943.

It might have been even more useful to compare net urban-rural barter terms of trade—that is, the value of agricultural versus nonagricultural commodities. But the data available are very limited. Because of the inadequate statistics on "nonagricultural commodities," I used price data for rice, coffee beans, sugar, and salt. All were products commonly purchased by the *fallāḥīn,* although they also bought different "nonagricultural" products (such as cast hoes and sickles)[118] that are not included here. There is also no indication that these "nonagricultural" products were purchased on a large scale. The findings, and the variations in different agricultural commodities, are presented in Figure 2.18.

The results in Figure 2.18 are, as anticipated, more extreme than those in Figure 2.17 because the initial comparison of agricultural products is not with only nonagricultural products. The fluctuations are more extreme, and so are the returns (the aver-

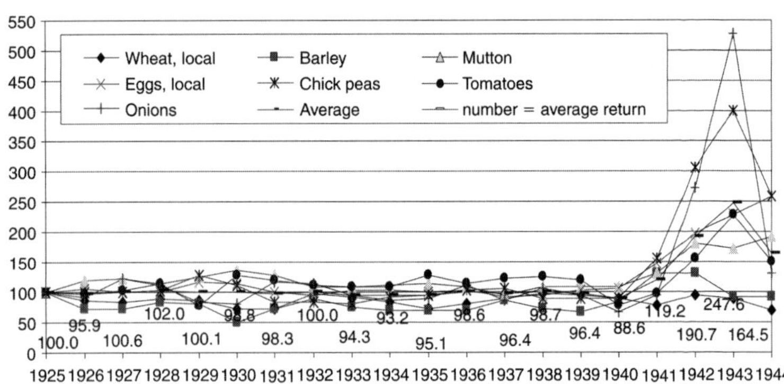

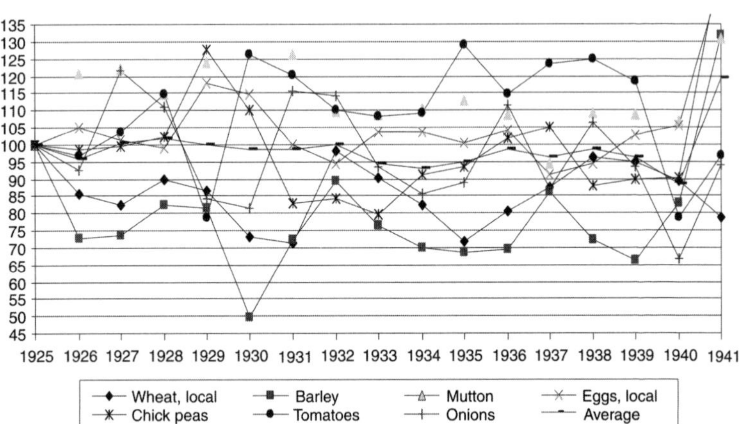

Figure 2.17 Index of Constant Prices of Agricultural Products
Sources: Government of Palestine, Department of Statistics, *Statistical Abstract of Palestine* (1938 and 1944–45), in Metzer, *The Divided Economy*, p. 241.

age return in 1940 was 91, but this had risen to 301 in 1943). Another notable difference is that while the earlier return for the years 1932 to 1935 showed a decrease in relative prices, the outcome in Figure 2.18 is of an increase (probably due to misrepresentation of the selected "urban prices" in the barter comparison). Together, the two comparisons—constant prices and barter—indicate fluctuations without significant change until

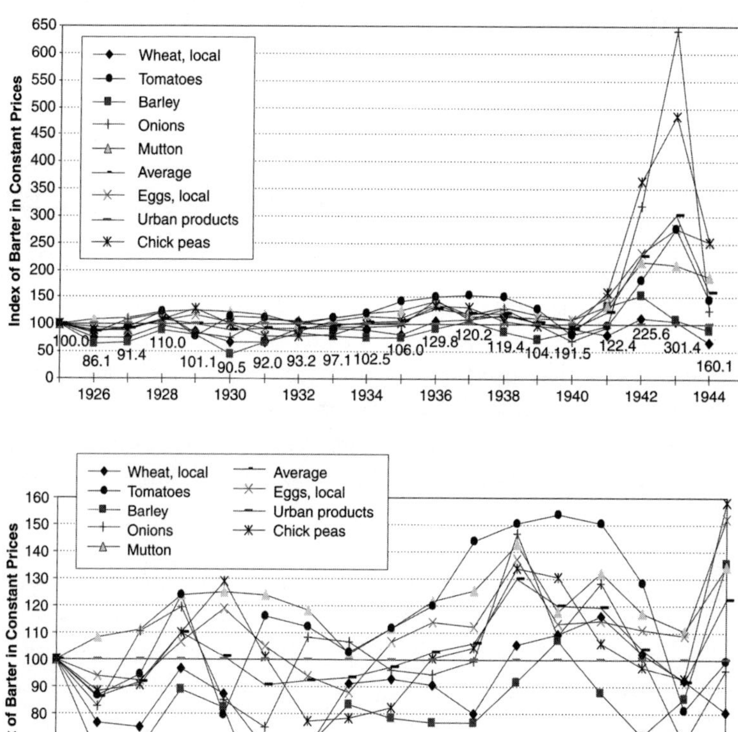

Figure 2.18 Index of Net Urban-Rural Barter Terms of Trade

Sources: Government of Palestine, Department of Statistics, *Statistical Abstract of Palestine* (1938 and 1944–45).

Notes: Because the prices for oranges in 1929 and 1930 and for watermelons for 1936 and 1938 were missing, the price was taken to be the average of the other rural products in the comparison. The prices of milk for 1929 and 1930 were likewise omitted, as there seems to be an error in the data (prices for those years are higher by 3800 and 7900 percent for the years on either side).

1940. The comparisons, however, clearly identify the dramatic changes in relative prices during the 1940s.

CONCLUSION

In principle, an expansion of irrigation could have brought significant changes in the Arab economy. It would have reduced the risk of crop failure, allowed a wider range of crops to be grown, multiplied yields, transformed arid lands into cultivated ones, and reduced seasonal unemployment. However, irrigation did not become widely used in the Arab sector during the Mandate period. Where easily accessed water was available, small-scale projects requiring comparatively little capital investment could be developed by individuals. But the government failed to create the long-distance projects that could have served as agricultural infrastructure. It also left unclear the implications of its ownership of all the water in Palestine. Consequently, private investment in irrigation was limited. The minor improvement that occurred in the quality of Arab land reflects a minor investment in land (most quantitative data are from the mid-1930s). The lack of significant investment in irrigation contributed to this. But at the same time, the amount of land in Arab possession diminished. These meant that there was a continual deterioration, per Arab rural inhabitant, in both quality and quantity of agricultural land.

The most notable increase in Arab livestock ownership between 1930 and 1943 was in hens and cocks and is related to governmental programs. There was a more modest but still significant increase in the number of cattle. These improvements seemed to occur mostly in the *fallāḥīn* villages. Although camels and goats (these were reported both in *fallāḥīn* and Bedouin areas) grew in total number, there was at the same time a decrease in the per capita rural inhabitant availability of these livestock (buffaloes show a decrease in both measurements). In other words, aggregately in the case of livestock as well, the demographic growth was higher than the growth in animals. The total value of the livestock in Arab ownership increased by about 33 percent between 1930 and 1943, but when population growth data are combined with these figures, a per capita rural inhabitant decrease of 7.6 percent is revealed.

Crop specialization in the Arab sector did not appear to change significantly during the Mandate. A modest change took place, probably mainly from the mid-1930s to the end of the Mandate period. Grains were obviously the main crop, followed by noncitrus fruit trees and vegetables. Market incentives determined the changes in vegetable cultivation. The relative increases in vegetable yields and in prices brought about a doubling of the lands covered by vegetables in the Arab sector between 1936 and 1945, reaching about 3.5 percent of total cultivated land. However, the diversion into vegetable production did not create as significant a change as was supposed by Metzer and Kaplan (for further discussion of their data, see Chapter 3). Instead, it was the relative increase in prices of agricultural foodstuffs (broadly defined) compared to other prices—thanks to the "miracle" of the 1940s—that caused the increase in agricultural net output.

Taking into account the low investment, the minor change in crops specialization, the probably far fewer differences than were predicted in a previous study on net return on vegetables (especially unirrigated vegetables) compared with grains, and the low (aggregate) progress in livestock, it seems reasonable to assume that if there was a positive change in income it should have been in the 1940s rather than before. The paradox between this tentative conclusion and the hitherto unchallenged narrative of sustained growth from the early years of the Mandate is discussed in detail in the following chapter.

On the historiographical level, a different and more reliable picture of Arab agriculture has now been established from that depicted by Kamen, who argues that there were "substantial changes" in the area devoted by Arabs to different crops. The evidence brought forward here suggests the opposite and highlights the importance of using a variety of sources.

NOTES

1. Walt W. Rostow, *The Stages of Economic Growth: A Non-Communist Manifesto,* 2nd ed. (Cambridge, 1960); William Arthur Lewis, *The Theory of Economic Growth* (London, 1956); Robert M. Solow, "A Contribution to the Theory of Economic Growth," *Quarterly Journal of Economics,* 70 (1956), pp. 65–94; Paul M. Romer, "Endogenous Technological Change," *Journal of Political Economy,* 98, no. 5 (1990), pp. S71–S102; Robert J. Barro, "Economic Growth in a Cross-Section of Countries," *Quarterly Journal of Economics,* 106, no. 2 (1991), pp. 407–44. See discussion in Debraj Ray, *Development Economics* (Princeton, 1998).
2. E.g., Government of Palestine, *A Survey of Palestine: Prepared in December 1945 and January 1946 for the Information of the Anglo-American Committee of Inquiry* (Jerusalem, 1946), pp. 105–06, 422.
3. Ibid.; Government of Palestine, Department of Statistics, *Statistical Abstract of Palestine 1944–1945* (Jerusalem, 1946), pp. 10, 217–19; David Grossman, *Hakfar ha'aravi 7e-bnota7: tahaliḥim bayeshuv ha'aravi be-'erez ishra'el batqufa ha'otmanit* (Jerusalem, 1994), pp. 55–130; Government of Palestine, Department of Agriculture and Fisheries, *A Review of the Agricultural Situation in Palestine, By E. S. Sawer, Director of Agriculture, Palestine* (Jerusalem, 1922), p. 4.
4. Government of Palestine, *A Survey of Palestine,* p. 310.
5. See Government of Palestine, Department of Agriculture and Fisheries, *Annual Reports* (Jerusalem, various years).
6. Moḥamad Yūnīs al-Ḥusayni, *Al-tatwūr al-'ijtimā'ī fi filasṭīn al-'arabiyyah* (Jerusalem, 1946), p. 96.
7. "The 'intensive' system, that is, farming under irrigation, permits a wide range of rotations and crops, and is capable of producing high yields and more than one crop in a year." Government of Palestine, *A Survey of Palestine,* pp. 310, 313; Dawson Shepherd, "Some Aspects of Irrigation in Palestine," *Palestine and Middle East Economic Magazine,* 8 (February 1933), pp. 63–65.
8. Government of Palestine, *A Survey of Palestine,* p. 326.

9. Government of Palestine, Department of Agriculture and Fisheries, *Annual Report for the Year 1944–1945,* p. 6.
10. In a drought year, the gap would have even been wider.
11. Government of Palestine, *Report of a Committee on the Economic Condition of Agriculturists in Palestine and the Fiscal Measures of Government in Relation Thereto, W. J. Johnson, R. E. H. Crosbie et al.* (Jerusalem, 1930), p. 4.
12. E.g., see Map 1.3.
13. As discussed below.
14. Government of Palestine, *Memorandum on the Water Resources of Palestine* (Jerusalem, 1947), pp. 2–3.
15. See broadly Amos Nadan, *The Arab Rural Economy in Mandate Palestine, 1921–1947: Peasants under Colonial Rule,* Ph.D. thesis, London School of Economics and Political Science, 2002, Chapters 1 and 2. The issue of capital is dealt in Chapter 4. In regard to credit, see George Hakim and M. Y. El-Hussayni, "Monetary and Banking System," Sa'id B. Himadeh (ed.), *Economic Organisation in Palestine* (Beirut, 1938), pp. 502–04.
16. Government of Palestine, *Memorandum on the Water Resources,* p. 12.
17. Government of Palestine, *Memorandum on the Water Resources,* pp. 5, 9; Elihu Grant, *The People of Palestine* (Philadelphia, 1921, reprinted 1976), pp. 18–19, 22–23.
18. Compare the areas referred to in the following extracts with the area under Arab possession in Map 3.1.
19. PRO/CO/733/174/9, 1929, Report on irrigation services by Dawson Shepherd, Irrigation Officer of Palestine, passim. See also his short essay, "Some Aspects of Irrigation in Palestine."
20. Grant, *The People of Palestine,* p. 145.
21. Charles Thomas Wilson, *Peasant Life in the Holy Land* (London, 1906), pp. 220–21.
22. PRO/CO/733/174/9, 1929, Shepherd, Report on irrigation services, p. 6.
23. Government of Palestine, *Memorandum on the Water Resources,* p. 6.
24. Sa'id B. Himadeh, "Natural Resources," Sa'id B. Himadeh (ed.), *Economic Organization in Palestine* (Beirut, 1938), p. 51. The assessment of 20 to 40 meters depth should not be taken for granted, but the borings were comparatively shallow. Wilson suggested that

"irrigation is carried on from large wells, 60 to 100 feet [about 18 to 30 meters] in depth." Wilson, *Peasant Life in the Holy Land,* pp. 220–21.

25. Government of Palestine, *Memorandum on the Water Resources,* pp. 6, 12.
26. Avraham Granovsky, *Land Policy in Palestine* (New York, 1940), p. 193.
27. Charles S. Kamen, *Little Common Ground: Arab Agriculture and Jewish Settlement in Palestine, 1920–1948* (Pittsburgh, 1991), pp. 173–93. This argument originated in the Jewish propaganda for land sales from Arabs to Jews. E.g., Jewish Agency for Palestine, "The Palestinian Arabs under the British Mandate," *Palestine Papers,* no. 4 (1930), pp. 33–35; Granovsky, *Land Policy in Palestine,* pp. 6–7.
28. E.g., Shmuel Hurwitz, *Ḥaqla'ut ba-mizraḥ ha-*'aravi (Tel Aviv, 1966), pp. 18–25.
29. Samuel Ludwig, for example, suggested that transfer of Jewish agricultural knowledge could stimulate progress in the Arab sector: Jewish Agency for Palestine, Economic Research Institute, *Jewish Agriculture in Palestine: A Progressive Factor in Middle East Economy, by Dr. Ludwig Samuel* (Jerusalem, 1946), p. 113. See also M. Smelansky, "Jewish Colonisation and the Fellah," *Palestine and the Near East,* 5, no. 8 (May 1930), pp. 146–59.
30. Zvi Sussman, "The Determination of Wages for Unskilled Labour in the Advanced Sector of the Dual Economy of Mandatory Palestine," *Economic Development and Cultural Change,* 22, no. 1 (1993), passim. especially p. 99. See also data on Arab and Jewish labor published in Government of Palestine, Department of Statistics, *Statistical Abstract of Palestine* (various years).
31. PRO/CO/733/268/10, November 1934, Officer Administering the Government of Palestine to Sir Philip Cunliffe-Lister, His Majesty's Principal Secretary of State for the Colonies (pp. 9–11, PRO pages).
32. PRO/CO/733/174/9, 1929, Shepherd. Report on irrigation services, p. 5.
33. This is explored in Chapter 5.
34. Discussed in the next chapter.
35. E.g., Interview with Al-'Othmān Sālim Maṣrāwa (Mr. Maṣrāwa, b. 1918, worked as a *fallāḥ* on his family farm until his village,

Safuriyya north, was destroyed in the 1948 war) (30 August 1998); interview with Mohammad Maṣrāwa (known as Bayrūti) from Reina (Ḥaj Maṣrāwa, b. 1929, was a *fallāḥ* in Safuriyya during the Mandate period) (19 August 1999); interview with Shraga Punq from Kibbutz Kfar Ha-makabi (Mr. Punq was an agriculture guide and a manager of vegetable production of his settlement during the years 1938 to 1948) (28 August 1998).

36. I have not found any evidence of such practice in my readings and interviews.
37. Montague Brown, "Agriculture," Sa'id B. Himadeh (ed.), *Economic Organization in Palestine* (Beirut, 1938), p. 119.
38. Granovsky, *Land Policy in Palestine,* p. 193. Granovsky held different positions in the Jewish National Fund from managing director to chair. He provides much information about irrigation in Jewish agriculture, including data on 372 borings by Jews during 1924 to 1936. But he deals mainly with the Jewish sector and adds that his measurements are "according to the information to hand, for which, however, no claim for completeness is made," so that it is doubtful how he reached the conclusion that only 16 new borings were made by non-Jews during those years.
39. Government of Palestine, *A Survey of Palestine,* p. 390; Government of Palestine, *Memorandum on the Water Resources,* pp. 4–5.
40. Government of Palestine, *A Survey of Palestine of Palestine,* p. 390.
41. Government of Palestine, *Memorandum on the Water Resources,* pp. 1–4; PRO/CO/733/174/9, 1929, Shepherd, Report on irrigation services, p. 4; Government of Palestine, *A Survey of Palestine of Palestine,* pp. 399–400.
42. For theoretical aspects relating to property rights, see Douglas C. North, *Institutions, Institutional Change and Economic Performance* (Cambridge, 1990).
43. PRO/CO/733/174/9, 1929, Shepherd, Report on irrigation services, p. 5.
44. Government of Palestine, *Memorandum on the Water Resources,* p. 5.
45. Discussed in Chapter 7.
46. Al-Ḥusayni, *Al-tatwūr al-'ijtimā'ī fi filasṭīn al-'arabiyyah,* pp. 96–97.

47. Government of Palestine, *Memorandum on the Water Resources,* pp. 13–31.
48. Kamen, *Little Common Ground,* pp. 194–95.
49. Government of Palestine, Department of Statistics, *Village Statistics, 1945* (Jerusalem, 1945).
50. Table 2.2 in Nadan, *The Arab Rural Economy,* based on Government of Palestine, *A Survey of Palestine,* pp. 314, 321–26, 339, 410, 422
51. Government of Palestine, Department of Agriculture and Fisheries, *Village Note Book* (undated blank books for the years 1935 to 1938 and 1943 to 1946; this source was found in the Israel Bureau of Statistics Library).
52. Government of Palestine, *A Survey of Palestine,* p. 250.
53. Although some statistics are available for the Beersheba subdistrict in the *Village Statistics* of 1945, it seems these are little more than a guess.
54. "The Department of Agriculture estimates the average annual area [for 1945] under wheat and barley together at 4,500 sq. kilometres." Government of Palestine, Department of Agriculture and Fisheries, *Annual Report for the Year 1945–46,* note on p. 33.
55. Government of Palestine, Department of Agriculture (Forests and Fisheries), *Annual Report 1926 by E. R. Sawer, Director of Agriculture and Forests,* p. 5; Government of Palestine, *A Survey of Palestine,* pp. 425–29. Some of the Arabs interviewed by the author mentioned that they used to graze their flocks on "public" areas (i.e., on those areas that they called the high commissioner lands, *'arāḍ al-mandūb*). E.g., interview with Abū 'Abdallah, from Mashhad (Abū 'Abdallah, b. 1921, was the *mukhtār*'s son in the Mandate period and later became the *mukhtār* of his village) (6 April 1999 and 17 August 1999); interview with Slīmān 'Adawī from Tur'an (Mr. 'Adawī, b. 1926–28, was a *fallāḥ* in the Mandate period and an agriculture adviser in Israel; he worked with some who had been agriculture advisers in the Mandate period) (5 April 1999).
56. Some of the administrative borders of different municipalities changed during the Mandate period: e.g., the note to Map of Palestine, *Index to Villages and Settlements,* December 1945 (Map Collection ISA).
57. See also Geremy Forman, "Settlement of Title in the Galilee:

Dowson's Colonial Guiding Principles," *Israel Studies,* 7, no. 3 (2002), p. 72.

58. ISA/(RG2)//L/88/45, 31 August 1945, A letter from the Acting Director of the Department of Lands Settlement to the Chief Secretary.
59. This view was particularly developed in Great Britain, Colonial Office, *Report on Immigration, Land Settlement* and *Development, by Sir John Hope Simpson* (London, 1930).
60. Kenneth W. Stein, *The Land Question in Palestine, 1917–1939,* 2nd ed. (London, 1985), pp. 102–08.
61. Government of Palestine, Department of Statistics, *Village Statistics, 1945.*
62. Al-Ḥusayni, *Al-tatwūr al-'ijtimā'ī fi filasṭīn al-'arabiyyah,* p. 96.
63. Government of Palestine, Department of Agriculture and Fisheries, *Village Note Book* (undated blank books for the years 1935–38 and 1943–46). This source was found in the Israel Bureau of Statistics Library.
64. For the meaning of "non-Jewish" sector, see above.
65. See Table 1.3 and Stein, *The Land Question in Palestine.*
66. Government of Palestine, "Supplement No. 2 to the Palestine Gazette Extraordinary No. 988 of 28th February 1940," in *Ordinances, Regulations, Rules, Orders, and Notices: Annual Volume for 1940,* pp. 327–39; Government of Palestine, *A Survey of Palestine,* pp. 260–71.
67. Government of Palestine, Department of Agriculture and Fisheries, *Annual Report 1941–42,* p. 3.
68. See *Annual Reports* of the Department of Agriculture and Fisheries for the years 1936–45.
69. Data for the Jewish share were left incomplete for 1941.
70. As discussed earlier, in regard to the *Village Statistics* and updates of agricultural returns.
71. Government of Palestine, *A Survey of Palestine,* pp. 320, 323.
72. E.g., ibid., p. 320.
73. E.g., ibid. Also compare the returns in the two parts of Table 2.5.
74. Since the sources for part A are similar, it will be more accurate to follow changes over time by comparing the results for 1936 and 1944 to 1945 in part A (i.e., keeping the results from the same source with similar weighting methods; as mentioned, the results for 1941 to 1942 are less exact).

75. Although officially the decrease is from about 85 to 80 percent, in fact it seems to be less dramatic, since the 1944 to 1945 statistics for "other field crops" include crops previously calculated as "grains and legumes" (Government of Palestine, *A Survey of Palestine,* p. 321). If "grains and legumes" are combined with "other field crops," the change between 1935 to 1945 is less significant—from 88.9 to 85.2 percent.
76. Government of Palestine, Department of Agriculture and Fisheries, *Annual Report 1945–46,* pp. 7–11, 33.
77. E.g., ibid., p. 23.
78. Government of Palestine, *A Survey of Palestine,* pp. 140–60, especially p. 142.
79. Brown, "Agriculture," p. 162.
80. As discussed below.
81. See especially, Grant, *The People of Palestine;* Government of Palestine, Department of Agriculture (Forests and Fisheries), *Annual Report 1925.*
82. 'Alī Nasūj al-Ẓāhir, *Shajārah al-zaytūn: tārīkhhā zirā'thā, 'amrāḍihā, ṣinā'thā* (Amman, 1947); Avraham Zinger, *Gidul Ha-Zayit* (Tel Aviv, 1985), pp. 31–36.
83. Government of Palestine, *A Survey of Palestine,* pp. 336–42, 356 (table); Government of Palestine. Department of Agriculture and Fisheries, *Annual Report 1946,* p. 7.
84. Government of Palestine. Department of Agriculture and Fisheries, *Annual Report 1941–2,* p. 3.
85. Government of Palestine, Department of Statistics, *Statistical Abstract of Palestine 1944–45,* p. 219.
86. Government of Palestine. Department of Agriculture and Fisheries, *Annual Report 1941–42,* p. 3.
87. Government of Palestine. Department of Agriculture and Fisheries, *Important Factors Governing Vegetable Growing in Palestine* (Jerusalem, 1938), p. 3
88. Government of Palestine, *A Survey of Palestine,* p. 326.
89. Government of Palestine. Department of Agriculture and Fisheries, *Important Factors Governing Vegetable Growing in Palestine,* p. 3
90. Metzer and Kaplan, *Mesheq yehudi 7e-mesheq 'aravi,* pp. 29–30, 44.
91. Metzer and Kaplan, *Mesheq yehudi 7e-mesheq 'aravi,* pp. 29–30, 44.

92. For the number of rural inhabitants, see Table 1.3.
93. The government's endeavors to promote a "green revolution" are discussed in Chapter 7.
94. See Government of Palestine, Department of Agriculture and Fisheries, *Annual Reports* (Jerusalem, various years)
95. As discussed in Chapter 3.
96. Largely because of the new form of measurement of the *Village Note Books* (see the earlier discussion).
97. For the reasons for different crop specialization between Arabs and Jews and for more detailed segregation, see Nadan, *The Arab Rural Economy,* Chapter 2.
98. Discussed in Chapter 7.
99. E.g., Government of Palestine, Department of Statistics, "Enumeration of Livestock," *General Monthly Bulletin of Current Statistics* (August 1943), p. 237.
100. Government of Palestine, *A Survey of Palestine,* p. 543.
101. Government of Palestine, Department of Agriculture (Forests and Fisheries), *Annual Report for the Years 1927 to 1930,* p. 13.
102. Ibid., for 1931 and 1932, p. 109.
103. The only difference is in "geese, ducks, and turkeys," where the number grows at faster rate between 1937 and 1943 than between 1930 and 1937. Yet as can be seen in Figure 2.11, these birds are of little account. Government of Palestine, Department of Statistics, *Statistical Abstract of Palestine 1944–45,* p. 235.
104. Brown, "Agriculture," p. 165. Also Government of Palestine, Department of Agriculture (Forests and Fisheries), *Annual Report* 1941, p. 9.
105. The vast majority of livestock import was for slaughter. E.g., Government of Palestine, Department of Customs, Excise, and Trade, *Statistics of Imports, Exports and Shipping for the Year Ended 31st December 1930* (Alexandria, 1931), pp. 179–80, 295; Government of Palestine, *Statistics of Foreign Trade for the Years Ended 31st December, 1942 and 1943: Compiled and Published by the Department of Statistics in Collaboration with the Department of Customs, Excise and Trade* (Jerusalem, 1946), pp. 6–7, 67.
106. Aaron Gertz (ed.), *Statistical Handbook of Jewish Palestine* (Jerusalem: Jewish Agency for Palestine, Department of Statistics, 1947), pp. 164–65.

107. Interview with Mohammad Ḥasūna from Abu Ghosh. Ḥaj Ḥasūna (b. 1929) was a *fellah* also employed as wage-laborer in Jerusalem during the Mandate period) (31 July 1999).
108. See Nadan, *The Arab Rural Economy,* Chapter 2.
109. E.g., interview with Mohammad Aḥmad Abū Aḥmad (Abū Riaḍ) from Nazareth (Abū Riaḍ, b. 1918, was a butcher and merchant of animals and meat during the Mandate period and the third generation in that family business) (28 August 2000); interview with Yūsif and Fārūk Ya'aqūb from Nazareth (these are the grandsons of 'Abdallah Yūsif Ya'aqūb, a merchant and money-lender; they—and especially Fārūk Ya'aqūb, the older one—used to work with the grandfather in his business) (25 March 1999).
110. E.g., Government of Palestine, *Blue Book 1931* (Jerusalem, 1932), p. 346.
111. E.g., interview with Slīmān 'Adawī; interview with Khalid Zu'abī (Abū Raf'at) from Nazareth; interview with Abū 'Abdallah (during the Mandate period Abū Raf'at was a *fallāḥ* in the Nein village who also worked in Nazereth) (25.3.1999).
112. Wilson, *Peasant Life in the Holy Land,* p. 5.
113. Grant, *The People of Palestine,* p. 131.
114. Interview with Abū 'Abdallah.
115. E.g., Government of Palestine, Department of Agriculture and Fisheries, *A Review of the Agricultural Situation in Palestine, by E. S. Sawer,* pp. 12–13.
116. E.g., Brown, "Agriculture," pp. 173–78
117. Government of Palestine, *Blue Book 1931* (Jerusalem, 1932), p. 346. As was officially advised in 1931, "the only true nomads in Palestine today are the Bedu inhabitants of the Beersheba Sub-District." Government of Palestine, *Census of Palestine 1931: Report by E. Mills, Assistant Chief Secretary* (Alexandria, 1933), vol. 1, p. 328. While the Department of Agriculture mentioned poultry in the Arab sector, it referred to *fallāḥīn* ownership (e.g., Government of Palestine, *Report of the Department of Agriculture and Forests for the Years 1931 and 1932,* p. 135). In addition, nomads raised few four-legged animals other than sheep, goats, and camels. This seems to suggest that the share of the Bedouin in poultry was also low.
118. Wilson, *Peasant Life in the Holy Land,* pp. 73–75; Grant, *The People of Palestine,* pp. 90–91, 145–46. Also interview with

Nimir Qasim Muṣafa from ‘Ein Mahil (Mr. Muṣtafa (b. 1910) spoke about his childhood in the Ottoman period and his life under the Mandate; in the Mandate period, he was a *fallāḥ* and shopkeeper; from 1937 he was also the *mukhtār* of his village) (18 August 1999).

· THREE ·

Growth, Income, and Development

The broad trends of growth, development, and income in the Arab rural economy are examined in this chapter. The first section deals with national accounts and assesses the reliability of the statistics for the Arab rural economy. It is argued that the prevailing view of high growth in real terms in this sector during the 1920s and 1930s is not well founded. Instead, the overall trend was probably of little growth or even stagnation and was certainly deterioration in regard to per capita measurements. However, the 1940s was a different period with high and sustained per capita growth.

The second section discusses wages, employment, and human development. While changes in net agricultural output in Arab farms undoubtedly had a bearing on income in *fallāḥīn* society, other influences on income were employment levels in nonfarm occupations and the earnings derived from these. During the Mandate period, no significant improvement in *fallāḥīn* income occurred until the 1940s.

It is widely recognized that trends in levels of well-being, quality of life, or what is now known as human development are important when dealing with socioeconomic change, and these trends are included here. The only clear long-term trend in human development was a steady improvement in the Arab rural sector and also in the Arab sector as a whole. This was closely related to progress in health and education and resulted from government spending in these areas.

THE DEBATE OVER GROWTH IN THE ARAB AGRICULTURAL SECTOR

The study by Metzer and Kaplan (1991) together with Metzer's subsequent research (1998) are the most comprehensive examinations of economic growth in Mandate Palestine. They are also valuable for distinguishing between data for the Arab and Jewish economies. Generally speaking, the work of these authors combines data that they constructed for the interwar period for the Arab and for Jewish sectors (discussed in greater detail below), together with the available official (government) segregated statistics between Arabs and Jews for the 1940s. Their analysis suggests that both sectors or economies experienced significant real growth during the Mandate period.[1] This is important at a comparative Middle Eastern level. Apart from Palestine, only Iraq, with its emerging oil economy, seems to have experienced growth in per capita income during these years.[2]

According to Metzer and Kaplan, there was a huge gap in product per capita between the Arab and Jewish sectors; the Jewish one, on average, was higher by 2.7 times.[3] However, as can be seen from Figure 3.1, the Jewish and the Arab economies did not always show the same patterns in per capita incomes, especially during 1929 to 1933, when Arab income per capita remained more or less stagnant, while Jewish income more than doubled.

A Rural-Based Economy

The main reason for such differences seems to be that incomes in the Arab sector, unlike the Jewish, were largely dependent on agriculture. It is true that agriculture generated only between 28.4 and 40.8 percent of the output in the Arab sector, with an average of 35 percent (Figure 3.2; the averages are for the years

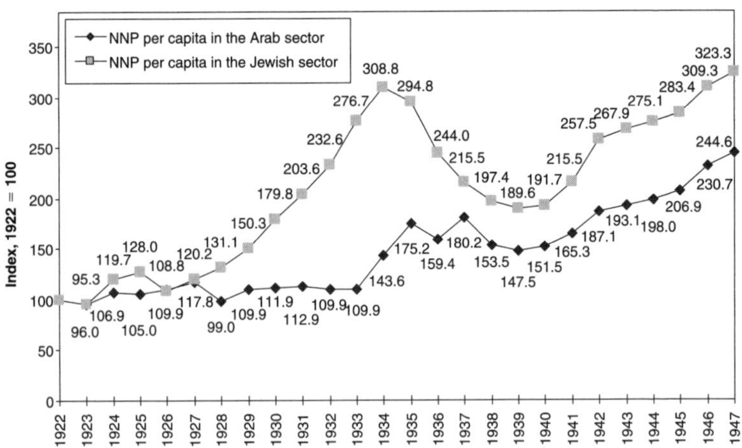

Figure 3.1 Trends in Arab and Jewish Net National Product per Capita, 1922 to 1947 (constant prices)
Source: Metzer, *The Divided Economy,* p. 242.

1922 to 1939, 1942, and 1944 to 1945). Still, in Metzer and Kaplan's view, agriculture might have "'formed' the trends in the [total] product's growth rates"[4] in the Arab sector. Indeed, one strong correlation that was almost unchanging in the pre–World War II period of 1922 to 1939 was that between the growth rates of Palestinian Arab NNP and the output from agriculture (the coefficient correlation between the two stood at 0.958, $R^2 = 0.917$ linear regression, whereas the equivalent Jewish correlation was significantly lower, at 0.35, $R^2 = 0.122$).[5]

Further research is needed to explain the high correlation between the trends in the Arab urban and rural sectors. However, there is some evidence that a multiple effect of agriculture influenced this. The livelihood of the majority of Arabs was closely connected to agricultural production. They lived mainly in the rural areas, and about 65 percent of them in 1922 and 55 percent in 1945 were employed in agriculture (see Tables 1.3

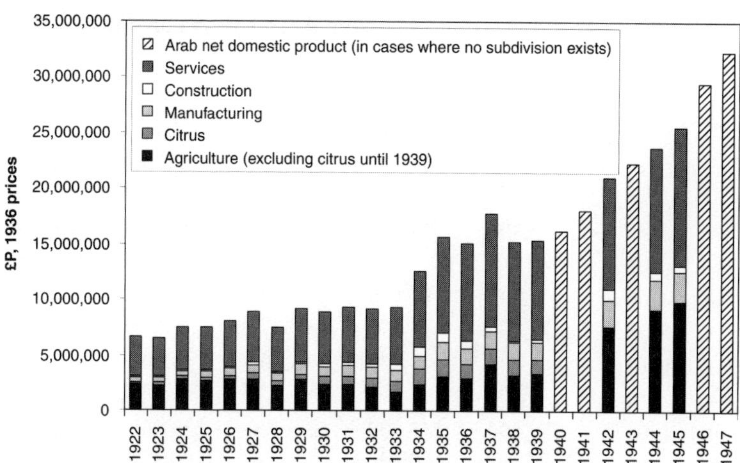

Figure 3.2 Arab Net National Product in Constant Prices, 1922 to 1947

Sources: Metzer, *The Divided Economy,* pp. 239, 241; Metzer and Kaplan, *Mesheq yehudi ve-mesheq 'aravi,* p. 46

Note: Data per sector is not available for 1940 to 41 and for 1946 to 1947.

and 3.1). In addition, a report from 1979 by Eliahu Eliashar (who was head of the Trade and Industry Bureau at the Department of Customs, Excise, and Trade during the Mandate) includes segregated data on manufacturing and industry between Arab and Jewish sectors from the 1928 survey (the British authorities did not allow publication of segregated data for political reasons). These suggest that about 75 percent of total Arab industrial produce came from agriculture-related manufacturing, such as olive and sesame oils, food, tobacco, milling products, and soaps (from olive oil)—industries that employed 38 percent of the total industrial and manufacturing Arab labor force.[6] In addition, the development of urban slums populated largely by first-generation immigrants from the countryside (who had migrated there mostly as a result of push factors from the villages and pull factors in urban areas but who often retained their part-time occupations in the villages)[7] also implies

Table 3.1 Sectoral Distribution of the Arab Labor Force in Mandate Palestine

	1922	1931	1935	1939	1945
Agriculture	124,300 (65.5%)	144,200 (63.5%)	145,100 (56.9%)	163,000 (58.2%)	186,000 (54.3%)
Services	53,300 (28.1%)	58,600 (25.8%)	76,400 (29.9%)	92,100 (32.9%)	109,000 (31.8%)
Manufacturing	9,100 (4.8%)	18,500 (8.2%)	19,900 (7.8%)	21,000 (7.5%)	30,300 (8.9%)
Construction	3,100 (1.6%)	5,700 (2.5%)	13,800 (5.4%)	3,900 (1.4%)	17,300 (5%)
Total	189,800 (100%)	227,000 (100%)	255,200 (100%)	280,000 (100%)	342,600 (100%)

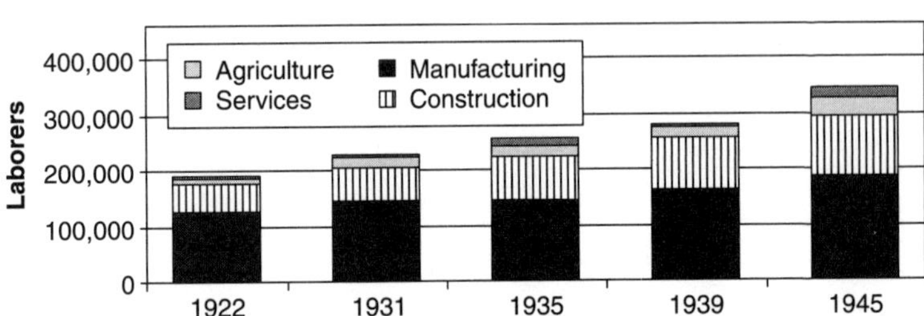

Source: Metzer, *The Divided Economy,* p. 219.

dynamics and a multiplier effect. This and the high rural-urban correlation may indicate that the factor market was working efficiently. Yet as discussed below, much caution is needed when interpreting the agricultural returns, and this high correlation should be viewed with a certain skepticism.

An Analysis of Metzer and Kaplan's Returns for Arab Agricultural Products

Since the analysis in this section often discusses returns from (statistical) linear regressions with time-series data, an explanation about the characteristics of such regressions and the analysis of their results is in order. Linear regressions help to analyze the relationship between two variables, X and Y, and calculations from the different data provide an equation for a line that best explains Y and X. In the example of Figure 3.3 (Data A), the production (output) of product Y is plotted against the years. In the first year, the output was 100 units (say, 100 tons), and for every subsequent year the output increased by five more units (for the second year it was 105, the third 110, etc.). The outcome of this calculated regression is that $Y = 5X + 95$ (e.g., in the second year, where $X = 2$, the output is 105; it is $Y = 5 * 2 + 95$). The line $Y = 5X + 95$ is also shown in the figure of Data A; note that this line moves through all the points because of the steady increase it represents.

Other kind of data are plotted in the Data B chart of Figure 3.3. Here the returns fluctuate (i.e., there is no steady increase). There is a statistical method of calculating a straight line that minimizes the sum of the squares of the vertical distances of the points from a single straight line. In other words, by means of calculation, we are able to find a straight line that best presents the way in which Y is influenced by X (providing that in this ex-

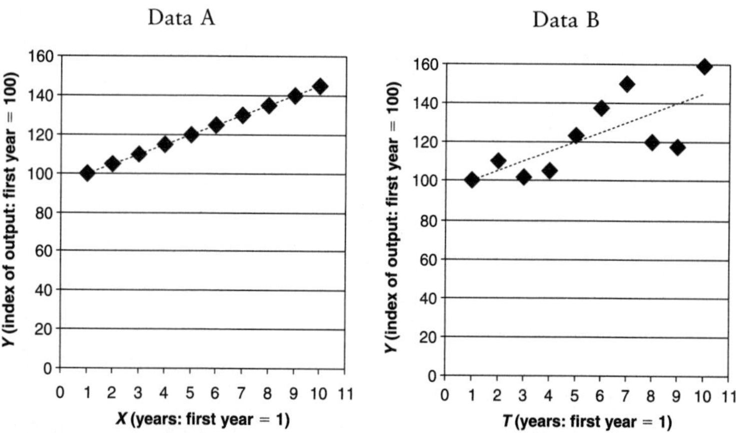

Figure 3.3 Linear Regression with Time-Series Data

ample *X* influences *Y*). It is possible, of course, to find the equation for such a line. In the example, the straight line in Data B moves through the same point as the straight line in Data A; therefore, they arrive at the same equation ($Y = 5X + 95$). Since not all the points are on the straight line in Data B, we should ask to what extent the straight line produced should be taken seriously.

In cases of uncertainty about the soundness of the returns, the calculation of the *coefficient of determination* (R^2) assists the analysis. The R^2 tells us what proportion in the returns of *Y*s fit the equation (the further the points are away from the line, the less consistent the trend). The highest value for R^2 is 1 (such as in Data A, where all the points are on the same line), while the lower score is zero. The returns for Data B are $R^2 = 0.55$ (i.e., only 55 percent of the returns are sufficiently represented by the line). This signifies an overall steady trend but one that is punctuated by many fluctuations. Our task is therefore not only to note the calculated trend line but also to ask how significant the outcome is. In fact, in cases of low R^2 the trend line is irrelevant to the analysis, since it hardly represents a clear trend; rather, it indicates many fluctuations. Finally, it is worth mentioning that the more returns available (that is, the more dots in a graph), the lower the possibility that an unusual return in a year distorts the results. Ultimately, statisticians would prefer to have more than 30 returns, yet the limitations of this study leave fewer returns to deal with. Equipped with these returns, we can make an informed analysis of Metzer and Kaplan's data.

According to these authors' figures on the net product of Arab agriculture (Figure 3.4), this particular sector (excluding citrus) experienced annual growth of 2.03 percent between 1922 and 1939 but had many fluctuations (R^2 is only 0.23). Yet where "agriculture including citrus" is concerned (Figure 3.5), the results suggest a quite sustained growth ($R^2 = 0.64$), representing an annual growth of not less than 3.42 percent. The government account for the years 1942 to 1945 suggests a more significant and sustained growth (9.13 percent, $R^2 = 1$) in "agriculture in-

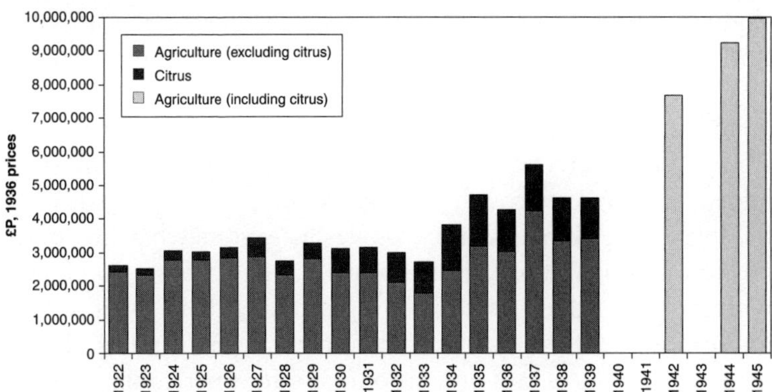

Figure 3.4 Net Product of Arab Agriculture

Sources: Metzer, *The Divided Economy,* pp. 239, 241; Metzer and Kaplan, *Mesheq yehudi ve-mesheq 'aravi,* p. 46.

Note: No data are available for the years 1940 to 41 and 1943.

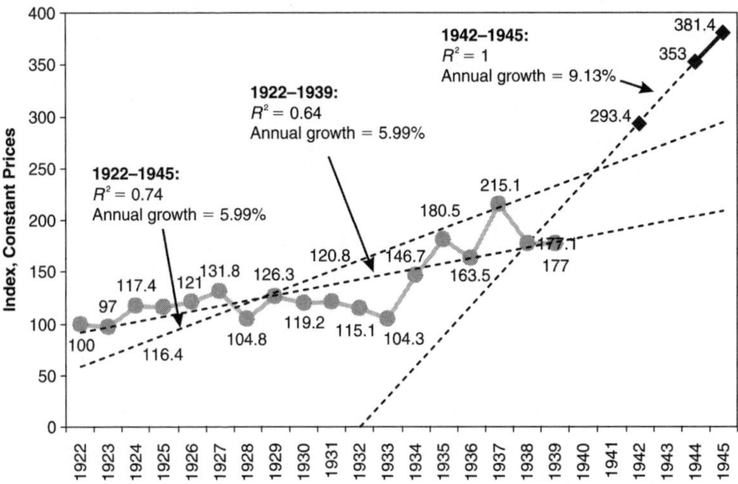

Figure 3.5 Index of Net Product of Arab Agriculture (Including Citrus)

Source: Figures 3.4.

cluding citrus" (no subdivision is available). Metzer and Kaplan's combined account (i.e., 1922 to 1939 with 1942 to 1945) concludes that during the Mandate period (here 1922 to 1945), the average annual growth in agriculture including citrus stood at 5.99 percent, with R^2 of 0.74—namely, a high and sustained agricultural growth (see Figure 3.5).

Metzer and Kaplan's story, however, is somewhat less optimistic when the returns from Figures 3.4 and 3.5 are combined with those of Table 1.3 (i.e., when discussing their "net product of Arab agriculture per rural inhabitant") (Figure 3.6). These data are, of course, not an approximation of per capita income in the rural areas, since the agricultural sector was not hermetically segregated from the nonagricultural sectors (as described below, many rural dwellers worked in nonagricultural occupations, and this trend was especially significant during the 1940s). The returns are therefore an approximation of income per capita *from agriculture* (according to Metzer and Kaplan) for those people who typically (and more so in the 1920s and 1930s) derived their main income from agriculture.

Figure 3.6 hints that between 1922 and 1939, Arab agriculture per rural inhabitant (excluding citrus) experienced an annual growth of 0.37 percent, signifying a low, yet positive growth. However, the two benchmark years of 1922 and 1939 hardly mark a sustained trend but rather do show a picture of many fluctuations ($R^2 = 0$). A major factor was the slump between 1927 and 1933, with a recovery taking place after 1933 and especially after 1937.

The story of "agriculture including citrus per rural inhabitant" for the years 1922 to 1939 is of a somewhat less fluctuating yet still unsatisfactory trend ($R^2 = 0.38$), with annual growth of 1.74 percent. The years 1942 to 1945 show a sustained and substantial upturn ($R^2 = 1$ with annual growth of 7.49 percent), while the overall trend for 1922 to 1945 is of sustained and high growth ($R^2 = 0.65$; annual growth = 4.3 percent). Overall, the most notable uncertainty is about "ordinary agriculture per ru-

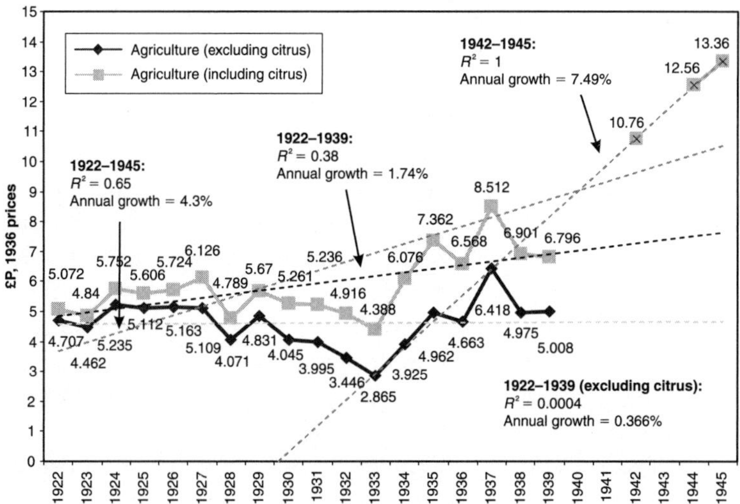

Figure 3.6 Net Product of Arab Agriculture per Rural Inhabitant

Sources: Table 1.3, Figure 3.4, and Figure 3.5.

Note: There are no consistent data about employment in citrus, yet it is clear that the vast majority of Arab agriculturists were employed in "ordinary agriculture" (98 percent in 1931; see the introduction). For this exercise, the returns for "agriculture excluding citrus" from Figure 3.4 were divided by the total Arab rural population in Palestine. In cases where R^2 was very low, the trend line was taken out, since it does not symbolize any decisive trend.

ral inhabitant." Here, the picture is of numerous fluctuations with no extensive growth. Still, the dominant trend derived from Metzer and Kaplan's data is of sustained and high economic growth during the Mandate period, with relatively higher growth in the 1940s. Population increase cuts into this growth, yet it still remained considerable. But to what extent are these returns accurate and therefore significant?

Measurement Constraints in Metzer and Kaplan's Data

If high-quality data on Arab agricultural output existed, the analysis of economic trends in the Arab rural sector would be easier and more precise. Let us assess the consistency of statistics on net product in Arab agriculture. The government published data on this for the years 1942, 1944, and 1945. As mentioned, Metzer and Kaplan decided to rely on it for the 1940s and constructed "national" accounts on gross and net product for Arabs and Jews for the 1920s and most of the 1930s. The method by which they calculated Arab agricultural output for 1921 to 1939 was to collect the statistics on crops produced in each year and on livestock for every year for all Palestine. The produce from livestock (milk, eggs, honey, wool, and organic manure) was usually calculated by multiplying the number of head of producing animals by what was believed to be their average produce.

But how reliable are the original data? Up to 1928, information on crops in government accounts is based on tithe returns.[8] In Chapter 2, we saw that between 1929 and 1934 the government used *Village Note Book* returns instead. These were reports by agricultural officers, based on some field inquiries in villages and a discussion of the results with *mukhtārs*.[9] At that time, the tax remained on produce. From 1935 to 1945, the returns continued to be based on field inquiries and discussions with *mukhtārs*. However, the tax system was then modified: it was no longer on produce (a tithe) but rather on type of land—the rural property tax. The most accurate returns were those in the two surveys of 1935 and 1945, taken for the purposes of this new tax.

Hence, crop returns for the years until 1929 were most likely to be underestimated because of underdeclaration. For 1929 to 1934, crop returns are also likely to be underreported. Under the *Village Note Book* system, the *mukhtārs* had some influence on the returns, and at that time *mukhtārs* and villagers paid tax according to their produce. It was therefore in their interest to make the returns appear lower, and this was probably the case. From 1935 onward, however, the data were collected only for statistical purposes, and because the tax was levied on property and not produce, the *mukhtārs* had little or no reason to bias the returns.

Metzer and Kaplan, aware to some extent of the underestimation problem, decided to add 10 percent to their data for the years 1921 to 1931 (although three of the sources they used suggested adding an average of 15 percent).[10] But as noted, the period needing adjustment was not only 1921 to 1931 but also 1921 to 1934, where it should have been on a special scale to reflect the different sets (1921 to 1928 and 1929 to 1934).

Even more questionable is the amount of adjustment needed. In such circumstances, any allowance has to contain an arbitrary element, however informed the guess. Still, why should 10 percent and not any other figure be viewed as reliable? In fact, the only other in-depth governmental study is that of Johnson and Crosbie (also very problematic), which suggests that 85 percent needed to be added to the declared returns of 1929.[11] If instead of 10 percent, an amendment of 85 percent had been adopted by Metzer and Kaplan, agricultural growth would have presented a very different picture.

Finally, as discussed above, the data for livestock raised in Palestine are far from accurate before 1930. Hence, the data on overall agricultural returns are likely to be inaccurate before 1935 and especially before 1930.[12] This creates a serious problem in the use of long-term time-series statistics for agricultural product.

After constructing their agricultural output figures, Metzer and Kaplan's next stage was to convert the figures from commodities into total cash value of consumer prices. But they collected prices for only five years (1921, 1927, 1931, 1935, and 1939), so that 14 out of 19 years were left uninvestigated. The average prices for 1921 and 1927 were used as a proxy for *all* prices in the 1920s, and the same technique was applied to the 1930s. This, of course, resulted in additional inaccuracy, since in reality prices were not fixed and were influenced by the changing supply of and demand for products.

Another problem is Metzer and Kaplan's use of "producer prices" to calculate product values. They estimated these prices to be 25 percent lower than the wholesale prices for 1921, 1927, and 1931 and 30 percent lower for 1935, and they reached these ratios by comparing redemption prices (prices used by the government to calculate the value of products for tax purposes) with wholesale prices. For 1939, no amendment was made, as they argue that the published prices were already given as producer prices. But how can one be sure that the methods used for calculating producer prices in earlier years were similar to "real" producer prices in 1939?

In any case, after calculating agricultural outputs and prices for all Palestine in the manner described, the estimated outputs were doubled by these estimated prices. The figure arrived at was regarded as the gross agricultural product. From this, the Jewish share was deduced, and the reminder was deemed to be the Arab share.

The last part of the calculation was of net agricultural product in the Arab sector. Yet as discussed in Chapter 2, there are no satisfactory data for such an assessment. Moreover, Metzer and Kaplan increasingly overvalued "net returns" compared with earlier calculations. In practice, this meant that growth rates in net Arab agriculture were lower than Metzer and Kaplan concluded. In addition, some years had very low "net" returns, which was very different from the comparatively successful years. Once again, Metzer and Kaplan's method of calculation does not reflect the significant diversities in yields: their "net" outcome varied only between 63.7 and 74.2 percent of the "gross."[13] Finally, they did not calculate the net product of Arab agriculture for the 1940s but used the published government accounts instead. Since there are no comprehensive data about the way in which these were constructed, it is possible that they were based on quite different methods of calculation. These many problems of distortion and inaccuracy call for considerable caution in using the data on product. Even so, they contain some important indications.

Reexamining Metzer and Kaplan's data with the "Years Separation" Method

As we have seen, the returns for product in Arab agriculture do not hold up as a single, long, and accurate time series. It is also clear that *some* of the inaccuracies can be overcome by discussing each comparable period separately (i.e., 1922 to 1928, 1929 to 1934, 1935 to 1939, or 1942 to 1945). However, by definition, such comparisons do not give an idea of trends between the comparable periods (i.e., we have no picture of the periods 1928 to 1929, 1934 to 1935, or 1939 to 1942). Figure 3.7 highlights each of these periods.

The returns for "agriculture excluding citrus" are our prime concern, since the vast majority of *fallāḥīn* were not engaged in citrus cropping as their main occupation. As can be seen in Figure 3.7, there was a significant increase in net product from 1923 to 1924. This may represent a recovery from the war period. However, no other significant trend can be seen for the entire period of 1922 to 1928 ($R^2 = 0.07$). The annual growth between the two benchmark years, 1922 and 1928, is slightly negative (−0.68). It could indicate fluctuations but not a steady trend—and certainly no economic growth in this first period. The second group of years, 1929 to 1934, shows a downturn from 1929 to 1933 but a significant recovery in 1934. Here, the tendency is clearer and more substantial. The annual growth is negative, at the high rate of −2.52 ($R^2 = 0.34$). It is important to note that if 1934 is omitted (i.e., only the years 1929 to 1933 are included), one gets a significant ($R^2 = 0.94$) and negative annual growth rate of −10.8 percent. The period 1935 to 1939, on the other hand, hints at moderate growth. The annual growth is 1.75 percent, but the R^2 is very low, due to an upward trend in one particular year, 1937. In fact, if this year is taken out, R^2 acquires the much stronger value of 0.69. This seems to suggest some positive growth during this third period. One cannot escape the conclusion that in spite of some fluctuations, the alternative analysis by the years separation method suggests that

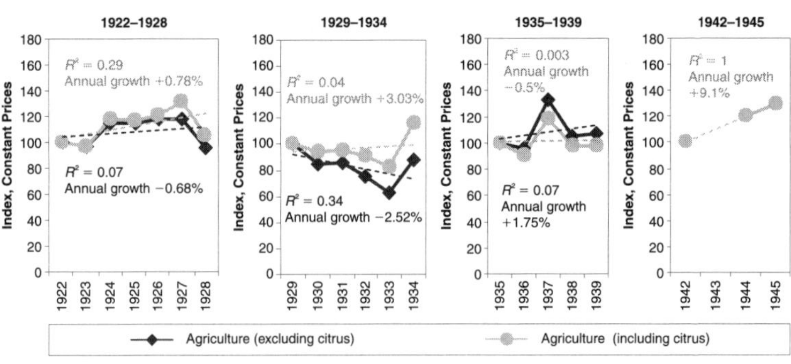

Figure 3.7 Trends in Net Product of Arab Agriculture

Sources: Metzer, *The Divided Economy,* pp. 239, 241; Metzer and Kaplan, *Mesheq yehudi 7e-mesheq 'aravi,* p. 46.

Note: Figures 3.7 and 3.8 show trends relative to the first year (100) in each of the discussed periods.

"agriculture excluding citrus" experienced an overall deterioration between 1922 to 1939. This accords with the findings in Chapter 2.

The returns for "agriculture including citrus" show a better outcome for 1922 to 1928. This indicates a more positive and sustained annual growth (+0.78 percent, R^2 = 0.29). But the picture for 1929 to 1933 is of considerable sustained deterioration (−4.67 percent, R^2 = 0.86), with a significant, atypical recovery in 1934. Consequently, the overall trend for this period is of much distortion (R^2 = 0.04), and the average annual growth return of 3.03 percent should be viewed as a noncharacteristic trend. The returns for the years 1935 to 1939 also reveal much fluctuation (R^2 = 0.003). Although those for the benchmark years, 1935 and 1939, are of low negative growth (−0.5 percent), the overall combination could represent stagnation with numerous fluctuations. The war years 1942 to 1945, however, present a pattern of high and sustained growth (9.1 percent, R^2 = 1).

While it is difficult to speak of a precise trend because of the many fluctuations and approximations, a cautious and indeed fair view would be to refer to a period of stagnation between 1922 to 1939 that is quite unlike the significant growth of the 1940s. In fact, use of the years-separation method on Metzer and Kaplan's data shows 1922 to 1939 in a different light: a deterioration in "agriculture excluding citrus" (versus the claim of moderate growth) and stagnation in the case of "agriculture including citrus" (versus high growth). These and the many uncertainties in the data call for a serious reexamination.

Not surprisingly, the trend in net product per rural inhabitant (the same technique that was used in Figure 3.6) tells a story of more deterioration overall for agriculture excluding citrus. Similar to the Figure 3.7 case, there were many fluctuations in the first period. Still, the trend is clear: apart from the postwar recovery years of 1923 to 1924, the general trend for 1922 to 1928 is of deterioration (Figure 3.8). More significant is the higher and sustained negative growth that can be seen for the 1929 to 1934 period (−4.08 percent, $R^2 = 0.49$), while the years 1935 to 1939 with their many variations could be described as near stagnation (an annual growth of 0.22 percent, $R^2 = 0.008$). In general, when the regular returns of Metzer and Kaplan for agriculture excluding citrus are used in a per rural inhabitant calculation, the story for 1922 to 1939 is one of low, yet positive growth (Figure 3.6). But using the years-separation method (Figure 3.8) suggests a very different picture—substantial negative growth.

When the years-separation method is not used, "agriculture including citrus per rural inhabitant" for 1922 to 1939 (Figure 3.6) depicts a relatively steady trend with an annual growth of 1.74 percent. But applying the years-separation method reveals many more fluctuations (R^2 is nearly zero in the periods 1922 to 1928 and 1935 to 1939). The general impression is of a deterioration from 1924 to 1933 (an annual growth of −0.96 percent for 1922 to 1928 and of −6.23 percent for 1929 to 1933), with, however, some recovery in 1934 (annual growth for 1929 to 1934 is therefore 1.38 percent). The period 1935 to 1939 also

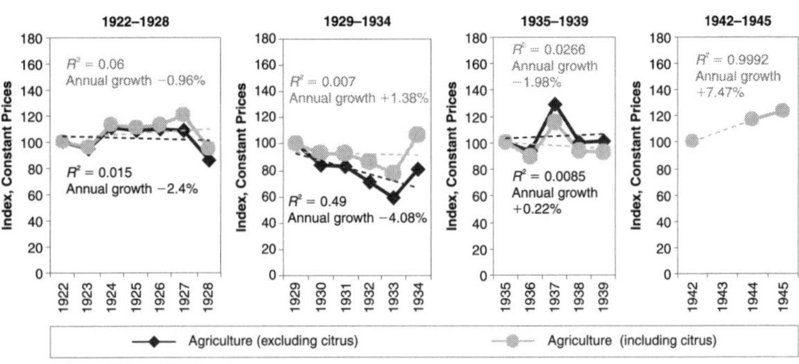

Figure 3.8 Trends in Net Product of Arab Agriculture per Rural Inhabitant

Sources: Table 1.3 and Figure 3.7.

displays many fluctuations, with an overall negative growth (−1.98 percent). These figures might represent stagnation or even some deterioration between 1922 and 1939, contrary to the original results. The findings in this and earlier sections call for an interpretation of the data that is quite different from that of Metzer and Kaplan. This is undertaken when another relevant aspect has been reassessed—Metzer's total factor productivity (TFP) growth.

Total Factor Productivity Growth in the Light of Measurement Constraints

The uncertainty about growth also casts doubt on Metzer's calculation of total factor productivity (TFP). This is a residual measure of how efficient an economy is at combining various resources[14] and was calculated by Metzer for the *entire* Arab economy. His TFP calculations for the Arab sector are based on his "net capital stock" statistics, his and Kaplan's national domestic product (NDP) statistics, and the size of the labor force. He gives two alternative equations with different factor shares: $TFP^*_1 = NDP^* - (0.4L^* + 0.6K^*)$, $TFP^*_2 = NDP^* - (0.8L^* + 0.2K^*)$, where TFP^* stands for the annual rates of change in percentage in Arab TFP, *NDP** for this change in Arab NDP, *L** for the change in the labor force, and *K** for the change in capital.[15] He also suggests high rates of TFP annual growth for the whole Arab economy in 1922 to 1947 (3.19 or 3.69 percent). If we take Metzer's data for 1922 to 1939 and insert it into his equations (he originally discussed 1922 to 1947), then the returns also postulate a significant annual TFP growth for the entire Arab sector during 1922 to 1939 (1.79 or 2.51 percent, depending on which equation is used) (Table 3.2).

To what extent is the story of TFP growth of the Arab rural economy similar to Metzer's account for the whole economy? If Metzer's data are used for the Arab rural economy (part B of Table 3.2), the picture is of significant positive TFP in this sector for 1922 to 1947 (3.22 and 4.03 percent), although the improvement appears more moderate for the years 1922 to 1939 (0.38 and 1.33 percent). But as demonstrated, the trend in product of Arab agriculture for the years 1922 to 1939 could be one of stagnation, even deterioration, with no economic growth at all. If this were the case, then the returns for *TFP** could only be negative.

A simple simulation that retains Metzer's data for the Arab agricultural sector yet places the returns of net product of Arab agriculture for 1939 in the cells of 1922 and 1939 (i.e., no growth) changes the TFP annual growth returns between 1922 and 1939 to −3.04 and −2.09 percent, depending on which equation is chosen. The trend for 1922 to 1947, according to this simulation, is better (0.81 and 1.63 percent). As already noted, the statistics for net product of Arab agriculture are underestimated in 1939, unlike the period commencing in 1940 (this is why the years-separation technique used for 1935 to 1939 dealt with it separately from 1940 to 1945), and the later the year, the more relatively overvalued are the returns on net product of Arab agriculture. It also means that in this simulation the TFP returns for 1922 to 1927 should have been lower. Hence, we are left with unanswered questions regarding TFP growth in the Arab rural sector, yet with the acknowledgment

Table 3.2 TFP Components

		1922	1939	1947
A. The Whole Arab Economy				
K (in thousand £P, 1936 prices)		22,246	43,312	57,057
L (in thousand persons)		194.0	280.0	369.9 (approx.)
NDP (in thousand £P, 1936 prices)		6,628	15,331	32,345
TFP^*	$TFP^*_1 = NDP^* - (0.4L^* + 0.6K^*)$ $TFP^*_2 = NDP^* - (0.8L^* + 0.2K^*)$	1922–39: $TFP^*_1 = 1.79$; $TFP^*_2 = 2.51$ 1922–47: $TFP^*_1 = 3.19$; $TFP^*_2 = 3.69$		
B. The Arab Rural Economy				
K (index—keeping the proportion from part A and hence dealing with the same growth rates)		100	194.7	256.5
L (in thousand persons)		124.3	163	194.4 (approx.)
Net product of Arab agriculture (in thousand £P, 1936 prices)		26,105	46,228	118,588
TFP^*	$TFP^*_1 = NDP^* - (0.4L^* + 0.6K^*)$ $TFP^*_2 = NDP^* - (0.8L^* + 0.2K^*)$	1922–39: $TFP^*_1 = 0.38$; $TFP^*_2 = 1.33$ 1922–47: $TFP^*_1 = 3.22$; $TFP^*_2 = 4.03$		
TFP^* (simulation)		1922–39: $TFP^*_1 = -3.04$; $TFP^*_2 = -2.09$ 1922–47: $TFP^*_1 = 0.81$; $TFP^*_2 = 1.63$		

Source: Metzer, *The Divided Economy*, pp. 139, 219, 241–42, 246.

Notes: Figures for the labor force are approximate. The average annual growth in the labor force between 1939 and 1945 was used as a proxy for its growth during the years 1945 to 1947. Although the agricultural data are part of the NNP series and not of NDP, the differences are negligible when dealing with trends. The use of Metzer's (p. 242) data suggests growth in Arab NDP of 5.1 percent during the years 1922 to 1939 and 9.8 percent during 1939 to 1947. The corresponding figures for NNP are 5.0 percent and 9.8 percent.

that the story of high TFP growth in agriculture is likely to be wrong and that the more accurate the data on net output, the more precise the discussion on TFP.

Another problem with the TFP calculation is the discussion of "net capital stock." Generally speaking, Metzer's "net capital stock" is a proxy measurement for the whole economy. However, it is based mainly on some calculations about construction and citrus data. Such a measure does not necessarily stand in proxy for other branches of the economy. This seems especially true for ordinary agriculture, particularly in light of the continual loss of land—a key component of "capital stock"—because of Jewish land purchase. The uncertainties urge the use of other indicators, together with these statistics, which can better capture macroeconomic performance, and such indicators will be proposed below.

Rethinking Growth in Arab Agricultural Products

The discussions above and in Chapter 2 call for a revision of the accepted view of growth in Arab agricultural products. As for investment, that vital engine of economic growth, very little aggregate investment was made in Arab land and irrigation during the Mandate period, which meant a continual deterioration in economic conditions per Arab rural inhabitant. We have already observed that crop specialization in the Arab sector did not change significantly under the Mandate, although a modest change took place when some lands were transferred into vegetable cultivation. The main reason for the low level of change seems to have been lack of market incentives.

As far as output per dunum is concerned, there was no noteworthy change except in vegetables (which remained on only about 3.5 percent of Arab cultivated land). Here the pattern is similar to that of investment: little change in production and probably an overall deterioration per Arab rural inhabitant. Likewise for livestock—an overall slower rate of increase than that for Arab rural inhabitants. On the "physical" level, any improvement seemed to be slower than population growth, reflecting a picture of deterioration.

As discussed above, however, the "miracle of the market" in the 1940s brought significant growth in Arab agricultural product, with relative prices of agricultural commodities increasing markedly as a result of changed military and political decisions. These may suggest that low growth in 1920s and 1930s was swallowed up by faster population increase—in other words, once again a negative growth per rural inhabitant.

But the narrative presented by Metzer and Kaplan is entirely different. They suggest a high and sustained growth in agricultural product, with an average annual rate of 5.99 percent for the period 1922 to 1945 (3.42 percent for 1922 to 1939 and 9.13 percent for 1942 to 1945), and their data propose lower growth, yet still positive per rural inhabitant (4.3 percent for 1922 to 1945, 1.74 percent for 1922 to 1939, and 7.49 percent for 1942 to 1945). However, as we have seen, Metzer and Kaplan's data suffers from many inaccuracies:

- A tendency to overestimate agricultural product in 1935 to 1939 compared with 1929 to 1934—and the latter period was overestimated in comparison to 1922 to 1928;
- A tendency to overestimate net return for the years 1935 to 1939, compared with earlier periods (because of higher vegetable production);
- The use of inaccurate data on the number of livestock for the years prior to 1930;
- The use of inaccurate prices of commodities for most of the investigated years and the use of noncomparable prices for the year 1939;
- Finally, as noted, their data are incomparable with the government data for the 1940s without further investigation of the nature of these data.

An alternative examination of Metzer and Kaplan's data by the years-separation method, dealing with each period separately, revealed that, generally speaking, the jumps in growth occurred between the subperiods and not within them. In other words, it is likely that the jumps occurred not because of increased agricultural output but because of the use of inaccurate and comparatively overvalued returns by Metzer and Kaplan for each subperiod. In addition, these returns might suggest that for most of the years during 1922 to 1939 there was an economic stagnation (with fluctuations) in Arab agricultural output and a deterioration per rural inhabitant. Furthermore, the negative long-term effect of Jewish land purchase should not be overlooked, even though this cannot be evaluated for the short periods under review.

Taking into account the returns on investment, crop specialization, livestock, and prices, the application of the years-separation method to Metzer and Kaplan's data and the issue of land purchase, it is evident that the most likely pattern was either of little growth or even of no growth at all in Arab agricultural net product during the period 1922 to 1939 and of continual deterioration in Arab agricultural net product per rural inhabitant. In such a situation, TFP growth could not have been positive. For the 1940s, however, there was very high and sustained growth, both overall and per rural inhabitant.

To give a rough idea of the broader meaning of this conclusion, a simple simulation might help. Taking the returns on average annual growth from Figure 3.5 between 1942 and 1945 (9.13 percent), and keeping this rate as it was the same between 1940 and 1945 (i.e., postulating that in these years such a huge growth existed), then the returns we get for 1940 are £P6,324,769 and £P9,956,880 for 1945 (all in 1936 prices). Using the same method that was earlier used—placing the returns for 1940 as if they were the returns for 1922 (i.e., assuming no growth)—we get a growth rate of 1.99 percent between 1922 and 1945. However, the overall growth per rural inhabitant (using the data from Table 1.3), shows a very low growth overall (0.36 percent). The use of these "returns" in the equation for TFP growth (Table 3.2) produces negative returns

(−1.03 and −0.22, depending on which equation is used). These returns should not be taken as accurate, yet they may be regarded as much closer to the real returns than those of Metzer and Kaplan's study, especially in regard to the outcomes for net Arab agriculture and per rural inhabitant.

WAGES, EMPLOYMENT, AND HUMAN DEVELOPMENT

Variations in net agricultural output of Arab farms affected total income in *fallāḥīn* society. Income was also influenced by employment levels and by earnings from nonfarm occupations. In addition, changes in levels of "human development" are discussed.

Wages and Employment

The evidence does not permit a clear picture of trends in wage employment, unemployment (and underemployment),[16] especially for the interwar period, largely because the main source for assessing nonfarm employment is questionable. As Rachelle Taqqu put it:

> Criteria for the definition of "unemployment" were furthermore a matter of political contention since the future of Jewish immigration was premised on the "absorption capacity" of Palestine. . . . [In regard to the statistics of unemployment collected by the Department of Statistics,] the sources of information were too varied, incomplete and inconsistent with one another to be reliable.[17]

Nevertheless, it can be assumed that wages for low-skilled labor in Mandate Palestine were determined by supply and demand (especially since the unemployed received no benefits) and by the wages offered in different sectors to the low skilled. The word "unskilled" is not used here, since most of what was categorized as work required a short period of training. Thus, when there were more alternatives or less unemployment, wages were assumed to rise, and vice versa. An increase in real wages, then, can also give an indirect indication of an increase in the incomes of *fallāḥīn* and other low-skilled laborers.

For the present study, real wages for Arab low-skilled labor—those in jobs requiring at most a short period of training—were collected for noncitrus agriculture and construction (available for the years 1931 to 1946) and are shown in Figure 3.9.

The sources for this figure give the lowest and the highest wages and not averages. For example, in summer 1936 the lowest number recorded in construction was 100 mils and the highest 180, while in agriculture it was 100 and 120. The midpoint between the two margins is represented in Figure 3.9 (140 for construction and 110 for agriculture). This gives some idea of trends but not an exact indication. In addition, payment in the noncitrus sector was usually in kind (see Chapter 4). It thus seems that the data on wages in agriculture were based on estimates and not on accurate prices.

Despite these constraints, certain major trends can be identified. First, daily wages in agriculture were lower than those in construction. There is no precise explanation of this phenomenon, but it is usually thought of as a mechanism that draws labor from the rural society into the cities.[18] There could also have been uncertainty about finding temporary jobs in the towns, which presumably "paid" a higher wage. Although low-skilled labor is assumed to involve a short period of training, this may have been longer in the construction industry and hence resulted in a higher wage. In addition, the findings may reflect the cost of transport from villages to towns (many made such a journey to work),[19] and the low quality of the figures for payment in kind.

Second, despite the differences between the two sets of data, it can be seen that the two groups showed similar trends (the data plotted on wages from agriculture against those of construction give an R^2 of the linear regression as 0.87). This suggests that the labor market in the Arab economy was not segmented between rural and urban occupations, and it is another indication of the factor market working efficiently. It also relate to the rationality of peasants, in an economic sense (an issue discussed in

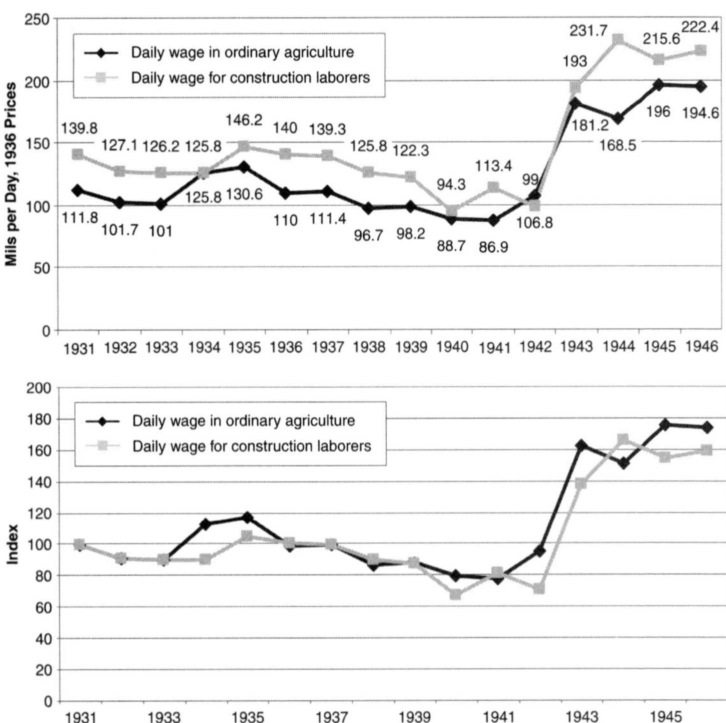

Figure 3.9 Daily Real Wages for Low-Skilled Arab Labor in Noncitrus Agriculture and Construction

Sources: Government of Palestine, Department of Statistics, *Statistical Abstract of Palestine* (various years); Government of Palestine, Department of Statistics, *General Monthly Bulletin of Current Statistics* (March 1944, p. 117; April 1946, p. 133; July 1946, p. 353; December 1946, p. 712; January 1947, p. 48); Government of Palestine, *A Survey of Palestine,* p. 741.

Notes: All prices are for the summer period (September to Oct) except for construction during 1940 to 1942, where the data are for March. Wages for agriculture are for Arab labor, in Arab employment, for general laborers in noncitrus agriculture. Wages for construction are for low-skilled Arab builders.

Chapter 4), where employment was absorbed in both sectors, with an equilibrating effect.

Third, despite a decline between 1931 and 1933, the main trend for 1931 to 1935 is moderately upward. This reflects a small increase in the relative demand for labor. However, during 1935 to 1939, there was a moderate decline, followed by a sharper one from 1939 to 1940. In 1940 and 1941, the figures were at their lowest. There was a marked increase from 1941 to 1944, and wages remained high between 1944 and 1946.

In terms of incomes for *fallāḥīn* farms, the wages data—especially bearing in mind the returns on product—provide additional support to the description given by many of the *fallāḥīn* in interviews that "the economic life of the *fallāḥīn* was very hard; the *fallāḥīn* were poor. But during the 1940s, *fallāḥīn* earned much more."[20]

The trends in employment during the 1930s appear to have several causes. The scarcity of land and lack of substantial investment in agriculture eventually meant that agriculture could not provide enough work for the expanding Arab labor force. At the same time, there was a decline in job opportunities for Arabs in the Jewish sector (see Chapter 1), and during the second half of the 1930s, there were possibly fewer opportunities in citrus. This intensified after the Arab Revolt of 1936 to 1939 began, although during the revolt some compensation was found in illegal and thus unrecorded opportunities for employment (see Chapter 1). The collapse in citrus cropping during World War II further reduced agricultural employment.[21] Hence, political as well as economic factors caused a significant slowdown in the second half of the 1930s, and the labor surplus was reflected in lower wages.

In the 1940s, the job shrinkage in agriculture continued, and the Arab Revolt ended, but an important determinant of the higher employment at this time was the war and military decisions. The 1940s are known as "the prosperity." In terms of employment for Arabs, Palestine during World War II became a large British military base, employing largely local labor.[22] Besides employment in the military, both Arabs and Jews were mobilized in a program designed to reduce dependence on outside sources of supply and to expand Palestine's industrial base.[23] While in 1939 the number of those working in Arab agriculture was estimated as 163,000 (see Table 3.1), at the peak of the prosperity the military employed about 35,000 Arab workers—mostly, it seems, of rural origin—and more Arabs went into other wartime occupations. In addition, the end of the war did not bring a significant change in the demand for labor because in 1944 the British military redefined their mission in the Middle East to include the creation of infrastructure for their garrisons and back-up forces. Further, the British believed that a strong army was necessary in the country while tensions were increasing following the discussions on the future of Palestine.[24] Nevertheless, some reduction in the number employed by the military seemed to take place, since in 1945 only about 28,000 Arab workers were employed by the War Department and in the Palestine troops.[25] All in all, the combination of different elements led to higher levels of labor-force participation with less unemployment and underemployment, and wages were therefore much higher.

The increased opportunities for work outside the villages caused a flow of both part-time and full-time migration away from the villages. Official surveys report that between 1939 and 1944, 47,000 Arab males left the agricultural labor force.[26] While this meant higher labor efficiency, there may also have been a contraction in employment in the rural economy.

In addition, higher wages led to more intensive forms of production. In 1945, when the citrus industry could again export fruits, not enough workers willing to be paid low wages could be found. Consequently, some equipment was imported, such as tractors, ploughs, and combine harvesters.[27] The effect of the 1940s wage boom can be seen in Table 3.3.

The evidence for the 1930s and 1940s suggests that while there was some increase in real wages for low-skilled laborers in the Arab sector during the first half of the 1930s, there was then

Table 3.3 Government Index of Volume of Wage Employment for the Total Population of Palestine, 1938 to 1946

Year	Index
1938	100
1939	102
1940	113
1941	141
1942	181
1943	221
1944	215
1945	224
1946	212

Sources: Government of Palestine, *A Survey of Palestine,* p. 732; Government of Palestine, *Supplement to Survey of Palestine,* p. 88.

a sharp decline until the early 1940s. However, wages increased significantly during the war years, reflecting the higher level of employment. The British decision to bring troops into Palestine and to employ local residents galvanized the labor market and brought relative prosperity during the 1940s.

Human Development

In addition to growth and revenue in monetary terms, the level of "well-being," "quality of life," or "human development" in a society is an important element of socioeconomic change. While each person may define "quality of life" differently, the intention is to focus on mainstream criteria that "people often value."[28] These are "a long and healthy life," "knowledge," and "a decent standard of living."[29] It is recognized that the concept of human development is broad and difficult to quantify and that many of its nonquantifiable elements require compromise; nevertheless, a simple composite measure is able to represent human development quite effectively.[30] The most common measurements are those of the United Nations' *Human Development Index*. This is based on the following elements: (1) longevity, as measured by life expectancy at birth (one-third of the weighting); (2) educational attainment, as measured by a combination of adult literacy and combined primary, secondary, and higher-education enrollment ratios (together, one-third); (3) real gross domestic product per capita (one-third).[31]

For the purposes of this research, a somewhat different human development index was constructed because of the limitations of the data available for the Mandate period. This method, using time series, has not previously been applied to the Arab economy or especially to the Arab rural economy. While the criteria are the same as the U.N. index, the measurements are different. I used the ratio of children who survive to age five, the proportion of Arab children age four to 14 who attend primary school (at any given time), and the NNP per capita (in spite of their limitations).

For each measurement, the highest positive score was ranked as 1. In this sense, 0.6 in attendance to school represents 60 percent of the highest score (it ranged between 21.4 to 60 percent attendance). An exception to this is the ratio of children who survive to age five, which represents the real ratio (ranging between 573 to 806 out of 1,000); otherwise it would have biased the overall picture by producing a higher weighting than the other two factors. Still, each component of the index can be followed separately in Figure 3.10. The results suggest a major improvement in well-being in the Arab sector throughout the Mandate period. Four stages can be seen: the 1920s, when "human development" did not show any significant change; the first half of the 1930s, when it showed a remarkable improvement; the second half of the 1930s, when the level appears unchanged; and the 1940s, when human development increased markedly, although less so than in the early 1930s.

Despite this significant improvement, the level remained extremely low. Even the lowest value of child mortality recorded meant that 20 percent of Arab children age 0 to 5 died (the high-

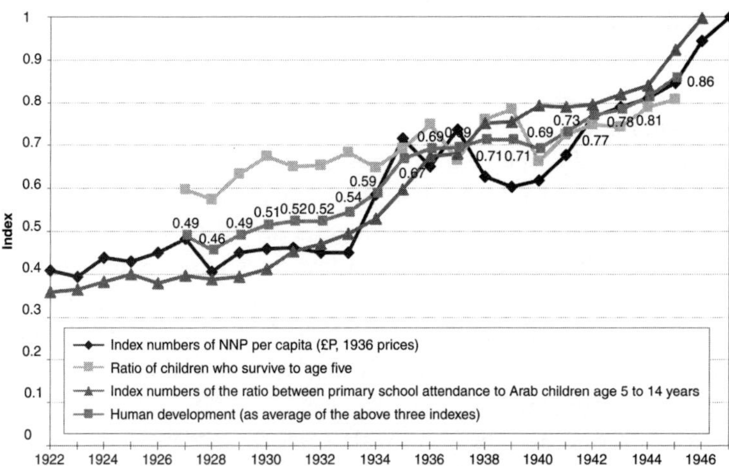

Figure 3.10 Raw Index of Human Development in the Arab Sector

Sources: For ratio of live children out of born children: Government of Palestine, Department of Statistics, *Vital Statistics Tables,* pp. 76, 78. For NNP per capita: Metzer, *The Divided Economy,* p. 242. For school attendance: Noah Hardi, *Education in Palestine* (Washington, DC: Zionist Organization of America, 1945), p. 124; Government of Palestine, Department of Statistics, *Statistical Abstract of Palestine* (1938 and 1944–45); Government of Palestine, Department of Education, *Annual Report for the Years 1943–44, 1945–46.* For Arab children age 5 to 14 years: Government of Palestine, *A Survey of Palestine,* vol. 3, p. 1164.

Notes: A gap in the data led me to take school attendance for 1943 as the average of 1942 and 1944. While information about the number of children age 5 to 14 was found for the years 1931 (census) and 1945 (estimates), it had to be estimated for the period, by using the calculated average annual population growth (of pupils) as a proxy for growth in each year. On infant mortality, the government assessed the measurements as less reliable for the years 1943 to 1945. It also revised the figures for 1922 to 1931. The originals are lacking (Government of Palestine, Department of Statistics, *Vital Statistics Tables* (Jerusalem, 1947), p. 57). This revision, somewhat biased the data for those years, and in fact, unlike Figure 3.10, infant mortality was higher during that period (i.e., fewer children remained alive and the line for these had to be lower) (Justin McCarthy, *The Population of Palestine: Population History and Statistics of the Late Ottoman Period and the Mandate* (New York, 1990), pp. 31–32)).

est value stood at 43 percent). As for literacy, the information from the survey of five villages in 1944, compared to that collected in the census of 1931, suggests that about 21.3 percent of Moslem males over age 7 were literate in these villages in 1931, compared to 29.1 percent in 1944 (the major increase was in the ages of seven to 13, from 28.8 to 55.6 percent). In fact, illiteracy was much more widespread, since the definition of literate was either one who could "read out a few lines from a newspaper" or "all children attending school and having completed one year." At the same time, in three of the five villages, "the teachers of the private schools have themselves enjoyed no more than elementary education."[32]

In addition, the level of Arab performance was extremely poor compared to that of Western countries in the same period. Metzer constructed an international comparison of human development for 1939 (unlike the present data, he did not show trends but rather a picture for a single year). He suggests that while Palestine's Arabs ranked at 0.182 (a different scale and weighting from my index), Western countries were on the opposite side of the scale. The United States, for example, scored as high as 0.954, the United Kingdom 0.881, and France 0.780. On the other hand, by Middle Eastern standards the Palestinian Arabs seemed to perform much better than the other countries examined. Egypt scored as low as 0.101 (55 percent of the level of Palestinian Arabs), and Turkey 0.086 (47 percent of the level of Palestinian Arabs).[33] Poor as they were, the improvement in human development of the Palestinian Arabs that occurred in the Mandate period seemed significant for the region at the time. A report on *Rural Education and Welfare in the Middle East* describes typical conditions:

> Consider for a moment the situation in Iran. The inhabitants of that country are estimated at approximately 15 millions. At least 85 per cent of these people are rural. Moreover, this element of the population produces, according to reliable authorities, about 90 per cent of the national income. And yet these millions, who mean so much to the nation's economy, live in poverty, for the

> most part are entirely without educational facilities, have practically no medical attention, are left more or less to themselves in matters of agricultural practice, and exist throughout most of the country under a type of feudalism that may be characterised as medieval.
>
> The situation is only slightly better in Iraq; no doubt considerably worse among the fellahs of Egypt, where 7 per cent of the population controls about 70 per cent. of the privately owned land. Much more favourable is the condition of the villager in Arab Palestine and Cyprus where feudalism is little known, education widely promoted, and the respective governments highly conscious of rural needs. The peasants of Syria and the Lebanon have enjoyed little in the way of direct assistance. . . . In Ethiopia, Eritrea, Arabia and large areas of the Sudan a majority of the people have hardly emerged from the tribal state. Their need of suitable education, better sanitation [and] some form of medical assistance is ever greater.[34]

One could argue that the increase in human development indicates an increase in the income of Arabs who invested more in education and health. But the phenomenon of higher investment in these sectors seems more likely to have occurred as a result of government action after 1930 (Figure 3.11). In regard to health, although there is as yet no comprehensive study of the impact of the government's measures (vaccinations, opening new clinics, etc.) on Arab society, it seems that their influence was significant. In fact, the government assessed that this was the sector in which its contribution was highest during the Mandate period and that "nowhere was there a greater need for, and nowhere has greater progress been achieved, than in the sphere of public health."[35] The rise in school attendance was another example of government activity, especially in rural areas (see below). Overall, while the glass may be seen as half empty, and some may argue that more could have been done in health and education,[36] it should be recognized that substantial improvement did occur.

The record of human development in the rural sector is not as

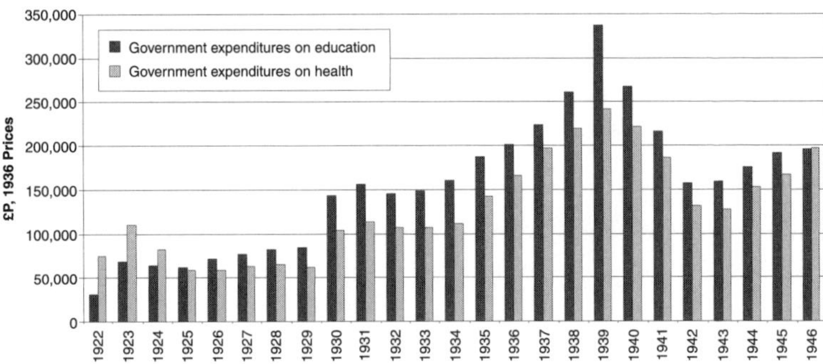

Figure 3.11 Government Expenditures on Health and Education

Sources: Government of Palestine, Department of Statistics, *Statistical Abstract of Palestine* (1939, pp. 113–15; 1940, p. 123; 1945, p. 81); Government of Palestine, *Report on the Accounts and Finances, 1946–47* (Jerusalem, 1948), p. 73.

impressive as for Arab society as a whole. Bearing in mind that the "raw index of human development in the Arab sector" consists of three parts, human development in the Arab agricultural sector is now compared with that of the Arab sector as a whole. Starting with the ratio of live children to children born, the answer is straightforward: there were no significant differences in child mortality between villages and urban areas.[37] In this sense, the "ratio of children surviving to age 5" in Figure 3.10 represents the rural situation fairly accurately.

There was a significant difference in child attendance in schools, with more receiving education in towns than in villages. The approximate ratio between Muslim children, who, as defined, "received education for some period or other," stood in 1946 at 1.34:1 for boys in towns over those in the villages (85% versus 63% of the totals), and 0.8:1 for girls (60% versus 75%).[38] Moslems were the majority of the Arab rural population in Palestine (Table 1.3), and the only noteworthy changes are those within this population, as the level of education of the Christian Arabs was comparatively high and did not seem to vary during the Mandate period: it stood at almost 100 percent attendance in primary schools.[39] The evidence therefore indicates almost no disparity in basic education between Arab rural and urban areas. Estimating that the ratio of boys to girls was approximately 1:1 and leaving aside the data on Christians, the ratio between urban and rural enrollment rates in primary education in 1946 is estimated as 1.05:1. Data for the year 1937 suggest that the disparity between Moslem urban and rural children was greater than in 1946, at 2.12:1 for boys and 15.37:1 for girls.[40] The lessening of the urban to rural enrollment gap in favor of rural enrollment should be largely attributed to government policy, since, unlike in urban areas, no significant effort had been made in public education in rural areas since 1922. However, the government began to promote Arab rural education from autumn 1934. In that year, 16,133 pupils entered Arab rural schools, and this number tripled to 49,000 in 1946 (for the school year 1945 to 1946),[41] while the total number of Arab pupils studying in 1934 was 57,542, and in 1945 to 1946, 124,927.[42] Overall, if one draws a line depicting the rate of child enrollment at school, the line representing Arab rural society is well below the "all Arabs" line in 1934; however, the gap between urban and rural figures decreases during the years.

Moving to the last component of the raw human development index, the net national product per capita in comparison to the product of the Arab sector per capita, certain points should be made. First, the data used relate only to agricultural produce. This means that the contribution of the rural economy to other sectors cannot be seen, either directly, through part-time employment, or indirectly. Second, it is clear that the product per capita was lower from agriculture than from other sectors in the economy because "agriculture" generated a smaller amount than its proportion of the population would suggest. It is therefore useful to compare changes in trends between the NNP per capita and the net product of Arab agriculture per rural inhabitant, bearing in mind that the result may say something about income trends *only in agriculture for the Arab rural sector as a whole.* It is most important to note, as discussed above, that the specific returns on product are the least accurate.

The evidence presented in Figure 3.12 confirms that there was a strong correlation between the Arab NNP and the Arab agricultural product between the two world wars ($R^2 = 0.83$). Second, it can be seen that from 1930 to the beginning of the war in 1939, the growth of agricultural product per capita was lower for "all Palestine." Third, the growth during the prosperity was faster in agriculture than in the aggregate measure of other sectors. Fourth, as the intention of this study is to focus on the noncitrus sector, it should be noted (see Figures 3.4 and 3.6) that much of the growth up to 1935 is ascribed to citrus, unlike in following years.

Taking into account the lack of information on nonagricultural income in the Arab rural sector, the following conclusions may be drawn. Until 1934, there was no significant improvement in "human development." On the one hand, income per capita did not show improvement (assuming that income from

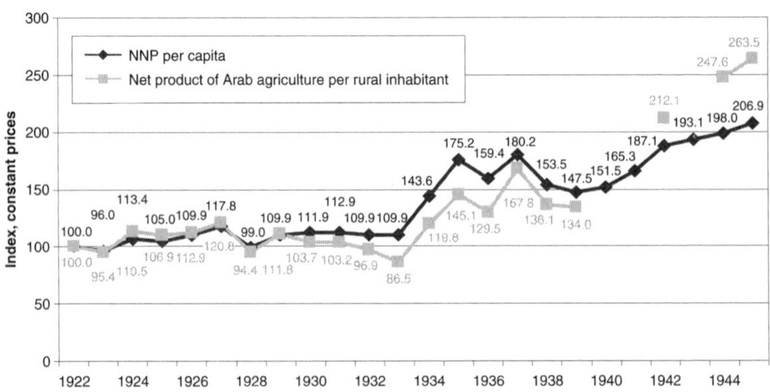

Figure 3.12 Net National and Agricultural Products per Capita

Sources: Government of Palestine, *A Survey of Palestine,* pp. 147–52, Table 1.3; Metzer, *The Divided Economy,* pp. 239, 241; Metzer and Kaplan, *Mesheq yehudi ve-mesheq 'aravi,* p. 46.

other sources did not change significantly). In educational enrollment, until the change of policy in 1934, no significant change occurred. The only improvement seen in those years was in the ratio of surviving children to children born, but this was for just a short period to 1930, after which it remained more or less stagnant. In that period, the advance in human development of the Arab rural sector as a whole was lower than that of the Arab sector as a whole.

The year 1934 was a turning point. The changes in government policy (see Chapter 1) led to a sustained improvement in education and even to an upward trend in the ratio of live children to children born. Product per capita—at least "officially"—also increased significantly from that year. The third phase began with the prosperity. It had a very positive influence on agricultural income. In addition, the government's education program continued to show results. No such positive change seems to have occurred in the ratio of live children to all children born.

Arab society generally, and Arab rural society in particular, experienced similar trends; signs of faster improvement were seen in education in the villages, as well as in product, during the prosperity, yet they were still less developed than in Arab society as a whole. The level of education was lower in the rural areas especially in the 1930s, as was the product per capita. The level of child mortality was quite similar between the two communities.

CONCLUSION

The array of evidence presented in Part 1 calls for a revision of the accepted view on the growth of Arab agricultural product. The leading commentators on the Mandate period, Metzer and Kaplan, suggested a high and sustained growth in agricultural product. However, it is argued here that the most likely picture is of little or even no growth in Arab net product during 1922 to 1939 and a continual deterioration in net product per Arab rural inhabitant. In such a situation, the TFP growth could not have been positive. The 1940s present a completely different scenario, of substantial economic growth in general, as well as per rural inhabitant. It seems that on average, we can speak of only very low growth per capita in the Arab rural sector during the Mandate period.

The findings for the 1930s and 1940s suggest that there was some increase in real wages for low-skilled laborers in the Arab sector during the first half of the 1930s and then a sharp decline until the early 1940s. However, wages increased substantially during the miracle years of the war, reflecting the higher level of employment. Even after the war, wages and employment remained high, since the British army continued to employ local workers. It was therefore the British decision to bring troops into Palestine and to employ local residents that galvanized the labor market and brought relative prosperity during the 1940s. Again, the conclusion is that it was the prosperity that pushed up income and not prewar policies or processes. The combination of employment, wages, and higher returns for net Arab agriculture highlights the significant change during these war years, unlike the relative malaise of the interwar period.

Instead, it was in the area of human development that pre-prosperity improvement took place. This was largely related to the government's concern to improve health conditions and rural education in the Arab sector, especially after the Disturbances of 1929.

NOTES

1. Jacob Metzer and Oded Kaplan, *Mesheq yehudi 7e-mesheq ʻaravi beerez ishrael: tozar taʻasuqa 7ezmiḥah betqufat hamandat* (Jerusalem, 1991).
2. Roger Owen and Sevket Pamunk, *A History of Middle East Economies in the Twentieth Century* (London, 1998), p. 7.
3. Jacob Metzer, *The Divided Economy of Mandatory Palestine* (Cambridge, 1998), p. 242.

4. Metzer and Kaplan, *Mesheq yehudi 7e-mesheq 'aravi,* p. 171.
5. Metzer, *The Divided Economy,* pp. 21, 26.
6. Calculated from Eliahu Eliashar, "Mifqad ha-ta'ashiya vehamelakha shel memshelet erez-ishrael 1928," *Riv'on le-kalkala,* 26, no. 101–02 (1979), pp. 248–56.
7. Government of Palestine, *A Survey of Palestine,* pp. 691–96; Mahmoud Yazbaq, *Hahagira ha'aravit leḥeyfa beyn hashanim 1933–1948,* M.A. thesis, University of Haifa, 1986.
8. E.g., Government of Palestine, Department of Statistics, *Statistical Abstract of Palestine, 1937–38* (Jerusalem, 1939), p. 42.
9. Government of Palestine, Department of Agriculture and Fisheries, *Village Note Book* (undated blank books for the years 1935–38 and 1943–46.) This source was found in the Israel Bureau of Statistics Library.
10. Metzer and Kaplan, *Mesheq yehudi 7e-mesheq 'aravi,* p. 21.
11. See Table 3.1.
12. As discussed below.
13. Metzer and Kaplan, *Mesheq yehudi 7e-mesheq 'aravi,* pp. 29–30, 44. See Chapter 2 for variations in yield returns.
14. This residual measure captures changes in the amount of output that can be produced by a given quantity of inputs. Intuitively, it measures the shift in production function. Many factors can cause such a shift: technical innovation, organizational and institutional changes, shifts in societal attitudes, fluctuations in demand, changes in factor shares, omitted variables, and measurement errors. However, the various factors comprising the TFP are not measured directly but lumped together as a residual "leftover" factor. They cannot be sorted out within the TFP framework—and this is exactly the source of its famous nickname: "a measure of our ignorance." Charles R. Hulten, "Total Factor Productivity: A Short Biography," [U.S.] National Bureau of Economic Research, Working Paper 7471, January 2000, pp. 1–75.
15. Metzer, *The Divided Economy,* p. 139.
16. Government of Palestine, *A Survey of Palestine,* p. 734.
17. Rachelle Leah Taqqu, *Arab Labor in Mandatory Palestine, 1920–1948,* Ph.D. thesis, Columbia University, 1977, p. 54.
18. Arthur W. Lewis, "Economic Development with Unlimited Supplies of Labour," *Manchester School,* 22 (May 1954), pp. 139–91.

19. Mahmoud Yazbaq, "Hahagira ha'aravit leḥeyfa 1933–1948: *Nituḥ 'al-pi meqorot 'arviyim,*" *Qatedra,* 45 (1987), pp. 131–46.
20. Interview with Abū 'Abdallah from Mashhad (Abū 'Abdallah (b. 1921) was the *mukhtār*'s son in the Mandate period and later became the *mukhtār* of his village) (6 April 1999 and 17 August 1999). Also interview with Raḍwan Salīm Bisharat (Mr. Bisharat, b. 1914, was a *fallāḥ* who lived in Ma'lul village) (22nd August 2000); interview with Mohammad Maṣrāwa (known as Bayrūti) from Reina (ḥaj Maṣrāwa, b. 1929, was a *fallāḥ* in Safuriyya during the Mandate period) (19 August 1999); interview with Maḍhib Nimir Sulṭī from 'Ilut (Mr. Sulṭī (b. 1934–35) is the son of a *fallāḥīn* family) (22 August 2000).
21. For employment in citrus, see Metzer, *The Divided Economy,* p. 143.
22. Rachelle Taqqu, "Internal Labor Migration and the Arab Village Community under the Mandate," Joel S. Migdal (ed.), *Palestinian Society and Politics* (Princeton, 1980), pp. 272–81.
23. Roger Owen, "Economic Development in Mandate Palestine: 1918–1948," George T. Abed (ed.), *The Palestinian Economy: Studies in Development under Prolonged Occupation* (London, 1988), p. 27.
24. Alon Kadish, "Ovdey maḥanot hazava kemiqre boḥan be-ḥeqer ha-ḥevra ha-falesṭinit" (forthcoming).
25. Government of Palestine, Department of Statistics, *National Income of Palestine 1944, P. J. Loftus, Government Statistician* (Jerusalem, 1946), p. 27.
26. Taqqu, "Internal Labor Migration," p. 265.
27. Government of Palestine, Department of Agriculture and Fisheries, *Annual Report for the Year 1944–45* (Jerusalem, 1946), p. 2.
28. UNDP, *Human Development Report 1990* (Oxford: Oxford University Press, 1990), p. 9.
29. UNDP, *Human Development Report 2002* (Oxford: Oxford University Press, 2002), p. 252.
30. "HDI," www.undp.org . For more about this debate, see N. F. R. Crafts, "Economic Growth in East Asia and Western Europe since 1950: Implications for Living Standards," *National Institute Economic Review,* 162 (1997), pp. 75–84; Partha Dasgupta and

Martin Weale, "On Measuring the Quality of Life," *World Development,* 20, no. 1 (1992), pp. 119–31.

31. UNDP, *Human Development Report 2002,* p. 252. See also Amos Nadan, "Reconsidering the Arab Human Development Report 2002," in Amnon Cohen and Elie Podeh (eds.), *Israel, the Middle East and Islam* (Truman Institute, 2004 forthcoming).
32. Government of Palestine, Department of Statistics, *Survey of Social and Economic Conditions in Arab Villages, 1944: Special Bulletin No. 21* (Jerusalem, 1948), pp. 32–33.
33. Metzer, *The Divided Economy,* p. 57.
34. Harold Boughton Allen, *Rural Education and Welfare in the Middle East: A Report to the Director General, Middle East Supply Centre, September 1944* (London, 1946), pp. 2–3.
35. Government of Palestine, *A Survey of Palestine,* p. 699.
36. Shepherd argues that there was improvement, yet not fast enough: Naomi Shepherd, *Ploughing Sand: British Rule in Palestine 1917–1948* (New Brunswick, 2000), pp. 126–78.
37. Child mortality data are available only for the Moslem population, the majority of the Arab population. The average mortality of Moslem children during 1927 to 1945 stood at 313.9 per 1,000 in all Palestinian towns and 315.8 in all villages. For the Christian population, only infant mortality (for those under one year old) is available. The average mortality of infants in this population during the years 1927 to 1945 stood at 155.4 per 1,000 in all Palestinian towns and 160.9 in all villages. Compiled from Government of Palestine, Department of Statistics, *Vital Statistics Tables,* pp. 19, 23, 61, 65, 76.
38. Government of Palestine, *A Survey of Palestine,* p. 716.
39. E.g., Government of Palestine, Department of Education, *Annual Report for the Years 1945–46* (Jerusalem, 1946), p. 5.
40. Noah Hardi, *Education in Palestine* (Zionist Organization of America, Washington DC, 1945), p. 125. Note that in the source, the figures are given for attendance in each age group, such as 5 to 6, 6 to 7, etc. The numbers presented above are the average of all the age groups between five and 14.
41. Government of Palestine, Department of Education, *Annual Report for the Years 1945–46,* p. 6. Note that in one source (Govern-

ment of Palestine, *A Survey of Palestine,* p. 716), it was mentioned that in 1945 the girls' attendance in villages was more than that in towns and also more than the boys in villages. This should be regarded as an error.

42. Government of Palestine, Department of Education, *Annual Report for the Years 1945–46,* p. 4; Hardi, *Education in Palestine,* p. 124.

Part Three

THE *FALLĀḤĪN* ECONOMY AND BRITISH REFORMS

· FOUR ·

The Rural Institutions of the Fallāḥīn

The high government spending on Arab agriculture outlined in Part 1 and the evident stagnation until the miracle of the prosperity discussed in Part 2 raise doubts about whether the government's efforts to improve the *fallāḥīn* economy delivered the success that it claimed. One intention of Part 3 is to assess these activities and their impact.

As mentioned in the introduction, the British administration's programs to assist the *fallāḥīn* were aimed, above all, at "rationalizing" the *fallāḥīn* and their institutions (defined by North as the "rules of the game" in a society). A policy of eliminating indigenous institutions and replacing them with Western-style ones lay behind the land and credit reforms in particular, although there were some direct services that were not based on this paradigm. A historical analysis is now needed to evaluate the British perception of the *fallāḥīn* as irrational and to compare the government's "rationalization programs" (Chapters 5 and 6) with its direct services (Chapter 7). These enable an assessment of the extent to which this perception affected the nature of government interventions. It is, however, important to stress that the reference is not to the concept of maximization that is often associated with rationality in neoclassical economics. This theoretical concept has been challenged recently, notably by Daniel Kahneman, winner of the Nobel Prize for economics in 2002, who states that "the idea that decision makers evaluate outcomes by the utility of final asset positions has been retained in economic analyses for almost 300 years. This is rather remarkable, because the idea is easily shown to be wrong."[1]

Another intention of Part 3 is to analyze the Arab rural economy in greater detail by taking a microperspective. The present chapter focuses on the structure of rural institutions in the capital-poor economy of the *fallāḥīn,* changes in those institutions, and the reasons for the changes.

THE EXTERNAL VIEW OF THE *FALLĀḤĪN* AND THEIR INSTITUTIONS

The belief that the *fallāḥīn* and their institutions were irrational was held widely by British administrators and some Zionist writers during the Mandate period. The broader position was that the culture or mental habits of Arab peasants gave rise to a conservative inability to make economic-related judgments and to adapt to change (in less politically correct language, the *fallāḥīn* were too ignorant to manage their farms wisely). It is important to note that the approach of such writers is not compatible with the familiar safety-first approach attributed predominantly to James Scott—that peasants understand the market and are logical, yet "are chary of commercial risks unless they have a solid subsistence foundation under them."[2] It is even further away from the approaches, of Theodore Schultz, who argued that "*there are comparatively few significant inefficiencies in the allocation of factors of production in traditional agriculture*" (italics in the original), and of Samuel Popkin, who subscribes to Schultz's main hypothesis but suggests an additional economic aspect to peasant cooperation—their motivation not only by maximization but also by insurance considerations.[3]

The supposed incompetence and lack of economic sense of the *fallāḥīn* were assumed to be highlighted by their failure to undertake certain improvements that were relatively common in the Jewish sector. In their book *The Arab Economy* (1944), Ze'ev Abrahamoviz and Izḥaq Guelfat doubted that the *fallāḥīn* knew how to allocate their resources efficiently. For example, referring to the use of manure on Jewish farms, they commented that "animal manure is almost not in use and heaps of animal manure have been and still are being gathered from time immemorial." Similarly, they described the plow used on *fallāḥīn* land as "probably more primitive than that used by the ancient Jews."[4] In the authoritative 1931 *Census of Palestine,* it was inferred that the *fallāḥīn* culture encouraged laziness: "In general, the life of the Arab peasant is [was] one of inactivity."[5] More important, it was argued in the influential British report by Johnson and Crosbie (1930), which proposed direct measures (later implemented) to improve the economic conditions of the *fallāḥīn,* that "the foremost need of the agricultural industry is rationalisation."[6] Not surprisingly, the Mandatory government decided to introduce measures to "rationalize" the *fallāḥīn,* and especially their institutions, by means of land and credit reforms.

On the other hand, no reference to lack of economic sense was made in sources written by those who were closely and directly connected with the *fallāḥīn* economy. This was the case, for instance, in the book on olive trees by 'Alī Nasūj al-Ẓāhir, the government inspector of fruits in the hill country from 1932 to 1947;[7] in Moḥamad Yūnīs al-ḥusayni's book on the socioeconomic development of the Arabs in Palestine, which includes much evidence based on his direct interaction with some *fallāḥīn* and Bedouins;[8] and in two separate semianthropological works about the *fallāḥīn* economy by the Reverend Charles T. Wilson and Elihu Grant.[9]

Could it be that the different perceptions of (1) those who knew the *fallāḥīn* economy from a distance and who believed in peasant irrationality and (2) those who knew it from within and who did not detect such a problem are closely related to the reliance of the former on a speculative preconception rather than on evidence or fieldwork? Perhaps, as Elihu Grant put it, among the *fallāḥīn* "there are [were] the lazy and the active as in any country;"[10] the *fallāḥīn* were well aware of how to allocate resources efficiently, such as using animal manure in a productive way; and because of their misconception, British reforms for the *fallāḥīn* were mistaken.

SAVING TRANSACTION COSTS: PRODUCTION, SUBSISTENCE, AND TRADE

The following two sections address the issues of part subsistence and part surplus production and of barter and money trade.

Part Subsistence, Part Surplus

According to the Census of 1931, 90.3 percent of the "earner" Arab farmers in the noncitrus sector were peasants, accounting for 51,837 farmers. The Census defined their occupation as "ordinary cultivation." The rest (9.7 percent; 5,569 "earners") were occupied mainly in the growing of "special products" such as vegetables and in the maintenance of nursery gardens (some of them were probably peasants).[11] Hence, the majority of the *fallāḥīn* were peasants.

The *fallāḥīn* primarily consumed their own agricultural products and sold the surplus to the market. Interviews with former *fallāḥīn* suggest that most of the crops they produced were what they consumed, especially wheat, olives, barley, and to a lesser extent fruits and vegetables.[12] Similarly, an inquiry into the diet of the population in Mandate Palestine from 1931 suggests that those Arabs who grew different products or raised animals had different diets based on their product specialization.[13] There is a similarity between this and the picture described by Grant in 1921, although Grant hardly spoke of vegetables:

> Wheat is the most important item for the well-to-do peasant. . . . Bread made of barley or of millet is used by the poorest people. . . . The peasants eat ripe olives, olive oil, figs, coffee [hummus and lentils are also mentioned].[14]

Besides meeting their own subsistence needs, *fallāḥīn* interacted with the market to obtain other household goods. As the above quotation shows, coffee, which was not grown in Palestine, was used by *fallāḥīn* and so was obviously purchased. All my interviews with former *fallāḥīn* indicate that they sold their own produce and bought some other products. This was also observed by Rosemary Sayigh in her interviews in Lebanon with former *fallāḥīn,* who had found refuge there after the 1948 war.[15]

The issue of safety-first tendencies is not in question here. Yet if peasants were "chary of commercial risks unless they have a solid subsistence foundation under them,"[16] such cautiousness probably could have had only a small influence on the crop specialization of the *fallāḥīn.* This is because cash crops in Palestine were also edible subsistence crops (which is not the case of, say, wheat and cotton cropping). The *fallāḥīn* were familiar with methods of fruit and vegetable conservation that enabled them to eat such crops all year long, just as they did with grains and legumes. Some vegetables and fruits, such as tomatoes, were perforated, dried, and later eaten in soup; other crops that were dried included okra, pepper, garlic, onions, plums, apples, and grapes.[17]

Knowing that *fallāḥīn* diets were based on their different product specializations, that the *fallāḥīn* diverted their crops into vegetables during the prosperity, and that physical factors inhibited the growing of more vegetables, it seems likely that *fallāḥīn* diets varied primarily in accordance with shifts in market incentives. Hence, in Palestine, the part-subsistence, part-surplus mode did not seem to move peasants away from the production of cash crops, since in their way of life there was no difference between cash and subsistence crops (certainly in the noncitrus sector). These findings also reflect Charles Kamen's study because he tried to forge a link between James Scott's theoretical hypothesis and the case of the *fallāḥīn.*[18] When dealing with the part-subsistence, part-surplus mode of production, Kamen argued that the "characteristics of the Palestine agricultural economy which drew frequent criticism were very similar to many of those which Scott listed."[19] Even so, an extensive theoretical discussion, accompanied by very meager evidence from Palestine, does not seem to support Kamen's claim that "it is unnecessary here to do more than outline the principal characteristics of peasant society in Palestine."[20] Indeed, his cardinal error is the belief that the *fallāḥīn* were either subsistence peasants or commercial farmers (i.e., that there were no part-subsistence, part-surplus peasants) and that there was a clear distinction between subsistence and cash crops.

Bearing in mind the discussion of crop specialization in Chapter 2 (Figure 2.6), especially in light of the lack of much relevancy of the safety-first paradigm, it becomes clear that the different ratio in factors of production between Arabs and Jews is highly relevant to the different crop specializations—that is, to the different types of land held in Arab and Jewish hands, the significantly different costs of labor in the two sectors, and the different availability of capital that could guide different modes of specialization.[21] Yet what is apparent from the comparison is that Jewish farmers chose to grow grains and legumes on about 50 percent of their land and that Arabs grew them on about 80 percent of their land (47.2 percent and 79.4 percent).[22] The fact that those whose response was not doubted—the nonsubsistence Jewish farmers—had a large share in grains and legumes may also imply that growing these crops on Arab farms was likewise a reliable response.

It was noted in Chapter 2 that some *fallāḥīn* owned land that was relatively more appropriate for vegetables (especially land that was irrigated). It was also observed from interviews in the Galilee that those with land on which irrigation could be easily developed grew vegetables as their principal crop. On such land, *fallāḥīn* tended to employ nonhousehold laborers. This is another indication that when market incentives were high enough to optimize crop choices in a less (or even non-) subsistence way, some *fallāḥīn* had no reservations about making the necessary changes.[23]

The key concept to which part-subsistence, part-surplus production seems to be related is not the British assumption of peasant irrationality, but its opposite—that this mode of production and consumption was a considered choice that allowed *fallāḥīn* to reduce onerous transaction costs, especially since the fundamental products they needed to obtain were staple crops, such as wheat, since bread was relatively more expensive and they therefore produced it themselves. In the words of a former *fallāḥ:*

> the *fallāḥ* was very poor and occasionally went hungry. He did not have enough money to buy food which was very expensive. He needed to grow his own food in order to survive.[24]

Another *fallāḥ* told a story about a peasant who loaded his donkey with as much foodstuff as the animal could carry and went to the city of Haifa to sell his goods. He sold them at a high price. Hungry and feeling well-off after that sale, he ordered a cheap meal of hummus with broad beans *(fūl)* in a local restaurant. But the normal restaurant price was higher than the payment he had received for his goods. Fortunately, the restaurant owner agreed to take what money he had. Back in the village, he told his friends what had happened, saying that a *fallāḥ* could sell a donkey load of hummus yet could not afford to buy with this money a small plate of hummus in the city.[25] This story demonstrates the relevancy of a transaction-cost analysis to the case of part-subsistence, part-surplus producers.

Together, these indications suggest that the *fallāḥīn*'s use of part-subsistence, part-surplus production was driven not by cultural or mental deficiencies but by their knowledge of transaction costs and the desire to avoid them. The differences between their modes of production and consumption and Jewish modes seem primarily to reflect the creation of a traditional practice in a capital-scarce economy, in which the main concerns of those who were poor (including those engaged in other occupations) were to obtain the cheapest kind of food—staples—and not to buy final or value-added products. They were able to produce what they most needed to consume. In the Jewish sector, on the other hand, capital was relatively plentiful, and people were able to purchase large amounts of finished goods. For the Jewish farmer, growing wheat did not mean that there would be more bread at home. For the *fallāḥ,* it meant exactly that.

The Fallāḥīn Preference for Barter over Money Trade

Mostly, a *fallāḥ* would sell to another *fallāḥ* not for money but in barter *(mubādalah),* which was the main form of payment in the villages. It was, for example, the usual means of payment when wheat was exchanged for a hen or used to pay for labor. Although not all villagers were engaged solely in agriculture, barter of crops was also common for nonagricultural products and services. The village barber, for instance, was paid in kind for his services once a year at harvest time, and a carpenter would receive measures of wheat in return for maintenance of plows and for other work.[26] This practice saved the transaction costs involved in the trading of produce through merchants. It was also easily done, especially since the main concern of those who were poor was to purchase the cheapest kind of food. Thus it was the scarcity of capital that determined the preference for barter over money trade.

Cash was paid when those providing the services (especially merchants selling commodities that they had had to purchase in cash) needed money more than staples. This was the case in the village shop, where commodities like tea, coffee, sugar, and rice were sold. Large villages (those with a few hundred inhabitants) had a butcher and shops that offered a wide variety of goods, such as shoes and furniture, as well as agricultural equipment (cast hoes, sickles, etc.). Although cash was the usual means of payment, *fallāḥīn* who did not have ready cash could usually defer payment until harvest time, and interest seemed to be included in the price.[27]

Payments in kind and repayment of loans were commonly delayed until the harvest of winter crops (wheat, barley, and olives), since that was when most *fallāḥīn* brought in the majority of their field crops (for further details, see Chapter 5). It was also the time when more milk was available, since mammals used to give birth during the spring, and hence more newborn animals could be traded (the males were usually set aside for meat).[28] Because of this output cycle (harvest and animal births coming together) and the need to pay off debts at harvest time, more agricultural produce was available in the market, bringing the prices of many commodities to their lowest point each year.

As can be seen in Figure 4.1, prices were lower after the harvest of winter crops (between April and June, varying in different agricultural years and in different parts of the country) and higher later on. Note that all crops available for all the period are winter ones; summer crops may have different trends. Olives were reaped in September to November. The commodities selected in Figure 4.1 are those in the lists for the period examined[29] and were sold directly by the *fallāḥīn* (for example, local wheat and not local flour; potatoes are excluded, as most were either imported or in Jewish hands).[30] To give a more comprehensive picture, the products in Figure 4.1 are divided into five groups, with the same weighting allotted to each product in a group: (1) wheat, (2) lentils, chickpeas, and onions, (3) hens and eggs, (4) milk, (5) meat (a less direct measurement, as it includes the cost of butchering).

At harvest time, it was expected that no one would tell a shopkeeper that he was unwilling to pay, as this was the only period where cash substitution in case of default could efficiently be charged.[31] Customarily, even other transactions with the money market were made at harvest time, since *fallāḥīn* seemed to sell all their surplus of crops and most of their surplus of animals then.[32] Prices fell significantly for as long as the market was flooded with agricultural commodities, and *fallāḥīn* accepted, in cash, the lowest possible price instead of waiting until demand (and prices) increased.

It may be argued that the reason for marketing field crops, in particular, immediately after the harvest is that the *fallāḥīn* did not have enough space for storage. This view is not well

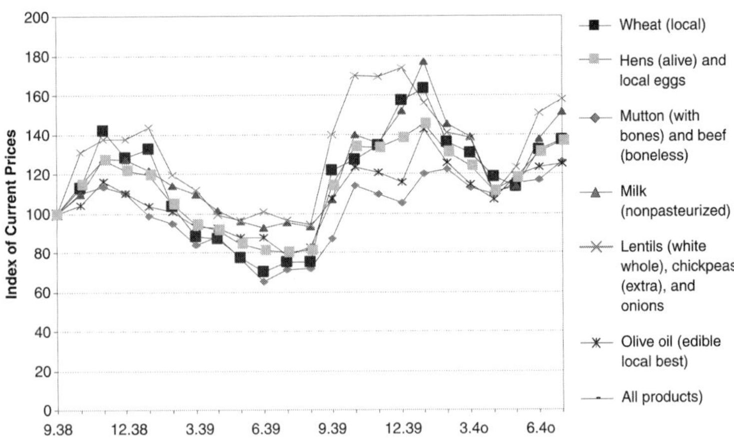

Figure 4.1 Index of Changes in Agricultural Commodity Prices

Source: Government of Palestine, Office of Statistics, *General Monthly Bulletin of Current Statistics* (various years).

Note: The same measurements of quantity and quality were taken for each product throughout the period examined.

founded, however. Indeed, storage of foodstuffs (especially of the main produce, grains and legumes) was not problematic. The *fallāḥīn* used to store food in their homes.[33] In 1930, an Arab household of 5.8 people held, on average, 40.25 dunums of field crops.[34] The average yield per dunum of grains and legumes was estimated at about 43.25 kilograms.[35] Hence, if such a household grew only grains and legumes, it had to store 1,741 kilograms per year. The Johnson-Crosbie report suggests that 766 kilograms of wheat were consumed per household per year, according to government estimates, and 920 kilograms according to the declared data collected from interviews.[36] These data, as indicated, are far from accurate. Yet they give some indication of the amount of produce consumed by the *fallāḥīn* or at least between 40 and 60 percent of it (let us assume 50 percent).

The question therefore is whether they could store about double the amount of grains that they did store (the "about double" estimate seems to be far higher than in reality, since it ignores the payments due to local shopkeepers at harvest time, as well as the consumption of foodstuffs other than wheat in the category "grains and legumes"). The differing weights of grains and legumes needed different storage capacities, although not widely different. Hence, the data for wheat, the dominant grain, is taken as proxy for all the grains and legumes: this was 150 kilograms per one *ardeb* (198 liters/0.198 cubic meters).[37] This meant that the *fallāḥ* used only about 1.15 cubic meters to store his consumption stock and needed no more than another 1.15 cubic meters for storing the marketable portion of his crop. There is also evidence of *fallāḥīn* storing their subsistence wheat in underground holes outside their houses, and reference was made by those interviewed to other ways of storing straw outside their houses.[38] There was clearly no problem with storage.

Indeed, other factors seemed to influence the response of the peasants. First and foremost, *fallāḥīn* needed to sell right after the harvest as this was when their payments were demanded, and they also had to buy other tools. After the harvest, there was an urgent need to buy various commodities for the coming ploughing, such as donkeys, oxen, or plows, and to repair agricultural tools, etc.[39] In addition, the moneylenders, the main source of credit, wanted their payments without delay, when the harvest was known to be available for payment or seizure.[40] It was also (as discussed in Chapter 5) that there were unwritten agreements between merchant-moneylenders and their borrower *fallāḥīn* in which *fallāḥīn* would sell all their cash-crop at harvest time and in exchange would receive assistance from the merchant-moneylenders in lean years. Finally, taxes were usually levied right after the harvest. From 1935, the payment date for the rural property tax was 1 April (previously, the date had been dependent on the High Commissioner's decision).[41]

Still, it would be foolish to think that *fallāḥīn* needed to make *all* their payments and purchases right after the harvest and could not wait a few months. Why did they rush? Why did they not optimize? When some former *fallāḥīn* were asked in interviews what wheat prices had been during the year, they replied that except at harvest time there was no price for wheat, since "everyone kept his own wheat."[42] Such answers seem to reflect other reasons for selling crops immediately after the harvest, particularly that *fallāḥīn* did not have reliable information about price trends during the year and therefore saw no advantage in keeping their produce a few months longer. This supports the assumption that they had difficulties with an economic-related judgment. However, since most of their interactions were through barter trade, it is likely that they were less knowledgeable about price trends.

Not surprisingly, the main winners from "premature" grain sales were wholesale merchants who were wealthy enough to finance holding the crop and could occasionally even get cheap credit.[43] Unlike the *fallāḥīn,* merchants showed close familiarity with the trends in price movements. Crop merchants had storage areas where commodities with a long shelf life could be stored until prices increased. Meat merchants used to delay the slaughter of some animals, raise them for a short period, and kill them when prices went up.[44]

Overall, the *fallāḥīn* operated soundly in their part-subsistence, part-surplus production and in barter trade. However, it seems that lack of knowledge—that is, imperfect information—and not their lack of common sense caused misjudgments in marketing. If government assistance was needed, it was surely in expert guidance of these practical *fallāḥīn* and not in structural change reforms, but the government did not identify this.

LABOR ALLOCATION

This section deals with labor allocation on *fallāḥīn* farms in the evolving situations of land scarcity, capital constraints, work opportunities away from the farms, technology, and livestock breeding.

Demographic Growth, Land Scarcity, and Labor Allocation

Considering Mandate Palestine as a unit, it is reasonable to assume that at the beginning of the Mandate era land for cultivation was not scarce. Although maps from the late Ottoman period show that the mountains were the most densely inhabited, much land in the valleys was not cultivated. The common explanation for the greater density of settlement in the mountains and consequently the more intense cultivation there is the lack of security in the plains because of frequent Bedouin raids, as well as the higher chances of malaria infection in valley swamps.[45]

But it can certainly be said of the subunits in Palestine that land was scarce in many areas at the beginning of the Mandate. As part of the comprehensive Ottoman reforms in the nineteenth century, known as *Tanẓīmāt,* land registration began. After the Land Law of 1858, only lands under cultivation were registered in the name of individuals. Uncultivated plots were registered in the name of the government, thus obstructing further expansion of the villages.[46] Concurrently, from the time of the land registration until the beginning of the Mandate, there was a significant increase in the village labor force because of population growth. The combination of land registration and a bigger labor force led, in practical terms, to a shortage of land (there was no substantial investment in labor-intensive agriculture to compensate for this,[47] although some improvements were made; see below). Indeed, although there is undoubtedly some degree of error in the population data for the late Ottoman period, it is clear that the Arab population significantly increased during that time. In 1850 and 1851, it was estimated at around 340,000; in 1914 and 1915, at more than double that (around 722,100; an annual growth of 1.2 percent per year).[48] This was mainly the result of natural increase, due to a steady improvement in longevity without significant change in birth rates, combined with immigration.[49] Although towns grew faster than villages, the higher population was absorbed mainly in rural areas, estimated as 233,500 persons (a rise of 90 percent) added to the rural population and 148,600 (186 percent) to the towns.[50]

In many cases in the later Ottoman period, land was not registered in the names of the *fallāḥīn* who cultivated it but in the names of urban and rural notables. Gabriel Baer gave several reasons for this, most important that *fallāḥīn* preferred not to register the land in their own names because they feared conscription of their sons into the Ottoman army (since the registration would take away their anonymity) and also because registration required a payment. In addition, notables used their knowledge of laws and their good connections with the administration to manipulate registrations.[51] Certain lands in the Jordan Valley were registered as the Sultan's property *(jiftlik)*, but other lands were sold—at attractive prices—by the Ottoman government to notables, mainly from Palestine, Lebanon, Syria, and Egypt (later, the *jiftlik* lands as well were sold by the Ottomans to other notables). These lands were mainly uncultivated areas and not associated with any village.[52]

With their population constantly growing, villagers coped with the difficulties of obtaining additional land in the late Ottoman period by turning to labor-intensive work, notably the building and cultivating of terraces.[53] *Fallāḥīn* also became part-time migrant laborers who found employment in the towns, in the new agrarian large-scale estates owned by big landlords (some of whom bought lands from the state), and in bigger neighboring farms.[54]

The Arab population increased during the Mandate for the same two reasons that it increased under the Ottomans—natural increase and, to a much lesser extent, immigration—yet the trends were much faster. While annual population growth stood at 1.2 percent per annum in the late Ottoman period,[55] the rate for the Muslim population in Mandate Palestine was around 2.9 percent and for Christian Arabs 3 percent,[56] with similar rates of natural increase in both villages and towns.[57] At the same time, agricultural land in Arab ownership decreased, and land improvement was outstripped by the demographic growth, creating a scenario of per capita deterioration in opportunities (see Chapters 2 and 3).

As in the Ottoman period, migration from rural to urban areas continued. There was a strong trend of *fallāḥīn* migration into towns, where they hoped to find part- and full-time employment and where many lived in temporary shelters and slums.[58] Evidence from the above-mentioned survey of social and economic conditions in five Arab villages in 1944 suggests that migration in the opposite direction was rare. Out of the 2,984 villagers living in the five villages, only 10 were born in towns and only nine outside Palestine.[59] Within this, however, the Arab rural population significantly increased (more slowly than the urban population) by 42.6 percent from 1922 to 1944 (see Table 1.3).

The Johnson-Crosbie report provides data about types of occupation in different sizes of farms measured in *faddān*s[60] (on average, a *faddān* is estimated to be about an acre; 1 *faddān* = 1.038 acres ≅ 4.15 dunums).[61] The report gives information about the number of *faddān*s in the possession of owner-cultivator family heads (i.e., not including the income of dependants) in the 104 Arab villages investigated that were considered a representative sample of the non-citrus-growing Palestinian Arab villages in 1930. A total of 23,573 family heads were found; among them, 63 percent were wholly or partly owner-cultivators—that is, they possessed land. The investigation suggests that of these owners, those in possession of more than two *faddān*s were not employed outside their farms; about half of those holding between one and two *faddān*s worked outside their farms; and those with less than one *faddān* had some kind of secondary occupation, as can be seen in Figure 4.2.[62]

This shows that in 1930 those who owned little land had to find outside employment. Hence, the push factor of land shortage was the main determinant for owner-cultivators to seek additional work at that time. Those "pushed" were owner-cultivator *fallāḥīn* who could not use their labor to full capacity. They therefore demonstrated efficiency in allocating some of their la-

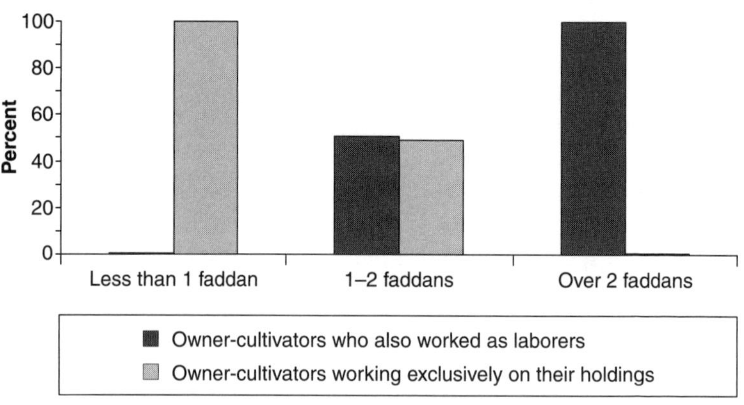

	Owners of Less than 1 faddān	Owners of 1–2 faddāns	Owners of over 2 faddāns	Owners of Trees Only
Owner-cultivators working exclusively on their holdings	3,873 (100%)	1,604 (49.2%)	Nil	Nil
Owner-cultivators also working as laborers	Nil	1,657 (50.8%)	8,396 (100%)	1,103 (100%)
Total	3,873 (100%)	3,261 (100%)	8.396 (100%)	1,103 (100%)

Figure 4.2 Modes of Occupation of Owner-Cultivator Family Heads, 1930

Source: Government of Palestine, *Report of a Committee on the Economic Condition of Agriculturists* (Johnson-Crosbie), p. 21.

bor elsewhere, as would be expected of rational economic actors.

The extent to which *fallāḥīn* landowning was restricted at the time of this investigation can easily be seen in Figure 4.3. Only 23 percent of the *fallāḥīn* were employed solely on their own lands; 43 percent of them did not have not enough land and were driven to seek additional employment; while 34 percent were not owner-cultivators at all. Bearing in mind that the jobs for low-skilled laborers outside agriculture were mostly unattractive until the prosperity years and that nonlandowners usually received much less than if they had been owners (see the discussion below on sharecropping, the primary mode of employment for so-called laborers), these figures suggest that significant gaps in income distribution in *fallāḥīn* society already existed by 1930.

Off-Farm Employment

As the Johnson-Crosbie report noted for 1930, employment outside farms was determined by lack of sufficient opportunities on them. The ebb and flow of the seasonal demand for labor also influenced the level of outside employment. Harvests or fruit picking were the peak time, and all members of the household—men, women, and children—went out to the fields.[63] Between April and June, the winter crop harvest created a considerable demand for labor because these were the main

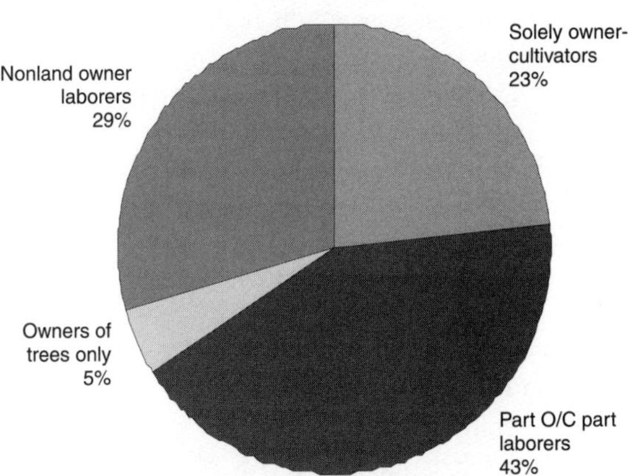

Figure 4.3 Occupations of Family Heads Dwelling in Villages, 1930

Source: Government of Palestine, *Report of a Committee on the Economic Condition of Agriculturists* (Johnson-Crosbie), p. 21.

ground crops of the *fallāḥīn*. Harvesting olives, the most important plantation crop, created a less significant demand and lasted from September to November in an average year, with different picking times in different parts of Palestine.[64] The need for casual labor created conditions in which migration of labor at peak times was not unusual, a phenomenon already observed at the beginning of the twentieth century (1906):

> The harvest in the southern part of Palestine, especially in the plains around Gaza, is much earlier than in central Palestine, and also more abundant, being often more than the people of the village can reap in a reasonable time. Consequently, they are glad to get help, and many of the *fallāḥīn* from the hills go to the plains to help in bringing in the wheat or barley. They generally receive as wages a certain quantity of cut corn, each day's amount being known as *kirweh*. . . . People will also not infrequently help friends and neighbours to bring in their harvest. This is especially the case if one has finished before another, or if anything delays the threshing. Sometimes a dozen or more men and women may thus be seen in line reaping, and it is astonishing to note the rate at which they will clear the ground. . . . Some of the hill villages have land both in the hills and in the plains, the latter being often at a great distance from their homes. Where this is the case, during the harvest in the plains (which, as already mentioned, is much earlier than in the hills, the difference being from a month to six weeks, according to the greater or lesser difference in altitude), the greater part of the population of the village goes down to the low ground for the harvest and threshing, locking up their houses, and leaving only a few people to look after the place. When the harvest in the high ground is ripe, they return to their homes.[65]

From the evidence in the 1931 census, one may think that this phenomenon had ceased to exist, as out of the 63,190 owner-cultivators and tenants it recorded (90.4 percent of them Moslems, 3.8 percent Christians, and 5.8 percent Jews), only 392 had a subsidiary agricultural occupation (19,197 were engaged in nonagricultural work).[66] Yet this does not seem to have been the case. A closer look at an unfilled "household schedule" that includes the instructions to interviewers suggests that the data did not cover such workers: the instructions were to count as subsidiary occupations only those pursued by "earners or dependents" for at least three months.[67] This would exclude information relevant to our case.

Even when members of *fallāḥīn* households found full-time employment outside their villages, many of them came back to the villages in their free time to assist in the household agricultural operation.[68] This practice and the practice of part-time employment suggest that the *fallāḥīn* did their best to find income to augment that from their farms. As we have also seen, at the peak harvest time almost nothing except agricultural work was done by household members. These are all strong indications that *fallāḥīn* did their best to maximize their available resources. Their impoverished situation was in general related to very limited opportunities and income for their labor and not to incompetence or laziness, as government officials assumed.

Technology in a Labor-Intensive Economy

Arab labor was notably much cheaper than Jewish labor.[69] Cheap labor, lack of capital, and lack of cheap credit[70] for Arab farmers seem to be why Arab cultivation practices remained labor- rather than capital-intensive. The prosperity during World War II increased the cost of labor. This encouraged a few minor changes toward less labor-intensiveness, such as wider use of motor pumps in the 1940s,[71] and at that time a small number of Arab farmers bought new tractors and other equipment.[72]

But for the vast majority of Arab farms there was no change in techniques during the Mandate period. *Fallāḥīn* continued to use simple agricultural implements. Apart from plows pulled by animals, agricultural equipment was manual. Wilson's (1906) and Grant's (1921) descriptions of agricultural equipment sold in village shops and of village occupations give some indication of these practices at the beginning of the Mandate era. In larger villages, the shops offered a variety of simple agricultural equipment, such as cast hoes and sickles.[73] In Galilee, where most of my own interviews were conducted, the same tools were mentioned as being in use throughout the Mandate period.[74]

As mentioned, land scarcity, combined with low labor costs, determined the creation and expansion of labor-intensive terrace farming in the hill country of Palestine:

> The terrace is to be found everywhere in the hill country . . . the walls [of the terraces] being often only a foot or eighteen inches in height. But sometimes [. . . the walls are] 7 or 8 feet, while occasionally they are much higher even than this.[75]

> The little iron-shod wooden plough is scattering along the terraces. Sometimes one of the oxen will be on a lower level. To go forward without slipping down the hillside is not easy. What cannot be ploughed is dug up with the pickaxe, and wheat or barley will find lodgement in every pocket of soil.[76]

It has also been noted that it was not uncommon to find descriptions of a *fallāḥ* ploughing with a plough that "is probably more primitive than that used by the ancient Jews" or claiming that "animal manure is almost not in use and heaps of animal manure have been and still are being gathered from time immemorial."[77] The problem with such arguments is that they are based on a patently external view of the Arab rural economy. The outsider's view of manure ignored the fact that "on Arab farms the bulk of farmyard manure is used as fuel"[78] and that use of a plow that seemed rather primitive compared with those in the Jewish sector ignores the relatively higher cost of a cast plow—widely used by Jewish farmers—over an iron-shod wooden plow. In general, the use of simple technology on the *fallāḥin* farms seems to have been a function of the low cost of labor and of the lack of capital and cheap credit. The simple technology was therefore based on a rationale to maximize profit.

Livestock Breeding and Labor Efficiency

The rearing of a small number of grazing animals was carried out in many cases by the women in the *fallāḥ* household. Women were also in charge of the rearing of chickens scavenging near the house.[79] It was not also unusual to see a landlord's animals being raised by the members of the tenant's household. In these cases, the tenant often had the right to consume part of the milk provided by the animal. He was usually paid in kind, customarily every third newborn animal. Other agreements on horses, which were needed by landlords for riding, were usually that a tenant received a mare to raise and to ride and had to give a newborn foal to the owner.[80] Hence, the agreement between the landlord and the tenant (see below) was often interlinked with other agreements.

In most villages, there was at least one herdsman for cattle and a shepherd for sheep and goats. This separation permitted grazing in different areas, especially as goats could eat lower-quality food than cattle. In the case of cattle, the herdsman was customarily paid in grains or other crops, whereas for goats and sheep the herdsman took every third or fourth animal born from each owner.[81] Here, too, the employer and employee secured their payment in a form of kind that could be consumed, thus avoiding unnecessary payment for transactions.

Generally speaking, livestock breeding is an example of managing labor efficiently. Women worked on the farms besides keeping house, yet when more attention was needed (especially when more animals were in hand), the animals were given to herdsmen to use labor more efficiently. This avoided employing a household member as a full-time herdsman and thus helped to maximize household income.

The evidence presented here indicates that the shortage of land was managed in sophisticated ways by the *fallāḥīn*. Those with enough land continued to cultivate it; those with insufficient land found outside employment. The *fallāḥīn* did not miss opportunities, such as harvests in other villages, to augment their income from temporary employment; and in peak times even former *fallāḥīn* came to assist their families. Efficient employment was also found in livestock breeding.

In a capital-scarce economy where labor was cheap, it was wise to use labor-intensive rather than capital-intensive methods of cultivation. And even though labor was cheap, it was used skillfully in a number of different tasks. In the face of such evidence, the British view that that the Arab peasants' culture or mental habits hampered their economic judgments and their ability to adapt seems irrelevant.

SHARECROPPING

Sharecropping seemed to be the predominant way in which *fallāḥīn* were employed on the land of others in the noncitrus farms.[82] The proportion of sharecroppers increased following the *Tanẓīmāt,* especially since land was no longer free and some was registered in the names of notables.[83] In addition, owner-cultivators who faced difficulties sold their lands, yet remained tenants on them:[84] "When one Arab sold land to another, the landowner changed, but the tenants remained, and those who laboured on the land for a regular or seasonal wage still continued to earn that wage."[85]

Three modes of sharecropping were dominant in the Mandate period: a simple tenant-laborer arrangement; joint farming; and a tenant-laborer in a rent-sharing model. In the simple tenant-laborer mode, the landlord contributed all the capital in the form of seeds, plough, stock, etc., and the tenant provided the labor (including nonfarm labor if necessary). Customarily, the landlord received three-quarters of the produce, and a quarter was left for the tenant. This was known as the *rub'* (quarter) agreement. Interviewers referred to the tenant employed under such an agreement as *ḥarrāth bi(al)rub'* (cultivator/ploughman for a quarter) and also regarded it as the dominant agreement. Joint farming was referred to as the second most prevalent form of sharecropping, where the tenant not only contributed the labor but also the inputs, such as working animals, seeds, etc. The tenant and landlord would determine ratios for sharing produce that were more than one-quarter in the tenant's favor. The third form of sharecropping, rent sharing, was practiced mainly on large farms, usually those of absentee landlords. The landlord left his land in the hands of a man or men who would manage the farm. The manager could work partly as a laborer, but his primary role was to employ others under a sharecropping agreement. The *fallāḥ* would receive one-quarter or less of the produce (usually not less than one-fifth).[86] The landlord and the manager agreed on the division of the remainder between themselves.

Although less common than the simple tenant-laborer agreement, joint farming seems to have become more frequent in Galilee during the Mandate period. Firestone's study of two Arab villages in the Jenin Subdistrict (ʻArraba and Zirʻin) also reveals that during the 1920s joint farming became more popular.[87] There seem to be two reasons for this. One was *fallāḥīn* indebtedness. When an owner-cultivator *fallāḥ* defaulted on a loan from a moneylender (who was in many cases a merchant), ownership of the land would be transferred from the *fallāḥ* to the merchant. Although the merchant would then become the landlord, in most cases the *fallāḥ* continued to be a tenant on that land.[88] This phenomenon of land transfer from owner-cultivators to merchants, with the former remaining to cultivate the land, was not unusual either in Palestine[89] or in the surrounding region. Doreen Warriner, discussing its occurrence in the Fertile Crescent during the nineteenth and twentieth centuries, calls it a process of peasants losing lands and argues that "this process has gone very far in Syria and northern Iraq."[90] One of the biggest merchants in Galilee, who acquired much land from defaulting *fallāḥīn*, used to rent the land to the same *fallāḥīn* on joint-share terms.[91] This is perhaps not surprising, as such agreements were established between urban merchants (who did not always have animal farms and other farming equipment) and *fallāḥīn* (who, although losing some lands in debt repayments, owned agricultural equipment). It thus seems that one of the reasons for the increase of joint farming is because the same labor with the same equipment could be obtained by the new landlord without the need of further investment. This may also explain the tendency to keep the same person on the land.

The second possible reason for the increase of joint farming (and which is not necessarily inconsistent with the first) is related to the theory of induced institutional innovation outlined in the introduction. According to this, changes in the demand for institutional change are induced by a shift in factor ratios. Such a change could occur when the value of land increased relative to that of labor because of the growing shortage of land and relative excess of labor. Agreements, especially new ones, were expected to reflect the new ratio rather than the 1:3 in favor of the landlord (similar to the olive agreements). In Figure 4.3, there is a category named "owners of trees only." Agreements for separate ownership of land and trees usually meant a form of tenancy where the landlord supplied the land and the tenant supplied the other inputs (i.e., he was a simple tenant-laborer in a rent-sharing model). At harvest time, tenant and landlord divided the fruits between them.[92] An indication of the increasing shortage of land (signifying an increasing surplus of labor) is the change in agreements in the villages around Ramah, as recorded in one of my interviews. In the early Mandate period, tenants in that area used to agree with their landlords that they would plant olive trees and invest all the capital and labor needed. In exchange, it was agreed that they would receive two-thirds of future yields. Later, however, when land became scarcer, new agreements allowed tenants only half of the yields. Not surprisingly, the tenant who recounted this story disliked the change.[93] Landlords may have wished to avoid upsetting their tenants and, even more, to avoid disputes over agreements. But it seems that many landlords, instead of creating an alternative institution to *murabb'ah,* which might have been costly and have led to disputes, chose the existing rent-sharing agreement to increase their share in a more disguised way. However, these two possible explanations for the change in agreement should be viewed only as postulates supported by *some* evidence, since limited evidence was found to support both. It is hoped that further research will shed more light on this phenomenon.

Sharecropping and the Paradigms of Marshall and Stiglitz

The classic criticism of sharecropping by Alfred Marshall in 1916 was that it is inferior to fixed rent (either in money or kind), since fixed rent induces maximization of outputs, whereas sharecropping precludes it. His argument was that if the concern of a tenant who supplies only labor is to maximize his own income, he will work harder in the case of fixed rent, since after paying the rent he gets 100 percent of the marginal return on his labor. Under sharecropping, however, his return is lower because he gets only a fraction of the marginal output for any input of labor. Hence, at the stage of production where returns start to diminish, the sharecropper-tenant is expected to stop investing his labor earlier than the fixed-rent tenant. Accordingly, if a *murabba'a* agreement is at issue, the tenant is expected to cease any investment when labor costs more than the 25 percent of the marginal output value.[94] On the other hand, Debraj Ray comments that "if we do observe sharecropping where theory tells us there should be none, then there is something wrong with this theory."[95]

Is there any evidence to suggest that something was wrong with the landlords and tenants in Mandate Palestine who chose to engage in sharecropping? Alternatively, is there evidence in our case study to suggest that something is wrong with the theory, as Ray suggests? The data do not permit us to compare yield returns in Mandate Palestine from sharecropping and fixed-rent agreements. However, there is evidence implying that the Marshallian logic is inappropriate when applied to the country's *fallāḥīn*, since it seems that both tenant and landlord had an interest in having the other party gain from the agreement. Customarily, the landlord was the one to decide which crops would be grown.[96] Yet even in the 1940s, when the income from wheat did not increase as much as that from other crops, especially on irrigated land (see Chapter 2), no *fallāḥ* in the interviews reported a shortage of wheat grown for subsistence. This is striking, since if a landlord is expected to want higher monetary returns from his land (generally speaking, he is unlikely to be interested in commodities for his subsistence), then he would have been expected to choose crops other than wheat. The implication is that the landlords in Mandate Palestine wanted their tenants to get enough. An obvious reason is that they wished their tenants to be in good shape. Hence, it is not surprising that there is evidence of a landlord also giving food and clothes to his tenants.[97]

But this is not the whole story. In the 1940s, when *fallāḥīn* incomes were significantly higher, it seems that the landlords could be assured that even if the most profitable investments in money terms were not the most profitable for the *fallāḥ* (who needed to pay transaction costs for out-of-farm food), the *fallāḥ* would survive. In these circumstances, why should a landlord need to ensure that the peasant got enough wheat? The landlord needed to consider other opportunities open to the tenant on the labor market, for if the tenant's income was lower than other opportunities, then the *fallāḥ* would look for employment elsewhere. By the same token, it can be assumed that the tenant preferred to have a well-off landlord who would be able to assist him, especially in a bad year. The tenant would also wish the landlord to gain, as otherwise the land he was cultivating might be sold. Moreover, as outlined above, the agreement with the landlord was in many cases interlinked with an agreement on rearing animals. If a landlord did not gain enough, this would affect the size of his herd and would directly affect the tenant.

Joseph Stiglitz built a model that treated sharecropping differently from Marshall. According to Stiglitz, "there is not an undersupply of labour (effort) as a result of a sharecropping system." However, when the capital is entirely provided by the landlord, "there is a greater return to closer supervision, and because of the non-convexity associated with supervision, a greater likelihood of using a wage system."[98] In our case study, the *murabba'a* agreement (where the landlord puts up all the capital) did not change into a wage agreement but rather into joint farming. The preference of another form of sharecropping (not based on wage labor) in cases where diversity in agreements was already agreed, may indicate that landlords and tenants viewed sharecropping as a much better system. It may have been preferred because it did not reduce productivity. Rather, it enabled a more efficient use of the combined factors of production of both landlord and tenant (especially in joint farming), and it also reduced risk for both parties since, unlike wage labor, there was an interlinked and long-term agreement that made landlord and tenant mutually responsible for the profit of both.

In addition, another compensating mechanism favored the tenant-landlord agreement. While many landlords were merchants and, as we have seen, the *fallāḥīn*'s knowledge of trends in the market were limited, sharecropping could be to benefit of the *fallāḥīn*. In one interview, a merchant-landlord was asked why the decision about what to grow in sharecropping was determined by the landlord. He replied, "we knew better how to assess what the prices in the next year would be."[99] Overall, sharecropping in Mandate Palestine seemed to be efficient, enabling a maximization of production.

The Effects of Government Intervention on Tenancy

As early as 1920, the military government sought to stem landlessness caused by Jewish land purchase by passing the Protection of Cultivators Ordinance. It empowered the district governor (later the director of lands) to withhold consent from any transfer of agricultural land until he was satisfied that the tenant would retain sufficient land for the maintenance of himself and his family. This ordinance failed to prevent transfers that left tenants landless; nevertheless, it created a mechanism of indirect compensation to tenants who left their lands as a result of sale:[100]

> [The ordinance of 1920] failed to achieve its purpose because tenants for the most part did not avail themselves of its provisions but preferred to divest themselves of their rights under the ordinance by declaring usually before a Notary Public, that they were not tenants entitled to its protection, and accepting monetary compensation for so doing. That tenants were induced to do this was due to their ignorance of their legal rights in those days and to unscrupulous pressure brought to bear upon them by the Arab "overlords," to whom they stood in a quasi-feudal relation. In fact, the principal [Jewish] land purchasing bodies at that time adopted a policy of not purchasing land unless all agricultural tenants had been removed from the land by the vendor before the sale. Thus the provision concerning retention of sufficient land for maintenance of the tenant and his family was evaded.[101]

Thus, Jewish land purchase continued in spite of the ordinance, which seemed merely to increase the cost of land for Jews. The government became increasingly concerned about the impact of this on the *fallāḥīn* and amended the ordinance in 1929. The payment that had to be made to tenants was raised not only to purchase the land but also to compensate for disturbance. Tenants, however, continued to behave as before, and the amendment was cancelled. The ordinance was further amended in 1932 and again in 1933. The final outcome was that landlords were unable to evict tenants who had cultivated the lands for at least one year, unless the landlord provided alternative land. In addition, the definition of tenants was changed to include a person who cultivated another's lands (including family members, as well as rent-sharing tenants). Finally, a landlord was forbidden to reduce the portion that a tenant received from the harvest.[102] This was important, since there had (previously) been some Arab landowners who managed to raise rents and hence forced their tenants off the land because they wished to transfer land without paying compensation.[103] Even so, the ordinance did not cause a significant decrease in such purchases. The rise in land prices for Jews after the ordinance may have somewhat reduced the amount of land they purchased, yet it was only on limited occasions that evicted tenants were compensated according to law; the majority were not compensated. Kenneth Stein argues that many of these evicted *fallāḥīn* lacked the legal knowledge or money to win lawsuits.[104]

However, a by-product of the 1933 amendment to the ordinance was that tenants used it as "an instrument to facilitate the exploitation of landlords by the tenants."[105] The ordinance encouraged the creation of "moral hazard," and some tenants refused to honor their obligations under the lease. After they had cultivated lands for more than a year, they refused to pay rents and continued to cultivate the land in following years. Some landowners, fearing this, did not use the tenancy agreements, and their land lay fallow, as can be seen in the government's *Survey of Palestine* (1946), which argues that the ordinance "retarded agriculture development in that landlords prefer to let their land lie vacant and fallow until they are able to develop it by themselves rather than to lease it to tenants whom they will not be able to remove."[106] At the same time, however, squatters who managed to cultivate such fallow fields (without the landowner's knowledge) obtained rights as "statutory tenants" under the ordinance.[107] This created an opposite mechanism, and it became sensible to look for "fine" tenants.

In spite of the increased risk, most landlords decided to let their lands. If the tendency for landlords to allow land to lie fallow rather than to lease it was dominant, one would expect to see a significant relative decrease in cultivated lands from 1935 to 1945, which did not happen (see Table 2.3). It seems that fear of squatters, combined with the desire to gain from leasing and the problems of evicting tenants, drove landlords to continue leasing their lands.

Under the Mandate, sharecropping in the Arab sector was common and seems to have been in the interest of both landlord and tenant. The Marshallian view of it as a system of undermaximization is far from supported by this evidence. On the contrary, in Mandate Palestine sharecropping seems to have been a means by which both peasants and landlords maximized profits. While Stiglitz did not see eye to eye with Marshall on the disadvantages of sharecropping, he envisaged it changing into a system of wage payment in instances such as the *murabb'ah*. This did not occur here, where the diversion was into another form of sharecropping. The government intervention between landlord and tenant did not appear to have significant influence on the transfer of lands from Arabs to Jews, but it had negative consequences for the Arab economy in that it deterred some landlords from fully utilizing their lands. If there was a misjudgment, it was not by the *fallāḥīn* or by non-*fallāḥīn* landlords but by the government.

THE PATRILINEAL SOCIOECONOMIC STRUCTURE OF THE ECONOMY

If the essence of the risk-aversion hypothesis is that peasants do not maximize profit because of their extreme risk-averse tendencies. It is true that the patrilineal socioeconomic structure of the *fallāḥīn* served to reduce risk. In the Arab rural sector of Mandate Palestine, the closer the kinship ties between peasants, the closer their economic ties, and the converse was also true. The well-known Arabic proverb that deals with disputes—"Me and my brother against our cousin, and me and my cousin against the stranger"—highlights the strength of these kinship ties. The closeness of interaction was seen in the creation of partnerships, where trust was central: patrilineal understandings were not signed in the manner of official contracts, as this would be regarded as *'ayb* (shame).[108] A man needed to trust his relatives if he expected them (as they expected him) to assist in times of crisis, such as food shortages.

The literature on peasant economics focuses on the concept of a peasant household. This is regarded as a social unit where peasants interact with each other in family relationships and share the same abode or hearth, where income is shared and resources are combined.[109] In the 1931 census, a *house* was defined as accommodation for a family eating from the same table, including other dependent persons such as widows and servants. This is a similar definition, in that people sharing the same abode (*dār* in Arabic) and eating from the same table indicates combined resources. Accordingly, the 1931 Census refers to the peasant household as a small unit of four to five persons.[110]

In the *fallāḥīn* society, kinship connections outside the *dār* were a significant basis for further economic integration. Several households tended to be part of a bigger association named *ahl,* which referred to a patrilineal kinship consisting of tens of people (originally meaning "those who occupy the same tent with one").[111] In many cases, members of an *ahl* lived in the same dwelling complex and shared certain resources and incomes. It was rare to see close integration without family ties. Brothers who had separate households but shared some income and expenditure on different fields—for example, joint purchase of plowing animals and mutual assistance in different work—were not uncommon, but this did not happen with remoter ties.[112]

A broader level of association was the *ḥamūla,* embodying different *ahl*s (there is no cross-affiliation of *ahls* into different *ḥamūla*s). The *ḥamūla* had communal responsibility for compensation *(diya)* in cases of homicide by one of its members; *ḥamūla* members used to give some assistance in case of need, to exchange gifts on special occasions, and to live in a specific quarter of the village;[113] and there were *mushā'* (communal land) associations on the *ḥamūla* level (see Chapter 6).

It was widely believed that a *ḥamūla* was and is an extension of an *ahl*'s genealogical tree or at least consisted of settled Bedouins from the same tribe. This was the case until the appearance of Scott Atran's paper in 1986, arguing that in the villages of Umm al-Fahim, Al-Birh, and 'Isfiya that he had investigated, "the constituent patrilineal units *(jeb)* of any one hamula are rarely connected genealogically."[114] Interesting as Atran's findings are, the villagers did not provide him with an alternative explanation for the emergence of the *ḥamūla*s. It might be that genealogical links existed, but the people in the villages were not aware of them. In addition, this does not deal with the concept of settled tribes. More important to the present study, even Atran admits that there were very close relationships among the *ḥamūla* members, as is expressed in this proverb: "Aid due to a member of the same *ḥamūla* was aid owed to a patrilineal kinsman."[115] This suggests that, at least in the minds of the people, *ḥamūla* meant kinship (even if not direct genealogical kinship).

The economic interactions within and between the *dār, ahl,* and the *ḥamūla* highlight that the closer the perceived kinship ties between peasants, the closer their economic integration. The economic blood-related association was essentially a system of risk reduction. For example, association in *ḥamūla* enabled a person to pay *diyah* and not to die in *faṣṣād* (revenge), while the *ahl* protected *dār*s from facing hunger, when, for example, their land was flooded. Hence, the patrilineal socioeconomic structure of the *fallāḥīn* economy was a way of reducing risk. The existence of trust and sound information about partners ensured less risk, which enabled efficiency in resource allocation. On the theoretical level, these findings are consistent with Popkin's suggestion about the role of insurance in some rural corporations.

CONCLUSION

This chapter examines the microstructure of the *fallāḥīn* economy and the changes that occurred in it. Four significant features emerged:

- Production was based largely on labor-intensive methods.
- The *fallāḥīn* used simple agricultural implements, which were much cheaper than the more modern equipment that was available.

- The *fallāḥīn* used various methods to reduce production and consumption costs and to increase income.
- Traditional institutions did not hinder sound economic functioning and in some cases even facilitated it.

The fundamental reason for the Arab economy continuing to be labor-intensive throughout the Mandate period was the cheap cost of labor compared to the cost of modern equipment. A second reason was the dearth of capital for purchasing expensive equipment. During the prosperity, however, a shift occurred in factor ratios. Arab labor became more expensive, and more money was available because of the relative increase in income from agriculture (excluding citrus). This caused some transfer into capital-intensive methods, yet it was modest—probably because the prosperity was perceived as a short-term wartime distortion of normal economic performance and because the purchase of modern capital-intensive equipment required a long-term investment. Also, in spite of the upturn, capital remained limited.

Various methods and institutionalized practices were used by *fallāḥīn* to reduce production and consumption costs. The essence of the part-subsistence, part-surplus production mode, as well as of barter trade, was to reduce transaction costs in a cash-poor economy. Thus the *fallāḥīn* consumed mostly basic, home-grown agricultural products and not final goods. Labor was managed efficiently and vigorously both on the farms and outside them to increase income through barter as well as in cash. Sharecropping was preferred, since it did not reduce productivity; rather, it enabled a better use of the combined factors of production of landlord and tenant. It also reduced risk, since, unlike wage labor, landlord and tenant were mutually responsible for achieving profit. We have also seen that, consistent with the theory of induced institutional innovation, dynamic changes in the traditional institution of sharecropping occurred because of a shift in factor ratios. Finally, the patrilineal socioeconomic structure of the *fallāḥīn* economy also proved efficient at reducing risk and enhancing labor productivity.

Two significant inefficiencies were noted, both of which seem to have occurred because of imperfect information: one was the tendency of *fallāḥīn* to sell all their surplus immediately after the harvest (i.e., they seemed unresponsive to price movements during the year), and the other is the Mandatory government's ill-advised intervention in tenancy arrangements. It is likely that the government failed to understand the broad consequences of its intervention (i.e., its information was imperfect). It would be incorrect to argue on the premise of marketing difficulties that the culture or mental habits of Arab peasants limited their ability to make economic-related judgments or to adapt to change. Ineffective marketing could have been a mistake, not a syndrome. On the whole, in a variety of *fallāḥīn* institutions, this was the only inefficiency found. With the benefit of hindsight, not only did the government have the expertise to advise on marketing; it chose an inappropriate form of intervention, a policy that represented a misjudgment both of commission and omission.

The external view of the Arab rural economy by British and some Zionist writers led them to see the differences between Arab and Jewish agriculture in terms of the irrationality of the poorer side. Instead, different factor ratios in the Jewish sector (more expensive labor and more capital) shaped their practices to become capital intensive, in the same way that the lack of these caused the Arab sector to become labor intensive. The reality was usually the opposite of the official view: competent economic-related judgments on the part of the *fallāḥīn* and a demonstrable readiness to change, if it was to their advantage, determined whether their conservative methods and institutions would be retained or modified.

NOTES

1. Daniel Kahneman, "Maps of Bounded Rationality: A Perspective on Intuitive Judgment and Choice," Tore Frangsmyr (ed.), *Les Prix Nobel 2002* (Stockholm, 2003), p. 460.

2. James C. Scott, *The Moral Economy of the Peasant: Rebellion and Subsistence in Southeast Asia* (London, 1976), pp. 23–24.
3. Theodore W. Schultz, *Transforming Traditional Agriculture* (London, 1964), p. 37; Samuel L. Popkin, *The Rational Peasant: The Political Economy of Rural Society in Vietnam* (London, 1979), pp. 31, 47.
4. Translated from Ze'ev Avrahamoviz and Izḥaq Guelfat, *Hamesheq ha-'aravi* (Tel Aviv, 1944), pp. 33–34.
5. Government of Palestine, *Census of Palestine 1931: Report by E. Mills, Assistant Chief Secretary* (Alexandria, 1933), vol. 1, p. 289.
6. Government of Palestine, *Report of a Committee on the Economic Condition of Agriculturists in Palestine and the Fiscal Measures of Government in Relation thereto, W. J. Johnson, R. E. H. Crosbie* et. al. (Jerusalem, 1930), p. 41.
7. 'Alī Nasūj al-Ẓāhir, *Shajārah al-zaytūn: tārīkhhā zirā'thā, 'amrāḍihā, ṣinā'thā* (Amman, 1947).
8. Moḥamad Yūnīs al-ḥusayni, *Al-tatwūr al-'ijtimā'ī fi filasṭīn al-'arabiyyah* (Jerusalem, 1946).
9. Charles Thomas Wilson, *Peasant Life in the Holy Land* (London, 1906); Elihu Grant, *The People of Palestine* (Philadelphia, 1921 reprinted 1976).
10. Grant, *The People of Palestine,* p. 130.
11. An additional 2,085 "earners" of "special products" were citrus growers. Government of Palestine, *Census of Palestine 1931* (1933), vol. 1, pp. 289–90.
12. E.g., interview with Mohammad ḥasūna from Abu Ghosh (ḥaj ḥasūna, b. 1929, was a *fallāḥ* who was also employed as wage laborer in Jerusalem during the Mandate period) (31 July 1999); interview with Muṣliḥ Aḥmad Yāsīn from Shafa 'Amr (ḥaj Yāsīn (b. 1923) is a son of an owner-cultivator *fallāḥ* who employed others on his lands) (22 August 1999); interview with Nimir Qasim Muṣafa from 'Ein Mahil (Mr. Muṣtafa, b. 1910, spoke about his childhood in the Ottoman period and his life under the Mandate; in the Mandate period he was a *fallāḥ* and shopkeeper; from 1937 he was also the *mukhtār* of his village) (18 August 1999); interview with Tatūr Jamāl from Reina (Mr. Jamāl, b. 1935, is the son of a *fallāḥīn* family) (20 August 1999).
13. I. J. Kligler and A Geiger, "An Inquiry into the Diets of Various

Sections of the Urban and Rural Population of Palestine," *Bulletin of the Palestine Economic Society,* 5, no. 3 (1931), pp. 1–72.

14. Grant, *The People of Palestine,* pp. 78–82, 85.
15. Rosemary Sayigh, *Palestinians: From Peasants to Revolutionaries* (London, 1979), pp. 18–24.
16. Scott, *The Moral Economy,* pp. 23–24.
17. Interview with Slīmān 'Adawī from Tur'an (Mr. 'Adawī, b. 1926–28, was a *fallāḥ* in the Mandate period and an agriculture adviser in Israel; he worked with some who had been agriculture advisers in the Mandate period) (5 April 1999); interview with Mohammad ḥasūna; Grant, *The People of Palestine,* p. 82.
18. Charles S. Kamen, *Little Common Ground: Arab Agriculture and Jewish Settlement in Palestine, 1920–1948* (Pittsburgh, 1991), pp. 36–37.
19. Ibid.
20. Ibid.
21. Amos Nadan, *The Arab Rural Economy in Mandate Palestine, 1921–1947: Peasants under Colonial Rule,* Ph.D. thesis, London School of Economics and Political Science, 2002, Chap. 2.
22. Government of Palestine, *A Survey of Palestine,* pp. 323, 339; Government of Palestine, Department of Agriculture and Fisheries, *Annual Report for the Year 1945–46,* pp. 7, 33.
23. Interview with Mohammad Maṣrāwa; Interview with Al-'Othmān Sālim Maṣrāwa (Mr. Maṣrāwa, b. 1918, worked as a *fallāḥ* on his family farm until his village, Safuriyya (north), was destroyed in the 1948 war) (30 August 1998); interview with Muṣliḥ Aḥmad Yāsīn; interview with Abū 'Abdallah from Mashhad (Abū 'Abdallah, b. 1921, was the *mukhtār*'s son in the Mandate period and later became the *mukhtār* of his village) (6 April 1999 and 17 August 1999).
24. Interview with Mohammad Maṣrāwa (known as Bayrūti) from Reina (ḥaj Maṣrāwa, b. 1929, was a *fallāḥ* in Safuriyya during the Mandate period) (19 August 1999).
25. Interview with Muṣliḥ Aḥmad Yāsīn.
26. Interview with Muṣliḥ Aḥmad Yāsīn; interview with Mohammad Maṣrāwa; interview with Nimir Qasim Muṣafa; interview with Tatūr Jamāl; interview with Sālim Moḥamad Abū Aḥmad (known as Abū 'Afif 'al-hishis') from Nazareth (Abū 'Afif, b. 1923, is the son of a family of owner-cultivators and landlords from Tel 'Adas;

during the Mandate period they moved to Nazareth, where the family continued to lease lands and also established a mercantile business, where they lent money to *fallāḥīn*) (21 August 2000); Wilson, *Peasant Life in the Holy Land,* pp. 73–75, 206–08, 242–43.

27. Wilson, *Peasant Life in the Holy Land,* pp. 73–75; Grant, *The People of Palestine,* pp. 90–91, 145–46. Also Interview with Nimir Qasim Muṣafa.
28. Interview with Sālim Moḥamad Abū Aḥmad; interview with Mohammad Aḥmad Abū Aḥmad (Abū Riaḍ) from Nazareth (Abū Riaḍ, b. 1918, was a butcher and merchant of animals and meat during the Mandate period); Interview with Mohammad ḥasūna; interview with Aḥmad Husayyn Gadir (Abū Salaḥ) (ḥaj Abū Salaḥ, b. 1924, is Bedouin in origin, from the Gadir tribe; during the Mandate he was a seminomadic agriculturist and was also employed in the Palestinian police; the interview was held in his tent next to Bīr Maksūr) (18 August 1999).
29. For the period selected, see the discussion preceding Figure 1.3.
30. Government of Palestine, Department of Agriculture and Forests, *Potatoes Growing in Palestine: Agricultural Leaflets, Series V1, Staple Crops, No. 5.* (RHs, 905.14 n.6, 1934), p. 4; Government of Palestine, *A Survey of Palestine: Prepared in December 1945 and January 1946 for the Information of the Anglo-American Committee of Inquiry* (Jerusalem, 1946), pp. 325–26.
31. In Chapter 5, the issue of defaults and charges in kind is discussed.
32. Interview with Sālim Moḥamad Abū Aḥmad; interview with Maḍhib Nimir Sulṭī from 'Ilut (Mr. Sulṭī, b. 1934–35, is the son of a *fallāḥīn* family) (22 August 2000); interview with Mohammad Aḥmad Abū Aḥmad.
33. Interview with Mohammad ḥasūna.
34. Government of Palestine, *Report of a Committee on the Economic Condition of Agriculturists* (Johnson-Crosbie), p. 4.
35. As average of the years 1936, 1939, 1942, and 1945: Government of Palestine, Department of Agriculture and Fisheries, *Annual Report* 1945–46 (Jerusalem, 1947), p. 33. Note that taxes were not paid at that time on produce, and the returns therefore seem to be better than those indicated, for example, by the Johnson-Crosbie investigation.
36. Government of Palestine, *Report of a Committee on the Economic*

Condition of Agriculturists (Johnson-Crosbie), pp. 6, 19. The calculation was done by finding the proportion between prices of dura and prices of wheat (p. 6) and accordingly finding the premium paid for wheat (p. 19) and calculating the amount in kilograms. Then the data was converted from a family of six to a family of 5.8.

37. Government of Egypt, Department of Statistics, *Al-'iḥṣa' al-sanawī al-'am lil-qūtr al-maṣri, 1925–1927* (Cairo, 1927), pp. 256–61; William F. Spalding, *Tate's Modern Cambist* (New York, 29th ed., 1929), p. 313. The data was taken for Egypt, since no data werefound for Palestine; yet no difference is expected because of this.
38. Interview with Maḍhib Nimir Sulṭī; interview with Mohammad ḥasūna.
39. Interview with Maḍhib Nimir Sulṭī; interview with Abū 'Abdallah; interview with Yūsif and Fārūk Ya'aqūb from Nazareth. These are the grandsons of 'Abdallah Yūsif Ya'aqūb, a merchant and moneylender. They—and especially Fārūk Ya'aqūb, the older one—used to work with the grandfather in his business (25.3.1999).
40. Moneylending is discussed in Chapter 5.
41. Government of Palestine, "Commutation of Tithes Ordinance, No. 49 of 1927," *Ordinances: Annual Volume for 1927* (Jerusalem), pp. 388, 391; Government of Palestine, "Rural Property Tax Ordinance. No 1. Of 1935," *Ordinances: Annual Volume for 1935* (Jerusalem), pp. 22–24.
42. Interview with Abū 'Abdallah; interview with Tatūr Jamāl; interview with Nimir Qasim Muṣafa; interview with Mohammad Maṣrāwa.
43. al-ḥusayni, *Al-tatwūr al-'ijtimā'ī fi filasṭīn al-'arabiyyah,* p. 201.
44. Interview with Yūsif and Fārūk Ya'aqūb; interview with Mohammad Aḥmad Abū Aḥmad.
45. See the map archive of the PEF. Also James Reilly, "The Peasantry of Late Ottoman Palestine," *Journal of Palestine Studies,* vol. 40, 1981, p. 8; Kenneth W. Stein, *The Land Question in Palestine, 1917–1939* (London, 2nd ed., 1985), pp. 64–66, 68–70, 223–25, 228–33; David Grossman, *Hakfar ha'aravi 7e-bnota7: tahaliḥim bayeshuv ha'aravi be-'erez ishra'el batqufa ha'otmanit* (Jerusalem, 1994), p. 131; Haim Gerber, "A New Look at the *Tanzimat:* The Case of the Province of Jerusalem," in David Kushner (ed.), *Pales-*

tine in the Late Ottoman Period: Political, Social and Economic Transformation (Jerusalem, 1986), p. 31.

46. Gabriel Baer, *Fellah and Townsman in the Middle East: Studies in Social History* (London, 1982), pp. 45–46.
47. Grossman, *Hakfar ha'aravi, passim.*
48. Justin McCarthy, *The Population of Palestine: Population History and Statistics of the Late Ottoman Period and the Mandate* (New York, 1990), p. 10.
49. Gad G. Gilbar, "Megamot bahitpatḥut hademografit shel hapalesṭinim, 1870–1987," *Sqirot,* 108, 1989, pp. 7–10.
50. These figures must be regarded with caution because of the uncertainties of the Ottoman data, which seem to be underestimates. See McCarthy, *The Population of Palestine,* pp. 2–8. The data for 1850 in the cities is calculated as an average between data available for 1840 (70,000) and for 1860 (90,000). Nonetheless, the data are reliable enough to demonstrate the main trend.
51. Gabriel Baer, *Mavo layaḥasim ha'agrariyim bamizraḥ hatikhon* (Jerusalem, 1971), pp. 53–58; Issa Khalaf, *Politics in Palestine: Arab Factionalism and Social Disintegration 1939–1948* (New York, 1991), p. 15; Jack Kno, *Ba'ayat haqarqa' basikhsokh hale'umi beyn yehudim le'aravim 1917–1990* (Tel Aviv, 1992), p. 17.
52. Fred M. Gottheil, "Money and Product Flows in Mid-Nineteenth Century Palestine: The Physiocratic Model Applied," David Kushner (ed.), *Palestine in the Late Ottoman Period: Political, Social and Economic Transformation* (Jerusalem, 1986), p. 225; Stein, *The Land Question,* pp. 14, 223–25.
53. For the latter, see Wilson, *Peasant Life in the Holy Land, passim;* Grossman, *Hakfar ha'aravi, passim.*
54. Grossman, *Hakfar ha'aravi,* pp. 284–85.
55. McCarthy, *The Population of Palestine,* pp. 27–37; Gilbar, *Megamot bahitpatḥut,* pp. 3–12.
56. Ibid., p. 3.
57. Government of Palestine, Department of Statistics, *Vital Statistics Tables* (Jerusalem, 1947), especially pp. 17–23, 59–65.
58. See especially Mahmoud Yazbaq, "Hahagira ha'aravit leḥeyfa 1933–1948: *Nituḥ 'al-pi meqorot 'arviyim,*" *Qatedra,* no. 45, 1987, pp. 136–37, 144. For descriptions of the slums in Palestine, see Government of Palestine, *A Survey of Palestine,* pp. 691–96.

59. Government of Palestine, Department of Statistics, *Survey of Social and Economic Condition in Arab Villages, 1944: Special Bulletin No. 21* (Jerusalem, 1948), p. 5. It is worth mentioning that the term "born in town" does not necessarily signify a migration from towns to rural areas. Because hospitals were in towns, it seems that there was an advantage in giving birth there rather than at home or in the clinics that existed in some villages and opened once a week. Government of Palestine, *A Survey of Palestine,* pp. 609–39.
60. The term *faddān* referred to a size of plot that could be ploughed in a given time (usually a day) by a plow yoked to a working animal or animals. The number of animals varied in different villages, showing that *faddān* was not strictly standardized throughout Palestine. Villages did not usually change the definition within a village, so the number of *faddān*s in each village was permanent. Grant, *The People of Palestine,* p. 132; Grossman, *Hakfar ha'aravi,* p. 29. In interviews, people referred to *faddān* as such. Interview with Jamāl 'Ilyās Khūri from Meghar (Mr. Khūri, b. 1905, was a *fallāḥ* and later a policeman during the Mandate period) (23 August 1999); interview with Uri 'Eliav from Tirat Zvi (Mr. 'Eliav, a settler who immigrated from the Netherlands, lived in the Beisan area from the 1930s; he was very interested in the life of the semi-nomadic Arab farmers who had lived in the area; he learnt Arabic and used to join in their activities, many of which are documented) (27 July 1999); interview with Nimir Qasim Muṣafa.

    The origin of this method of calculating land size seems to lie in earlier times of relative excess of land and shortage of labor, when arable lands were distributed among villagers according to their ability to cultivate them with the equipment they had. Ya'akov Firestone, "The Land-Equalizing *Mushā'* Village: A Reassessment," Gad G. Gilbar (ed.), *Ottoman Palestine, 1800–1914* (London, 1990), p. 93.
61. Roger Owen, *The Middle East in the World Economy, 1800–1914* (London, 2nd ed., 1993), p. xiii.
62. Government of Palestine, *Report of a Committee on the Economic Condition of Agriculturists* (Johnson-Crosbie).
63. Grant, *The People of Palestine,* pp. 40, 135, 137.
64. Al-Ẓāhir, *Shajārah al-zaytūn,* pp. 80, 88, 92, 94, 112, 116.
65. Wilson, *Peasant Life in the Holy Land,* pp. 206–08.

66. Government of Palestine, *Census of Palestine 1931* (1933), vol. 2, pp. 289–92.
67. Government of Palestine, *Palestine Census 1931: Household Schedule* (Jerusalem, 1931).
68. E.g., interview with Maḍhib Nimir Sulṭī; Mahmoud Yazbaq, Hahagira ha'aravit leḥeyfa 1933–1948.
69. Zvi Sussman, "The Determination of Wages for Unskilled Labour in the Advanced Sector of the Dual Economy of Mandatory Palestine," *Economic Development and Cultural Change,* 22, No. 1, 1993, passim (especially p. 99). See also the data on Arab and Jewish labor published in Government of Palestine, Department of Statistics, *Statistical Abstract of Palestine* (Jerusalem, various years).
70. Capital availability and credit are discussed in Chapters 1, 4, and 5.
71. E.g., interview with Al-'Othmān Sālim Maṣrāwa; interview with Mohammad Maṣrāwa; interview with Shraga Punq from Kibbutz Kfar Ha-makabi (Mr. Punq was an agriculture guide and a manager of vegetable production of his settlement during the years 1938–48) (28 August 1998). See the discussion on irrigation in Chapter 1.
72. Kamen, *Little Common Ground,* pp. 214–21.
73. Government of Palestine, *A Survey of Palestine of Palestine,* pp. 73–75; also Grant, *The People of Palestine,* pp. 90–91, 145–46.
74. Most of my interviewees referred to such equipment.
75. Wilson, *Peasant Life in the Holy Land,* p. 199.
76. Grant, *The People of Palestine,* p. 39.
77. Translated from Avrahamoviz and Guelfat, *Hamesheq ha-'aravi,* pp. 33–34.
78. Government of Palestine, *A Survey of Palestine of Palestine,* p. 313.
79. Government of Palestine, *Census of Palestine 1931* (1933), vol. 1, pp. 286–88; Montague Brown, "Agriculture," Sa'id B. Himadeh (ed.), *Economic Organization in Palestine* (Beirut, 1938), pp. 164–65.
80. Interview with Slīmān 'Adawī; interview with Ya'aqūb Nāṣir Waqīm; interview with 'Alī Abū Yūsif Zu'abī; interview with Jamāl 'Ilyās Khuri; interview with Mohammad Maṣrāwa; inter-

view with Tatūr Jamāl; interview with Nimir Qasim Muṣafa; interview with Abū 'Ātif Fāhūm; interview with Muṣliḥ Aḥmad Yāsīn; interview with Mohammad Maṣrāwa; also Hagana/105/178 "Ain Mahel: Intelligence Report.'

81. Interview with Slīmān 'Adawī; Interview with 'Alī Abū Yūsif Zu'abī.
82. There are no comprehensive data for regular employment, yet this picture emerges from the various secondary and primary sources used for this study. In interviews, for example, permanent wage employment was mentioned in only one case, while sharecropping featured in all the others.
83. It seems that the *fallāḥīn*'s purchase of lands from such rich landowners was rare. This is indicated in the fact that while such large estates were sold to Jews, they were sold as a single unit containing hardly any enclaves of other Arab property. See, broadly, Stein, *The Land Question.*
84. This was also mentioned in interviews, such as interview with Yūsif and Fārūk Ya'aqūb and interview with Mohammad Maṣrāwa.
85. PRO/CO/733/290/8 (February 1933), Secret Cabinet, "Policy in Palestine: Memorandum by the Secretary of State for the Colonies," p. 1.
86. In Sursoq's lands in the Jezreel Valley, the *fallāḥīn* received one-fifth: CZA/S25/9851, "Notes on the Protection of Cultivator Ordinance 1933–6 and the Land Disputed Possession Ordinance 1932–4," p. 1. For the rest, Ya'akov Firestone's study of two Arab villages, which was also skillfully summarized by Graham-Brown; interviews; and archival sources: Ya'akov Firestone, "Cash-Sharing Economics in Mandatory Palestine," *Middle Eastern Studies,* 11, no. 1 (1975), pp. 3–23 and no. 2, pp. 175–94; Ya'akov Firestone, "Production and Trade in an Islamic Context: Sharika Contracts in the Transitional Economy of Northern Samaria, 1853–1943" *International Journal of Middle Eastern Studies,* vol. 6, 1975, pp. 185–209; Sarah Graham-Brown, "The Political Economy of the Jabal Nablus, 1920–48," p. 115; interview with Mohammad ḥasūna; interview with Jamāl 'Ilyās Khuri; interview with Ya'aqūb Nāṣir Waqīm; interview with Nimir Qasim Muṣafa; interview with Yūsif and Fārūk Ya'aqūb; interview with Slīmān

'Adawī; interview with Abū 'Ātif Fāhūm from Nazareth (Mr. Fāhūm, b. 1927/28, is the son of Yūsif Fāhūm, the mayor of Nazareth during different years of the Mandate period; his father was also a landlord) (17 August 1999); Hagana/105/178 "'Ain Mahel: Intelligence Report"; CZA/S25/9851, "Notes on the Protection of Cultivator Ordinance 1933–6 and the Land Disputed Possession Ordinance 1932–4," p. 1.

87. Ya'akov Firestone, "Cash-Sharing."
88. PRO/CO/733/290/8 (February 1933), Secret Cabinet "Policy in Palestine: Memorandum by the Secretary of State for the Colonies," p. 1.
89. Discussed further in Chapter 5.
90. Doreen Warriner, "Land Tenure Problems in the Fertile Crescent in the Nineteenth and Twentieth Centuries," Charles Issawi (ed.), *The Economic History of the Middle East* (London, 1966), p. 77.
91. Interview with Yūsif and Fārūk Ya'aqūb.
92. Interview with Yūsif and Fārūk Ya'aqūb; Interview with Ya'aqūb Nāṣir Waqīm from Ramah (Mr. Waqīm, b. 1908, is the son of a *fallāḥīn* family who worked as an agriculturist in the late Ottoman and Mandate periods) (6 April 1999).
93. Interview with Ya'aqūb Nāṣir Waqīm.
94. Alfred Marshall, *Principles of Economics* (London, 7th ed., 1916), "Book VI, Chapter X," especially pp. 643–44. See also the discussion in Debraj Ray, *Development Economics* (Princeton, 1998), pp. 424–29.
95. Ibid., p. 429.
96. Interview with 'Alī Abū Yūsif Zu'abī from Daḥi (today from Nazareth) (Mr. Zu'abī, b. 1923, was a *fallāḥ* in the Mandate period) (26 March 1999); interview with Yūsif and Fārūk Ya'aqūb.
97. E.g., interview with Al-'Othmān Sālim Maṣrāwa.
98. Joseph E. Stiglitz, "Incentives and Risk Sharing in Sharecropping," *Review of Economic Studies,* 42, no. 2 (1974), pp. 220–21.
99. Interview with Yūsif and Fārūk Ya'aqūb.
100. ISA//BOX4431/02/4/10, Government of Palestine, *Report of the Committee Appointed to Consider the Necessity of Amending the Cultivators (Protection) Ordinance, R. E. H Crosbie, Chair-*

man (1943). See also CZA/S25/9851, 1937, "Protection of Cultivator Ordinance and Land Dispute Ordinance."

101. ISA//BOX4431/02/4/10, 1943, *Report of the Committee Appointed to Consider the Necessity of Amending the Cultivators (Protection) Ordinance.*
102. Ibid.; CZA/S25/9851, 1937, "Protection of Cultivator Ordinance and Land Dispute Ordinance." For an account on the inspiration behind the ordinance of 1933, see PRO/CO/733/290/8, February 1933, Secret, "Policy in Palestine: Memorandum by the Secretary of State for the Colonies."
103. Ted Swedenberg, "The Role of the Palestinian Peasantry in the Great Revolt (1936–9)," Ilan Pappe (ed.), *The Israel/Palestine Question* (London, 1999), p. 146.
104. See largely Stein, *The Land Question,* pp. 115–216.
105. Government of Palestine, *A Survey of Palestine,* p. 293
106. Ibid., p. 294.
107. Ibid., pp. 290–94; ISA//BOX4431/02/4/10, Government of Palestine, *Report of the Committee Appointed to Consider the Necessity of Amending the Cultivators (Protection) Ordinance.*
108. E.g., interview with Abū 'Abdallah.
109. E.g., Ellis, *Peasant Economics,* p. 14.
110. In the 1931 census, a *house* was defined as an accommodation for a family eating from the same table, including other dependent persons such as widows and servants. Both mentioned definitions of house and household, although not exactly the same, seem to more or less correspond with each other. According to the 1931 census, in Arab rural areas of the Nablus subdistrict, for instance, the average number of people per house was 4.4; in the Nazareth subdistrict the average was 4.7. Government of Palestine, *Census of Palestine 1931: Population of Villages, Towns and Administrative Areas, by E. Mills,* (Jerusalem, 1932), introduction and pp. 59–66, 73–76.
111. 'Ahl,' *The Encyclopaedia of Islam,* 1999, CD edition (author not mentioned).
112. E.g., interview with 'Alī Abū Yūsif Zu'abī (his father and uncle used to cultivate lands together). The *ahl* custom of economic integration where a father and his married adult sons cooperate can be found in some families in the postpeasantry era. Interview with Maḍhib Nimir Sulṭī; interview with Tatūr Jamāl.

113. Amnon Cohen, *'ḥamūla'*, in *The Encyclopaedia of Islam,* 1999, CD edition.
114. Scott Artan, "Hamula Organization and Masha' Tenure in Palestine," *MAN,* vol. 21, no. 2, 1986, p. 274.
115. Ibid., p. 281.

· FIVE ·

Credit for the Fallāḥīn: *An Illusory Shift*

The British decision to reform the supply of credit to the *fallāḥīn* was made after the Disturbances of 1929. The high-interest informal system of moneylending was replaced by a cheaper, formal credit system of bank loans, a change that the government considered to be successful. New evidence, however, primarily from the archives of Barclays Bank and from interviews with Palestinian Arabs who were involved in the informal credit system (*fallāḥīn* and moneylenders), suggests that both the government's actions and the structure of the credit systems should be reassessed.

The term *credit* is here taken to mean the provision of money, goods, or services that are to be paid for later. *Formal credit* refers to the system of bank credit operated under state laws. Direct loans from the government are not included (but continued only on a modest scale).[1] *Informal credit* refers to credit that is provided by traditional, nonbanking institutions; in Mandate Palestine, it refers to moneylenders who operated illegally on the black market. Two other concepts are related to the principal-agent relationship in which one person motivates another to act on the former's behalf. The first, *moral hazard,* refers to post-contractual opportunism, where the benefit of a transaction to one party depends on the actions of the other party; however, the latter may not have any incentive to take the beneficial action after a contract has been signed between the two. The second concept, *strategic default,* is a specific case of moral hazard in which a borrower is able to repay but refuses to do so. (A situation in which a borrower is not able to pay and therefore does not do so is called *involuntary default.*

The theoretical basis of informal credit systems and their interactions with formal systems has been developed by Debraj Ray. While the exploitation approach to the informal system perceives the moneylender primarily as abusing the borrower, Ray regards the informal credit market as generally competitive, where the lender does not have a monopoly, and the borrower has significant bargaining power to negotiate comparatively low interest rates. He further suggests that moneylenders can often provide more attractive loans than banks because they have better information on borrowers and can make better use of guarantees in cases of default. In addition, Ray considers that loans taken out by groups with mutual guarantees have the potential of performing better than direct loans, since this arrangement can provide closer supervision. On the other hand, he is alert to the possibility that such schemes might indirectly promote strategic default. These observations, as we shall see, are relevant to this study.[2]

THE HISTORICAL DEBATE: DID THE GOVERNMENT SUCCEED OR FAIL?

In the 1946 *Survey of Palestine,* the Mandatory government claimed that following its rationalization of the credit regime, which entailed a high degree of government intervention, the provision of credit underwent a profound shift from an informal system to a formal one. It stated that "the practice of borrowing from moneylenders is no longer followed by the majority."[3] On the other hand, it conceded that the accuracy of this statement was controversial: "Non-Arab bankers held that [Arab] indebtedness to moneylenders and merchants is now negligible; while

Arab bankers thought it still to be considerable."[4] There was also uncertainty about the evidence:

> In most agricultural countries there exists the problem of unproductive indebtedness of the farmer to professional moneylenders and traders. Everywhere this problem presents serious difficulties to the investigator. The difficulties are inherent in the fact that the debts are not recorded, and securities which the moneylenders and traders hold are usually promissory notes or contracts of sale drawn up so as to conceal the exact nature of the transaction, showing the borrower as having received a larger sum than has actually been advanced to him. The investigator must therefore rely on oral evidence collected from the borrowers themselves, and the truth is frequently obscured out of suspicion of the reason underlying the inquiry. Thus the investigator is liable to the pitfall of drawing conclusions from evidence which it is difficult or impossible to subject to adequate tests. A similar situation exists in Palestine.[5]

As this suggests, investigators of the informal system had to rely on oral evidence. My own interviewees in Galilee repeatedly claimed that the only viable option for credit-seeking *fallāḥīn* was to approach moneylenders, who were usually local wholesale merchants. They further stated that it had been difficult to get loans from banks.[6]

Several recent studies have discussed the issue of credit availability for the *fallāḥīn*. Yet the controversy has not been resolved. Kamen counted the number of Arab agriculturists who received loans from Arab cooperative societies, the Agricultural Mortgage Bank, and direct loans from the government. He concluded that loans from the formal sector were insignificant.[7] But the data he uses, especially for cooperative societies, are not comprehensive. Also, he does not deal with the two other options for formal credit—the comparatively extensive provision of credit by the short-term crop loans scheme of 1935 (explained below) and direct loans from banks. Nor does he supply any evidence on loans by moneylenders after the change in government policy, which included measures to suppress moneylenders. Further, he does not provide evidence on the need of the *fallāḥīn* for loans in the period after the Johnson-Crosbie investigation in 1930. Kamen's account therefore gives no indication of how much credit was needed by the *fallāḥīn* and how much was supplied by the formal sector and by the informal one.

Roza El-Eini discusses the issue of credit to *fallāḥīn* in the Mandate period in four essays (1996–97). Her work deals more with the government's political agenda than with the impact of its policies on the Arab rural credit system or the overall structure of the formal and informal systems. She provides interesting material, especially on the establishment of the Agricultural Mortgage Bank, but leaves the economic controversy unresolved.[8]

Metzer acknowledged that the sources he used to study the provision of credit to peasants are "scanty." Even so, he infers that the government achieved a partial, yet significant success in its attempt to institutionalize the provision of rural credit and that government activities had "reduced the dependence of Arab peasants on private moneylenders, which was rather substantial prior to World War II."[9] The present study, using a number of new sources, proposes more definite answers to some of these vexing questions.

THE NEED FOR LOANS AND THE RELUCTANCE OF BANKS

Theoretically, there is a distinction between credit for consumption and credit for production. In practice, this distinction is blurred in small households that are also production units. It is clear, however, that the *fallāḥīn* were not enthusiastic about taking loans with defined rates of interest, especially high-interest loans in the informal sector (the custom of deferring payments to shopkeepers is here excluded, since interest seemed to be included in the price of goods; see Chapter 4). A *fallāḥ* would usually take a loan after crop failure (to maintain a certain low standard of living while he still had enough seeds for sowing) or in cases of special need (such as to purchase a working animal after an old one had died).[10]

At the beginning of the Mandate period, credit to the *fallāḥīn* was available principally from moneylenders in the black market, who commonly charged an interest rate of 30 percent per annum.[11] Banks had to comply with Ottoman law, which prohibited interest in excess of 9 percent—a law that remained in force throughout the period.[12] Banks were reluctant to give loans to *fallāḥīn* at low rates of interest. As early as 1919, the military administration reached an agreement with the Anglo-Egyptian Bank (which became part of Barclays Bank in 1925) that the latter would provide £P576,312 in short-term loans in Palestine (typically, this meant loans repayable in full within 12 months) at an interest rate of 6.5 percent, with up to a 9 percent penalty on arrears,[13] but by 1923 it was already clear that the bank was unwilling to continue lending unless the government in London provided security for unpaid loans. London was not yet ready to do this.[14]

In addition, four banks—Barclays Bank, the Ottoman Bank, the Arab Bank, and the Arab National Bank *(bank al-'ummah al-'arabiyyah)*—were supposed to provide formal credit for Arab agriculture.[15] The government collected limited information from banks about agricultural loans, and surviving files do not differentiate between loans to Arabs and those to Jews. Consequently, no comprehensive government-source information was available for the present study.[16] There is, however, limited evidence on the operations of the last three banks. It suggests that the two Arab banks generally did not provide loans to *fallāḥīn*. They lent only to Arab agriculturists via the Arab National Fund *(ṣandūq al-'ummah al-'arabiyyah)*, a political organization whose principal function was trying to prevent land transfer from Arabs to Jews.[17] The credit granted by the Fund seems to have been very limited. In 1945, it issued the insignificant sum of £P1,635 in loans, and the total credit it either loaned or had available to issue for land purchase at that time was a modest £P149,016.[18] Information on the Ottoman Bank was found for short-term crop loans, apparently its main area of agricultural lending. Since these loans were not direct but coordinated via the government, they are discussed in that context below.

Unlike other banks, Barclays Bank was comparatively active in lending to *fallāḥīn.*[19] In the late 1920s, at a time where even many rich merchants and businessman did not receive credit from foreign banks,[20] Barclays started a unique program to facilitate credit for comparatively wealthy *fallāḥīn,* without the backing of government guarantees. Loans were given according to a mutual security system: small groups of two or more borrowers signed contracts with the bank in which they undertook collective responsibility for the failure of any member to pay as required. Interest rates did not exceed the permitted 9 percent,[21] and the bank noted that *fallāḥīn* did whatever they could to retain this source of credit:

> The farmer made every effort to repay us, even if it meant selling livestock, which he might be obliged to repurchase subsequently at a higher price.[22]

> We see with regard to Haifa branch that branch manager states quite clearly that debtors confessed that the 1935/6 loans were repaid chiefly with borrowed money [from moneylenders].[23]

Thus, even among those who were fortunate enough to receive such loans, there were *fallāḥīn* who took out (illegal) high-interest loans from moneylenders to repay their loans to the bank when facing difficulties. At that time, the informal system provided backing to the formal one. Such loans were taken out mostly to retain the ability to get further low-interest loans from the bank and not to be subjected to confiscation of collateral. The documents show that the formal loans were repaid to the bank fairly reliably. In 1932, £P60,000 was issued in this way, and in 1936 £P248,000 was loaned to 16,331 borrowers in some 420 villages.

It is likely that the reverse also occurred, with the formal system providing backing to the informal one in time of breakdown. This worried the general director of Barclays Bank during the *fallāḥīn*'s economic crisis of 1938 (discussed below), although he found no proof of it:

> it might be found that instead of our advances having relieved borrowers from recourse to Moneylenders, we were being repaid by such recourse, the Moneylenders in turn being repaid from lending by the Bank—a vicious circle which would probably mean loss eventually either to the Moneylenders or the Bank.[24]

After the crisis of 1938 many of Barclays' loans remained unpaid, and the bank decided to end them.[25] It therefore joined the other banks in a reluctance to make loans without better security.

GOVERNMENT PERCEPTIONS AND CONSEQUENT STRATEGIES

The experience of the banks, and especially of Barclays, showed that an interest rate of 9 percent was not realistic in the long run, especially without the support of moneylender activity. The government, however, insisted that this rate was satisfactory for legal credit operations. What it did not realize, as Barclays Bank did, that farmers made every effort to repay loans. The conclusion that "strategic default" was the main cause of breakdown in payments was reached (without extensive investigation) by C. F. Strickland, who planned the credit reform in Palestine: "It is obvious that 9% is not a possible rate for a merchant to allow to a cultivator in a distant village, whose inclination and intention is frequently to avoid repayment if he can."[26]

Not surprisingly, when the government decided to reform the supply of credit to the *fallāḥīn* following the Disturbances of 1929, the ruling on the maximum interest rate was not even considered for amendment. Rather, most government policies, in accordance with official thinking, were planned to restructure the credit regime so as to prevent strategic defaults, on the assumption that this would make low-interest loans more attractive to banks. The alternatives were to create credit cooperative societies, to provide short-term crop loans, or to establish an agricultural mortgage bank. Another aim was to outlaw moneylenders, who were considered to be exploitative lenders in comparison to banks and therefore an obvious target. By whatever means, the government intended to "rationalize" the *fallāḥīn* and their surrounding institutions, in a mode similar to that outlined in Marx's discussion of capitalist colonialism, which resulted in a policy of replacing indigenous institutions with Western-style ones.[27]

LONG-TERM LOANS AND THE AGRICULTURAL MORTGAGE BANK

Unlike the programs dealing with short-term loans (repayable in full within 12 months), the Agricultural Mortgage Bank was set up to give long-term loans. It was also the only program that Strickland seemed to dislike:

> In almost every village when I asked the *fellahin* to offer their own solution for their difficulties they replied with a demand for an agricultural bank. . . . They were merely repeating the catch-word which they had heard from other people.[28]

Predictably, Strickland's approach reflects the British perception that the *fallāḥīn* were too ignorant to understand what was good for them. Yet it is also a rare example of considering what they had to say. Indeed, in response to these demands, an Agricultural Mortgage Bank was created. The intention was to facilitate loans for the improvement and development of mortgaged agricultural properties, such as by the introduction of fruit farming and irrigation, as well as paying off debts to moneylenders.[29]

The government wished to persuade monetary institutions to join this endeavor, yet from the beginning they were not enthusiastic, even though the government granted £P150,000 to the Agricultural Mortgage Bank in place of any security. But it failed to persuade the Arab banks to participate in its new mortgage bank. This, again, shows the tendency of Arab banks not to give loans to farmers. Still, some institutions took part, and the balance of the Agricultural Mortgage Bank's capital (£P335,000) was advanced by non-Arab banks and financial institutions such as Barclays Bank, the Ottoman Bank, the Anglo-Palestine Bank, Prudential Assurance, Guardian Assurance, and the Palestine Corporation. Even then, the motives for joining the new bank were not purely a response to economic strategy but, as in the case of the Anglo-Palestine Bank, more of a political strategy:

> To return to our conclusions, it is precisely the aspect of the situation which I mentioned last—Government showing its solicitude for the Arabs—that dictated to us the necessary to avoid the impression being created that we objected to Arab interests being protected.[30]

Loans were issued by the Agricultural Mortgage Bank between 1936 and 1938 and totaled £P425,000 in 670 loans at an interest rate of 8 percent. With no further inducement to invest, the bank's partners did not continue to make loans available.[31] The contribution of the Agricultural Mortgage Bank to the *fallāḥīn* was assessed by Horwill in 1936 and by Hoofien in 1938:

> The operations of this company (which are limited to settled areas where "title" is secure), whilst they should in due course benefit the *fallah* who is able to obtain financial assistance therefrom, increase his present indebtedness, as it is a general policy of this company only to advance money for fresh development. It is improbable, moreover, that the *fellah,* heavily in debt, would use the monies to full advantage when he knows that the results of his labour would be for the benefit of his creditor.[32] (Horwill, 1936)

> The Company [the Agricultural Mortgage Bank] is not really an agricultural Mortgage Company at all. Every word that has been said by Mr. C. F. Strickland in his report on Agricultural Credit (1930) about the unfitness of a central agricultural bank to deal with the credit problem of the Arab peasant has come true. The Company has done nothing whatsoever for the grain-growing peasant and it has already spent all its available funds. Practically

> the whole of its money has gone towards meeting the credit needs of orange growers, large and medium, mainly medium. Scarcely any small growers of the ten dunam type have benefited.[33] (Hoofien, 1938)

Only half of the loans were given to Arabs, and these were mostly to citrus growers who were a small proportion of Arab agriculturalists. In practical terms, then, although the *fallāḥīn* might have influenced the decision to establish the bank, for most of them it was irrelevant. This is not surprising. The banks involved in the Agricultural Mortgage Bank followed the pattern of giving loans only to the most creditworthy borrowers, like citrus growers, whose irrigated orchards faced little natural hazard and were prospering at that time.[34] In view of the risk of default, it seems that the banks ultimately wanted their loans repaid and did not wish to enter the long process of liquidating the land that was used as collateral by the Agricultural Mortgage Bank (see below).

Also, the government believed that no development would take place on "unsettled lands" under the *mushāʿ* form of tenure (see Chapter 6). Loans by the Agricultural Mortgage Bank were therefore offered only on "settled" lands. Because the government's land settlement program made slow progress,[35] loans could be given only in restricted areas—mainly the plains.[36] Overall, the vast majority of the *fallāḥīn* did not receive loans from the Agricultural Mortgage Bank, and its associated institutions were not economically motivated to continue such activity.

THE ARAB CREDIT COOPERATIVES

The main government strategy for replacing the old system by a new one was derived from C. F. Strickland's report. While describing *fallāḥīn* debts as extensive, Strickland suggested that the government should not itself deal with the debts but should create an alternative credit system that would reduce dependence on moneylenders.[37] He believed that setting up small cooperative societies of 50 to 100 members would be the best way to provide short-term credit to *fallāḥīn*.[38] Mutual guarantee, he thought, would solve two major problems. The first was "strategic default." As noted above, the *fallāḥ* was considered to be a person "whose inclination and intention is frequently to avoid repayment if he can." Strickland considered that the use of mutual guarantee would reduce this tendency among individual *fallāḥīn*, as they would be watched by their fellows. Second, he believed that with the assistance of the registrar of cooperative societies—a government official—there would be a better selection of creditworthy borrowers.[39] The *fallāḥ* would learn

> to watch his expenditure and submit it to the criticism of his fellow members, to be punctual in payment, and to be loyal to his society rather than to those creditors who are the cause of his failure. . . . In a cooperative credit society he rapidly becomes borrower and lender at the same time.[40]

Strickland envisaged the emergence of a system of cooperative societies as the leading credit system of Palestine:[41]

1. The government would arrange sources for short-term loans.
2. Societies would be created by the demand of villagers. There could be more than one society in a village. As a precaution, the registrar of cooperative societies would make sure that the people in the societies were well prepared for the idea of managing credit cooperative societies.
3. The societies would be managed by equality of voting power among the members and have their own treasurer, who would be chosen from the members and guided by the registrar's staff.
4. Loans would be given to societies at 8 percent interest. The societies would charge 12 percent interest from the members (eventually the rates stood at 6 and 9 percent, respectively).[42]

5. As societies proved themselves efficient in repaying loans and raising their own capital, they would become eligible to borrow from external commercial institutions, without government mediation. This would become another source for increasing their capital.
6. The cooperative movement would develop into an extensive credit system, coordinated by a successful cooperative central bank. The bank would not need a government guarantee and would be a vehicle for investment by the public (buying shares) and by commercial banks.
7. Cooperative societies would have many other functions in the villages besides the provision of short-term credit. They would market milk, barley, etc. In addition, a cooperative society would be a "valuable agency which can be found in a village for the promotion of agriculture, education and public health."[43] The cooperatives would also be able to give long-term loans to their members.
8. F. G. Horwill, who described Strickland's plan as an "admirable proposal," suggested adding another angle: that in the "event, say, of total failure of a crop" the government would assist the cooperative societies, as a response to accurate information which would be submitted by the latter about the needs of the *fallāḥīn.*[44]

The Performance of the Arab Credit Cooperative Societies

Throughout the Mandate period, Barclays Bank remained the sole financial institution that dealt with the Arab credit cooperative societies.[45] The bank gave loans only on recommendations from the Registrar of Cooperative Societies, who also advised the sum to be lent to a society each season.[46] The registrar looked for small trustworthy groups of cultivators who also trusted each other, so that the selection process was meticulous. In 1934, for example, "out of 60 villages in which propaganda was carried on during the year only 18 were selected."[47]

The progress of the cooperative movement was comparatively fast during the agricultural years 1933 to 1934 through 1937 to 1938 inclusive. Starting in 1933, 14 cooperatives were established, and 263 members received a total of £P3,303. All loans were repaid during that period, and accordingly the number of cooperatives increased to 121, with 5,121 members receiving £P59,832 (all 1936 prices, see Table 5.1). Until September 1937 the cooperatives created their own funds, amounting to £P13,691 (£P13,595 in current prices). The movement seemed very promising at that stage.[48]

However, the general strike in April 1936—the first phase of the Arab Revolt of 1936 to 1939—slowed the progress of the movement because the general insecurity discouraged Barclays from making loans:

> The Disturbances created abnormal difficulties in the collection of our agricultural advances to the villagers being unable to dispose of their crops in the usual way to move out of their villages. . . . In view of the unsatisfactory political situation and uncertain outlook, we have not considered it advisable to proceed with our policy of expansion and our proposals involve an increase of only £P32,000 over last year's figure.[49]

Hence it is not surprising that although from 1936 to 1937 the number of cooperatives and their members significantly increased, the capital advanced by the bank grew only moderately and was even less than planned (see Table 5.1).

The revolt reached its peak during the summer of 1938 and dwindled in 1939 with the military reconquest of the country. The revolt brought financial difficulties for the *fallāḥīn* because much of their fixed capital was seized or destroyed either by bands of Arabs or by the British collective punishments in villages.[50] In 1938, the losses caused by the revolt coincided with a poor harvest. The *fallāḥīn* and especially owners of smallholdings or tenants (who were paid by a share of the produce)[51] had little to sell and faced difficulties in raising the necessary cash. Understandably, there were problems of loan repayment that year (see Table 5.1).

A similar picture of low repayment occurred in 1939, although the yield that year was much higher than in 1938. It is hard to assess the losses suffered by the *fallāḥīn* during the suppression of the revolt, which may have caused greater hardships than it did in the previous summer. The problem of repayment may have been compounded by a late effect of the circumstances in 1938, so that in 1939 the members of cooperatives were indebted both to cooperatives and to moneylenders. The fear of inability to service bank debts is clearly demonstrated in extracts from a Barclays' report in 1938.[52] Not surprisingly, the bank was cautious in granting loans that year, yet remained under an obligation to do so:

> Briefly, our policy at the present time is to maintain our valuable connection with those borrowers who hitherto have been punctual, honest and worthy of the accommodation accord, but naturally in many cases what was considered right and proper a year or even six months ago must now be revised in the light of the abnormal conditions prevailing.[53]

Following its losses in the two consecutive years of 1938 and 1939, the bank reconsidered the granting of loans to *fallāḥīn,* either to cooperatives or in direct advances, unless it had the protection of government securities.[54] Essentially, the bank lost faith in the cooperatives and wished to have the debts repaid. It withheld loans for 1940 and 1941. In November 1940, an agreement was reached for 1942 and subsequent years to grant £P50,000 per year for lending to cooperative societies, conditional on the government giving a 50 percent guarantee for future loans as well as for earlier unpaid loans and on the registrar of cooperative societies and the bank jointly selecting the borrowers. Any losses would be split equally between the government and the bank:

Table 5.1 Arab Credit Cooperative Societies, 1933 to 1947

Advanced for the Year (issued the year before)	Number of Societies Registered as Active	Total Number of Members	Capital Advanced by Barclays Bank (£P 1936 prices)	Unpaid Capital by Cooperatives (£P 1936 prices; notes)		Amount of Wheat Produced in This Year (index)	Unpaid Capital (£P current prices)	Capital Advanced by Barclays Bank (£P current prices)
1933	14	263	3,303	0		42.5	0	3,270
1934	32	911	13,691	0		79.3	0	13,595
1935	61	2,422	40,766	0		100	0	39,013
1936	68	2,731	49,629	0	1936 Arab strike, later developing into an extensive Arab revolt	72.8	0	49,629
1937	121	5,121	60,242	0	Arab revolt	122.1	0	59,459
1938	121	5,121	53,810	48,433	The apex of the Arab revolt; a drought year	42.5	45,043	50,043
1939	121	5,121	59,832	49,731	Diminishing role of the Arab revolt; military reconquest of the country	85.4	44,310	53,310
1940	N.A	N.A	3,349	N.A	Cessation of bank lending	130.4	N.A	3,583
1941	N.A	N.A	N.A/0?	N.A	Cessation of bank lending	86.5	N.A	N.A/0?
1942	101	N.A	6,054	N.A	Agreement with the government for guarantee (not exceeding £P50,000) and compensation for earlier years	100	N.A	11,617

1943	78	N.A	9,952	N.A	Loans under the government agreement	63.2	N.A	23,199
1944	90	N.A	23,177	N.A	Ditto	55	N.A	About 55,000
1945	101	N.A	N.A	N.A	Ditto (not exceeding £P65,000)	55.9	N.A	N.A
1946	125	6,500	N.A	N.A	Ditto (not exceeding £P140,000)	N.A	N.A	N.A
1947	143	9,565	108,527	N.A	Ditto (no information about the limits for this year); the bank faced problems in collecting loans	N.A	N.A	292,698
1948	138	About 9,000	0	0	No loans granted, presumably because of the uncertain political conditions in 1947	N.A	0	0

Sources: Barclays/11/825; Barclays/11/559; Barclays/11/356; ISA/(RG2)/BOX479/v/3/40/vol. 1; Government of Palestine, *Cooperative Societies in Palestine: Report by the Registrar of Cooperative Societies on Developments during the Years 1921–1937,* pp. 9, 46; Government of Palestine, *A Survey of Palestine,* p. 360. For wheat yield: Government of Palestine, Department of Statistics, *Statistical Abstract of Palestine 1944–45;* Government of Palestine, Department of Agriculture and Fisheries, *Annual Report 1945–46* (1947), p. 20. For the Arab revolt (besides Barclays and ISA sources): Yoval Arnon-Ohana, "Heybetim 7hevratiyim 7vepoli7tiyim betno'at hamered ha'aravi, 1936–1939," Danin, 'Ezra (ed.), *Te'udot vedmoyot miginzei haknufiyot ha'arviyot beme'ora'ot 1936–1939* (Jerusalem, 1981), introductory pages, pp. 25–34; Yoval Arnon-Ohana, *Fala7hiym ba-mered ha-'aravi be-'erez yishrael 1936–1939* (Tel Aviv, 1978).

Note: Returns for wheat are suspected to be underestimated for 1933 to 1934 (see discussion before Figure 2.5).

> The High Commissioner [of Palestine] thinks it most desirable that this cooperative movement, which was started with strong Government encouragement, should be kept alive, and ultimately a proposal emerged whereby the Bank would continue to finance the Arab Co-operatives up to a period of five years, subject to annual review and subject to a Government guarantee in respect of 50% of capital loss. The societies considered unsound would be debarred from further advances and the amount advanced would be on seasonal lines and would not exceed £P50,000 except by arrangement between the Bank and the Government. It is proposed that the Government guarantee should have a retro-active effect as regards borrowings which are known already to be bad.[55]

Only the best-functioning cooperatives already in existence could be kept going.[56] As shown in Table 5.1, their number was reduced from 101 in 1941 to 78 in 1943. The registrar did not find the movement in good shape, and accordingly loans did not reach the target of £P50,000.

During World War II, Palestine experienced agricultural prosperity,[57] and Barclays considered the cooperative movement to be sounder but still insisted on 50 percent compensation from the government in cases of default. In 1944, the bank granted £P5,000 more than the limit of £P50,000 (Table 5.1). Later, it asked for the guarantee limit to be raised to £P60,000 for 1945 and about £P100,000 for 1946 (after pressure from the registrar, it was increased to £P140,000).[58] Even this increase was conditional on government guarantees. Loans were not granted in 1948, probably because of the uncertain political conditions.[59]

Two main concepts guided Strickland in proposing the establishment of cooperative societies—that they would reduce the risk of strategic defaults and that with the assistance of the registrar, the cooperative societies would function properly. In fact, the cooperatives resorted to strategic default to a higher degree than borrowers who took loans directly from banks. Although a Barclays memorandum commented on the valiant efforts made by farmers to repay the bank,[60] the attitude of members of cooperatives was different. According to the same source:

> The attitude of the Arab Cooperative Societies was disappointing as they showed little or no desire to honour their debts to the Bank and the Registrar had been able to extract little influence over them in the matter.[61]

This lament is supported by evidence from the registrar.[62] Various factors explain the greater likelihood of cooperative societies to default. As mentioned, banks wished to get their loans repaid and were not interested in acquiring land. Indeed, Barclays did not usually go to court in cases of loans owed by the Arab cooperative societies—even though 98.3 percent of their mutual guarantor members owned land. Instead, the bank preferred to seize crops for recouping unpaid loans.[63] Even then, there was a high risk that the full loan would not be repaid:

> Mr. Clark [the local director of Barclays Bank in Palestine] said that crop charges did not provide satisfactory security. The charge was registered but the man could move his crop off the land to the threshing floor and he had time to sell it before the sum due was paid. Seizure was the only certain way of getting money, but this provided great difficulties in practice. [64]

Unlike the short-term crop loans, the government did not help the bank to recover unpaid loans. The registrar's policy was to avoid official intervention in the form of administrative (executive) action because in his view this would damage the delicate relationship between the bank and its borrowers. He considered that the bank should resolve its problems with debtors peacefully.[65] Hence, the power of the creditor in regard to cooperative societies was weak—weaker than it was with short-term crop loans or loans made in the informal sector (discussed below). It is possible that *fallāḥīn* who were unable to repay all their debts (as in the "involuntary default" of 1938 and 1939), chose first to repay individual loans rather than the cooperatives, since the penalty for defaulting was lower with the latter than with any other option. Hence, in the case of involuntary default, the cooperatives were the first to lose, in contrast to moneylenders, who would seize the security or take the easily arranged loans given under the Security Loans Ordinance, which permitted seizure of movable agricultural crops and equipment.

It could be argued, in line with Ray's theory, that the defaults were deliberate, "strategic defaults" because borrowers wished to take the money and run. This does not seem to be the case, however, at least until 1938. In fact, members of cooperatives regularly repaid their loans (see Table 5.1). It is reasonable to assume that strategic default came about only after the bank changed its policy to withhold additional lending from farmers in distress (see Table 5.1). Certainly, from that date, it was clear that further loans were unlikely to be given. Bearing in mind the collection problems faced by the bank, borrowers were left with very little motivation to repay debts.

Another reason for default is that the registrar's staff, who were charged with selecting creditworthy borrowers, did not do their job as expected. The local director of Barclays Bank in Palestine complained that in some cases the registrar's staff were part of "political intrigue and the money lent had been diverted to improper purposes."[66] On another occasion, he wrote that it "is not surprising that certain of the senior Arab officials of the Registrar's Department took an active part in the rebellion."[67]

Corruption in the cooperative societies lay behind a number of defaults and hindered the development of some cooperatives. The method of supervision also seemed to reflect a mistaken approach in Strickland's plan. After the 1948 war, with the country now under Israeli rule, Barclays Bank tried to collect loans issued to cooperatives for the year 1947. Representatives from the bank went to some of the villages in an attempt to collect the loans. In the village of Kfar Rai, a representative found that the secretary of the cooperative took payments from members but did not transfer them to the bank (all members remained debtors because of the mutual guarantee).[68] In another village, which

I visited in 1999, members had not received loans since the early years of the cooperative because their treasurer argued that "the system did not succeed." The treasurer would not let anyone see the documents of the cooperative society that were in his possession, arguing that they included "top secret material."[69] According to the lists available in Barclays Bank, in 1947 that society had 35 members who borrowed £P661.[70] Strickland's intention was that there would be supervision and inspection of society treasurers by the auditor of the registrar of cooperative societies, but the auditor merely had to check the books and was under no obligation to meet members of the cooperatives.[71]

MOVABLE SECURITIES FOR SHORT-TERM LOANS

In the belief that the *fallāḥ*'s "inclination and intention is frequently to avoid repayment if he can,"[72] the government initiated another program, a cheap one as far as it was concerned. Like the cooperative societies, this program ignored the problem of earlier debts.[73] The idea was to enable both the landowner and the tenant *fallāḥīn* to obtain bank loans,[74] and the collateral chosen for this scheme, enacted in the Short-Term Crop Loans (Security) Ordinance of 1935, was any agricultural movable security. This meant much more than crops:

> The term "crops or other agricultural produce" [i.e., the collateral] shall mean any crops or produce including felled timber, animals, fodder, marine produce (including fish), agricultural, industrial and fishing implements, machinery, boats, tackle nets, and generally all things used in connection with agriculture.[75]

The bank's ability to lend against such securities was protected quite effectively. First, the borrower had "to make a statutory declaration before a Notary Public giving particulars of all liens, charges or agreements for further sales affecting such crops or agricultural produce,"[76] and for false declaration he would be subject to fine and/or imprisonment. Second, while banks had to register these loans with the government in each subdistrict (after the payment of a nominal fee), they were assured that in cases of default, a bank would be assisted by the administration to levy a charge on such movable assets.[77]

This scheme was comparatively more appealing to banks than previous schemes. The government had made provision for a faster and more effective levy on existing movable property, which allowed banks to recoup bad debts without having to liquidate land. This was quite different from the immovable collaterals of the Agricultural Mortgage Bank or the problem experienced by cooperative societies in making use of their collaterals because of the registrar's policy of nonintervention. In addition, the requirement that borrowers make a statutory declaration before a notary public enabled the bank to obtain better information on collaterals and thus to select more promising borrowers.

In the end, this least costly program was the most successful. Even so, its impact should not be overestimated. The impression is given in the *Survey of Palestine*'s comments about the "short term seasonal credit by the banks since 1935" that the supply of credit had significantly increased and that formal credit came to be the leading credit regime after the new ordinance had been passed that year:

> The provisions of this ordinance have enabled the principal banks and financial institutions . . . to make short term seasonal advances of considerable amount—some millions of pounds—to cultivators.[78]

This is not supported by any other evidence. The *Survey* provides a full account to the last pound for every type of loan given to agriculturalists. None of them reached even one million pounds. A phrase such as "some millions of pounds" is therefore inappropriate. It implies that no comprehensive data were collected or, alternatively, that the truth has been disguised. The consistent oral evidence from the *fallāḥīn* whom I interviewed was that bank loans were usually unattainable.[79] Finally, if the scheme was so successful, why then did the government have to intervene repeatedly, as in the case of cooperative societies, to create loans for *fallāḥīn?*

Among the few available documents about loans is a *Register of Charges (on) Short Term Crop Loans* in Lydda district for the agricultural years 1944 to 1945, 1945 to 1946, and 1946 to 1947.[80] Compared to other parts of Palestine, Lydda was privileged for several reasons. The district contained a larger proportion of high-quality land than the average.[81] It had more irrigated land, better yields, and more citrus groves. Its real estate values were probably also higher because Jewish land purchase was concentrated in that area.[82] Certainly, Lydda district had distinctly more "settled" lands than the rest of Palestine. It is therefore likely that banks were more willing to give loans here than in many districts. Hence, one would expect that the level of *formal* loans granted in Lydda district would be higher than the Palestine average.

Records of loans in the Lydda register include details like the name of the borrower (or borrowers, in cases of loans to small groups), the name of the village, a description of the plot/s whose crops were secured for repayment, the name of the company or bank granting the loan, the amount borrowed, and the dates of registration and expiration, as illustrated in Document 5.1. The use of the register permits the identification of the amounts of all loans given by banks and branches for each year; all villages where loans were granted (except one, the name of which could not be traced); and the ability, in most cases, to recognize whether the borrowers were Arabs or Jews (judging by their names). According to the register, loans by the Anglo-Palestine Bank and by the Tel Aviv branch of Barclays Bank were issued to Jews. Other branches of Barclays Bank and the Ottoman Bank made loans only to Arabs (except for one case of a loan of £P184 made to a Jew by the Jaffa branch of Barclays). No other bank, most significantly neither of the Arab banks, gave loans. Figures for loans granted to Arabs, with the estimated Arab population and Arab cultivable lands taken from the *Village Statistics,* are presented in Table 5.2. Out of 82 Arab

SUB DISTRICT Lydda

REGISTER OF CHARGES SHORT TERM CROP LOANS

1946/1947

Serial No. over Company's No.	Date of Registration	Name of Creator of charge	Name of Village	CHARGE					
				Date of Execution	Description	Amount L.P.	Amount Mils	Term date of Expiry	Name of Company

Document 5.1 Register of Charges (on) Short-Term Crop Loans of Lydda District

Source: ISA/(RG81)/BOX1418/2796, Register of Short-Term Crop Loans, Jaffa and Ramle Sub-Districts (i.e., Lydda District).

Note: This is a copy of one of the pages from the source.

rural municipalities in Lydda district, loans were granted only in 24, or 29.3 percent of them. Even in these localities, only a minority of villagers benefited from the loans (see Table 5.2). Figure 5.1 shows that 60 percent of the loans given were under £P120, but together these small loans made up a mere 26.8 percent of the total. The rest was loaned in larger sums, presumably to wealthier clients. According to the 1930 Johnson-Crosbie report, an average *fallāḥīn* household required an average loan of £P72.2 in 1945 prices (£P27 in 1929 prices).[83] Since we know that incomes from agriculture were higher in the 1940s than in 1929 because of the prosperous war years, one would expect

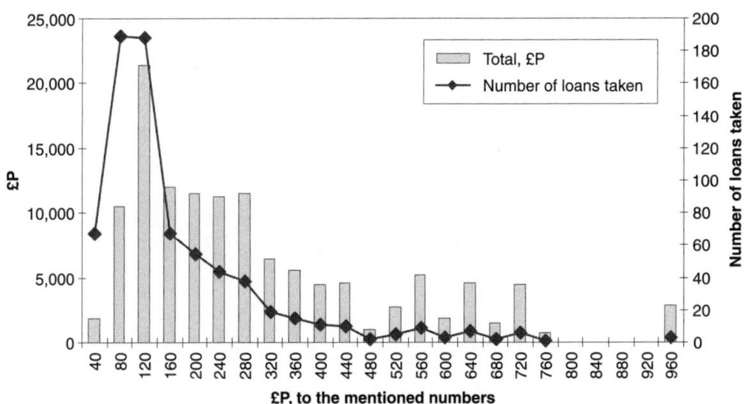

Figure 5.1 Distribution of Arab Short-Term Loans in Lydda District, 1944 to 1947

Source: ISA/(RG81)/BOX81/1418/3796, Register of Short-Term Crop Loans, Lydda District.

that a *fallāḥīn* household needed to borrow less in that decade. The higher sums borrowed imply, yet again, that loans tended to be given to richer *fallāḥīn.*

As shown in Table 5.2, banks made loans available only to certain villages. Evidence from Barclays suggests that this was related to the perception of a village as a whole, insofar as they tried to hold a village collectively responsible for repayments:

> It should be clearly understood that we are not prepared to consider lending any fresh money in any village until the entire debts owed by the village to the Bank have been cleared, including the village Cooperative Societies. We intend to insist upon the recognition of village responsibility.[84]

Out of seven villages in which Arab credit cooperative societies were active in Lydda district in the 1940s, six received short-term loans, partly or wholly from Barclays, as shown in Table 5.3. There was therefore, as implied in the above quotation, some correlation between villages that had cooperative societies

Table 5.2 Short-Term Crop Loans for Arabs, Lydda District, Agricultural Years 1944 to 1945 through 1946 to 1947

A. Branches Lending to Arab Farmers

	In 1945		Agricultural Year 1944–45			Agricultural Year 1945–46			Agricultural Year 1946–47		
Rural Municipalities	Estimated Arab Population	Arab Cultivable Lands (in dunams)	Number of Loans	In £P	Average per Dunam (in mills, thousandth £P)	Number of Loans	In £P	Average per Dunam (in mills)	Number of Loans	In £P	Average per Dunam (in mills)
1 Abu Kishk	1,900	6,772	2	670	98.9	26	6,627	978.5	24	7,232	1,067.9
2 Arab el-Muweilih	360	2,772	0	0	0	8	2,598	937.2	8	2,493	899.3
3 Beit Nabala	2,310	12,031	7	365	30.3	15	789	65.5	15	784	65.1
4 Biyar ‘Adas	300	4,798	2	190	39.5	11	2,360	491.8	9	1,758	366.4
5 Deit Tarif	1,750	7,729	1	40	5.1	4	190	24.5	2	85	10.9
6 Fajja	1,200	3,215	2	485	150.8	5	873	271.5	4	763	237.3
7 Innaba	1,420	11,248	0	0	0	5	319	28.3	5	319	28.3
8 Jaffa (rural)	unknown	1,095	0	0	0	0	0	0	1	75	68.4
9 Jalil	660	9,866	2	250	25.3	17	3,918	397.1	16	3,442	348.8
10 Jammasin	1,810	812	1	55	67.7	4	140	172.4	4	130	160
11 Kafar ‘Ana	2,800	13,923	7	805	57.8	29	2,644	189.9	23	2,162	155.2
12 Kheiriya	1,420	6,795	1	75	11	25	5,896	867.6	26	6,339	932.8
13 Lydda	unknown	18,409	10	1,355	73.6	38	6,475	351.7	29	5,625	305.5
14 Majdal Yaba	1,520	15,616	4	735	47	30	4,582	293.4	28	4,436	284
15 [illegible]	[illegible]	[illegible]	0	0	0	13	1,226	181.9	12	1,122	166.5

16 Qula	1,010	2,871	0	0	0	0	0	0	1	104	36.2
17 Rantiya	590	3,576	0	0	0	14	2,829	791.1	10	1,333	372.7
18 Safiriya	3,070	10,210	17	1,580	154.7	20	2,108	206.4	10	1,157	113.3
19 Salama	6,730	5,362	3	615	114.6	14	2,385	444.7	13	1,850	345
20 Saqiya	1,100	5,101	2	895	175.4	14	2,758	540.6	19	3,309	648.6
21 'Sasf' ('nomads'/ unreadable?)	unknown	unknown	0	0	0	1	128	0	0	0	0
22 Sawalmeh	800	5,651	0	0	0	9	1,887	333.9	7	1,695	299.9
23 Sheikh Muwannis	1,930	10,983	0	0	0	47	9,912	902.4	45	8,846	805.4
24 Yahudiya	5,650	17,115	3	315	18.4	10	1,085	63.3	7	891	52
24 Total, receiving r. municipalities	42,960	216,280	64	8,430	46.1	359	61,729	337.8	318	55,950	306.2
82 Total, Lydda District	108,660	628,205 (544,700 exc. citrus)	64	8,430	13.4	359	61,729	98.2	318	55,950	89
Average loan			131.7			194.1			175.9		

B. Branches Lending to Jews

Agricultural Year 1944–45			Agricultural Year 1945–46			Agricultural Year 1946–47		
No. of loans	In £P	Average Loan	No. of loans	In £P	Average Loan	No. of loans	In £P	Average Loan
12	6,640	553.3	28	10,810	386.1	28	9,906	353.8

Sources: ISA/(RG81)/BOX81/1418/3796. For lands and population: Government of Palestine, Department of Statistics, *Village Statistics, 1945*.

Table 5.3 Loans Provided to Cooperative Societies in Lydda District

	Name of the Society	Loans Approved 1935–40 (£P)	Loans Approved 1946–47 (£)P
1	**Beit Nabala**	401	475
2	**Deir Tarif**	176	130
3	**Innabe**	914	46
4	**Kafar 'Ana**	277	130
5	**Qula**	246	110
6	**Rantiya**	120	90
7	Barfiya	0	130
8	Beit 'Inan	397	0
9	Jimzo	816	0
10	Rantis	300	0
11	Salame	3,146	0
	Total: 11 societies	6,793	1,111
Average per year, 1945 prices		2,970	994
Average per dunam per year, in mils (thousandth £P), Lydda district, 1945 prices		4.8	1.6

Source: ISA/(RG2)/BOX479/V/3/40/Vol. 1, "Cooperative Societies Accounts"; Barclays/11/825, "Credit Cooperative Societies, season 1947/8," Table 5.2.
Note: Villages in bold are the six mentioned previously.

and those that received short-term crop loans from Barclays Bank. The bank believed that "village responsibility" would encourage villagers who borrowed from it to exert pressure on problematic borrowers to repay outstanding loans to enhance the credibility of the village as a whole. In the bank's view, the fear of being refused future loans because of default by others encouraged villagers to provide information that could be used to select "creditworthy" borrowers. Yet it is possible that this behavior cost the bank some creditworthy potential borrowers, as it limited its operations to villages with which it was familiar. In addition, borrowers might have given the bank only limited information, fearing that mistakes would damage their chances of getting further loans.

THE HISTORICAL DEBATE RECONSIDERED: FORMAL CREDIT AND THE *FALLĀḤĪN*

The credit needs of the *fallāḥīn* clearly varied from year to year, depending on yields and incomes, and it can be assumed that high-interest loans were taken out only in cases of necessity. To what extent, then, did the supply of formal credit help the *fallāḥīn?*

An investigation by the government of 88 of the 125 Arab cooperative societies in December 1945 (by which time loans would have been taken out for both summer and winter crops for the agricultural year 1945 to 1946), found that 51.2 percent of members who borrowed from their cooperatives also needed to borrow from other sources. Of these, 51.4 percent obtained loans at an annual rate of 12 percent or less ("cheap credit" from "formal" and "informal" creditors), and the rest (48.6 percent) had to pay higher rates. Thus, not only did members have to borrow from other sources, but 24.9 percent of these loans were from the informal sector (probably more, since illegal loans at rates of 9 to 12 percent were regarded as "cheap credit").[85] In other words, even members of cooperative societies who were fortunate enough to have access to formal loans also needed to borrow from the informal sector.

In the same year, an inquiry was made by Barclays Bank into 86 Arab cooperative societies that were customers of its Haifa, Nazareth, Nablus, and Jerusalem branches. It showed that, on average, a member of a cooperative owned 77.5 dunums of land (again indicating that they belonged to the more affluent sector of Arab society—see Figures 4.2 and 4.3—and possibly that the majority of them were not tenants). In 1945, £P109,541 was loaned by Barclays Bank to these societies, which between them owned 307,861 dunums, so that the average loan per dunam was 355.8 mils.[86] The survey did not include loans from other sources (either formal or informal, including Barclays Bank itself), unlike the government's survey of 88 societies. Hence, it is likely that in 1945 much more money was borrowed per dunum by these societies.

Against this, the sums lent in Lydda district, where banks tended to lend more, are small: less than 100 mils (1.6 + 98.2) per dunum (see Tables 5.2 and 5.3). These loans coexisted with continued borrowing by the *fallāḥīn* from the informal sector for most of their needs. Moreover, formal-sector loans were available only to a minority who satisfied the conditions of the cooperative societies and the short-term crop loans scheme. Even when short-term loans were given to small groups of borrowers, the latter were usually from the same *ahl* (a father and two sons, for example).[87] The Barclays archives indicate that loans issued by the cooperative societies were restricted to some of the villagers, who were in many cases relatives of one another.[88] Loans, therefore, were concentrated not only in a few households but in certain *ahl*s. Compared to what was needed, the evidence is that both the cooperative societies and the short-term crop loans scheme issued a small amount of loans to a small number of borrowers, who represented only a fraction of Arab rural society, and even these select clients had to borrow elsewhere to survive.

MONEYLENDING: AN EFFICIENT CREDIT SYSTEM

To restrain the activities of moneylenders, the government decided to enforce more strictly the law that prohibited the charging of interest above 9 percent. Shortly after the establishment of the Mandate, the high commissioner for Palestine issued the Usurious Loans (Evidence) Ordinance, 1922. This allowed courts to use oral evidence in preference to written documentation in the case of interest rates on loans exceeding 9 percent.[89]

This idea was reformulated in the Usurious Loans Ordinance, 1934. To reduce pressure on debtors, another law, the Imprisonment Debt Ordinance of 1931, limited the type of offences for which a person could be imprisoned for debt and laid down a maximum term of 21 days in jail[90] (in the case of the short-term crop loans, the maximum was one year in jail, giving this scheme another comparative advantage).

Moneylenders and the Law of Low-Interest Rates

Given that the rate of interest was limited by law to 9 percent, banks were largely unwilling to give low-interest loans except to a small number of people whom they considered creditworthy. In contrast, moneylenders, as Strickland noted in 1930, encountered few problems in circumventing this law:

> Since the Turkish Law prohibits a rate of interest in excess of 9% the pro-note is drawn up in a form concealing the exact nature of the transaction; either it shows that the borrower has received a larger sum than that which was actually paid, *e.g.* £P15 instead of £P10, or a fictitious sale of goods is included in the terms, and if the goods change hands at all they are immediately returned to the lender. The case of a cat which carried two tablets of soap across a table from the creditor to the debtor, who thereupon agreed to buy for £P50 "the load of soap borne by this animal" may be mythical, but indicates a common method of evading the law.[91]

In 1936, Horwill argued that the Usurious Loans Ordinances of 1922 and 1934 were likely to be ineffective:

> The provision of this Ordinance can only be applied when there is sufficient evidence to satisfy the court that usurious interest has been charged. Usually, in such cases, the only evidence will be the sworn testimony of the debtor, unsupported by any other evidence, as against the sworn testimony of the money-lender, supported by documentary evidence. It is very doubtful whether such evidence of the debtor will suffice to satisfy the Court.[92]

In a few cases, such as one in the District Court of Jaffa, oral evidence by a debtor, endorsed by two witnesses, was accepted as sufficient to prove an illegal interest rate on a loan.[93] But consistent with Horwill's observations, in most cases the debtor's oral evidence was against that of the lender, who also had documentary proof. For example, in a case taken to the Supreme Court, an agreement was reached between a lender and a debtor. The only recorded figure was the sum that had to be paid by a certain date. The principal and interest were not identified (this, as we shall see, reflected the main system of loan registration in Galilee). The judgment was that "there is no evidence . . . to suggest that the amount secured by the mortgage included interest in excess of a legal rate."[94] Similarly, another appeal to the same court was defeated on grounds that "oral evidence is not admissible to contradict the contract of a written document."[95] Examining judgments, one discovers that not many cases reached the court.[96] This is hardly surprising, as debtors, and especially other *fallāḥīn,* would refrain from testifying against a moneylender because to do so would preclude them from receiving further loans:

> It is true that the legal rate of interest is 9 percent per annum. This law is a dead-letter. . . . no *fellah* would dare to defend himself by means of this law, as he would unquestionably close to himself the door of the moneylender for ever. Without the moneylender he cannot live.[97] (Hope Simpson's Report)

The same evidence emerged from an interview with the heirs of a moneylender:

> If a man would have taken inappropriate action against a creditor, everyone knew it, and he would have never ever got any loan from any creditor.[98]

In retrospect, knowing that the government had proved unable to establish a comprehensive supply of formal credit for *fallāḥīn,* the latter were fortunate that the government also failed in its policy to ban high-interest moneylending, as otherwise no credit would have been available to them. The alternative would have been even higher interest rates in the informal sector because the danger of effective prosecution would have raised lender risk.

The Merchant-Moneylender and Interlinked Transactions

In 1939, W. J. Johnson, the treasurer for Palestine, argued that "the village money lender is also the local grain merchant."[99] Strickland implied the same.[100] Interviews confirmed that throughout the Mandate period most moneylenders were also wholesale merchants. In formal terms, loans had to be repaid to merchants in cash during or directly after the harvest, but the *fallāḥīn* frequently sold the yield to the merchant-moneylender.[101] Horwill argued that the *fallāḥ* often had to sell his crops to the merchants, and the sum received was below the market price:

> [The *fallāḥ* is] cajoled into selling his next crop to the moneylender at a figure well below the market price under the threat that no further assistance from the latter will be forthcoming if he does not do so.[102]

Bearing in mind the earlier discussion of the tendency of the *fallāḥīn* to market all their surplus of field crops to merchants (even in cases were no loans were taken), it might be the case that the *fallāḥ* knew that a moneylender would provide safety net in cases of crisis but tended to market his surplus anyway at harvest time to maintain good relations with (and hence the commitment of) the merchant-moneylender. Moneylending was an interlinked transaction, where a contract in the goods market was simultaneously a contract in the credit market.[103]

Even in cases of default, the transaction remained interlinked. Like the bank, the merchant-moneylenders typically did not want to recover the security but preferred to get the loan repaid (preferably in kind).[104] Even so, moneylenders would not give loans to those tenants or laborers who did not own land that could be offered as security. It seems that in the case of default a merchant-moneylender could be more effective, since, unlike the bank, the moneylender regarded land as a good security:

> Q: Why did merchants give loans to *fallāḥīn?*
> A: It was worth doing so. The merchant had the power to get the money back. If a *fallāḥ* would not repay his debt at harvest time, the merchant came with his strong men and took the debt [in kind] by the use of force. Hence, when the merchant gave a loan, he secured himself to get wheat, barley, etc. But if the merchant could not get his loan back, he would take the land. My family also received some lands in this way.[105]

Although land was the second security (the first being the crop), the acquiring of either crops or land in cases of default served the same interlinked motivation. When land was given in place of unpaid debt, the debtor usually continued to cultivate it, although ownership passed to the merchant. From then on, the supply of produce was even better secured because the merchant owned a share in the crops.[106]

Having a second (desirable) form of security gave the moneylender a comparative advantage, since even though it may not be used, the outcome could not favor the lender. Indeed, in an exceptional case where olive trees were given as security (that is, not the land but only the olives on it), a moneylender found that a "mysterious" arson attack had occurred in the plantation and that all his (the moneylender's) trees were destroyed. Accordingly, the *fallāḥ* who owned the land continued to cultivate it without any obligation to the moneylender.[107]

Finally, another indication that land was a part of an interlinked transaction is the unwillingness of meat merchants to give loans to *fallāḥīn,* from whom they could obtain land as security.[108] For meat merchants, however, animals were the preferred security. Like the bank, they would have to sell land to release the funds. They were also reluctant to lend because animals were movable property and could easily vanish.

As discussed, because of their political motivation, the offers made by Jews for agricultural land were usually above market value. In one interview, a merchant-moneylender was mentioned as a person who also sold land to Jews.[109] Some merchants therefore seemed tempted into selling land to the Jews, but this seems to have been a minor part of their business activities.

Characteristics of the Informal Credit Market

Oral evidence suggests that often only one or two significant moneylenders operated in a village, even though in principle others could have done so as well. Some moneylenders used to refer to villages as "ours" or "others."[110] In the case of villages near Nazareth, only a few major moneylenders active in the area were named in interviews. In the village of Mashhad, I was shown the village's register of "Land Settlement" from 1943 (Document 5.2). According to this, six parcels were mortgaged, all to the same moneylender, ʻAbdallā Yūsuf Yaʻaqub.[111] Like other moneylenders, he would register only the loans he considered to be higher risk (see below),[112] so that he probably arranged even more loans to that village.

It is hard to determine why villages tended to deal with only one or a few moneylenders. One hypothesis is that there was a moneylenders' cartel. If this were true, we would expect that moneylender-merchants would unite to "exploit" and "extract surpluses" from *fallāḥīn* and that interest rates would rise during the 1940s as the *fallāḥîn* shared in the general prosperity (see Chapter 2). In fact, interest rates remained virtually unchanged throughout the Mandate: the most common nominal interest rate in the informal credit sector remained at about 30 percent.[113]

An alternative hypothesis is more plausible—that of competitive market development. In this scenario, the village money market is "contestable" in the sense that if the incumbent moneylender charged an excessively high rate, competition would come in. On the other hand, no newcomer would intrude lightly because the entry price would be high, in the sense that the newcomer would lack the incumbent's detailed knowledge of the

LAND SETTLEMENT OF PALESTINE.
SCHEDULE OF RIGHTS (Lands in Divided Ownership)

District — Sub-District — Village — Name of Block — No. of Block — Serial No.

No. of Parcel	Category of Land	Area of Parcel	Names and addresses of Persons entitled to Rights	Shares	Nature of Rights	Remarks	Other Rights affecting Parcel	FEES: Survey	FEES: Registration	FEES: Partition	FEES: Court

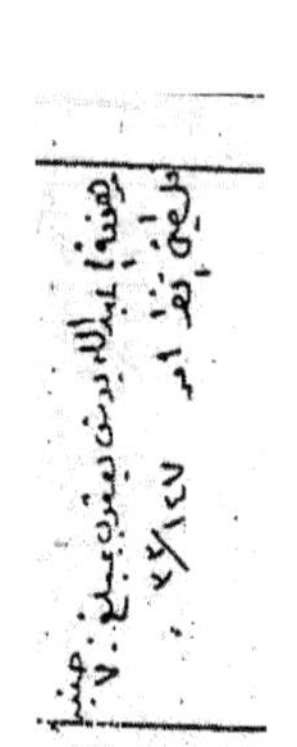

Document 5.2 Mashad's Register of Rights

Note: This is a copy of one of the pages from the source.

village. Naturally, imperfect information was a deterrent to lending. When a merchant-moneylender developed close connections with borrowers in a village, he would obtain better information. His risk was therefore reduced, and he could lend at a lower rate.[114] As the case of a leading moneylender in Nazareth suggests, his background knowledge about the villagers enabled him to discriminate among potential borrowers:

> A good man received a loan "by giving his word," without signing a document. An average man received a loan after signing a document. A bad man did not receive a loan.[115]

Because of the interlinked nature of the transaction, the competition remained largely among the wholesale merchants. For the *fallāḥīn,* it meant that the merchant-moneylender who offered the best deal remained in the village. The result was that the *fallāḥīn* probably got the best deal available.

Tenants, Laborers, and Ribā

Since moneylenders tended to lend to landowners, the tenants and laborers, who did not own land, were in a difficult position. In general, because they were responsible neither for engaging other labor nor for providing equipment,[116] their credit requirements for directly agricultural purposes were negligible. They could, however, have needed loans "purely" for personal consumption. Such loans, as discussed in Chapter 4, were customarily not secured and were repaid when the *fallāḥīn*'s liquidity position was better, usually at the winter harvest.

It is interesting to note that the prohibition of charging *ribā* (interest, or high interest, depending on interpretation) on loans under Islamic law *(sharī'a)* had little or no influence on the credit market. It is clear that, as in many other Moslem societies,[117] the law was ignored or circumvented in Mandate Palestine. However, moneylending was not regarded as an honorable occupation. Indeed, some interviewees withheld the names of moneylenders, wishing to protect them from the shame *('ayb)* involved in this occupation. However, Christians in Galilee[118] and Jews in Hebron (whose ancestors had lived there since before the first *'aliya* of 1882)[119] seemed to fill the role of moneylenders beyond their proportion in the population. The fact that neither group had a religious objection to charging interest may have influenced the development of mercantile activity in these communities.

An important question that remains unanswered is where the moneylenders obtained funds for the loans. It is likely that prior to the establishment of the Arab banks, a large number of merchants did not obtain bank loans at all. In fact, one of the reasons for urging the establishment of the Arab Bank was the need of Arab merchants for a supply of formal credit.[120] In later years, there are indications that wholesale merchants received loans from banks,[121] but it is unlikely that these provided sufficient credit for the informal sector. An example of this was found in an interview with a merchant-moneylender who stated that his father (in the same household) used to have a current bank account but that the bank would not give him loans.[122] No doubt this issue would benefit from further research.

CONCLUSION

This discussion began with the historical controversy about the success or failure of the government of Mandate Palestine to change the credit system from an informal into a formal one. Using a variety of sources, it has now been established that most of the credit for the *fallāḥīn* throughout the Mandate period was provided by informal lending.

Nevertheless, credit reform brought some improvement. It meant that a comparatively small number of more prosperous *fallāḥīn* enjoyed cheap credit. The program with most impact was the Short Term Crop Loans Ordinance of 1935. Paradoxically, the more expensive schemes—the credit cooperative societies and the Agricultural Mortgage Bank—were the least influential, representing high expenditure with very limited returns.

The most important reason for the failure to replace the informal system by a formal one was the government's misunderstanding of the logic of credit supply in Palestine. It believed that high-interest moneylending was caused by the tendency of the *fallāḥīn* to "strategic default" and by the exploitative practices of moneylenders. However, Palestine's moneylenders, consistent with Ray's theory, operated in a competitive market where the lender who offered the best deal remained. A scenario of "exploitation" was unlikely to occur in such an environment—and did not seem to.

The main reason for nonpayment was not "strategic default" but "involuntary default." No *fallāḥ* wished to default to a moneylender who had little hesitation about appropriating the collateral. Default to banks was also very undesirable because the *fallāḥ* would be unable to get further low-interest loans from them and could also lose his collateral. Defaults were more likely to occur in cases where the creditor had less power of confiscation; this was especially so with the cooperative societies. In cases of "involuntary default management," when a debtor who took out more than one loan had some of the money and needed to choose which loan to pay off, the cooperatives were more attractive because the consequences of evading payment were less severe. Finally, in cases of "involuntary default," it is likely that debtors hid their movable assets to minimize personal damage.

For the bank, taking land as collateral could embroil them a long process of liquidation. It therefore preferred to seize crops or other movable assets when recovering unpaid loans. For the merchant-moneylender, however, both kinds of collateral were sound, since they could use land for crop production. The risk involved in defaults was therefore higher to banks, giving the moneylender a comparative advantage.

Competition in the informal credit market meant that high rates of interest were realistic. It was no coincidence that moneylenders set such rates, that most banks were unwilling to give low interest loans, and that the few banks willing to venture into this area realized that without government backing they were unable to operate efficiently.

Natural hazards were a determinant of high risk. The lands of the *fallāḥīn* were largely unirrigated and therefore dependent on rainfall. Crop yields varied greatly from one year to another. In low-yield years, the *fallāḥīn* could not repay their debts. Insecurity was a subsidiary determinant of risk. The crisis of 1938 was caused by an unusually poor harvest combined with the general deterioration during the Arab Revolt of 1936 to 1939. On the other hand, local tranquillity, especially in a period of significant economic upturn like the prosperity of the 1940s, had the opposite effect of reducing risk.

Imperfect information about borrowers also contributed to risk—typically, not on the likelihood of strategic default but on the assets available for liquidation. This was particularly relevant to bank operations. The moneylender had the advantage of close connections in the village and clients who also owned land, to him a desirable guarantee. The bank was likely to be less well informed. It also sought information on movable properties, which a debtor could easily conceal, especially following "involuntary default."

Understanding the particular risks involved in bank lending may also explain why the short-term crop loans scheme was a comparative success. Better information was collected about movable collateral, which helped in the selection of more "creditworthy" borrowers, and the government's assistance in cases of default was generous. Most of these low-interest loans were probably granted after the crisis of 1938 and to comparatively wealthy *fallāḥīn,* and it is not known if they were a success in the long run.

Since the government's attempts at "rationalizing" credit by doing away with the "informal" system were unsuccessful, the *fallāḥīn* were fortunate that it also failed to enforce the Usurious Loan Ordinance. Otherwise, they would have been left without adequate sources for credit, or the moneylenders would have gone underground while charging even higher interest rates. The dependence of the *fallāḥīn* on moneylenders also undermined the ordinance, since "no *fellah* would dare to defend himself by means of this law, as he would unquestionably close to himself the door of the moneylender forever. Without the moneylender he cannot live."[123]

The extremely limited success of the government in bringing about change was because its efforts were largely exhausted on policies aimed at overturning long-established and proven indigenous institutions and imposing Western-style ones in their stead, most of which could not survive without ongoing government spending. This conclusion leads us to a discussion of the alternatives that could have been utilized to assist the *fallāḥīn.*

NOTES

1. Government of Palestine, *A Survey of Palestine: Prepared in December 1945 and January 1946 for the Information of the Anglo-American Committee of Inquiry* (Jerusalem, 1946), pp. 349, 353. This is discussed in Chapter 7.
2. Debraj Ray, *Development Economics* (Princeton, 1998), pp. 529–86.
3. Government of Palestine, *A Survey of Palestine,* p. 367.
4. Ibid., p. 366.
5. Ibid., p. 364.
6. E.g., interview with Khalid Zu'abī (Abu Raf'at) from Nazareth (during the Mandate period, Abu Raf'at was a *fallāḥ* in the Nein village who also worked in Nazereth) (25 March 1999); interview with Al-'Othmān Sālim Maṣrāwa (Mr. Maṣrāwa, b. 1918, worked as a *fallāḥ* on his family farm until his village, Safuriyya (north), was destroyed in the 1948 war) (30 August 1998); interview with Slīmān 'Adawī from Tur'an (Mr. 'Adawī, b. 1926–28, was a *fallāḥ* in the Mandate period and an agriculture adviser in Israel; he worked with some who had been agriculture advisers in the Mandate period) (5 April 1999); interview with Yūsif and Fārūk Ya'aqūb from Nazareth (these are the grandsons of 'Abdallah Yūsif Ya'aqūb, a merchant and moneylender; they—and especially Mr.

Fārūk Ya'aqūb, the older one—used to work with the grandfather in his business) (25 March 1999); interview with 'Alī Abū Yūsif Zu'abī from Daḥi (today from Nazareth) (Mr. Zu'abī, b. 1923, was a *fallāḥ* in the Mandate period) (26 March 1999); interview with Abū 'Abdallah from Mashhad (Abū 'Abdallah, b. 1921, was the *mukhtār*'s son in the Mandate period and later became the *mukhtār* of his village) (6 April 1999 and 17 August 1999); interview with Ya'aqūb Nāṣir Waqīm from Ramah (Mr. Waqīm, b. 1908, is the son of a *fallāḥīn* family who worked as an agriculturist in the late Ottoman and Mandate periods) (6 April 1999).

7. Charles S. Kamen, *Little Common Ground: Arab Agriculture and Jewish Settlement in Palestine, 1920–1948* (Pittsburgh, 1991), pp. 242–46.
8. Rosa I. M. El-Eini, "The Agricultural Mortgage Bank in Palestine: The Controversy over its Establishment," *Middle Eastern Studies,* 33, no. 4 (1997), pp. 751–76; "Government Fiscal Policy in Mandatory Palestine," *MES,* 33, no. 3 (1997), pp. 570–96; "The Implementation of British Agricultural Policy in Palestine in the 1930s," *MES,* 32, no. 4 (1996), pp. 211–50; "Rural Indebtedness and Agricultural Credit Supplies in Palestine in the 1930s," *MES,* 33, no. 2 (1997), pp. 313–37.
9. Jacob Metzer, *The Divided Economy of Mandatory Palestine* (Cambridge, 1998), p. 110.
10. E.g., interview with 'Alī Abu Yusif Zu'abī; interview with Yūsif and Fārūk Ya'aqūb.
11. Government of Palestine, *Report of a Committee on the Economic Condition of Agriculturists in Palestine and the Fiscal Measures of Government in Relation Thereto,* W. J. Johnson, R. E. H. Crosbie, et al. (Jerusalem, 1930), pp. 2 –27.
12. Ibid., p. 2; Government of Palestine, *The Banking Situation in Palestine with a Commentary on the Co-operative Society Movement, by F. G. Horwill* (Jerusalem, 1936), pp. 90–91.
13. Government of Palestine, *A Survey of Palestine,* pp. 348–49; also George Hakim and M. Y. El-Hussayni, "Monetary and Banking System," Sa'id B. Himadeh (ed.), *Economic Organisation in Palestine* (Beirut, 1938), p. 498.
14. El-Eini, "The Agricultural Mortgage Bank," p. 752.
15. E.g., Ze'ev Avrahamoviz, and Izḥaq Guelfat, *Hamesheq ha-'aravi*

(Tel Aviv, 1944), pp. 106–10; M. Atar, *'Sheney habanqim ha'arviyim,' Haaretz,* 20 August 1947.

16. E.g., ISA/(RG2)/BOX135/F/734/1/40, "Analysis of Customers' Liabilities to Banks and Certain Cooperative Societies."
17. The Arab National Bank controlled the Arab National Fund. The latter dealt with agriculture and aspects of national land purchases. Loans for agriculturists by the two Arab banks were given only via this institute. For the Arab Bank, see Arab Bank, *Twenty-five Years of Service to Arab Economy, 1930–1955* (Amman, 1956), p. 44.
18. *Šandūq al-'ummah al-'arabiyyah, taqrīr majlis al-aidārah al-mukarrim 'ila al-jam'iyyah al-'umūmiyyah al-'ādiyyah lil-'ai'ādah sanah 1945* (Jerusalem, 1946), pp. 4–10.
19. Government of Palestine, *A Survey of Palestine,* pp. 348–64.
20. Joseph Vashitz, "Temurut ḥevratiyut bayeshuv ha'aravī shel ḥeyfah betqufat hamandaṭ habriṭī: soḥarīm ve-yazamīm aḥerīm," Avi Bareli and Nahum Karlinsky (eds.), *Khalkhala veḥevra betqufat hamandaṭ* (Jerusalem, 2003), pp. 398–99.
21. E.g., Government of Palestine, *Report by Mr. C. F. Strickland of the Indian Civil Service on the Possibility of Introducing a System of Agricultural Co-operation in Palestine* (Jerusalem, 1930), p. 7.
22. Barclays/11/565, 11 September 1944, "Memorandum on Advances to Native Cultivators (Palestine)."
23. Barclays/11/317, 20 January 1938, a letter from the General Manager, Barclays Bank, to the Local Directors in Jerusalem.
24. Ibid.
25. Barclays/11/565, 11 September 1944, "Memorandum on Advances to Native Cultivators (Palestine)."
26. Government of Palestine, *Report by Mr. C. F. Strickland,* p. 10.
27. Karl Marx, "The Future Results of British Rule in India," *New York Daily Tribune,* 8 August 1853, reprinted in Shlomo Avineri, *Karl Marx on Colonialism and Modernization* (New York, 1969), pp. 132–39.
28. Ibid., p. 5.
29. El-Eini, "The Agricultural Mortgage Bank," pp. 754, 768.
30. CZA/S25/7052, 5 December 1933, Moshe Shertok to A. Lurie.
31. Government of Palestine, *A Survey of Palestine,* p. 351.

32. Government of Palestine, *The Banking Situation in Palestine* (Horwill), p. 81.
33. CZA/S25/7052, 31 May 1938, "The Future of the Government Agricultural Mortgage Bank," S. Hoffien.
34. Government of Palestine, *A Survey of Palestine,* p. 354.
35. For the progress of land settlement, see maps in Government of Palestine, Department of Land and Survey, *Annual Reports* (Jerusalem, various years)
36. Government of Palestine, *A Survey of Palestine,* pp. 339, 724. See also El-Eini, "The Agricultural Mortgage Bank," p. 770.
37. Government of Palestine, *Report by Mr. C. F. Strickland,* p. 3.
38. Ibid., pp. 4, 6, 30.
39. Ibid., pp. 4, 6, 16, 30.
40. Ibid., pp. 4–5.
41. For the following points, see ibid., pp. 5–8, 10, 16, 23–24, 26–28, 32.
42. Government of Palestine, *A Survey of Palestine,* pp. 348–63; also Hakim and El-Hussayni, "Monetary and Banking System," pp. 457–61.
43. Government of Palestine, *Report by Mr. C. F. Strickland,* p. 23
44. Government of Palestine, *The Banking Situation in Palestine* (Horwill), p. 84.
45. E.g., Barclays/11/825, "Arab Cooperative Credit and Thrift Societies," 1948.
46. E.g., ISA/(RG2)/BOX479/V/3/40/Vol.1, "Notes of a Meeting between Mr. Clark and the Financial Secretary on the 5th October, 1940."
47. Government of Palestine, *Cooperative Societies in Palestine: Report by the Registrar of Cooperative Societies on Developments during the Years 1921–1937* (Jerusalem, 1938), pp. 41, 43.
48. Ibid., p. 43.
49. Barclays/11/317, 16 December 1936, "Agricultural Loans in Palestine," a letter from the Local Director in Palestine to the General Mangers, London.
50. See Chapter 1.
51. See Chapter 4.
52. Barclays/11/317, 20 January 1938, letter from the General Manager, Barclays Bank, to the Local Directors in Jerusalem.

53. Barclays/11/356, 7 September 1938, "General Conditions—Advances," by the Local Manager, Palestine.
54. Barclays/11/565, 11 September 1944, "Memorandum on Advances to Native Cultivators (Palestine)."
55. Barclays/11/369, 11 November 1940, "Arab Co-operative Societies."
56. Barclays/11/369, 11 November 1940, "Telephone from Colonial Office."
57. See Chapters 2 and 3.
58. See various correspondences ISA/(RG2)/BOX479/V/3/40/Vol.1, especially from November 1943 onward. Barclays/11/825, "Memorandum Regarding Correspondence with the Government of Palestine on Advances to Arab Cooperative Societies."
59. Barclays/11/825, 14 November 1947, a copy of a letter from the Registrar of Cooperative Societies to all District Commissioners, in which he says that action taken by Barclays Bank due to the existing conditions is understandable.
60. Barclays/11/565, 11 September 1944, "Memorandum on Advances to Native Cultivators (Palestine)."
61. Ibid.
62. See the case of Betuniya: ISA/(RG2)/BOX479/V/120/33, 17 October 1940, a letter from the Registrar of Cooperative Societies to the Jerusalem District Commissioner. See also ISA/(RG2)/BOX479/V/3/40/Vol. 1.
63. Government of Palestine, *Cooperative Societies in Palestine: Report by the Register,* p. 47.
64. ISA/(RG2)/BOX479/V/3/40/Vol.1, "Note of a Meeting Between Mr. Clark and the Financial Secretary on the 5th October, 1940."
65. See the response of the registrar to the only known case of seizing the loans of cooperative societies in a village: ISA/(RG2)/BOX479/V/120/33, 17 October 1940, a letter from the Registrar of Cooperative Societies to the Jerusalem District Commissioner. See also ISA/(RG2)/BOX479/V/3/40/Vol.1.
66. ISA/(RG2)/BOX479/V/3/40/Vol. 1, "Notes of a Meeting Between Mr. Clark and the Financial Secretary on the 5th October, 1940."
67. Barclays/11/356, 30 November 1939, a letter from the Local Manager in Palestine to the General Managers in London.
68. Barclays/11/825, 7 and 8 September 1949, "Kufr Rai."

69. The name of the person and village are held by the author.
70. Barclays/11/825, list for 1947/48 season.
71. Government of Palestine, *Report by Mr. C. F. Strickland,* p. 19.
72. Ibid., p. 10.
73. Government of Palestine, *The Banking Situation in Palestine* (Horwill), p .80.
74. Ibid.
75. Government of Palestine, "Short Term Crop Loan (Security) Ordinance, 1935: Rules Made by the Officer Administering the Government under Section 9," *Supplement no. 2 to the Palestine Gazette,* 4.10.1935, pp. 959–60.
76. Ibid.
77. Government of Palestine, "An Ordinance to Provide Security for Short Term Loans on Crops," *Palestine Gazette,* 16 May 1935, pp. 415–17; Government of Palestine, "Notice of Enactment," *Palestine Gazette,* 25 June 1935, p. 550; Government of Palestine, *A Survey of Palestine,* p. 350.
78. Government of Palestine, *A Survey of Palestine,* p. 350.
79. E.g., interview with Nimir Qasim Muṣafa from 'Ein Mahil (Mr. Muṣtafa, b. 1910, spoke about his childhood in the Ottoman period and his life under the Mandate; in the Mandate period he was a *fallāḥ* and shopkeeper; from 1937 he was also the *mukhtār* of his village) (18 August 1999); interview with Mohammad Maṣrāwa (known as Bayrūti) from Reina (Ḥaj Maṣrāwa, b. 1929, was a *fallāḥ* in Safuriyya during the Mandate period) (19 August 1999); interview with Jamāl 'Ilyās Khuri from Meghar (Mr. Khuri, b. 1905, was a *fallāḥ* and later a policeman during the Mandate period) (23 August 1999); interview with Slīmān Aḥmad Slīmān Muhammad from Bu'eina (Mr. Muhammad, a Bedouin by origin, was a seminomadic *fallāḥ* during the Mandate period) (23 August 1999); interview with Tatūr Jamāl from Reina (Mr. Jamāl, b. 1935, is the son of a *fallāḥīn* family) (20 August 1999); interview with Khalid Zu'abī; interview with 'Alī Abū Yūsif Zu'abī; interview with Slīmān 'Adawī; interview with Ya'aqūb Nāṣir Waqīm; interview with Abū 'Abdallah; interview with Muṣliḥ Aḥmad Yāsīn from Shafa 'Amr (Ḥaj Yāsīn, b. 1923, is a son of an owner-cultivator *fallāḥ* who employed others on his lands) (22 August 1999).

80. ISA/(RG81)/BOX1418/2796, Register of Short Term Crop Loans, Jaffa and Ramle Sub-Districts (i.e., Lydda District). This file was catalogued by mistake in the ISA as "Citrus Loans of the Ottoman Bank": (1) Each page in the register was entitled "register of charges short term crop loans" for Jaffa and/or Ramle subdistricts, and not otherwise. (2) The loans in that register were not given by the "Ottoman Bank" alone but also by Barclays Bank and the Anglo-Palestine Bank. (3) Registration of citrus loans was found in the Accountant General's files in the same archive. The amounts of loans given to citrus growers in those years in Ramle and Jaffa subdistricts were totally different. See ISA/(RG6)/BOX1942/79, Government of Palestine, Accountant General's "monthly return on (citrus) loan transaction," February 1948. (4) As archivists in ISA advised, mistakes in cataloguing Mandate files are not unusual.
81. Government of Palestine, Department of Statistics, *Village Statistics, 1945* (Jerusalem, 1945). The figures are for all Mandate Palestine, excluding the arid subdistrict of Beersheba.
82. Kenneth W. Stein, *The Land Question in Palestine, 1917–1939,* 2nd ed. (London, 1985), p. 210.
83. Government of Palestine, *Report of a Committee on the Economic Condition of Agriculturists* (Johnson-Crosbie), p. 26.
84. Barclays/11/356, 9 February 1939, "Overdue Agricultural Loans and Discounts for All Seasons to and Including 1938, by the Local Director in Palestine."
85. Government of Palestine, *A Survey of Palestine,* pp. 366–67. Unfortunately, the information in this source is limited.
86. Barclays/11/825, "Arab Cooperative Societies, season 1944/45."
87. ISA/(RG81)/BOX1418/3796, "Register of Charges Short Term Crop Loans."
88. Barclays/11/825, 16 August 1949, lists of members in three Arab cooperative societies are appended to correspondence with the Haifa branch.
89. CZA/S25/10395, 1924, a letter from the Vice Grand Rabbi of Hebron to the Palestine Zionist Executive.
90. Government of Palestine, *The Banking Situation in Palestine* (Horwill), p. 80.
91. Government of Palestine, *Report by Mr. C. F. Strickland,* p. 10.
92. Government of Palestine, *The Banking Situation,* p. 80.

93. C.A 16/1943 in the District Court of Jaffa, Daoud Smouha v. Mohammed El-Duwah, *Selected Cases of the District Courts of Palestine, 1943,* pp. 278–79.
94. H.C 74/1935, As'ad Warwar v. Chief Execution Officer, Nablus and Adla Nuweis, *Law Report of Palestine 1934–5,* pp. 378–79.
95. H.C 102/1936, Hassan Yasin Abu Hadel vs. Saleh Saleh, *Law Report of Palestine 1937,* pp. 140–41.
96. See, broadly, *Current Law Report, Law Report of Palestine, Collection of Judgements* and other law collections for the Mandate period, available in the Law Library of the Hebrew University, Jerusalem.
97. Great Britain, Colonial Office, *Report on Immigration, Land Settlement* and *Development, by Sir John Hope Simpson* (London, 1930), p. 68.
98. Interview with Yūsif and Fārūk Ya'aqūb.
99. ISA/(RG6)/BOX1928/1101/2, 13 November 1939, "Note by the Treasurer on the Issue of Agricultural Loans in 1939."
100. Government of Palestine, *Report by Mr. C. F. Strickland,* p. 10.
101. As was argued in interviews: interview with Yūsif and Fārūk Ya'aqūb; interview with Sālim Moḥamad Abū Aḥmad (known as Abū 'Afif 'al-hishis') from Nazareth (Abū 'Afif, b. 1923, is the son of a family of owner-cultivators and landlords from Tel 'Adas; during the Mandate period they moved to Nazareth, where the family continued to lease lands and also established a mercantile business, where they lent money to *fallāḥīn*) (21 August 2000).
102. Government of Palestine, *The Banking Situation in Palestine* (Horwill), p. 80.
103. For theoretical remarks on interlinked transactions, see Frank Ellis, *Peasant Economics: Farm Households and Agrarian Development* (Cambridge, 2nd ed., 1993), pp. 156–60; Ray, *Development Economics,* pp. 561–72.
104. E.g., Interview with Yūsif and Fārūk Ya'aqūb; Interview with Sālim Moḥamad Abū Aḥmad.
105. Interview with Sālim Moḥamad Abū Aḥmad.
106. E.g., PRO/CO/733/290/8, February 1933, Secret, Cabinet, "Policy in Palestine: Memorandum by the Secretary of State for the Colonies," p. 1; interview with Yūsif and Fārūk Ya'aqūb.

107. Interview with Yūsif and Fārūk Ya'aqūb.
108. Interview with Mohammad Aḥmad Abū Aḥmad (Abū Riaḍ) from Nazareth (Abū Riaḍ, b. 1918, was a butcher and merchant of animals and meat during the Mandate period).
109. Interview with Khalid Zu'abī.
110. Especially the interview with Yūsif and Fārūk Ya'aqūb.
111. Mashad's Register of Rights (1943). This was shown to me by Mr. Mohammed Mar'ī.
112. Interview with Yūsif and Fārūk Ya'aqūb; interview with Sālim Moḥamad Abū Aḥmad.
113. Great Britain, Colonial Office, *Report on Immigration* (Hope Simpson), p. 68; Government of Palestine, *The Banking Situation in Palestine* (Horwill), p. 80. E.g., from interviews: interview with Abu 'Abdallah; interview with 'Alī Abu Yusif Zu'abī; Interview with Nimir Qasim Muṣafa.
114. For a theoretical approach, with some historical indications of such segmentation and the rationing behind such a credit system, see Ray, *Development Economics,* especially pp. 406, 536–37, 540–43.
115. Interview with Yūsif and Fārūk Ya'aqūb.
116. Ya'akov Firestone, "Cash-Sharing Economics in Mandatory Palestine," *Middle Eastern Studies,* 11, no. 1 (1975), pp. 3–23 and no. 2. pp. 175–94; Ya'akov Firestone, "Production and Trade in an Islamic Context: Sharika Contracts in the Transitional Economy of Northern Samaria, 1853–1943," *International Journal of Middle East Studies,* 6 (1975), pp. 185–209. E.g., from interviews: interview with Ya'aqūb Nāṣir Waqīm. Also Hagana/105/178, "'Ain Mahel: Intelligence Report."
117. Gareth Austin and Kaoru Sugihara (eds.), *Local Suppliers of Credit in the Third World, 1759–1969* (London, 1993), p. 5; Rodney Wilson, *Banking and Finance in the Arab Middle East* (New York, 1983), pp. 70–98.
118. As observed in interviews, for example, Abū 'Ātif Fāhūm from Nazareth (Mr. Fāhūm, b. 1927–28, is the son of Yūsif Fāhūm, the mayor of Nazareth during different years of the Mandate period; his father was also a landlord) (17 August 1999).
119. CZA/S25/10395, 1924, a letter from the Vice Grand Rabbi of Hebron to the Palestine Zionist Executive about the Usurious

Loan Ordinance of 1922. He sought to persuade the government to change the ordinance, as it could have brought losses for the richer Hebron Jews who made loans to nearby villages.

120. Vashitz, "Temurut ḥevratiyut bayeshuv ha'aravī shel ḥeyfah betqufat hamandaṭ habriṭī," pp. 398–99.
121. ISA/(RG2)/BOX135/F/734/1/40, 1941–1946, "Analysis of Customers' Liabilities to Banks and to Certain Credit Cooperative Societies"; Barclays/11/317, 20 January 1938, a letter from the General Manager, Barclays Bank, to the Local Directors in Jerusalem; Moḥamad Yūnīs al-Ḥusayni, *Al-tatwūr al-'ijtimā'ī fi filasṭīn al-'arabiyyah* (Jerusalem, 1946), p. 201.
122. Interview with Sālim Moḥamad Abū Aḥmad.
123. Great Britain, Colonial Office, *Report on Immigration (Hope Simpson),* p. 68.

· SIX ·

Land Reform and Mushā' *Lands*

According to the British administration, the *mushā'* (communal land) in Mandate Palestine was an archaic and "irrational" system, an obstacle to investment that blocked any chance of development. Officials argued that "under this system . . . no one [had] any inducement to improve his land."[1] Another supposed disadvantage was that the *mushā'* encouraged "overparcelling." It is therefore not surprising that the government devoted considerable efforts to land reform in its land-settlement program, which was aimed at dividing *mushā'* into individual—preferably consolidated—permanently owned plots.[2] Both the British perspective and the outcome of land reform are examined below.

THE SYSTEMS OF *MUSHĀ'* IN THE LEVANT

The word '*mushā'*' has several meanings, most of them about the joint property rights of a group of people. The group can vary from several people to the population of a country.[3] Common grazing lands, for example, were termed *mushā'* on the Druze mountain of Hawran.[4] However, discussions about *mushā'* usually refer to its meaning as land tenure, which is how it is used here.

The essence of the *mushā'* was—and still is, where it exists—that commonly held land was divided into equal shares, and after a set period all the shares were redistributed among the shareholders (who were sometimes also the landowners, as when a tenant leased another's shares), so that a person who was allotted a fraction of the *mushā'* land (a share or more or even a fraction of a share) would begin to cultivate lands he had not cultivated in the previous distribution. In other words, under this system a shareholder obtained access to a portion of the land he shared but did not get a long-term designated plot or plots. Each share usually included a similar proportion of different kinds of land with regard to soil type, topography (e.g., certain land in the hill and in the valley), distance from the village, etc.[5]

Although the essence of the *mushā'* remained the same, it was not a homogeneous system. There was a major division between the "open-ended" and "quantified-share" *mushā'* and their subtypes. In the open-ended *mushā'*, the number of shares was determined by *nonland* factors (which varied from one *mushā'* establishment to another). These could be the number of persons, either *dhukūr* (the number of males of any age, clan heads, or grown males) or other nonland factors of production usually counted in *faddāns* (plow-related units comprised of a number of plows, plow animals, males capable of plowing, or plow teams). Before each redistribution, the units of the agreed factor (e.g., the *dhukūrs*) were counted, and the land was divided into equal shares, totaling the same as the quantity of the agreed factor. The land was then redistributed among the members according to the share to which they were entitled (e.g., if by *dhukūr*, a household of a father and two boys associated with a *mushā'* of 50 males would receive three shares out of 50). Typically, no one was allocated a plot he had cultivated in the previous distribution.[6]

By contrast, in the quantified-share *mushā'* only the amount of land was counted, no matter what the number of plows, males, etc. If there were, say, 50 shares in a quantified-share *mushā'* and each share included three dunums, a change in nonland units belonging to a household—the number of plows, *faddāns, dhukūrs,* etc.—would not affect that household's portion in the land.[7]

Although, as Haim Gerber put it, "the history of the institution [*mushāʿ*] is extremely obscure,"[8] there is a tendency to view the open-ended *mushāʿ* as the original form from which the quantified-share *mushāʿ* emerged.[9] The fact that there were quantified-share *mushāʿ* in which shares were called *faddān*s seems to support this claim.[10] According to Ya'akov Firestone, there was an economic reason for this changing pattern—land scarcity. Based largely on his study of Ottoman and Mandate Palestine, he maintains that because land became scarce, due to a greater increase in population than in cultivated land (technological change was negligible at that time), the open-ended *mushāʿ* changed into quantified-share. In this respect, land registration hemmed in the village because the cultivation of additional plots was more difficult. He speculates that registration itself did not lead to quantification, since deeds could be given for shares.[11]

For Brigit Schaelber, the *mushāʿ*'s "logic has to be sought in a realm other than economics . . . it is rather the very expression of the community."[12] She thus suggests indirectly that the origins of *mushāʿ* "irrationality" lay in the peasants' culture and ingrained conservatism, as British policymakers had concluded. She argues that in the Hawran highlands, "the events that caused the transition from 'open-ended' to 'fixed-share' redistribution are . . . political"[13]—namely, that greedy sheikhs tried, and to some extent succeeded, in manipulating the *mushāʿ* system in such a way that they were allotted the better lands. Moreover, this attempt by the sheikhs to seize *mushāʿ* lands encouraged other shareowners to divide their lands permanently, hoping to retain rights to the property. She maintains that the Ottoman land registration in the name of individuals (i.e., not in the manner described by Firestone) also encouraged partition and, furthermore, that distribution continued for a certain period after registration.[14]

Nevertheless, this does not prove Schaelber's argument that the logic of the *mushāʿ* had nothing to do with economics, and her own case study reveals an ambiguous division between politics and economics. Those who had shares in the *mushāʿ* acted exactly as might be expected from rational economic actors, so it is difficult to maintain that the realm of economics did not influence their activities in any way. The peasants moved to change *mushāʿ* lands into *mafrūz* (permanent partition of plots) only when there was a need to ensure continuity of property rights and access to the means of production. Before that, under the *mushāʿ* system, these were already sustained. This in itself indicates that economic reasoning was incorporated into the *mushāʿ*. The *mushāʿ* was also connected to various out-of-village political-economic forces, such as the avaricious sheikhs mentioned above; and the decision to register land was aimed above all at increasing production and the Ottoman government's income.[15] *Mushāʿ* therefore should not be viewed as unrelated to economics; a wider perspective (here, political-economic) can help to throw light on the system, its creation, its modification, and even its termination.

There is a tendency to see equality as inherent in the open-ended *mushāʿ*.[16] But as Martha Mundy observed, the level of equality is not always certain, since real equality is based on equality of income in terms of money or kind.[17] It should be understood, however, that certain subtypes of the open-ended *mushāʿ* could even increase inequality: based on a *faddān* unit, a household could be left without any land at all if its plow was broken, and according to the *dhukūr* system, as the following Arab proverb refers, "a father of daughters is a poor man [*miskīn abū al-banāt*]."[18]

Thus, any investigation into the equality of the open-ended system needs to pay attention to its different subtypes. As for the quantified-share *mushāʿ*, given that it was not built on ratios such as land/labor, land/males, or land/mouths (the latter typified the Russian commune),[19] it can be said that it was not organized on the principle of equalization.

In a sense, there were likely to be fewer variations in the quantified-share *mushā‘*, since distribution was solely according to the amount of land (and not according to men, plows, etc.). Nevertheless, there were variations in this system. In ‘Ain-Mu‘ammariya lands (Jordan), for example, quantified-share *mushā‘* was part of a more complicated system in which village lands were divided into two areas: grazing and cultivated lands. These were swapped each year, so that the area previously cultivated became grazing lands, and vice versa, and the cultivated area was also redistributed every year.[20] Here, the possession of herds determined a "modified" system of *mushā‘*.

It would seem that the primary group associated with *mushā‘* was the village.[21] This was not the case in Mandate Palestine, however, where the group could consist of people who were from a few villages or a single village or who were linked to a *ḥamūla* or to some smaller, usually family-linked association (discussed below).[22]

There were also differences in the frequency of distribution. Mundy suggests that this was related primarily to different geographical settings and livestock ownership.[23] She stresses the necessity to understand that *mushā‘* was not a uniform system across the Levant:

> We should be wary of reifying the notion of *mushā‘*: at issue is not a uniform system of tenure but an idiom of cultivators for thinking of relations within the village, to the fisc and to land, in terms of shares. On the ground in villages with most land held in shares, we find variety in the actual patterns of laying out land, the crop rotations, the collective disciplines in production, the organization of animal production, and the articulation of men and women to domestic and descent groups. The challenge is to understand how such socio-economic structures differed systematically between micro-regions.[24]

So far, the discussion suggests that although there was a common "essence" of *mushā‘* land tenure, there were wide-ranging varieties, or "divisions" and "sub-divisions" of it. Even in the quantified-share type—a system that apparently embodied fewer variations—much diversity can be found. The reason for the emergence of different variations is not always clear. Still, the many forms do not indicate that the logic of *mushāʿ* has to be sought in a realm other than economics.'[25] The reasons for the pattern changing from open-ended to quantified-share *mushāʿ* can be found in political economics or even in pure economics. The explanations of geographical aspects and livestock ownership determining different varieties of *mushāʿ* highlight a certain level of economic motivation, toward maximization (the appropriate use of geographical location to increase production and revenue) and innovation (the modified system required for animal husbandry). Still, the many diversities emphasise the need to study both the economic and the noneconomic aspects of the *mushāʿ*, to look at specific areas (such as Mandate Palestine), and then to use the findings as a basis for comparison.

CHARACTERISTICS OF THE *MUSHĀʿ* IN MANDATE PALESTINE

Despite the existence of subtypes, Mandate Palestine's *mushāʿ* lands shared many characteristics. They were primarily quantified-share.[26] The determined period for redistribution was usually two years,[27] although variations existed,[28] and a shareholder was customarily allotted plots that were different from those he had held before.[29] A shareholder was entitled to diverse categories of land. In Deir Ed Dubban, for example, shareholders were entitled to plots in two different areas of the village, one more appropriate to summer crops and the other to winter crops. In other cases, the division was according to irrigated and nonirrigated lands, types of soil, and so forth.[30] It is worth mentioning that while the main basis of crop rotation in Palestine was the two-year system (a year with a summer crop and a year with a winter crop),[31] *mushāʿ* does not seem to have discouraged crop rotation. A farmer knew that his yield would not be high if he cultivated the same crop in two successive years.

Information that I gathered in interviews in Galilee with people engaged in the Arab rural economy indicates that the *dār* (household) was mostly connected to a *mushā'* held by the *ahl* and/or by the *ḥamūla*.[32] These modes of association were not a matter of chance; the patrilineal socioeconomic structure of the *fallāḥīn* served to reduce risk.[33] Also pertinent is Shukrī 'Āraf's observation of *mushā'* being held together by the people of a few villages, or a single village, or a *ḥamūla* or some smaller association[34] (possibly of the *ahl* type). These challenge the overemphasis in the literature on the *ḥamūla*.[35]

BRITISH INTERPRETATIONS AND THE RESULTANT REFORM

Ernest Dowson, who designed the land-settlement program in Palestine, admitted that the British obligation to the Jews accelerated the need for a new order in land registration.[36] This, however, was not the main reason for initiating the land settlement policy. Dowson, formerly the financial adviser and director-general of surveys to the government of Egypt, believed in the need to combine land settlement (the examination and registration of rights to land by cadastral methods) and land reform (in this case the partition of *mushā'* lands and consolidation of plots), hoping that this would ease investment and hence the development of lands,[37] and facilitate the replacement of the Ottoman tax system. He argued that the tax system, based mainly on a tithe, provided too little information for efficient collection and "was excessive in amount, economically vicious in principle and operated most vexatious[ly] and inequitably."[38] In regard to the *fallāḥ*, Dowson believed that land registration, along with the partition of the *mushā'*—which was regarded as "a most serious handicap on economic development"—would significantly improve the *fallāḥ*'s economic condition:

> Owing to the failure of the Land Registers there was no security right to land, no basis for economical borrowing for agricultural needs, and uncertain encroachments both on public and private domain. . . . The periodic re-appointment of village lands, so widely practised in accordance with the system known as mesha‘ [*mushā*‘], was a most serious handicap on the economic development of the country and the improvement of the position of the peasantry.[39]

Dowson needed no more than a three-day visit to Palestine to formulate the scheme:

> It is necessary to summarise briefly the position as it existed when I first visited Palestine for three days in November 1923, at the invitation of Sir Herbert Samuel [the High Commissioner for Palestine at that time], as well as the steps subsequently taken. My original impressions were outlined in a letter dated 9th November of that year to the Chief Secretary, the late Sir Gilbert Clayton. This was followed up on the 7th December followed by some fuller "Notes on Land Tax, Cadastral Survey and Land Settlement."[40]

Dowson's conclusions and recommendations were accepted by the Mandate government. They were even enhanced in the Johnson-Crosbie report, where the advice to abolish the *mushā*‘ by partition was buttressed by the notion that *mushā*‘ lands "could not be developed":

> Under this system the village lands are divided into the requisite number of shares, and each shareholder is allotted the number of shares or the fraction of a share to which he is entitled. At the end of a prescribed period—usually two years [administered by the elders of the village], to suit the crop rotation—the shares are re-allocated, and each shareholder moved to a fresh holding. Consequently, no one has any inducement to improve his land. . . . while it remains, it is useless to expect that land will be weeded or fertilised, that trees will be planted, or, in a word, that any development will take place. . . . no improvements can take place in something like half of the area of the country until the musha‘ system of tenure is abolished.[41]

Lewis French, the first director of the Development Department, was deeply involved with Land Department activities in 1931.[42] Worried by the slow progress of the formal procedure of land settlement and the tendency of the *fallāḥīn* to prefer "over-parcelling," French suggested encouraging the partition of the land by agreement: "Almost any partition, however officially bad, is better than no partition at all,"[43] he declared. Still, C. F. Strickland of the Indian Civil Service, who came to advise the Mandate government on the introduction of a system of agricultural cooperation, criticized a case of agreed settlement because it resulted in "over-parcelling":

> The holdings of the cultivators consist at the present, in the majority of cases, of a number of scattered strips and patches of land in all directions around a village. The system of inheritance also tends to a progressive sub-division of each holding. It is clear that this fragmentation and sub-division materially reduces the value of the *fellah*'s [*fallāḥ*'s] holding as a working farm. . . . The allotment of strips at Samakh is a striking instance of the evil which results from following the wishes of the people. The partitioning officer, being associated with a committee with which he had to reach agreement, was unable to carry out a radical plan of re-allotment, and though he reduced the number to four strips for each person, the strips are of enormous length, and I found one measuring 2,150 metres from end to end and 4½ metres in width. The lie of the land does not appear to necessitate this curious elongation; it is merely the result of old habit and prejudice. The Land Settlement Ordinance gives the Settlement Officer considerable powers to reject a scheme put forward by the people, if unsatisfactory, and to insist on a better scheme of his own.[44]

The registration of *mushā‘*, if not partitioned by agreement between the villagers and the settlement officer, entailed the collection of information about the value of the various plots belonging to a *mushā‘*, the crops it was possible to grow on each plot and the shares of the owners.[45] After an "improved division" of the land had been proposed, there were certain levels of appeal to the courts or to the officers responsible for land settlement, until a final decision could be taken. The numerous disputes about the partition of *mushāʿ* lands suggest that agreed partitions must have been limited in number. These were the main reasons for the slow progress of land settlement and explain why the settled area in 1947 amounted to no more than 50 percent of the villages.[46]

Land registration after settlement was expensive, amounting to about 3 percent of the land's value.[47] During registration the price of land tended to become much higher than its agricultural value because the process was proceeding simultaneously with the rising demand for land for Jewish national purposes.[48] Registration fees for small plots were higher than those paid for large ones. In May 1946, for example, the landowners of the village of Mujeidil were required to pay 250 mils per dunum for the registration of small plots (two dunums or less), and only 120 mils per dunum for plots larger than two dunums. The villagers could pay either in one sum or by installments, which added 20 percent to the total cost.[49] The fees for registration of two dunums amounted to at least one-third of the *gross* income per dunum of wheat.[50] The higher fees for small plots were intended as an incentive to consolidate. But it also meant that the cost of registration weighed more heavily on the poor, whose entire property was one small holding.

Toward the end of the Mandate, the government claimed that land settlement was the most important measure taken to increase agricultural productivity[51] and that "the feeling of security which derives from a good title has promoted development in areas where stagnation had long prevailed."[52] It is my intention to demonstrate that land settlement, far from bringing about this dramatic positive shift, instead had negative results.

INSTITUTIONAL CHANGE AND THE *MUSHĀʿ*

In the introduction, we saw that while North tends to give greater weight to economic outcomes varying as a result of institutional change, Ruttan and Hayami's theory of induced institutional innovation pays more attention to economic incentives leading to institutional change. Firestone's argument that the shift of *mushāʿ* from open-ended to quantified-share was induced by changes in relative factor scarcities (land-labor ratios) is consistent with the theory of induced institutional innovation. According to Firestone, this change occurred as a response to local demand from *mushāʿ* shareholders (i.e., the innovations happened endogenously).[53] This may imply that an endogenous process occurred, in the manner described by the induced institutional innovation theory.

However, most of the literature on the *mushāʿ* in Mandate Palestine regarded it as an institution that was dependent on an archaic path that was inherited from past agreements and was in need of replacement by the more permanent *mafrūz*. Such a change, it was argued, should stimulate investment and development.[54]

In general, scholars have viewed the *mushāʿ* as an example of North's path-dependent institution, and agree that there was a need for institutional change to promote development. Also—in accordance with the theory of induced institutional innovation—that there was a demand for an institutional change from *mushāʿ* into *mafrūz* land tenure. However, there is no agreement on whether this change had to be done exogenously by the government or done endogenously by the members of the *mushāʿ*. Those who oppose intervention have maintained that a significant reduction of the area under *mushāʿ* was happening through an endogenous mechanism in which *mushāʿ* lands became *mafrūz*.[55] Others have tended to argue that although some replacement could have occurred endogenously to achieve a massive change the government had to intervene.[56]

Neither is there any clear consensus on the extent to which *mushāʿ* was practiced or on a systematically endogenous process that caused its diminishing incidence. Scholars have tended to view the diminution of *mushāʿ* as resulting both from endogenous and exogenous processes. According to Raphael Patai (1947), "in 1917 . . . about 70% of the villages' lands were still cultivated under the musha'a system. . . . circa 1940 only about 25% of the village lands remained musha'a."[57] Patai's sources for these figures are not known, but his underlying assumption is that some endogenous change took place in parallel with land settlement (which was not implemented throughout the country; see Map 6.1). On the basis of Patai's doubtful evidence (compare, for example, his estimate for 1917 with the following returns for 1923), Kamen argues that the *mushā'* was declining—and not only because of land settlement. He declares that the "disadvantages for the development of cultivation, which had been noted by foreign observers, were also evident to the peasants."[58] Both Patai and Kamen therefore seem to assume that there must have been a diminishing incidence of *mushā'* because it was in the interest of all parties to replace it with *mafrūz,* while at the same time inferring that the government's land reform was very welcome.

Only two comprehensive inquiries into *mushā'* have furnished estimates. These were the Musha' Committee of 1923 and the Johnson-Crosbie report of 1930, which covered "cultivable lands" of about 3,876,000 and 1,070,000 dunums, respectively. A comparison of these two investigations shows a reduction in the proportion of land under *mushā',* from 56 percent in 1923 to 44 percent in 1930. The Johnson-Crosbie Committee, aware that its results "show a rather lower proportion than the former *mushā'* land," explained that the "result is affected by the large proportion of villages in the Northern District and Jerusalem Division (80 out of 104), where the proportion [of *mushā'* land] is much lower than [in] the Southern District." The investigators concluded that "from a comparison of the two sets of estimates, it may be summarised that something like half of the cultivable land of the country is *musha'*."[59] According to an early survey (1923) in the Gaza and Rafah area, only 23 percent of the land was under *mushā'*.[60] This estimate is much lower than that of the 1923 Musha' Committee of the same year. Hence, there is insufficient evidence to support the argument for an endogenous, one-way process (i.e., only a diminution of *mushā'*).

In my interviews, villagers referred to cultivated land as *mushāʿ* (or *mashāʿ* in colloquial Arabic[61]), but they also spoke of their grazing lands as *mushāʿ*.[62] Al-ḥusayni mentioned grazing lands being entitled as *mushāʿ*, in addition to forests and threshing floors.[63] Shukrī ʿĀraf described cases of villagers naming their *mafrūz* lands as *mushāʿ al-balad* (the *mushāʿ* of the village).[64] It is not known if the estimates of *mushāʿ* refer only to the investigated system or also to grazing, *mafrūz,* and other lands. It is therefore doubtful if even the figure of 50 percent *mushāʿ* lands is accurate.

Information gathered in interviews suggests that there were instances of *mafrūz* being changed into *mushāʿ*.[65] The 1944 survey of five unnamed Arab villages gives some support to these testimonies. The land settlement of one of these villages, "Village A," took place in 1934. The 1944 survey 10 years later indicated that 295 dunums (4.47 percent of the village lands) were held in *mushāʿ*. These were divided between seven *mushāʿ* groups: two with two members (with 12 and 86 dunums, respectively), one with five members (with 72 dunums in total), and four groups of six and more members (with 11, 16, 22, and 31 dunums, respectively).[66] Land settlement, then, did not end the practice of *mushāʿ*, but it reduced its incidence.

However, when dealing with *endogenous* mechanisms, it is no less likely that the overall effect was not to diminish the incidence of *mushāʿ* but rather to increase it. *Mushāʿ* was a living institution, and, contrary to Kamen's argument, the disadvantages that "had been noted by foreign observers" were not necessarily "evident to the peasants." *Fallāḥīn* did not tend to ask the government to intervene in breaking up the *mushāʿ*. In fact, nowhere in my reading (including village correspondence with the government and with the Arab Higher Committee in the Israel State Archives) did I come across such a case. This, from the perspective of rational choice, throws doubt on the claim that *mushāʿ* was predominantly inefficient.

It has been noted above that endogenous institutional change was not one-directional; *mafrūz* changed into *mushāʿ* and vice versa. Also, that the database is insufficient to determine the overall direction of the endogenous process. Could it be that the theory of induced institutional innovation is irrelevant to the one-directional change from *mushāʿ* to *mafrūz* in Mandate Palestine, given that no change was needed because the institution was already efficient? In fact, the endogenous creation of new *mushāʿ* implies efficiency, according to this theory.

CONSIDERATION OF THE HALF-EMPTY, HALF-FULL GLASS

As noted, the British saw only disadvantages in *mushāʿ*, especially in its unsuitability for investment and its waste of resources through overparcelling. These and related considerations are now discussed.

Firestone was the first to challenged the inadequacy of the investment paradigm, while advocating (indirectly) the induced institutional innovation theory. He argued that there were investment options in "*mushāʿ* villages" (villages in which *mushāʿ* was widely practiced). According to Firestone, investment occurred *only* as a result of the transfer of *mushāʿ* lands into *mafrūz,* a transfer that happened endogenously in association with the shift to cash-crop-oriented farming or, less often, when land was required for trade with nonvillagers.[67] Hence, as long as land remained *mushāʿ*, no investment could be made: "In the key areas of investment and improvement . . . ownership and enterprise were as a rule individual in the first place, and not subject to equalisation, in the *mushāʿ* communities."[68] However, this approach is erroneous, as suggested even in Firestone's own study. He argues that most or all of the plots were *mushāʿ* in the Ottoman period and that on such land no investment was made. But an analysis of maps of rural Palestine in the nineteenth century, especially of the hill country, shows that many plots were covered by fruit trees.[69] These trees, and especially the predominant olive, had been planted for several thousand years.[70] This clearly challenges the idea that "no one [had] any inducement to improve his land. . . . while [the *mushāʿ*] remains, it is useless to expect that land will be weeded or fertilised, that trees will be planted, or, in a word, that any development will take place.'[71]

I agree with Firestone that investment was possible in *mushāʿ* villages, but for an entirely different reason. Investment was enabled not only by endogenous *ifrāz* (transforming land to *mafrūz*), but was possible both on *mushāʿ* and *mafrūz* lands. My interviews shed light on two ways in which *mushāʿ* lands were improved. The first was joint investment by the members. In the case of tree planting, all members made the decision to plant, and the investment was shared, as well as the yield in due course.[72] The second was when a shareholder in a *mushāʿ* wanted to make an individual investment. He would ask his fellow members to give him a permanent plot. They would either agree on a permanent division or would arrange a *qurʿa,* a lottery, to decide it[73] (this was different from the *qurʿa* conducted from time to time to decide temporary division—in effect, a redistribution).[74] In practical terms, it was a transition of land from *mushāʿ* into *mafrūz,* although the land continued to be called *mushāʿ* and to retain its formal ownership.

In unusual cases where no agreement was reached on permanent division, disputes ensued. The person might then decide on his own investment (such as the planting of trees), without receiving authorization from the other members. He knew, as they did, that uprooting his trees would bring about violence and even *faṣṣād*s (revenge killings). A solution could finally be found by agreeing to compensation.[75] It would be a mistake to argue that disputes were inherent in the *mushāʿ* and that this institution should therefore be uprooted. Rather, the origin of the *mushāʿ* was traced back in some interviews to cases where the lands of an ancestor were inherited by his masculine heirs, who, instead of dividing the lands permanently, agreed to own the property jointly.[76] This illustrates a fundamental advantage of the *mushāʿ*: it helped to avoid disputes within families over the parcelling of inherited land (i.e., it reduced unnecessary risk). It was not surprising that in the process of trying to overturn *mushā'* by land reform, many more conflicts emerged.[77]

Two anthropologists, Rosemary Sayigh and Scott Atran, have pointed to the advantages of the institution of *mushā'* and explained why the so-called overparcelling was wise economically. Atran gives examples of risk spreading in the event of natural hazards or raids. The possession of plots separated one from another may also have been seen as an advantage by the *fallāḥīn* because they could cultivate summer crops and winter crops in the most appropriate places, thus making better use of land and labor.[78]

Sayigh raises the issue of the Islamic inheritance law, which requires the division of land (or shares, in the case of *mushā'*) among the inheritors. In a land-scarce economy, this division increases the ratio of labor to land.[79] In addition, *mushā'*, integrated as it was into the patrilineal economic structure, facilitated a highly efficient use of labor. Given the trust among members of an *ahl,* the owner of a small plot could rent his share to a fellow member and find full-time occupation off the land, while still receiving a portion of the produce.[80]

It can be concluded, therefore, that the British looked at the half-empty glass and were unaware that even that half was rather full. Investment on *mushā'* was indeed possible. This could be done either collectively or individually. Further, *mushā'* was not in opposition to *mafrūz,* and the two systems coexisted. Lands were transformed from *mushā'* into *mafrūz* and the other way round. The waste of time in overparcelling (because of the logistics of moving from one parcel to another) was offset by the benefits of working a number of parcels. The *fallāḥīn* saw an advantage in having several plots, rather than a single consolidated one (because of a better use of land and greater spread of risk). In addition, *mushā'* reinforced the patrilineal economic system that served to reduce risk as well as to increase labor efficiency. It also seems that the fewer the incidences of *ifrāz,* the fewer the disputes over inheritance.

The *mushāʿ* system in Palestine thus differed considerably from what the Mandatory government believed. In particular, it did not have the disadvantages ascribed to it. Certainly, it was incorrect that "no improvements [could] take [place] . . . until the mushaʿ system of tenure is abolished."[81] On the contrary, there were many advantages in allowing this system to flourish. Even so, one might wish to argue that although the government was mistaken, some of its activities were successful (e.g., the land reform attracted relatively more investment than would otherwise have been the case). The next task therefore is to try to assess the impact of land reform on the *fallāḥīn.*

DID LAND SETTLEMENT HELP DEVELOPMENT?

The data collected for tax purposes as *Village Statistics*[82] help to assess the influence of land settlement on investment in Arab farms. These two surveys of villages in Palestine that were undertaken in 1935 and 1945 provide information about the number of dunums in the villages under 16 categories of land quality (see Table 2.2). Generally, the movement of a piece of land from one category to another between these two benchmark years may be taken as a proxy for investment on that land. If between 1935 and 1945 additional capital was invested in, say, 100 dunums in a village and those lands became better irrigated, more fully planted or benefited from the removal of stones, for example, then one could expect that in the second survey the 100 dunums would have been classified in a higher category. Changes in categories of land thus reveal changes in investment.

In general, as shown in Table 2.2, the lower the land category, the higher the development. This is especially clear for Categories 5 to 16. Categories 1 and 2 (citrus) reflected a highly intensive irrigated crop. Yet because during World War II citrus trees were uprooted and the land converted to irrigated vegetables,[83] a change from categories 1 or 2 to 5 does not automatically mean that the land was underdeveloped. Bananas (category 3) were an insignificant crop and therefore ignored in the later comparison. Finally, any change in category 4 from one period to the next does not indicate a change in investment in agriculture. Not all categories are distinguished in the *Village Statistics*. Categories 1 and 2, 5 to 8, 9 to 13, and 14 to 15 are combined. Hence, a change in the quality of land from, say, 10 to 9 cannot be seen, but a change from 9 to 8 can be. The data provide an indication of investment but not in detail.

To assess the level of change caused by land settlement, a comparison is now made between the level of investment (using tax categories as a proxy for investment) in villages where land settlement was undertaken and the level in villages where it was not. Information about the settlement dates for villages was taken from maps and sketches. Maps showing the progress of land settlement up to December 1945 and sketches of progress up to 1935 and 1937 make it possible to recognize most of the villages that were "surveyed" (in many instances, the least problematic of them were "settled") or "settled" (i.e., all disputes were officially settled, and it was assumed that no lands remained under *mushā'*)[84] up to 1935, without indications for specific years. This procedure also gives some indications of the villages settled during 1935 to 1937 and 1937 to 1945.[85] More recent sketches provided by Gavish contributed to the mapping inquiry.[86]

If the reform had been the very significant "lift" for development, via increased investment, that Dowson and others believed, then settled lands would have been improved and unsettled ones would not. Or in less black-and-white terms, settled lands would have shown faster improvement than unsettled ones. Hence, if Dowson was correct, a comparison of investment during 1935 to 1945 in villages that were settled (i.e., not the merely the surveyed ones) before 1935 with those that were not would show faster development in the settled villages (remembering that there were *mafrūz* lands in unsettled villages as well). If the reform was indeed a lift, then the most striking figures should be found in the comparison between those villages that were surveyed and settled during 1935 to 1937 and the unsettled ones. If the reforms were necessary, then massive investment would have followed on lands that had previously been "blocked from development," on the assumption that an owner had waited for reform on his co-owned land to invest. In this context, it is worth mentioning that incomes on *fallāḥīn* farms increased significantly during the 1940s,[87] and more money became available for investment. Data about the actual year of settlement between 1937 and 1945 are unclear and have not been used, so that the criterion is lands settled either before 1935 or during 1935 to 1937.

A cross-sectional comparison between settled and nonsettled lands is inadequate for this case study. Indeed, as Map 6.1 indicates, land settlement was much more intensive on the plains. This was chiefly because there was pressure on the authorities to settle as much land as possible. Given the surveying techniques in use at that time, the plains were the area where the investigation had been carried out fastest, and the surveyors therefore preferred to deal with those areas, as they would provide a more productive picture to the government. Even so, they progressed more slowly than expected, to a large extent because of the need to solve disputes over land in the villages. The plains therefore remained the major settled areas in the Mandate period.[88] But they were also the areas most suitable for irrigation because wells bored there could reach underground water.[89] If the settled plains are compared with the unsettled hills in a cross-sectional manner, the results might identify some differences, but these can be attributed to geographical variations rather than to land settlement.

Since it was not feasible to compare all the settled villages in Palestine with all the unsettled ones, settled Arab villages were compared with neighboring unsettled Arab villages, in areas where there were few geographical differences (e.g., settled villages in a hilly area with others in the same area). To avoid bias, only villages that bordered an investigated village were included. These provide a much more accurate comparison but narrow

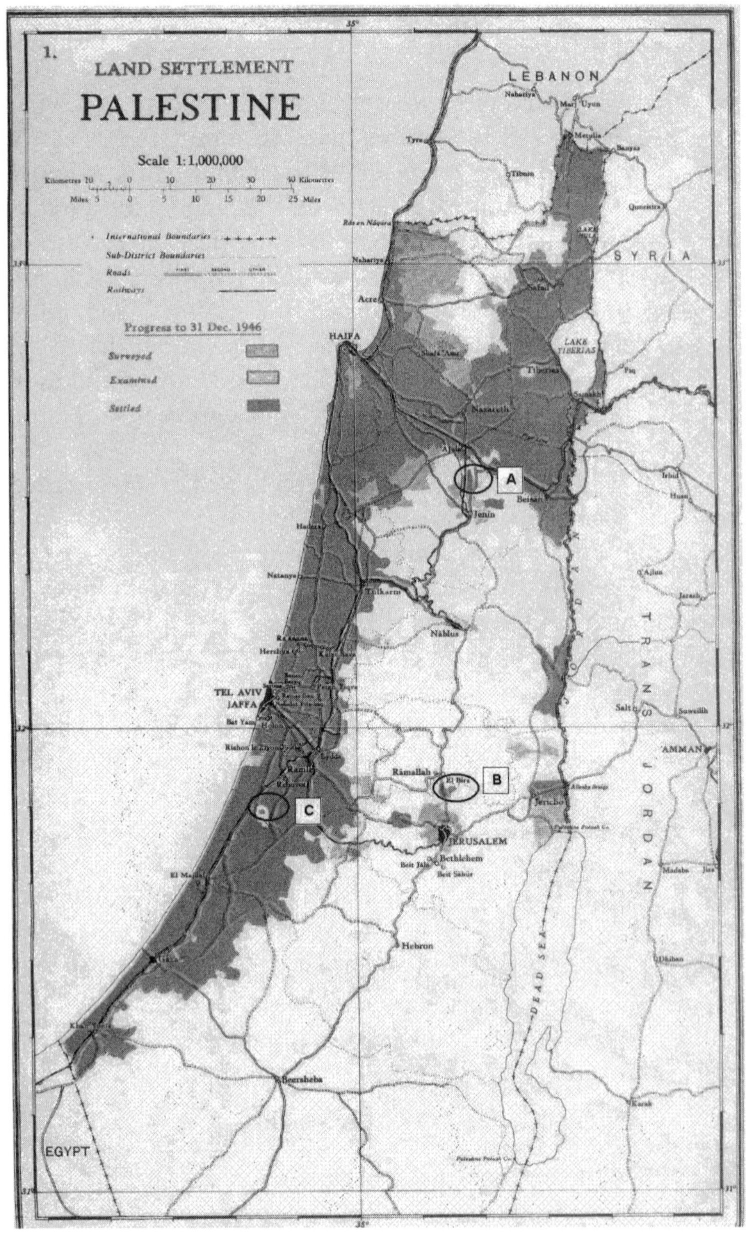

Map 6.1 Progress of Land Settlement, 1946

Source: Government of Palestine, Commissioner for Lands and Surveys, *Annual Report 1946.*[90]

the discussion to specific case studies. Hence the number of observations is limited (although all cases found have been used).

Noncomparable cases, where the quantity of land belonging to the village changed significantly between 1935 and 1945, also had to be eliminated. In Beit Qad (southeast of Muquibila), for example, a settled village in the hill country surrounded by unsettled villages, there was an unexplained increase of 11.2 percent in village lands in the period 1935 to 1945. Similarly, in Idnibba (southeast of Bash-Shit), a settled village with two adjacent unsettled villages, there was an increase in the village lands of 37.1 percent. Information about the villages that were selected, before elimination, is given in Table 6.2 at the end of this chapter.

Case A (Hill Country)

Muquibila was already settled in 1935, unlike El-Yamun, Kafar Dan, Jalama, and Sandala, the surrounding villages, which were not settled during the Mandate period (the group of villages in this category is marked A in Map 6.1). If Dowson and Simpson were right, one would expect more investment in Muquibiliya than in the surrounding villages because in the latter "no one [had] any inducement to improve his land . . . [and] it is useless to expect that improvements can take place."[91] But as can be seen in Table 6.1 (also in Table 6.2), there were no significant investments in either the settled or the unsettled areas. Paradoxically, the opposite of what was expected by the reformers occurred. While there was no development on the settled lands (in fact, there was even some—albeit relatively insignificant—underdevelopment of the settled village lands), there were certain indications of investment in unsettled villages (especially Kafar Dan and Jalama; see Table 6.2), where lands were transferred from categories 9 to 13 to categories 5 to 8.

Case B (Hill Country)

The village of Judeira was surveyed and settled during 1935 and 1937, unlike its neighbors. Hence, if land settlement had a

Table 6.1 Total Trend of Changes (Settled Versus Unsettled), in Percentages

	Categories 1–2	Category 3	Categories 5–8	Categories 9–13	Categories 14–15	Uncultivable	Built on Area	Roads, etc.	In Jewish Hands
Hill case A (S)	0	0	0	−0.46	0	−0.08	0	+0.55	0
Hill case A (U)	0	0	+0.69	−0.7	0	−0.01	0	0	0
Hill case B (S)	0	0	+0.88	0	−0.98	+0.44	−0.1	0	−0.24
Hill case B (U)	0	0	+0.18	−0.81	−3.75	+3.78	−0.05	+0.14	+0.51
Valley case C (S)	+0.16	0	+0.16	−6.84	0	−0.13	0	+0.16	+6.5
Valley case C (U)	−0.02	0	+0.02	0	0	0	0	0	0

Note: Settled villages are designated *S*, and unsettled villages *U*.

strong impact on investment, then Judeira should show a very significant change, as it "waited to be rescued by land settlement" (unlike the surrounding villages of Er-Ram, Rafat, Bir Nabalah, and Kafar 'Aqab). But again, apart from a very small transfer of lands from categories 14 and 15 to categories 9 to 13, there is no sign of investment in the settled village. On the contrary, there is an indication of some transfer from categories 14 and 15 to category 16 (uncultivable), seemingly representing underdevelopment of lands. But neither is there any indication of investment in the unsettled villages.

An interim conclusion from the hill-country examples (A and B) is that new investment was insignificant on both settled and unsettled lands and that these case studies show no change in the level of investment between settled and unsettled villages. In sum, the massive investment intended to be released by land reform did not occur.

Case C (Coastal Plain)

Bash-Shit village was not settled until 1945, unlike its comparable neighboring villages Yasur and El-Mughar, which were settled before 1935. As with cases A and B, significant signs of investment were not seen in either settled or unsettled villages. The only significant feature that case C furnishes is that in the settled villages many lands were transferred into Jewish hands, unlike in the unsettled ones.

The three examples point in the same direction. First, they give additional support to the earlier argument that, contrary to the belief of the reformers and scholars, there is no evidence that land settlement led to more investment. Another noticeable feature is that no substantial changes in investment on Arab farms and no major shift into intensive farming occurred from the mid-1930s to the mid-1940s[92] or, more specifically, during the prosperity of World War II. The most significant finding is that in case C, the only one from the coastal plain, about 6.5 percent of the settled lands were transferred into Jewish ownership. This

Table 6.2 Base Data for Cases A, B, and C

	Categories 1–2	Category 3	Categories 5–8	Categories 9–13	Categories 14–15	Category 16	Built on Area	Roads, etc.	In Jewish Possession	Total	Change in percent 35–45
Case A											
Muquibila, 35 (S)	0	0	194	6,454	0	349	12	119	0	7,128	
Muquibila, 45 (S)	0	0	194	6,421	0	343	12	158	0	7,128	0
El-Yamun, 35	0	0	6,636	11,191	0	2,413	58	63	0	20,361	
El-Yamun, 45	0	0	6,636	11,191	0	2,413	58	63	0	20361	0
Kafr Dan, 35	5	0	2,510	3,919	50	771	37	36	0	7,328	
Kafr Dan, 45	5	0	2,680	3,749	50	774	34	36	0	7,328	0
djustrightJalama, 35	0	0	0	4,863	0	897	15	52	0	5,827	
Jalama, 45	0	0	86	4,777	0	897	15	52	0	5,827	0
Sandala, 35	0	0	2	3,109	0	99	7	32	0	3,249	
Sandala, 45	0	0	2	3,109	0	99	7	32	0	3,249	0
Taken Out:											
El-Mazar, 35	0	0	125	5,325	104	9,434	9	29	0	15,026	
El-Mazar, 45	0	0	229	5,221	0	9,013	9	29	0	14,501	−3.5
Ti'inik, 35	0	0	360	18,973	0	387	4	115	2,690	22,529	
Ti'inik, 45	0	0	194	2,726	0	3,707	0	0	0	6,627	−70.6

Case B											
Judeira, 35 (S)	0	0	235	1,080	254	424	9	1	41	2,044	
Judeira, 45 (S)	0	0	253	1,080	234	433	7	1	36	2,044	0
Er-Ram, 35	0	0	427	781	2,100	1,782	20	14	450	5,574	
Er-Ram, 45	0	0	441	782	1,509	2,364	14	39	449	5,598	0.4
Rafat, 35	0	0	582	911	1,136	1,123	21	4	0	3,777	
Rafat, 45	0	0	582	912	1,053	1,205	21	4	0	3,777	0
parBir Nabalah, 35	0	0	963	529	318	652	24	3	147	2,636	
Bir Nabalah, 45	0	0	962	408	375	689	21	4	233	2,692	2.1
Kafar ‘Aqab, 35	0	0	809	574	2,221	1,897	10	30	0	5,541	
Kafar ‘Aqab, 45	0	0	829	553	2,183	1,862	10	30	5	5,472	−1.3
Taken Out:											
Beit Hanina, 35	0	0	1,505	848	989	2,015	30	6	0	5,393	
Beit Hanina, 45	0	0	3,072	4,300	4	7,353	219	86	805	15,839	193.6
Case C											
Bash-Shit, 35	70	0	647	17,558	0	205	58	15	0	18,553	
Bash-Shit, 45	66	0	651	17,558	0	205	58	15	0	18,553	0
Yasur, 35 (S)	505	0	174	12,752	0	223	35	321	2,379	16,389	
Yasur, 45 (S)	636	0	180	12,173	0	173	35	322	2,871	16,390	0
El-Mughar, 35 (S)	1,850	0	41	10,856	0	1,186	31	338	1,088	15,390	
El-Mughar, 45 (S)	1,772	0	86	9,261	0	1,194	31	387	2,659	15,390	0

Note: Settled villages are designated *S*, and unsettled villages *U*.

presumably reflected transactions made between April 1935 (the first survey for *Village Statistics*)[93] and the Land Transfer Regulation in February 1940, which prohibited any further transfer of land from Arabs to Jews in the coastal plain.[94]

INCREASED JEWISH LAND PURCHASE IN SETTLED AREAS

In Chapter 1, we saw that the *fallāḥīn* were significantly disadvantaged by Jewish land purchase, especially the poorest *fallāḥīn*—the tenants. They also lost their jobs in times of higher unemployment, which continued until the prosperity of the 1940s. Certainly, a large proportion of the land sold was not in *fallāḥīn* ownership, but Arab lands on the whole were not improved as a consequence of Jewish land purchase.

We have noted that Jews preferred to buy plots from big owners and that when the availability of large estates diminished as a result of progressive land purchase, they targeted owners of smaller estates. When buying smaller plots, Jews preferred to buy *mafrūz* rather than *mushā'* land, the latter being regarded as a complicated and expensive purchase[95] to the degree that "the *masha'a* system removed large areas of Palestine from the [Jewish acquisition] market."[96] Indeed, the Jewish share of Palestine's *mushā'* lands was negligible compared with that of *mafrūz* lands,[97] since unless they bought 100 percent of the shares (especially of large estates), it was virtually impossible to create a Jewish settlement. Arab participants in *mushā'* were usually unwilling to let Jews establish a permanent plot from *mushā'* purchases. The transfer of a large plot into Jewish hands meant the erection of a Jewish settlement, prohibiting further use of that land by Arabs. Thus, it was in the personal interest of many of the *mushā'* shareholders to object to such transfers because they also worked on the lands of others (according to the Johnson-Crosbie investigation, about 65 percent of landowners were additionally employed on the farms of others),[98] in addition to their obligations to their *ahl* or *ḥamūla* relatives in the village (who could likewise be damaged by such a transfer). In addition, assisting Jewish settlement was regarded as immoral at a national level and was risky as well.[99] There were thus serious disincentives for participants in the *mushā'* to allow Jews to engage in *ifrāz,* and this was a considerable deterrent to Jewish land purchase.

Mushā', in conjunction with the institution of the *waqf,* a nonnegotiable religious endowment, hindered the sale of lands to Jews. The Grand Mufti of Jerusalem, *Al-ḥajj* Amin Al-Hussaini, headed the Supreme Muslim Council in charge of *waqf* lands. Through the bank of the Arab Higher Committee, *bank al-'ummah al-'arabiyyah,* he bought—for endowment—small parcels of lands in the *mushā'* of the villages Taybe, 'Atil, and Jeita, since even if the *waqf* owed only a very small part of *mushā'* land, neither any part nor the whole of that *mushā'* could be sold unless a settlement was arranged.[100] However, pure private lands, known as *mulk,* could be dedicated as *waqf,* whereas most of the lands in Mandate Palestine were *mīrī*[101] (lands defined as state-owned, although in practice they were used and traded as if they were private: the state leased these lands for long periods, and the lease was renewable at the lessee's request). *Al-ḥajj* Amin Al-Hussaini made strenuous attempts to change the law to permit *mīrī* lands to be dedicated as *waqf* to hinder the transfer of land from Arabs to Jews, but the government did not agree to a change[102] (the inability to reassign *mīrī* lands as *waqf* was probably the only significant difference between the *mulk* and *mīrī* forms of tenure). All in all, the *mushā'* constrained Jewish land purchase.[103]

On the other hand, land settlement helped land purchase by Jews, who preferred to purchase settled *mafrūz* lands. Not surprisingly, Jewish land purchase reached a peak during the time of land settlement, as described by 'Āraf[104] and Stein:

> Jewish buyers often bought musha' shares during the land-settlement process. Often the schedule of rights to musha' shares was posted to allow potential claimants the opportunity to challenge

> the schedule before it was structurally recorded. At that point, land was sometimes transferred into Jewish ownership. When time came for official registration of the shares or the designation of right to those shares, these unofficial transfers were entered in the Land Registry books and legalised, since they now appeared in the posted schedule.[105]

Naturally, the Jewish demand for *mafrūz* lands increased the price of *mushā'* plots that were transformed into *mafrūz*.[106] Land settlement thus gave the green light to land purchase. The story of Jewish land purchase is more complicated than the notion that "the *only* [italics in original] factor limiting the pace and scope of Jewish land purchase prior to and after the institution of the Mandate was insufficient funding."[107]

Reflecting on the quantitative discussion, one may ask why cases A and B, unlike C, do not significantly support the claim that Jewish land purchase increased due to land settlement. The answer seems to be that cases A and B were enclaves of settled villages in an unsettled area (see Map 6.1). In such conditions, the ultimate target of establishing large territorial zones could not be accomplished, in contrast, case C was a settled village in settled area. A comparison of Maps 6.1 and 1.1 supports this argument. It is evident that the areas settled during the Mandate period were also the areas where Jewish purchase of land was most extensive.

Knowing that the most significant effect of land settlement was not investment but the acceleration of land transfer from Arabs to Jews; that land purchase was destructive for the *fallāḥīn;* that the inherent advantages of the *mushā'* system were wiped out by land reform; that the reform was intended to improve the economic conditions of the *fallāḥīn,* although it failed to achieve this; and that in parallel with its attempts to secure and increase land settlement for Arabs, the British tried to restrain Jewish land purchase, one cannot escape the conclusion that the land-settlement policy was destructive to the Arab rural economy and in reality worked against the Mandatory government's own objectives.

CONCLUSION

The accepted wisdom of government officials and scholars was that where the *mushāʿ* system prevails, "no one [had] any inducement to improve his land. . . . it is useless to expect that land will be weeded or fertilised, that trees will be planted, or, in a word, that any development will take place." Guided by these premises, the policy of the Mandate government was to uproot the *mushāʿ* system in favor of *mafrūz* lands. But it was again the British paradigm of *fallāḥīn* irrationality that led the government into another ill-advised, Marxist-style reform.

This study of the *mushāʿ*, as part of a set of institutions suggests that it did not constrain development. Investment in *mushāʿ* lands took place either jointly by their members or by established semipartition mechanisms. The advantages of having a system of many plots were that it spread the various hazards and cultivated crops in the most appropriate places. By so doing, *fallāḥīn* could avert the risk of complete disaster. The close association between the *ahl* and the *mushāʿ* seemed to increase labor efficiency. The equal division of inherited land among heirs within the *mushāʿ* system reduced the likelihood of disputes. Finally, crop rotation was part of the *mushāʿ* system. Hence, the *mushāʿ* was an informal and efficient/rational institution, path-dependent but not in an anachronistic manner. There was, in fact, no need to eradicate the *mushāʿ* by land reform.

The Department of Land Settlement administered the registration of rights to lands. Such registration, however, could have been done without any reform and, in the case of *mushāʿ*, through registration of shares. The advantages gained from land registration[108] were outweighed by the disadvantages of land settlement. Land settlement meant abandoning the benefits of *mushāʿ* by consolidating plots and hence increasing risks; it created disputes in families and might also have reduced labor efficiency. Hence, the reform nullified the advantages inherent in the system. In addition, land settlement was costly both to the *fallāḥīn* and the government. Paradoxically, the most significant effect of land settlement was the transfer of lands from Arabs to Jews, an unexpected and destructive by-product of the reform. In short, the land-settlement program designed to assist the *fallāḥīn* economy severely undermined it instead.

NOTES

1. Government of Palestine, *Report of a Committee on the Economic Condition of Agriculturists in Palestine and the Fiscal Measures of Government in Relation Thereto, W. J. Johnson, R. E. H. Crosbie et al.* (Jerusalem, 1930), p. 44.
2. For the land settlement, see Martin Bunton, "Demarcating the British Colonial State: Land Settlement in the Palestine *Jiftlik* Villages of Sajad and Qazaza," Roger Owen (ed.), *New Perspectives on Property and Land in the Middle East* (Harvard, 2000), pp. 121–58. These issues are explored in this chapter.
3. Wher's definition of *mushāʿ*: "widespread; (well-)known, public; general, universal; common, joint; joint (or collective) ownership, joint tenancy (Isl. Law); public property, public domain." Hans Wehr, *A Dictionary of Modern Written Arabic* (Wiesbaden, 1966), p. 498.
4. Birgit Schaebler, "Practicing *Mushaʿ*: Common Lands and the Common Good in Southern Syria under the Ottomans and the French," in Owen, *New Perspectives,* p. 245.
5. For example, ibid., p. 246.
6. Ya'akov Firestone, "The Land-Equalizing *Mushāʿ* Village: A Reassessment," in Gad G. Gilbar (ed.), *Ottoman Palestine, 1800–1914* (London, 1990), pp. 91–129; Martha Mundy, "La propriété dite *mushaʿ* en Syrie: une note analytique à propos des travaux de Ya'akov Firestone," *Revue du Monde Musulman et de la Méditerrannée,* vol. 79–80, no. 1–2 (1996), pp. 274–76; Schaebler, "Practicing *Mushaʿ*," p. 246; André Latron, *La vie rurale en Syrie et au Liban: Etude d'économie sociale* (Beirut, 1936), pp. 56, 81; Moḥamad Yūnīs al-ḥusayni, *Al-tatwūr al-'ijtimāʿī fi filasṭīn al-ʿarabiyyah* (Jerusalem, 1946), pp. 109–10.
7. Firestone, The Land-Equalizing; Schaebler, Practicing *Mushaʿ*, pp. 254–55; Al-ḥusayni, *Al-tatwūr al-'ijtimāʿī fi filasṭīn al-ʿarabiyyah,* pp. 109–110.
8. Haim Gerber, *'Mushāʿ,' The Encyclopedia of Islam* (CD Edition:

Leiden, 1999). See also Shukrī ʿAraf, *Al-qaryah al-'arabiyyah al-filasṭīniyah: mabnī wa-'istiʿimālāt 'arāḍī* (Tarshīḥā, 1996), p. 76.

9. For example, Firestone, "The Land-Equalizing"; Schaebler, "Practicing *Mushaʿ*," pp. 254–55; Al-ḥusayni, *Al-tatwūr al-'ijtimāʿī fi filasṭīn al-ʿarabiyyah,* pp. 109–10.
10. Elihu Grant, *The People of Palestine* (Philadelphia, 1921 reprinted 1976), p. 132; interview with Jamāl 'Ilyās Khuri from Meghar (Mr. Khuri, b. 1905, was a *fallāḥ* and later a policeman during the Mandate period) (23 August 1999); Interview with Nimir Qasim Muṣafa from ʿEin Mahil (Mr. Muṣtafa, b. 1910, spoke about his childhood in the Ottoman period and his life under the Mandate; in the Mandate period, he was a *fallāḥ* and shopkeeper; from 1937, he was also the *mukhtār* of his village) (18 August 1999).
11. Firestone, "The Land-Equalizing," especially pp. 91–96, 106–07.
12. Schaebler, "Practicing *Mushaʿ*," p. 288.
13. Ibid., pp. 254–55.
14. Ibid., pp. 254–55.
15. Roger Owen, *The Middle East in the World Economy, 1800–1914* (London, 2nd ed., 1993), pp. 116–18.
16. Firestone, "The Land-Equalizing"; Schaebler, "Practicing *Mushaʿ*," p. 288; Mundy, "La propriété dite *mushaʿ* en Syrie." Al-ḥusayni, *Al-tatwūr al-'ijtimāʿī fi filasṭīn al-ʿarabiyyah,* pp. 109–10.
17. Mundy, "La propriété dite *mushaʿ* en Syrie," pp. 280–82.
18. ʿĀraf, *Al-qarya,* p. 78.
19. Dorothy Atkinson, *The End of the Russian Land Commune 1905–1930* (Stanford, CA, 1983), pp. 1–19, 28.
20. Lucine Taminian, "ʿAin," Martha Mundy and Richard S. Smith (eds.), *Part-Time Farming: Agricultural Development in the Zarqa River Basin, Jordan* (Irbid, 1990), pp. 16, 20.
21. Schaebler, "Practicing *Mushaʿ*," p. 288; Mundy, "La propriété dite *mushaʿ* en Syrie," p. 276.
22. ʿĀraf, *Al-qarya,* p. 76; Scott Artan, "Hamula Organization and Mashaʿ Tenure in Palestine," *MAN,* vol. 21, no. 2 (1986), pp. 271–95. This issue will be discussed later.
23. Mundy, "La propriété dite *mushaʿ* en Syrie," p. 281.
24. Martha Mundy, "Qada' ʿAjlun in the Late Nineteenth Century: Interpreting a Region from the Ottoman Land Registry," *Levant,* vol. 28 (1986), pp. 84–87.
25. Schaebler, "Practicing *Mushaʿ*," p. 288.

26. Firestone, "The Land-Equalizing," pp. 93, 122.
27. Government of Palestine, *Report of a Committee on the Economic Condition of Agriculturists* '(Johnson-Crosbie), p. 44.
28. Al-ḥusayni, *Al-tatwūr al-'ijtimā'ī fi filasṭīn al-'arabiyyah,* p. 111.
29. Government of Palestine, *Report of a Committee on the Economic Condition of Agriculturists* (Johnson-Crosbie), p. 44; Al-ḥusayni, *Al-tatwūr al-'ijtimā'ī fi filasṭīn al-'arabiyyah,* p. 111. According to one of my interviewees, the rule was not strictly enforced for a former *fallāḥ* who moved to a different plot; if a member requested keeping the same plot or plots for another round, he was usually permitted to do so. Interview with Khalid Zu'abī (Abū Raf'at) from Nazareth (during the Mandate period, Abū Raf'at was a *fallāḥ* in the Nein village who also worked in Nazareth) (25 March 1999).
30. 'Āraf, *Al-qarya,* pp. 76–78; Al-ḥusayni, *Al-tatwūr al-'ijtimā'ī fi filasṭīn al-'arabiyyah,* p. 110.
31. Government of Palestine, *A Survey of Palestine: Prepared in December 1945 and January 1946 for the Information of the Anglo-American Committee of Inquiry* (Jerusalem, 1946), pp. 310–11. As mentioned in this source, there were also cases of three-year rotation (a cycle consisting of a winter crop, another type of winter crop, and a summer crop). No crop rotation was practiced in the light soil areas (especially of the Beersheba subdistrict), which were unsuitable for many crops, and hence barley was sown year after year.
32. For example, Interview with Khalid Zu'abī; also Interview with Tatūr Jamāl from Reina (Mr. Jamāl, b. 1935, is the son of a *fallāḥīn* family (20 August 1999). About the *Ḥamūla,* see Amnon Cohen, "*ḥamūla,*" *Encyclopaedia of Islam* (CD edition: Leiden, 1999). As mentioned in Chapter 4, *ahl* referred to a patrilineal kinship group made up of several *dārs,* and the *ḥamūla* to a broader association encompassing some *ahls,* usually linked patrilineally.
33. See Chapter 4.
34. 'Āraf, *Al-qarya,* p. 76; see also Al-ḥusayni, *Al-tatwūr al-'ijtimā'ī fi filasṭīn al-'arabiyyah,* p. 110.
35. For example, Artan, "Hamula Organization," pp. 271–95.
36. Dov Gavish, *Qarqa vemapa: mehesder haqarqa'ot lemapat ereẓ yishra'el* (Jerusalem, 1991), pp. 2–3, 150.

37. Bunton, "Demarcating," pp. 121–22, 148, 150.
38. Ernest M. Dowson, *Progress in Land Reforms, 1923–1930* (Kent, 1930), p. 4.
39. Ibid., pp. 4–5.
40. Ibid., p. 1.
41. Government of Palestine, *Report of a Committee on the Economic Condition of Agriculturists* (Johnson-Crosbie), pp. 44–45, 55.
42. Gavish, *Qarqa vemapa,* p. 183.
43. Government of Palestine, Palestine Development Department, *Agricultural Development and Land Settlement in Palestine (First and Supplementary Reports), by Lewis French, Director of Development* (Jerusalem, 1931), pp. 12–13.
44. Government of Palestine, *Report by Mr. C. F. Strickland of the Indian Civil Service on the Possibility of Introducing a System of Agricultural Co-operation in Palestine* (Jerusalem, 1930), pp. 43–44.
45. Gavish, *Qarqa vemapa,* p. 173; Government of Palestine, *Report by Mr. C. F. Strickland,* p. 44. For more on the process of land settlement, see Bunton, "Demarcating," pp. 137–47.
46. Up to 1946, out of about 1,000 Arab villages in Palestine, 473 were settled, 102 were in the process of settlement, and the rest were not settled at all. Gavish, *Qarqa vemapa,* pp. 115–205.
47. Government of Palestine, *A Survey of Palestine,* pp. 239, 547.
48. This matter is explored later in this chapter. For prices of lands purchased by Jews, see Jewish Agency for Palestine, *Land and Agricultural Development in Palestine* (London, 1930), p. 52.
49. ISA/(RG2)//L/135/46, "Land settlement Fees: Petitions."
50. The data are available for 1944. That year, one kilogram of wheat was worth 18.3 mils (while this is the average value for the year as a whole, *fallāḥīn* who sold directly after the harvest received much less; moreover, *fallāḥīn* were paid in the producer price—i.e., less than the wholesale price). Average wheat production per dunum that year stood at 39.6 kilograms. Government of Palestine, Department of Statistics, *Statistical Abstract of Palestine, 1944–45* (Jerusalem, 1946); Government of Palestine, Department of Agriculture and Fisheries, *Annual Reports 1944–45 and 1945–46* (Jerusalem). For the tendency of *fallāḥīn* to sell immediately after the harvest when prices were at their lowest, see Chapter 4.
51. Government of Palestine, *A Survey of Palestine,* pp. 342–43.

52. Ibid., p. 237.
53. Firestone, "The Land-Equalizing," especially pp. 91–96.
54. Ibid., pp. 91–96. Mohammad al-ḥizmāwī, *Mulkiyah al-arāḍī fī filasṭīn 1918–1948* (Acre, 1998), p. 48; 'Āraf, *Al-qarya,* pp. 76–78. For a survey of these attitudes to the *mushā'*, see Dan Rabinowitz, *Antropologiya vepalesṭinim* (Ra'anana, 1998), pp. 61–73.
55. For example, Firestone, "The Land-Equalizing"; see also Charles S. Kamen, *Little Common Ground: Arab Agriculture and Jewish Settlement in Palestine, 1920–1948* (Pittsburgh, 1991), pp. 136–37.
56. Raphael Patai, "Musha'a Tenure and Co-operation in Palestine," *American Anthropologist,* vol. 51, no. 3 (1949); Government of Palestine, *Report of a Committee on the Economic Condition of Agriculturists* (Johnson-Crosbie); Government of Palestine, Palestine Development Department, *Agricultural Development and Land Settlement* (Lewis French), p. 12.
57. Patai, "Musha'a Tenure," p. 441.
58. Kamen, *Little Common Ground,* pp. 136–37.
59. Government of Palestine, *Report of a Committee on the Economic Condition of Agriculturists* (Johnson-Crosbie), pp. 44–45. See also Gabriel Baer, *Mavo layaḥasim ha'agrariyim bamizraḥ hatikhon, 1800–1970* (Jerusalem, 1971), p. 70.
60. Gavish, *Qarqa vemapa,* pp. 18–19, 134.
61. Baalbaki also mentioned this form *(mashā')* as a synonym for *mushā'*: Rohi Baalbaki, *Al Mawarid: A Modern Arabic-English Dictionary* (Beirut, 13th edition, 2000), p. 1044.
62. Interview with Maḍhib Nimir Sulṭī from 'Ilut (Mr. Sulṭī, b. 1934–35, is the son of a *fallāḥīn* family) (22 August 2000); Interview with Raḍwan Salīm Bisharat, (Mr. Bisharat, b. 1914, was a *fallāḥ* who lived in Ma'lul village) (22 August 2000); Interview with Mohammad ḥasūna from Abu Ghosh (ḥaj ḥasūna, b. 1929, was a *fallāḥ* who was also employed as wage laborer in Jerusalem during the Mandate period) (31 July 1999); Interview with Jamāl 'Ilyās Khuri; Interview with Slīmān 'Adawī from Tur'an (Mr. 'Adawī, b. 1926–28, was a *fallāḥ* in the Mandate period and an agriculture adviser in Israel; he worked with some who had been agriculture advisers in the Mandate period) (5 April 1999).

63. Al-ḥusayni, *Al-tatwūr al-'ijtimā'ī fi filasṭīn al-'arabiyyah,* p. 111.
64. 'Āraf, *Al-qarya,* p. 79.
65. Interview with Khalid Zu'abī; Interview with 'Alī Abū Yūsif Zu'abī from Daḥi (today from Nazareth) (Mr. Zu'abī, b. 1923, was a *fallāḥ* in the Mandate period) (26 March 1999); Interview with Taṭūr Jamāl.
66. Government of Palestine, Department of Statistics, *Survey of Social and Economic Conditions Arab Villages, 1944: Special Bulletin no. 21* (Jerusalem, 1948), pp. 54–55, 58, 66.
67. Firestone, "The Land-Equalizing," pp. 92, 120–23.
68. Ibid., p. 119.
69. See the Map Archive of the PEF; Beshara Doumani, *Rediscovering Palestine: Merchants and Peasants in Jabal Nablus, 1700–1900* (Berkeley, CA, 1995).
70. See, broadly, 'Alī Nasūj al-Ẓāhir, *Shajārah al-zaytūn: tārīkhhā zirā'thā, 'amrāḍihā, ṣinā'thā* (Amman, 1947).
71. Great Britain, Colonial Office, *Report on Immigration, Land Settlement and Development, by Sir John Hope Simpson* (London, 1930), pp. 44–45, 55.
72. Interview with 'Alī Abū Yūsif Zu'abī; Interview with Abū 'Abdallah from Mashhad (Abū 'Abdallah, b. 1921, was the *mukhtār*'s son in the Mandate period and later became the *mukhtār* of his village) (6 April 1999 and 17 August 1999).
73. Interview with Abū 'Ātif Fāhūm from Nazareth (Mr. Fāhūm, b. 1927–28, is the son of Yūsif Fāhūm, the mayor of Nazareth during different years of the Mandate period; his father was also a landlord) (17 August 1999); Interview with Taṭūr Jamāl; Interview with 'Alī Abū Yūsif Zu'abī; Interview with Slīmān 'Adawī.
74. Al-ḥusayni, *Al-tatwūr al-'ijtimā'ī fi filasṭīn al-'arabiyyah,* pp. 109–111.
75. Interview with 'Alī Abū Yūsif Zu'abī (he argued that many disputes emerged between relatives as a result of land settlement). On this point, see Gavish, *Qarqa vemapa,* pp. 115–205.
76. Interview with Khalid Zu'abī; Interview with 'Alī Abū Yūsif Zu'abī; Interview with Taṭūr Jamāl. Such an observation does not solve the question about the origin of the *mushā',* yet it does give an indication of its origin in *some* cases.

77. Bunton, "Demarcating the British Colonial State," p. 139; Gavish, *Qarqa vemapa,* pp. 115–205.
78. Artan, "Hamula Organization," pp. 271–95.
79. Rosemary Sayigh, *Palestinians: From Peasants to Revolutionaries* (London, 1979), p. 33.
80. As mentioned earlier, Firestone, too, suggests that trust was important. However, he deals only with trust between relatives who were landlord and tenant, without discussing relations with the rest of the family. Firestone, "The Land-Equalizing," p. 119.
81. Government of Palestine, *Report of a Committee on the Economic Condition of Agriculturists* (Johnson-Crosbie), pp. 44–45, 55.
82. Government of Palestine, Department of Statistics, *Village Statistics, 1937* (data collected in 1935: Jerusalem, 1937). Government of Palestine, Department of Statistics, *Village Statistics, 1945* (Jerusalem, 1945).
83. Government of Palestine, Department of Agriculture and Fisheries, *Annual Report 1941–42* (Jerusalem, 1942), p. 3.
84. At least at the time of settlement, remembering that later on, as in the case of Village A from the inquiry of five villages in 1944, *mafrūz* lands became *mushā*ʻ.
85. Government of Palestine, Commissioner for Lands and Surveys, *Annual Reports* 1935 and 1937. ISA/Maps Collection: Map 649, "Progress of Land Settlement, 31.12.1945" and Map 207, "Palestine: Index of Villages and Settlements, Dec. 1945."
86. Gavish, *Qarqa vemapa.*
87. See Chapter 3.
88. See, broadly, Gavish, *Qarqa vemapa.*
89. Government of Palestine, *Memorandum on the Water Resources of Palestine* (Jerusalem, 1947); see more in Chapter 1.
90. More accurate and detailed maps were used for the study (especially, ISA/Maps Collection/ Map 649, "Progress of Land Settlement, 31.12.1945," and Map 207, "Palestine: Index of Villages and Settlements, Dec. 1945"). While it appears from this map that there are other cases to investigate, it is important to stress that this is not the case. First, the map does not distinguish between Jewish and Arab villages (the intention is to examine the latter). Second, areas cultivated by Bedouins, especially in the Beersheba subdistrict, were not surveyed for the rural property tax (these areas con-

tinued to pay the tithe). Third, there are many cases that could not be compared because of uncertainty about settlement dates, such as those around Lakes Tiberias and Hula (i.e., these were settled some time during 1938–45; the criterion is lands settled either before 1935 or in 1935–37—see earlier discussion). Fourth, there are cases where the amount of land registered for villages changed dramatically, hence the two sets of data are not comparable (e.g., Beit Qad).

91. Great Britain, Colonial Office, *Report on Immigration, Land Settlement and Development* (Hope Simpson), pp. 44–45, 55.
92. This is another example of the case of investment in Arab farms discussed in Chapters 1 and 2.
93. Government of Palestine, *Village Statistics 1935,* p. 3.
94. For example, Government of Palestine, *A Survey of Palestine,* pp. 58–59.
95. Baer, *Mavo layaḥasim,* p. 178; Yossi Katz, *Beḥazit haqarqa': qeren kayemet leyisrael beterem hamedina* (Jerusalem, 2001), pp. 38, 97, 166.
96. Warwick P. N. Tyler, *State Lands and Rural Development in Mandatory Palestine, 1920–1948* (Brighton, 2001), p. 8.
97. ISA/Map Collection/Land in Jewish Possession as at 30.6.1947.
98. Government of Palestine, *Report of a Committee on the Economic Condition of Agriculturists* (Johnson-Crosbie), p. 21.
99. See, for example, ISA/(RG2)/BOX326/653, 15.5.1947, Šudki al-Ṭabariyy's letter to the Arab Higher Committee.
100. Yehoshua Porath, *Mehamehumot lameridah: hatnu'a ha'aravit hapalestinit, 1929–1939* (Tel Aviv, 1978), pp. 122–28.
101. See, for example, "Land Appeal 44/36 Ameereh el Khalidi vs. Director of Lands et. al.," *Current Law Reports,* vol. 2 (1937), pp. 42–47.
102. Porath, *Mehamehumot lameridah,* pp. 124–26.
103. See also ḥizmāwī, *Mulkiyah al-arāḍī,* p. 48.
104. 'Āraf, *Al-qaryah,* p. 78.
105. Stein, *The Land Question,* p. 71.
106. Interview with Yūsif and Fārūk Ya'aqūb from Nazareth (these are the grandsons of 'Abdallah Yūsif Ya'aqūb, a merchant and moneylender; they—and especially Mr. Fārūk Ya'aqūb, the older one—used to work with the grandfather in his business) (25 March 1999).

107. Stein, *The Land Question,* p. 37; also quoted in Warwick, *State Lands,* p. 9.
108. The records left to the British by the Ottomans were restricted to a few areas in Palestine: Ruth Kark and Haim Gerber, "Land Registry Maps in Palestine During the Ottoman Period," *Cartographic Journal,* no. 21, 1984, p. 30; Gavish, *Qarqa vemapa,* pp. 18–19.

· SEVEN ·

Government Agricultural Services: Limited Relief

The colonial government's agricultural policy and its expenditure on agricultural technology represent various attempts to improve the conditions and practices of Arab farmers. The following discussion covers the modest attempts to initiate a "green revolution" in the Arab sector through assistance with animal breeding, agricultural advice and methods of communicating with the *fallāḥīn,* and direct government loans to agriculture.

In 1943, an article in the popular Arabic newspaper *Al Difa* claimed to be based on some inquiries in villages and described the economic conditions of the *fallāḥīn* as much better (as a result of the wartime prosperity). It also stated that the *fallāḥīn* had asked the government for support in four ways:

- Direct government loans for agriculture;
- Guidance from government agricultural advisers;
- More and cheaper chemical fertilizers, as these were usually too expensive to buy; and
- More roads to rural areas because these significantly enhanced marketing.[1]

It is hard to assess how much the arguments put forward in the article represented the views of the *fallāḥīn* as a whole. The assistance requested, however, was for an intensification of some existing programs—all quite limited in their operations and none of which challenged the so-called irrational institutions of irrational *fallāḥīn*.

THE DEPARTMENT OF AGRICULTURE'S BUDGET

The national accounts of the government of Palestine leave uncertain the size of total government spending on agriculture.[2] However, the picture is clearer for agricultural technology, since this was carried out mainly by the Department of Agriculture. The phrase "expenditure on agricultural technology" refers to financing improved techniques and instructing farmers in their use, with the aim of increasing agricultural production or preventing its decline. This was done by offering alternatives, without banning any other technologies. Table 7.1 shows that on average, the main expenditure by the Department of Agriculture was on cultivation (about 40 percent) and that it was followed by livestock breeding (31 percent). "Other agricultural spending" accounted for 14 percent (this usually meant additional spending on cultivation and livestock in unexpected circumstances such as cattle plague and the locust campaign). Nine percent went on administration, and 6 percent on education.

Although information for certain years, especially during the World War II period, is missing, it seems that during the war, expenditures on agricultural technology increased but were not necessarily initiated by the Department of Agriculture. At that time, the (Anglo-American) Middle East Supply Centre in London took steps to increase production via new technologies and, through the War Supply Board in Palestine, directed the government of Palestine on investment.[3] The figures on government spending to farmers during the war show a sharp increase. At the end of the war, government spending dropped sharply. This seems to be related to a new policy, expressed by the government as "the greatly increased prices obtained by farmers . . . during the war left them generally with ample resources to finance further development."[4]

Table 7.1 also reveals a major rise in spending after the Disturbances of 1929. This was due not only to increased budgetary expenditure but also to departmental sales, especially the proceeds of animal breeding and cultivation, which constituted about 94 percent of the total. The change following the disturbances was therefore not as significant as one would have thought—probably because the biggest share of the budget was allocated to land and credit reforms.

NOTE ON THE SPENDING ON AGRICULTURAL INFRASTRUCTURE

The spending on agricultural technology is invariably related to investment in the rural infrastructure.[5] As discussed in Chapter 2, no direct investment was made in large-scale irrigation. Where it existed, irrigation enabled the cultivation of many more varieties of crops and generated income that could help to fund the acquisition of newer technologies.

Road building could also assist the *fallāhin.* Palestine was a small country without long distances between towns and villages, so that animal transport served marketing purposes fairly well. Even so, there was an obvious advantage in having better transport routes. One of the government's two main objectives in road building was to facilitate trade, including agricultural products, and the other was to extend military control:

> The opening up of the country by means of roads has not only enhanced the agricultural and trade potentials of the country but has facilitated the maintenance of public security by making it possible to control remote and lawless areas previously inaccessible during certain periods of the year.[6]

In 1922, at the beginning of the Mandate, there were about 450 kilometers of roads; in 1936, about 1,247; in 1939, 2,277; and

Table 7.1 Expenditure on Agriculture by the Department of Agriculture, £P 1936 Prices

Year	1923	1924	1925	1926	1927	1928	1929	1930	1931	1932	1934	1935	1936	1937	1945
Cultivation	6,944	6,710	4,904	4,938	8,107	8,090	13,661	19,882	19,909	19,766	56,146	80,893	94,937	103,221	16,995
Animal breeding	9,263	8,558	7,294	7,570	16,838	13,847	17,395	24,192	26,442	30,044	34,943	45,506	42,649	46,548	31,681
Other agriculture spending	1,664	2,058	2,100	11,635	4,412	10,260	14,724	40,887	15,610	10,984	16,265	16,596	8,688	10,258	0
Agricultural education	229	218	193	237	183	162	325	40	1,972	1,393	12,890	14,292	13,697	15,327	6,700
Administration	2,868	2,187	1,920	2,573	2,492	2,967	4,357	5,367	7,739	7,690	7,747	11,507	13,584	14,339	14,768
Total expenditure	20,968	19,731	16,411	26,953	32,032	35,326	50,462	90,368	71,672	69,877	127,991	168,794	173,555	189,693	70,144
Revenue from government	17,665	16,814	13,658	24,105	27,399	30,433	44,209	75,328	52,384	50,633	80,598	92,547	88,392	93,962	61,617
Nongovernment revenues	3,304	2,916	2,752	2,848	4,633	4,893	6,254	15,039	19,288	19,243	47,392	76,247	85,163	95,732	8,527

Source: Government of Palestine, Department of Agriculture, *Annual Reports* (various years).

Notes: The Department of Agriculture was responsible for fisheries and in some years for forests as well. However, apart from "administration," the accounts permit a separation of agriculture from other categories. Loans to farmers do not seem to be included in the Department's accounts and are discussed later in this chapter.

in 1945, 2,660. This represented an average annual increase of 7.5 percent between 1922 and 1936, 22.2 percent between 1936 and 1939, and 2.6 percent between 1939 and 1945.[7] The sudden expansion of road building during the Arab Revolt of 1936 to 1939 occurred mostly in rural areas, in response to the insurrection:

> A programme of road construction commenced early in 1938 on grounds of public security in order to provide communication to areas hitherto inaccessible to wheeled traffic and in order generally to facilitate the movement of troops and police. This programme was completed in 1940, and the total length of roads built there under was about 840 kilometres.[8]

While there was a trend toward higher investment in agricultural technology after the Disturbances of 1929, no direct investment in agricultural infrastructure occurred, and it was the need to facilitate military operations during the revolt that led to the considerable expansion of public roading.

LIMITATIONS OF THIS INQUIRY

Information for this discussion is scarce in many respects. There are records of different departmental activities, but frequently the details needed to assess their full impact are lacking. For example, improved veterinary services would be expected to reduce animal mortality from diseases, but data for such ratios are not available. Further, while the Department's policies were intended to upgrade agricultural conditions, there could have been cases where "improvements" made them worse or were inapplicable to most Arab farms.

Nevertheless, the services and recommendations provided by the Department followed detailed investigations into what the impact of these was likely to be.[9] This may suggest that the aggregate effect of departmental activities was positive. To facilitate the analysis, the working hypothesis here is that all activities, if implemented, were effective—unless found to be otherwise. By definition, this leaves some room for misinterpretation and, indeed, for further scientifically expert interpretation, especially by agroscientists.

THE MODEST GREEN REVOLUTION

The term "green revolution" refers to gains in agricultural productivity as a result of improved plant varieties and/or extensive use of fertilizers and pesticides. Although the term was not in use in Mandate days, it nevertheless fits some activities carried by the Department of Agriculture in Palestine.

The Use of Fertilizers

Various departmental reports suggest that during the 1930s and especially the 1940s, there was higher use of fertilizers and pesticides such as urea and sulphate ammonia.[10] In 1937, the Department observed that "increased purchase [import] of artificial fertilisers continues to reflect the efficacy of departmental efforts in experiments and demonstrations and in the propaganda in villages."[11] Data for 1932 to 1936 about imports to Palestine of all kinds of fertilizers and "import of chemical fertilisers" reveal that the former was only slightly higher than the latter—about 9 percent—so that most of the imported fertilizers were chemical. Such imports, following the Department's method, can stand as a proxy for the use of all artificial fertilizers and are presented in Figure 7.1.

The figures show a significant rise in the import of chemical fertilizers from 1932 to 1933. It remained high until the outbreak of World War II, when imports were restricted. But for *fallāḥīn,* this increase was a drop in the bucket. Because they tended not to use fertilizers, unlike the constantly expanding Jewish agriculture,[12] only an increase of thousands of percent would mark a significant change for them. In addition, the transfer of land from Arabs to Jews is likely to have caused higher fertilizer use—in the Jewish sector. Officially, the Department reported that "the extension in the use of chemical fertilisers is apparent on Arab lands both on intensive and extensive

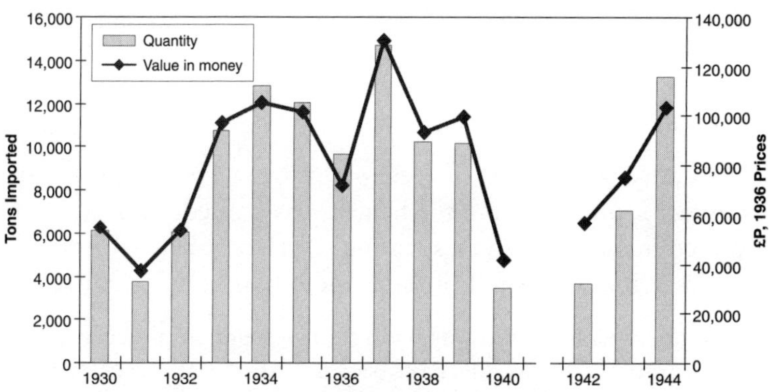

Figure 7.1 Import of Chemical Fertilizers into Palestine, 1930 to 1944

Source: Government of Palestine, Department of Statistics, *Statistical Abstract of Palestine* (various years).

holdings. The appointment of agents in villages by distributing firms has increased sales."[13] Such an increase probably occurred but on a limited scale. If, as the Department maintains, these firms had agents in villages, then it could be that the high cost of fertilizers meant a low demand for them.

Agricultural Research Stations and the Benefits from Jewish Research

One of the Department's main objectives was to supply better-quality seeds to achieve higher yield. It researched the suitability of high-yield varieties and benefited from the extensive Jewish knowledge in this area and the assistance of Jewish agricultural research institutes, either for nominal payment or none at all. The Jewish Agency's Agricultural Research Station in Rehovot investigated diseases of vegetables and fruit trees (including citrus) in the Arab sector, tested cereals and seeds, researched new machinery, and so forth.[14] The Jewish Agency seemed motivated to assist the *fallāḥīn,* in the hope that more intensive agriculture would make more land available for Jewish purchase. Indeed, as a report of 1930 observed:

> There was no room for a single additional settler if the standard of life of the Arab villager was to remain at its existing level . . . [until the implementing of] close settlement on the land and intensive cultivation by both Arab and Jews.[15]

In this way, a spillover of technology from the Jewish to the Arab sector occurred. But the benefit was limited, as B. A. Keen reported in 1945 after investigating the Department of Agriculture's activities on behalf of the Middle East Supply Centre:

> Palestine organisation for agricultural investigation presents special features [in the Middle East] because of the existence of a parallel Jewish organisation staffed by able investigators and advisory specialists. Certain of the scientific departments of the Hebrew University: the Rehovot Experiment Station is engaged, both in research and technology, on problems in the various agricultural systems developed for the Jewish Settlements, and in citrus culture; Mikveh Israel also has an extensive programme of investigation. In practice, the Government has taken note of the Jewish agricultural work while paying special attention to the problems of the Arab cultivators. It has utilised the services of Rehovot as far as feasible, by grants to cover certain investigations of general importance to Palestine which could more suitably done at Rehovot than elsewhere. It cannot be said that this arrangement has been very satisfactory. Experience has shown that it could be a useful supplement to, but not a substitute for, the Government's research and technological work.[16]

In addition to this limited spillover, Keen reported that the government's arrangement of its research stations could have been more efficient:

> At present the Government has an experiment station at Acre, and various sub-stations that are engaged mainly in multiplication and distribution of better tree and plant varieties, while the sub-station of Beersheba is now developing dry-farming cultivation studies. The distribution and programme of the sub-stations are satisfactory, although more are needed to cover the different conditions. But it is questionable whether Acre is the best place for the one experiment station. It is in the limited marshy region of the northern

> coastal plain, whereas much of the Arab agricultural activities are in the upland and hill regions and the dry-farming area of the Negev.[17]

It appears that in spite of assistance from the advanced Jewish experimental stations and additional research, the returns were unsatisfactory for the Arab sector. Nevertheless, better seeds suited to particular areas were available from the regional stations.

The Use of New Varieties of Seeds in fallāḥīn Farms

The chief way which the Department tried to increase productivity was to use high-yielding varieties. In cases of crop failure, the government helped farmers by supplying grain seeds on loan, often high-yield varieties suitable for unirrigated lands. Other high-yield varieties were sold to farmers at attractive prices, and some were even given free.[18]

What was the impact, in terms of productivity, of these more "suitable" seeds? Unfortunately, a quantitative analysis of productivity changes is problematic. It is widely acknowledged that productivity can best be measured by calculating total factor productivity, but as noted in Chapter 3, this is not feasible here since much information is missing. The cost of different outputs in money and kind, and more so the different inputs, are far from adequately reported. In addition, while the main intention is to measure the productivity effect of improved varieties, the returns cannot be differentiated because the results (especially on nonirrigated lands) would also include returns on natural factors, the impact of which is hard to assess. In the case of Palestine, the separation is even more problematic because Arab output data cannot be separated from the total. Further, statistics on production are inexact prior to 1935 (discussed in Part 2). The implications are that the present analysis has to focus on qualitative evidence.

Bearing in mind that grains and legumes were the dominant crops grown unirrigated in Arab farms, the use of improved seeds could have been critical for the *fallāḥīn*. Surprisingly, even when the seeds reached the *fallāḥīn*, the government reported that they were hardly used:

> The wheat and barley seed used by the Jewish farms is good, an admirable system of seed improvement has been developed and through the years there has been a steady improvement in the quality. Much time has been devoted by the Department of Agriculture to trying to bring about an improvement in the quality of seed used on Arab lands, but there has been little or no general improvement. The quantities of seed which are distributed to them are very soon dissipated and become mixed with inferior seed on the threshing floors. Seventy-four tons of grain seed of improved varieties were distributed by the Department in 1944.[19]

As this suggests, it was not that these seeds were regarded as untrustworthy. Indeed, *fallāḥīn* sowed them on their lands but did not perceive the seeds as better quality. Hence, they were "very soon dissipated and [became] mixed with inferior seed on the threshing floors."[20] This points to a communication failure between the Department and the peasantry. It may have been that such information was relatively new. *Al Difa* reports in 1935 that government farms had failed to find good high-yield varieties of wheat.[21] Nevertheless, the input of 74 tons of seeds in a country producing 98,938 tons of wheat and barley[22] (assuming that these seeds were indeed better, as the government maintained), mostly from Arab farms, seemed to produce negligible returns. Presumably, if the Department had explained more effectively the advantage in using such seeds, the returns on this investment would have been more significant.

Unlike its work with grains, the Department argued that during World War II it succeeded in its efforts with fruit production—although at the time, such changes were not expected to show an immediate upturn in yields because of the longer fruiting cycle of trees:

> Advice is given regarding the planting and cultivating of olives, summer fruits, citrus, sub-tropical and tropical fruits and vines.

> There has been a very large expansion in planting, particularly in the hills, with a great demand for budded plants and seedlings from the Government nurseries. During the war years it has not been possible to meet the demand but arrangements have now [1945] been made to expand production considerably.[23]

The yield per dunum from vegetables appeared to increase significantly (see Chapter 2), which might have been a result of departmental activity. First, as the Department stated, an increase in vegetable production and productivity was its main achievement with high-yield varieties:

> Particular attention has been given to the extension of the areas of vegetable production and to improved methods; success has attended these efforts. Potatoes may be quoted as an example: before the war only negligible quantities were grown but in 1944 some 50,000 tons were produced. Some ten million vegetables seedlings were distributed from Government stations annually during the war.[24]

Second, unlike grains (where seeds from the threshing floor were taken for planting)[25] and fruit (where seedlings of many trees grew naturally),[26] it would have been much cheaper to purchase seeds from the Department at the prices offered[27] than, for example, to let tomatoes rot and collect the seeds. The large number of vegetable seeds and seedlings produced by the Department could find its way to the *fallāḥīn* directly or, more likely, via third parties such as merchants. If so, high-yield varieties of vegetable seeds could filter into *fallāḥīn* farms whether or not *fallāḥīn* were aware that these seeds were improved (and the impression from my interviews is that they lacked this knowledge).

Overall, the information about the level of success with the new varieties is too sparse to give a full picture. Still, it is clear that some of the failure was the result of communication problems in the area that most needed improvement—grains and legumes. Fruits seemed to have been upgraded on a small scale, with a more significant improvement for vegetables.

ASSISTANCE FOR ANIMAL BREEDING

The Department assisted animal husbandry in three ways: protection of grazing, veterinary services, and improvement of livestock.

Protection of Grazing

While, as the Department noted in 1946, "there has not been any appreciable progress towards improving the methods of grazing and feeding in the Arab villages,"[28] the protection of grazing—the essence of Arab livestock breeding[29]—was crucial to the *fallāḥīn*. The government certainly aimed to provide it:

> Both by direct action and by example and instruction, the Department of Forests and Agriculture and the Soil Conservation Board in their respective spheres seek to bring large areas under cover of vegetation, to introduce scientific systems of soil conservation both in the hill areas and on the plains and to increase both the agricultural qualities of land and also the yield of stock.[30]

Government agencies tried to gain the attention of cultivators mainly through radio broadcasts.[31] These, it seems (see below), hardly penetrated into Arab villages. In addition, the many terraces in Arab villages in the Ottoman period imply that Arab farmers had long been aware of the need to conserve soil.[32] Hence, the overall influence of activities to encourage soil conservation on cultivated lands appears to have been minor.

However, the government's soil conservation activities were mostly concentrated in noncultivated areas. Trees were planted to reduce soil erosion, and by controlling grazing[33] an attempt was made to "put an end to the ravages of soil erosion and the encroachment of sand dunes."[34] Following the designation of an area as a forest reserve, apart from a few exceptions, *fallāḥīn* from nearby villages were permitted to graze their herds in the forests for a nominal fee. Others, such as nomads, could not graze livestock in such reserves. In effect, the *fallāḥīn* received a kind of grazing right that gave them an advantage over nomads and probably enjoyed better returns on pasturing because of the government's measures.[35]

At the same time, the protection of these commons by the increase in forest reserves also strengthened the government's *de facto* control of land at the expense of the *fallāḥīn*'s ability to extend their areas under cultivation. The cultivated land in forest reserves was better controlled, which effectively brought to a halt the expansion of *fallāḥīn* farms, in spite of their growing need to utilize more land:

> Except during the lengthy disturbances of 1936–1939, comparatively little land was lost to the State by illegal encroachment and cultivation.[36] . . . The system of reservation has more than fulfilled all expectations; in many localities settlement officers have recorded as State Domain the whole forest reserve and nothing else.[37] (Government report, 1945)

> There has in the hills been a widespread attempt to cultivate the lands which were previously regarded as the grazing ground of the village, or which were public "forests" on the neighbouring mountain slope.[38] (Director of the Department of Land Settlement to the Chief Secretary, 1945)

The government's soil conservation policies had two consequences for the *fallāḥīn*. They gave them the privilege of using lands for grazing, and some of the grazing areas were improved. But the policies also reduced the *fallāḥīn*'s access to "free" arable land in forest reserves. In 1945, forest reserves were about 751,000 dunams[39] (about 12.6 percent of the "category 16" lands).[40]

Veterinary Services

The government's veterinary services concentrated on the control of animal diseases and the inspection of slaughterhouses and meat. They treated many epidemics, such as sheep and goat pox, foot and mouth disease in cattle, and Newcastle disease in poultry. They conducted investigations and inspections of animal health, and when outbreaks of disease occurred, direct treatment was given, usually by vaccination of healthy animals and the slaughter and quarantining of sick ones. The level of success of these services is, of course, hard to assess since it is based on a "what if" question without a control group (there is no data on treated versus untreated groups). Nevertheless, different reports by the Department seem to suggest that its efforts indeed contributed to both Arab and Jewish livestock breeding.[41] It is not unusual to encounter assertions such as this, from an annual report:

> In September a severe outbreak of African horse-sickness occurred. It was introduced from Egypt. Fortunately, it proved possible to obtain sufficient quantities of vaccine from South East Africa to bring the disease under effective control by the middle of November. Altogether it spread to 335 localities and resulted in the loss of some 1,500 horses and mules. Had it not been the early arrival of the vaccine the losses might have been catastrophic.[42]

The claim about sufficient vaccinations appears to be correct. Evidence about anthrax vaccinations of cattle, sheep, and goats in the Lydda district suggests that animals were vaccinated in 120 localities (118 of them Arab), covering about 62 percent of the goats, 71 percent of the sheep, and 124 percent (reflecting underrecording and animal migration) of the cattle.[43] The veterinary services therefore appear to have contributed significantly to the *fallāḥīn* economy.

Improvement of Livestock Quality

During breeding periods, the Government Stock Farm in Acre loaned selected sires to farmers free of charge. These were bulls, male goats, rams, stallions, and jackasses. A very few animals were also sold to villagers. The aim of the policy was to improve the country's livestock.[44] But the numbers seemed far too small to make a significant difference, at least in the short term, as Table 7.2 indicates.

As we saw in Chapter 2, the number of poultry increased substantially under the Mandate. The Department's role in that was

Table 7.2 Ratio of Uncastrated Male Animals on Acre Farm Compared to the Rest of the Country, 1936 to 1937

	Acre Farm, 1936	Proportion of Total in the Country, 1937
Bulls	58	0.8% (total 7,044)
Stallions	5	0.09% (5,587)
Jackasses	15	0.05% (29,164)
Ewes	261	1.5% (17,557)
Goats	119	0.7% (17,906)

Source: For Acre Farm: Government of Palestine, *Annual Report of the Department of Agriculture and Forests for the Year Ending March 1936,* pp. 149–50. For the rest of Palestine: Government of Palestine, Department of Statistics, *Statistical Abstract of Palestine 1943,* p. 87.

significant. It established hatcheries from which many pedigree chicks were sold, as well as many hatching eggs, at what were claimed to be "most reasonable prices."[45] The success of the poultry promotion is described in Keen's report:

> The relative ease of working and handling poultry on a large scale has led to a useful development in the supply of birds to farmers and to some war-time extension. Thus in Palestine the Government has two large hatcheries at Jerusalem and Acre to produce day-old chicks. In the season May-June 1943, 500,000 chicks were sold [probably to both farmers and merchants]. . . . The scheme is a useful illustration of what could be done with proper precautions in peace-time to distribute better-class birds throughout the Middle East.[46]

A much smaller contribution was made to beekeeping. The Department's Poultry and Bee-Keeping Division promoted beekeeping in the form of "short courses for beginners, control of disease, destruction of hornets, loans to beginners and sale of duty-free sugar for bee-feeding." However, beehives were best placed in citrus groves[47] and so were unsuitable for most Arab farms. In addition, few *fallāḥīn* seemed to attend the courses. In 1934, two two-week courses of practical instruction in beekeeping were held. The attendance at the Arabic course was 27 farmers, with 25 at the Hebrew one.[48] The volume of loans registered for beehives in 1934 to 1937 also implies that the number of Arab farmers involved was small, as was the amount of money they received (Table 7.3).

FARMING ADVICE: METHODS OF COMMUNICATION

Any program aimed at improving agricultural production or preventing its decline among the *fallāḥīn* would be doomed without adequate communication. A communication failure between the Department and the peasantry has already been noted in the case of wheat and barley seeds. How prevalent was this?

The Lack of Professional Agricultural Instructors

In the late 1920s, the Jewish philanthropist Sir Ellis Kedoorie left a bequest to the British government for educational purposes in Palestine. After long legal arguments, the High Commissioner decided in 1931 to split the bequest and establish two agricultural schools: one for Jews near Mount Tabor and one for Arabs in Tulkarm.[49] The intention was that the training received in the Arab schools would be transferred into Arab villages by the now better-educated agricultural advisers and would assist the progress of the *fallāḥīn*. In practice, the educational level of that school was not high enough, nor were its graduates sufficiently integrated into the Arab rural sector, as Keen describes:

> There is a marked contrast as between Arab and Jew in the facilities for training and supply of the subordinate officers, especially

Table 7.3 Beehive Loans, 1934 to 1936

	Arabs			Jews			
	Number of Loans	£P	% of Total	Number of Loans	£P	% of Total	Total in £P
1934	47	212.5	65.9	20	110.0	34.1	322.5
1935	134	668.735	49.0	93	698.29	51.0	1367.025
1936	22	97.5	45.3	12	118.055	54.7	215.555
Total	203	978.735	51.4	125	926.345	48.6	1905.08

Source: ISA/(RG6)/BOX1931/1101/8, "Beehive Loans."

> those in direct contact with the farmers. The Jewish community is well provided with facilities for agricultural instruction: the WIZO schools, as at Nahalal (for women only); the Jewish Farmers' Federation School at Pardess Hanna; the large Mikveh Israel school. Recently, the Hebrew University has opened a college at Rehovot as part of its new Faculty of Agriculture. On the Arab side there is only the Kedoorie Agricultural School at Tulkarm, which has had so far an unfortunately chequered career. Originally the two Kedoorie schools were expected to produce the future agricultural officers, but experience has shown that the scholars of Mount Tabor are absorbed by the Jewish colonies, while those from Tulkarm are inadequately trained. Further, their entry into the Agricultural Services can only be as on occasional replacements, as the Department of Agriculture is fully staffed on its existing (but inadequate) basis. . . . It would be improved if the school became the responsibility of the Department of Education, and at the suggestion of the Department of Agriculture the transfer has now been made. . . . the country is too small to sustain an institution for the exclusive purpose of training a junior agricultural staff, and yet it is the outdoor staff of this class that are in closest contact with the farmers, and on whom, therefore, the possibility of agricultural improvement really depends.[50]

Media Communications

One way of handling with the problem of "inadequate" field staff was to develop indirect communication. *Mukhtār*s in Arab villages were expected to convey information from the Department of Agriculture to the *fallāḥīn*. Much of this was delivered to *mukhtār*s in the form of leaflets. These were about insects and pests and how to control them; notes on animal breeding, high-yield varieties of seeds and seedlings, manure, and soil conservation; advice on cultivation of different fruits, vegetables, and grains, and so forth.[51] Not surprisingly, of 96 people in Jaffa and Ramleh subdistricts who received the "Advice to Citrus Growers as to Spraying against Red Scale" leaflets in 1936, 65 were *mukhtār*s, and 31 were "land owners."[52]

The small number of leaflets does not necessarily indicate that only a few farmers were aware of their content. Since the majority of the *fallāḥīn* were illiterate,[53] and many of the *mukhtār*s were either illiterate or had low literacy skills,[54] it was expected that, if read, this would be done by "collective reading." This practice is better known in regard to newspapers, as explored by Ami Ayalon—the gathering of people, usually at the *mukhtār*'s house, to hear the news read aloud by a literate person.[55] It could also be done for agricultural leaflets, although the sophisticated language that these tended to use may have left some of the points unclear (as did radio programs; see below).

Still, newspapers sporadically backed up leaflets in much simpler language, as in the agricultural advice to *fallāḥīn* in *Al-karmil al-jdīd,*[56] and the "*fallāḥ* page" (*ṣaḥīfah al-fallāḥ;* a name that changed over time) in *Al Difa,*[57] which primarily offered advice on cultivation in response to readers' questions. In addition, newspapers occasionally carried advertisements about different technologies that were aimed at illiterates as well, like the advertisement shown in Document 7.1 with pictures of different bugs and the words "Keating's powder . . . kills all these insects."

Another medium by which the Department tried to communicate with farmers was a weekly radio program called *Talks to Farmers* in Arabic (Tuesdays) and Hebrew (Mondays). These programs carried extensive information and included much that was in the leaflets. But the system's Achilles heel was that radio sets were rare in villages. Some radios were lent to villages by the Department but not many. At the end of 1937, 70 had been supplied to Arab villages (22 in the Northern Division, 19 in the Western, and 29 in the Southern),[58] a very small number for about a thousand Arab villages. Moreover, many of the *fallāḥīn* did not listen to the program. The Department discovered that a main constraint was that its talks were not given in popular speech but in a more elaborate and technical form of Arabic that reflected the written language. Officials therefore changed the style and worked to make the programs more attractive.[59] Even so, the village audience as reported by *mukhtār*s was negligible. In the three villages in Gaza subdistrict where radio sets were

ان الصراصير ، والخنافس ، والبق ، والناموس ، والذباب ، وجميع الحشرات تنقل الامراض ، وتحمل الميكروبات وتزعج الناس ، اما طريقة محاربتها وقتلها وابادتها فهي ان ترش كيتنج .

كل شيء غير كيتنج يدوخ الحشرات ولا يقتلها فتعود اليك بعد ساعة . أما كيتنج فانه يقتل الحشرات قتلا فلا ترجع ابداً ، رش كيتنج حول السرير وفي المطبخ وغرف النوم او رش سائل كيتنج فيقتل جميع الحشرات

KEATING'S

كيتنج سائل ـ وكيتنج بودرة

الوكلاء : المستودع ـ الشركة المصرية البريطانية التجارية

مصر ـ سوريا وفلسطين

فرع فلسطين : يافا — شارع يافا — تل أبيب تلفون ١٠٦٢

Document 7.1 Agricultural Advertisement, 1936
Source: Al Difa, 1 July 1936.

available, it was reported that, on average per village, 37 persons came to listen to the *Talks*.[60] This figure may be inflated upward because of the fear that if attendance was low, the radio sets would be taken back by the Department, as indeed happened.[61] There were other problems as well: the supply of batteries was not always adequate, and *fallāḥīn* repeatedly complained that the language was still too complicated and asked for "simple language, i.e. public language when broadcasting as it is easy for the fallaheens to understand the talks so that they could understand."[62]

Although some of the knowledge that the Department wished to convey to the *fallāḥīn* failed to reach them, it nevertheless achieved some success.

Demonstration Plots

In an *Al Difa* article referred to earlier, *fallāḥīn* asked for more guidance from governmental agricultural advisers.[63] This could be viewed as a call for increased direct contact with the villages. Insofar as contact occurred, it was mainly in certain locations outside the villages—the demonstration plots. These were intended as an alternative way of teaching the use of better technologies. The leading government farm for agricultural research and guidance in Acre had eight subsidiary stations in different regions. In these stations and in a few plots in nearby villages, new methods of cultivation were demonstrated to farmers, alongside guidance on the use of manure, fertilizers, high-yielding seeds, and new types of crops. Fertilizers and other supplies could be acquired from the stations.[64] In addition, after agreements between the government and the Jewish Agency, the Jewish experimental and guidance farms in Rehovot and Kiriat 'Anavim were—at least officially—opened to Arabs.[65]

There are no comprehensive data about the number of *fallāḥīn* who attended these plots and stations. Some indeed visited stations and even bought various materials. But they seemed to be mainly from the farms adjacent to the limited number of demonstration plots.[66] Communication with the *fallāḥīn* via this channel was not very effective. Much attention, for example, was given by the Department to the control of the *scythris temperatella* pests (known as El-Duda [*al-dūdah*] in departmental correspondence), which caused significant losses in grain yield in the valleys. Three ways were found to control the El-Duda: to use legumes in crop rotation more often, to use a variety of fertilizers, and to use deep plowing. Yet two main problems emerged. First, there was a paucity of demonstration plots where the *fallāḥīn* could learn about these remedies. In the agricultural year 1936 to 1937, after several years of departmental operations against the El-Duda, there were only six such plots in the Southern District, two in the villages in Gaza subdistrict, and four in the Jaffa and Ramle subdistricts.[67] Second, even if a *fallāḥ* had learned about the new techniques, implementation of the advice given on the stations was not always practical for poorer *fallāḥīn*. The adoption of deep plowing equipment was too expensive; as reported, "only wealthy *fallāḥīn* can afford this practice."[68] Fertilizers were also expensive.

The fact that the advice could have been too costly for an ordinary *fallāḥ* to follow could also have discouraged attendance at the farms and plots. In a village where an interviewee stated that no *fallāḥ* went to see the farms, he explained this was because it was clear to them that "we knew better than them how to do olive seedlings."[69] He may have been right about the seedlings, but no check was made of whether any other kind of advice or support was available. It seems that information (or misconception) about one unsuitable or inadequate kind of service led to a preconception about other services. The demonstration plots were therefore useful only to a limited number of *fallāḥīn*.

The relatively small number of demonstration plots, their distance from most of the farms, and the limited knowledge of the *fallāḥin* about activities at the plots led to lack of confidence in their applicability. Further, a perception of the cost of new technologies hardened as information and materials trickled into Arab villages. More spending on demonstration plots and on more direct promotion of services in the villages—such as visits from agricultural advisers—was needed. In spite of the government's efforts, it seems that funds for communication were too light. The result was that some important information, including the actions taken to follow up government inquiries, did not reach its target.

GOVERNMENT LOANS

Assistance in Cases of Distress

The government gave loans to farmers in cases of crop failure, which was usually the result of lack of rain and devastation caused by mice, floods, earthquakes, and so on.[70] The interest rate on these was as low as 5 percent per annum and 9 percent on arrears. Such rates (see Chapter 5), were tempting compared to other options. Most of these loans were made before 1940 and were usually in kind (commonly wheat and barley) to encourage *fallāḥīn* who did not have enough grain for sowing. But loans were also given in cash—for example, to buy plow animals where there had been a heavy loss of these.[71] A senior official wrote in 1939:

> I am directed by the High Commissioner to inform you that with the approval of the Secretary of State, His Excellency has decided to provide seed loans in kind for normal sowing amounting to 2,500 tons seed wheat, 500 tons seed barley, 200 tons seed lentils at an estimated cost of £P. 30,000.
>
> These loans will be limited to villages and settlements which have no cash or creditworthiness for the purchase of seed for normal sowing, especially those which have been affected by the failure of the last season's crops. Loans will be made according to need, irrespective of Arab or Jewish demand.[72]

According to the Director of Agriculture and Fisheries, G. G. Masson, the government believed that it gave loans to "farmers who were most needy."[73] It worked on the assumption that the *mukhtār,* the government's local watchman, handled the matter properly:

> The mukhtars who are remunerated by Government are Government watchmen. It is considered that there is little to fear of any loss [on seed loans]. Firstly, Government has under paragraph 5(a) of the Short Term Crop Loans (Security) Ordinance 1935, priority over any other money lender to recover debts, the mukhtar and elders are signatories of the contract, and guarantors of the loan are in a stronger position to safeguard Government interests than Agents of the money lenders, and finally the money can be collected in the usual way by the machinery at the disposal of the District Administration.[74]

However, giving loans to needy villages was no guarantee that they would reach the neediest individuals. The fact that the "*mukhtār* and elders" were "signatories of the contract" gave them no incentive to allocate such loans to those whom they regarded as the least creditworthy borrowers, usually the poorest,[75] because a failure by the poor to repay meant that the government would demand repayment from the signatories, among others, because "the village collectively . . . held responsibility for due repayment as a first lien to Government of all or any of the village crops collectively in the event of default."[76] In addition, individual borrowers usually had to have two guarantors with good security. In 1930, for example, the Northern District Commissioner was instructed to approve each loan only on reliable information that the guarantors of each borrower were of "good standing."[77] The poor, especially those from poor *ahl*s, were unlikely to have such guarantors. In this respect, the government seemed unwittingly to have created a problem between principal and agent because the attitude of the *mukhtār*s and elders was a disincentive to allocate loans to whom were mainly directed.

In addition, expecting the *mukhtār*s (and in some cases other notables) to handle the distribution of loans, given that they wished to get such loans for themselves, was like getting the mouse to watch the cheese. It was surprising to discover in interviews that while many *fallāḥīn* did not know that *mukhtār*s received such assistance, those who were more aware of the interaction between notables and the government knew that assistance was given but believed that the *mukhtār*s and their associates often kept it for themselves.[78] On the other hand, not all the *mukhtār*s were dishonest. "Our *mukhtār* received [on loan] wheat from the government and distributed it to everyone in the village," said a former *fallāh* whom I interviewed. Both he[79] and another *fallāḥ* interviewed considered that the government's grain distribution (usually wheat) in cases of shortage was vital.[80]

The Accountant General's files in the Israel State Archives contain information about such loans, which is presented in Table 7.4. This table suggests that loans were usually issued to a restricted number of villages. Further, even within these selected villages, few people received them. While it is impossible to trace the number of recipients of loans that were registered in the names of borrowers and their associates (or "co."), the information about agricultural loans for 1933 to 1934 and fodder loans in 1934 to 1945 (both in Ramallah subdistrict) implies that on average, 10.5 loans were issued per village. Given the need for good security for loans, the risks from collective guarantee, and tendencies for "rent-seeking,"[81] it seems that although planned for the village as a whole, the recipients were usually the better-off and/or those associated with the *mukhtār*s.

Such loans accounted for most of the government's rural lending in the period up to 1939. Among less frequent kinds of loan were those for beehives (see Table 7.3). At the same time, some long-term loans were given in the hill country and others to encourage farmers to grow more forage crops (Table 7.5).[82] A closer look at Table 7.5 reveals a surprising feature. On the one hand, some better-off borrowers in the selected (yet poor) villages seemed to receive the loans and also had good guarantors. On the other hand, many of the loans were not repaid, especially during the years 1930 to 1935, as illustrated in Figure 7.2. The

Table 7.4 Loans Issued in Cases of Distress, 1929 to 1935

Year	Loan Type	Information	Remarks
1929–30	Agricultural loans in Nablus subdistrict	Loans amounting to about £P590 were issued to 116 borrowers and their associates in several Arab villages.	Average loan: £5.09. Wheat was issued as loans.
1930–1	Agricultural loans in Nazareth subdistrict	"The number of seed loans issued is 1,141 amounting LP. 6962,500 mills" (i.e., £P6962.5).	Average loan: £P6.1.
1933–4	Agricultural loans in Ramallah subdistrict	Loans amounting to £P300 were issued to 98 borrowers in 7 Arab villages.	Average loan per individual: £P3.06. Average loan per village: £P42.86.
1933–34	Fodder loans in Ramallah subdistrict	Loans amounting to £P203 were issued to 160 borrowers in several villages.	Average loan per individual: £P1.27. Average loan per village: £P16.57
1934–5	Fodder loans in Ramallah subdistrict	Loans amounting to £P580 were issued to 341 borrowers in 35 Arab villages.	Average loan per individual: £P1.7. Most loans were of one kantar (288.45 kilograms) of barley, equal to £P1.75. Average loan per village: £P16.57
1934–5	Agricultural loans in Nablus subdistrict	Loans amounting to £P1490 were issued to 96 borrowers "& Co." in 3 Arab villages.	Average loan per "borrower & co.": £P15.52. Average loan per village: £P15.52.

Source: Lists in ISA/(RG6)/BOX1928/1101/2, and letters in that box: 20 November 1930, Treasurer to Chief Secretary regarding seed loans; 9 May 1931, District Officer, Nazareth to Treasurer.

Note: The lists for 1929 to 1930 are those in Arabic attached to a letter from the District Officer in Nablus to the District Commissioner of the Northern District, 23 July 1931.

reason for this paradox is related not to inability to pay but rather to the government's lack of will to collect the loans. The government continually remitted loans and was apparently not eager to collect them during those years. When it became more active, much more was recovered (see Table 7.5 for 1936 and 1939). As the Treasurer explained, the high level of repayment in 1919 to 1923 was in contrast to 1930 to 1935:

> The high percentage of collections in the period 1919–23 was due to the energetic action taken by District Commissioners for recovery at the time when the farmer could repay.[83]

In fact, as the Treasurer observed in 1939, there was high demand for loans, partly because of a wish to "obtain from the Government something for nothing."[84] This is support by interviews, where the issuing of seed loans was regarded by borrowers as a contribution from the government. The decision to become determined to collect loans in 1939 evidently paid off.[85]

The Long-Term Loans of the Mid-1940s

The government changed its loan scheme during the 1940s. First, as can be seen from comparing Table 7.5 with Table 7.6, the amount of money given as loans in agriculture significantly increased. Second, the objectives of the loans were changed. Although from 1940 to 1944 some were provided as assistance in cases of distress,[86] these were limited. Most of the money—81 percent—was lent to citrus growers. It was aimed at avoiding a collapse resulting from the import restrictions during the war.[87] Citrus (see Figure 2.6) was grown by a small number of Arab farmers, but the total was almost equally divided between Arabs and Jews. The loans, as can be seen in Table 7.6, were divided in the same proportion.

Government policy for the noncitrus sector during World War II was supervised by the Middle East Supply Centre. Loans to these farmers were intended mainly to increase food production in the hope of achieving self-sufficiency.[88] The aim was to

Table 7.5 Direct Government Loans to Arab and Jewish Farmers, 1919 to 1939 (all Palestine, current prices)

	Description	Issued, £P	Written Off	Outstanding in 1945
1919–23	Agricultural loans	576,319	26,814	1,278
1927	Beersheba (drought) loans	19,980	547	0
1928	Northern District (seed) Loans	19,366	10,218	0
1930	Agricultural loans	29,980	15,708	528
1931	Agricultural loans	17,137	4,581	28
1932	Agricultural loans	53,537	30,778	360
1933	Agricultural loans	57,259	33,797	353
1933	Fodder loans	20,720	17,575	611
1934	Agricultural loans	6,313	4,408	17
1935	Agricultural loans	4,988	4,106	41
1936	Agricultural loans	33,019	1,074	1,510
1935–38	Hill development	33,098	0	3,171
1935–38	Other loans	7,263	418	995
1939	Agricultural loans	28,355	816	31
Total		907,334	124,026	8,923

Source: Government of Palestine, *A Survey of Palestine*, p. 349.

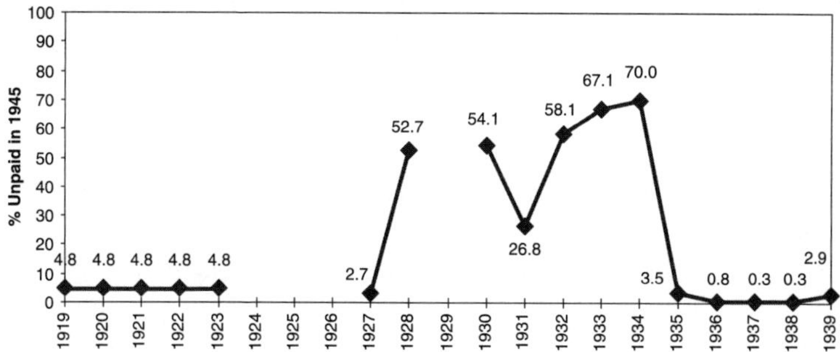

Figure 7.2 Ratio of Unpaid Loans Issued to Farmers, 1919 to 1939
Note: The ratio was calculated as a combination of the sums written off and outstanding in 1945, against the issued loan (see Table 7.5).

enlarge the area under cultivation and to farm already cultivated plots more intensively.[89] Of these loans, 53 percent were medium term, most of them repayable in five years. They were for irrigation, vegetables, fodder, livestock, diversification of farming in citrus areas, cropping under improved rotation, auxiliary farming, and purchase of tractors and boats, and some went to the Rehovot Farm. About 47 percent were short-term, one or two years, and were given for deep plowing for cereal cultivation and for the purchase of fertilizers and grain seeds.[90]

The loans to increase food production, however, were given mainly to Jews, who, as discussed in Part 2, held a much smaller share of agricultural land. The reason seemed to be that the government considered them better able to increase production.[91] It seems these particular loans were almost nonexistent in 1945 to 1947:

> After October, 1944, the issue of further loans were stopped save in a few exceptional cases. Government considered that the greatly increased prices obtained by farmers for their produce during the war left them generally with ample resources to finance further development without the need of further loans.[92]

Overall, a limited number of modest loans were provided by the government to Arab farmers in both periods discussed—1919 to

Table 7.6 Direct Government Loans to Arab and Jewish Farmers, 1940 to 1944 (all Palestine, current prices)

	For the Increase of Food Production			For Citrus		
	Issued, £P	Written Off	Outstanding in 1945	Issued, £P	Written Off	Outstanding in 1945
1940	104,735	0	2,099	443,295	0	350,133
1941	221,555	0	8,737	533,280	0	443,176
1942	359,805	0	19,529	609,965	0	538,534
1943	165,483	0	6,831	753,715	0	691,545
1944	5,000	0	180	718,505	0	706,607
1945 (estimates)	0	0	0	600,000	0	600,000
Total	856,578		37,376	3,658,760	0	3,329,995
Arab and Jewish shares	Jews 67.5 / Arabs 32.5 (0% 50% 100%)			Jews 53 / Arabs 47 (0% 50% 100%)		

Source: Government of Palestine, *A Survey of Palestine*, pp. 353–56.

1939 and the 1940s—and only a small fraction of those allocated in the 1940s went to the *fallāḥīn.*

CONCLUSION

It is clear that substantial investment in agricultural technology could have boosted the *fallāḥīn* economy. The government believed that it should help to provide such technologies not only because the *fallāḥīn* could not develop them on their own but also because they were usually unable to obtain the necessary inputs of high-yield seed varieties, fertilizers, vaccinations, and so forth. Indeed, many *fallāḥīn* had so little that they sometimes even lacked seeds for sowing after a bad harvest.

Although government spending rose after the Disturbances of 1929, funds for agricultural technology were very limited, especially since most of the government's contribution to the *fallāḥīn* was already committed to two other projects: the largely failed credit reform and the destructive land reform. The Department of Agriculture managed to add some money from the sales of products and services, but even so, the budget for agricultural technology remained quite small.

As a result, few agricultural experiments could go ahead, agricultural education was underresourced, and only a small number of free or subsidized services could be offered to the *fallāḥīn.* Nevertheless, the Department achieved significant results in combating animal diseases, in supporting poultry breeding, and probably in distributing high-yield vegetable seeds as well. But the lack of capital, imperfect information about the *fallāḥīn,* and the dishonesty of some of the *mukhtārs* created a syndrome in which the main beneficiaries of government assistance were well-off *fallāḥīn* or the associates of *mukhtār*s and were not the poor *fallāḥīn* whom the government originally intended to help on grounds that they had the greatest potential to rebel. In time of crisis, the government was especially interested in assisting these *fallāḥīn* and provided loans to "villages in need" via their *mukhtārs.* However, the *mukhtār* was also the guarantor for loans (and feared defaults) and usually had an interest in obtaining them for himself and his associates. Consequently, many loans intended for the poorest *fallāḥīn* did not reach their destination.

Another area in urgent need of government investment was agricultural infrastructure—especially irrigation—since in most cases a *fallāḥ* could not set up an irrigation project on his own. At no time, however, did the government focus on this, and in some ways it even blocked development (see Chapter 2). The upgrading of existing roads was of some benefit to the *fallāḥīn*. In its building of new roads, government investment was driven primarily by the determination to control the country. Hence, during the Arab Revolt of 1936 to 1939, road development was extensive in the Arab rural areas. The improvement in rural infrastructure was therefore incidental.

Looking at the picture as a whole, the area of government spending that could have most benefited the *fallāḥīn* was agricultural technology and infrastructure, notably irrigation, but such investment as occurred was too small and too piecemeal, largely because of expenditure on other, ill-advised, *fallāḥīn* "rationalization" programs.

NOTES

1. "'Isti'idād al-fallāḥ al-'arabī," *Al Difa,* 5 January 1943.
2. Government of Palestine, Department of Statistics, *Statistical Abstract of Palestine* (Jerusalem, various years): for 1939, pp. 113–15; for 1940, p. 123; and for 1944–45, p. 81; Government of Palestine, *Report on the Accounts and Finances, 1946–7* (Jerusalem, 1948), p. 73.
3. B. A. Keen, *The Agricultural Development of the Middle East: A Report to the Director General Middle East Supply Centre, May 1945* (London, 1946), pp. 24–29, 80–82; Martin W. Wilmington, *The Middle East Supply Centre* (London, 1971), pp. 12, 90–94; Rachelle Leah Taqqu, *Arab Labor in Mandatory Palestine, 1920–1948,* Ph.D. thesis, Columbia University, 1977, p. 49.
4. Government of Palestine, *A Survey of Palestine: Prepared in De-*

cember 1945 and January 1946 for the Information of the Anglo-American Committee of Inquiry (Jerusalem, 1946), p. 354.

5. Infrastructure: The capital assets of a country available for public use, including roads, water systems, and other public utilities. Investment in rural infrastructure is intended to assist the rural economy.
6. Government of Palestine, *A Survey of Palestine,* p. 859.
7. Government of Palestine, *Statistical Abstract of Palestine 1944–45,* p. 251; Government of Palestine, *A Survey of Palestine,* p. 861.
8. Government of Palestine, *A Survey of Palestine,* pp. 859–60.
9. See the many descriptions of such activities in Government of Palestine, Department of Agriculture, *Annual Reports of the Department of Agriculture and Forests for the Year Ending March 1934;* as well as for the years ending March 1935, 1936, 1937, and 1938.
10. Government of Palestine, Department of Agriculture, *Annual Report for the Year 1945–46* (Jerusalem, 1945), pp. 31–32.
11. Ibid., for the year ending March 1937, p. 8.
12. This issue was expanded in Nadan, *The Arab Rural Economy,* chap. 2.
13. Government of Palestine, Department of Agriculture, *Annual Report for the Year Ending March 1937,* p. 19.
14. Much evidence about such activities was found in ISA. See especially files in Boxes 663–64 (AG/35) and also the correspondence in ISA/(RG7)/BOX4177/F/14/A/11/9 and PRO/CO/733/229/10, 5 December 1932, Chaim Arlosoroff, the Jewish Agency for Palestine, to Sir A. G. Wauchope. See also correspondence in ISA/(RG7)/BOX4177/F/14/A/11/9.
15. Great Britain, Colonial Office, *Report on Immigration, Land Settlement* and *Development, by Sir John Hope Simpson* (London, 1930); Government of Palestine, *A Survey of Palestine,* p. 27.
16. Keen, *The Agricultural Development of the Middle East,* pp. 80–81.
17. Ibid., p. 81.
18. Government of Palestine, *A Survey of Palestine,* pp. 114, 343–46. See also Government of Palestine, Department of Agriculture, *Annual Report for the Year 1945–46,* pp. 34–41; Montague Brown, "Agriculture," Sa'id B. Himadeh (ed.), *Economic Organization in Palestine* (Beirut, 1938), p. 161.

19. Government of Palestine, *A Survey of Palestine,* p. 344.
20. Ibid.
21. "Šaḥifah al- fallāḥ: zirā'ah al-hanṭah," *Al Difa,* 4 January 1943.
22. Government of Palestine, *Statistical Abstract of Palestine 1944–5,* p. 226.
23. Government of Palestine, *A Survey of Palestine,* pp. 344–45.
24. Ibid., p. 344. Another example is in Government of Palestine, Department of Agriculture, *Annual Report for the Year 1944–45,* p. 6.
25. As mentioned earlier.
26. E.g., interview with Ya'aqūb Nāṣir Waqīm from Ramah (Mr. Waqīm, b. 1908, is the son of a *fallāḥīn* family who worked as an agriculturist in the late Ottoman and Mandate periods) (6 April 1999); interview with Ya'aqūb Nāṣir Waqīm from Ramah (Mr. Waqīm, b. 1908, is the son of a *fallāḥīn* family who worked as an agriculturist in the late Ottoman and Mandate periods) (6 April 1999).
27. A. F. Nathan, Assistant Director of Agriculture and Forests, "Report of the Agricultural Service for the years 1931 and 1932," in Government of Palestine, Department of Agriculture, *Annual Report for the years 1931 and 1932,* p. 16.
28. Government of Palestine. Department of Agriculture, *Annual Report for the Year 1944–45,* p. 8.
29. See Chapter 4.
30. Government of Palestine, *A Survey of Palestine,* p. 343.
31. Government of Palestine, Department of Agriculture, *Annual Report for the Year 1944–1945,* p. 46.
32. See the Map Archive of the Palestine Exploration Fund, London.
33. Government of Palestine, *Memorandum on the Water Resources of Palestine* (Jerusalem, 1947), pp. 5, 13; Government of Palestine, *A Survey of Palestine,* pp. 423–34. See also "*Al-muḥāfaẓah 'ala al-turbah al-jabaliyyah,*" *Al-Difa,* 23 May 1945.
34. Government of Palestine, *A Survey of Palestine,* p. 343.
35. Government of Palestine, Department of Agriculture, *Annual Report* for *1926 by E. R. Sawer Director of Agriculture and Forests,* p. 5; Government of Palestine, *A Survey of Palestine,* pp. 425–29.
36. Land could be transferred to individuals who gained the rights of statutory tenants; see discussion in Chapter 4.
37. Government of Palestine, *A Survey of Palestine,* p. 427.

38. ISA/(RG2)//L/88/45, 31 August 1945, Acting Director of the Department of Lands Settlement to Chief Secretary.
39. Government of Palestine, *A Survey of Palestine,* p. 429.
40. See Table 2.3.
41. E.g., Government of Palestine, Department of Agriculture, *Annual Report for the Year Ending March 1936,* pp. 87–156; ibid., for the year ending March 1937, pp. 31–61; Government of Palestine, *A Survey of Palestine,* pp. 327–31.
42. Government of Palestine. *Annual Report of the Department of Agriculture for the year 1944–45,* p. 9.
43. ISA/(RG7)/BOX4167/F/6/9, August–September 1947, correspondence between the Conservator of Forests and the Director of Veterinary Services. They tried to understand the cause of the difference between the animals enumerated and those vaccinated. They concluded that this was related to the different timing of the vaccination compared with the enumeration (there was flock migration in-between), which they also suspected was combined with undercounting in the enumeration.
44. Government of Palestine, Department of Agriculture, *Annual Report for the Year Ending March 1936,* p. 120; ibid., for the year ending March 1937, p. 39.
45. Ibid. for the year ending March 1934, pp. 72–73. For village incubators in 1947, see ISA/(RG7)/BOX667/60/12, 24 October 1947, "Village Incubator Scheme."
46. Keen, *The Agricultural Development of the Middle East,* pp. 73–74.
47. Government of Palestine, Department of Agriculture, *Annual Report for the Year Ending March 1934,* pp. 73–74.
48. Ibid.
49. PRO CO/733/173/12, 19 June 1929, Officer Administering the Government of Palestine to Sidney Webb, P.C., His Majesty's Principal Secretary of State for the Colonies.
50. Keen, *The Agricultural Development of the Middle East,* p. 82.
51. ISA/(RG7)/BOX628/AG/5/1, various years, "Agricultural Leaflets."
52. ISA/(RG7)/BOX631/11/12, c. 1936–37, "Advice to Citrus Growers as to Spraying Against Red Scale."
53. See Chapter 3.

54. Ylana N. Miller, *Government and Society in Rural Palestine, 1920–1948* (Austin, TX, 1985), pp. 60–61.
55. Ami Ayalon, *Reading Palestine: Printing and Literacy 1900–1948* (Austin, TX, 2004).
56. E.g., "Naṣā'j 'ila al- fallāḥīn," *Al-karmil al-jdīd,* no. 1837, 1935.
57. E.g., "Saḥīfah al-fallāḥ," *Al Difa,* November 1935, p. 6.
58. ISA/(RG7)/BOX652/AG/61/2, 9 December 1937, "Circular No. 50 to all Heads of Services," by the Director of Agriculture and Fisheries of Palestine.
59. Ibid.
60. ISA/(RG7)/BOX653/AG/67, 14 August 1939, Agricultural Inspector in Gaza to Agricultural Officer in Jaffa.
61. ISA/(RG7)/BOX653/AG/67, 31 May 1940, Director of Agriculture and Fisheries to Chief Agricultural Officer and Agricultural Officers in Tel Aviv, Jerusalem and Haifa, "talks to farmers—radio sets."
62. ISA/(RG7)/BOX653/AG/67, 14 August 1939, Agricultural Inspector in Gaza to Agricultural Officer in Jaffa.
63. "'Isti'idād al-fallāḥ al-'arabī," *Al Difa,* 5 January 1943.
64. Government of Palestine, *A Survey of Palestine,* pp. 114, 343–46. See also Government of Palestine, Department of Agriculture, *Annual Report for the Year 1945–46,* pp. 34–41 and for 1942, p. 5; Brown, "Agriculture," p. 161.
65. Government of Palestine, *A Survey of Palestine,* pp. 342–47. See more details of the agreements in PRO CO/733/229/10.
66. Interview with Slīmān 'Adawī from Tur'an (Mr. 'Adawī, b. 1926–28, was a *fallāḥ* in the Mandate period and an agriculture adviser in Israel; he worked with some who had been agriculture advisers in the Mandate period) (5 April 1999); interview with Būlus Ḥanna Būlus from Acre (Mr. Būlus, b. 1910, was a notable landlord with urban businesses during the Mandate; he also participated as a "full-time" rebel in the Arab Revolt; today he is a poet famous in the Arab world) (18 August 1999). Many other interviewees were asked about visits to the farms and plots and responded negatively.
67. ISA/(RG7)/BOXES631-2/AG/11/1/6, correspondence regarding El-Duda.
68. Ibid.
69. Interview with Ya'aqūb Nāṣir Waqīm from Ramah (Mr. Waqīm,

b. 1908, is the son of a *fallāḥīn* family who worked as an agriculturist in the late Ottoman and Mandate periods) (6 April 1999).

70. E.g., ISA/(RG6)/BOX1928/38, correspondence about agricultural loans.
71. For the latter, see ISA/(RG6)/BOX1928/1101/2, 16 August 1934, A. G. Wauchope (High Commissioner for Palestine) to Sir Philip Cunliffe-Lister (His Majesty's Principal Secretary of State for the Colonies).
72. ISA/(RG6)BOX1928/1101/2, 25 November 1939, Chief Secretary to District Commissioners and Director of Agriculture and Fisheries.
73. ISA/(RG6)BOX1928/1101/2, 24 October 1939, Director of Agriculture and Fisheries to W. J. Johnson, Treasurer.
74. ISA/(RG6)BOX1928/1101/2, 10 November 1939, Director of Agriculture and Fisheries to W. J. Johnson, Treasurer.
75. See Chapter 5 for a similar case in regard to bank loans.
76. ISA/(RG6)BOX1928/1101/2, 25 November 1939, Chief Secretary to District Commissioners and Director of Agriculture and Fisheries.
77. ISA/(RG6)BOX1928/1101/2, 25 November 1930, Chief Secretary to District Commissioner of the Northern District.
78. Interview with Slīmān 'Adawī; interview with Abū 'Ātif Fāhūm from Nazareth (Mr. Fāhūm, b. 1927–28, is the son of Yūsif Fāhūm, the Mayor of Nazareth during different years of the Mandate period; his father was also a landlord) (17 August 1999); interview with Mohammad Ḥasūna from Abu Ghosh (Ḥaj Ḥasūna, b. 1929, was a *fallāḥ* who was also employed as wage laborer in Jerusalem during the Mandate period) (31 July 1999); interview with 'Amiram Argaman from Kibuz Ḥamadiya (Mr. Argaman, b. 1928, grew up in the Jewish settlement of 'Atlit and studied in Haifa; he had close connections with Arabs who lived in villages adjacent to 'Atlit) (29 August 2000).
79. Interview with Raḍwan Salīm Bisharat (Mr. Bisharat, b. 1914, was a *fallāḥ* who lived in Ma'lul village) (22 August 2000).
80. E.g., interview with Raḍwan Salīm Bisharat; interview with Jamāl 'Ilyās Khūri from Meghar (Mr. Khūri, b. 1905, was a *fallāḥ* and later a policeman during the Mandate period) (23 August 1999).
81. Rent-seeking behavior: Behavior that improves the welfare of someone at the expense of the welfare of someone else.

82. Government of Palestine, Department of Agriculture, *Annual Report for the Year Ending March 1935,* p. 5.
83. ISA/(RG6)BOX1928/1101/2, "Note by the Treasurer on the Issue of Agricultural Loans in 1939."
84. Ibid.
85. Ibid. and Figure 7.5.
86. E.g., Government of Palestine, Department of Agriculture, *Annual Report for the Year 1943–44,* p. 3.
87. Government of Palestine, *A Survey of Palestine,* pp. 353–57.
88. Government of Palestine, Department of Agriculture, *Annual Report for the Year Ended March 31, 1941,* p. 4.
89. Ibid., p. 23.
90. Government of Palestine, *A Survey of Palestine,* p. 353.
91. See Table 7.5. For the positive attitude of the Middle East Supply Centre toward Jewish agriculture, see Keen, *The Agricultural Development of the Middle East,* pp. 24–27.
92. Government of Palestine, *A Survey of Palestine,* p. 354.

Conclusions

The question of the precise trends in net Arab agricultural product throughout the Mandate period is at present unanswerable and will probably remain so because of the many uncertainties in surviving data about output and to some extent about prices. But a close analysis of a wide range of material gives us an approximate picture of trends and challenges the conclusion of Metzer and Kaplan that the years 1922 to 1939 were characterized by high and sustained growth in Mandate Palestine. The story is rather one of little or no economic growth, and when this is combined with the relatively strong demographic growth during this period, a pattern of continual deterioration per capita becomes apparent. This result is derived not only from a careful reconsideration of Metzer and Kaplan's data but also from the use of alternative direct data on output as well as of indirect quantitative and qualitative data, most of which were not included in earlier studies. Together, these reveal an aggregate lack of investment in land, irrigation, and new technologies, as well as a burgeoning increase in human population that outstripped the modest increase in livestock. In such a context, total factor productivity growth in the Arab rural sector could not have been positive.

The 1940s were markedly different. Government statistics on net Arab agricultural product for this decade (the figures used by

Metzer and Kaplan) are much more accurate and reliable and support the scenario of high and sustained growth. However, this occurred chiefly because of an increase in relative prices of agricultural foodstuffs and not as a result of significant agricultural development or government policies. However, some successes in the government's "green revolution" undergirded the increase in production, and this was enhanced by a limited investment in technology. The relative lift in prices during the prosperity, as the World War II years were known, was due mainly to changes in the regional security situation—the constraints on shipping and the development of Palestine into a large military base—causing an increase in demand for agricultural foodstuffs. At the same time, the income for *fallāḥīn* from farm and nonfarm employment rose sharply, especially from new, military-related jobs. This reduced the longstanding unemployment and underemployment of the *fallāḥīn* and provided higher real wages for low-skilled laborers in general. By 1943, real wages had doubled, in constant prices, from their 1940 level.

By definition, a comparison of outputs between two distant benchmark years overlooks the movements in between, especially when average annual growth is assessed between the benchmarks. As there is a tendency to use this method in some literature, it is worth mentioning that data comparing the benchmark years of 1922 and 1945 appear to suggest little growth per capita, because of the notable upturn of the prosperity years.

The question of the overall influence of the Jews on the *fallāḥīn* is not, of course, a simple one. The impact of the direct integration of the Arab rural sector into the Jewish sector, as a result of the government's transfer of funds from the Jewish economy into the Arab rural economy, cannot be accurately assessed. Still, the macro trends in Arab agriculture between 1922 and 1939 may suggest that this interaction largely failed to stimulate the Arab rural economy. But any economic assessment has to take into account the ethnonational conflict, which drove the

British to conclude that "The possibility of war being the opportunity for rebellion in Palestine will depend on the strength of the forces which we [British] have in the country." This fear of further uprisings, and Britain's determination to retain control of the country, led to an indirect inward transfer of colonial resources from outside Palestine. Thus the violence between Arabs and Jews in Palestine "gave a hand" to the prosperity, and one cannot escape the conclusion that although there was a short-term economic deterioration during the Arab Revolt of 1936 to 1939, the long-term effect of violence was to substantially boost the *fallāḥīn* economy.

The primary mission of the British in Palestine was to hold and administer the country. After the Disturbances of 1929, the Mandatory government believed that Arab urban migration should be discouraged to reduce discontent. The main tool for this was the improvement of economic conditions in the Arab villages. Thus the government helped the *fallāḥīn* by reducing taxation and by supplying some agricultural services.

But the seriously flawed paradigm of *fallāḥīn* "irrationality" that guided British policymakers led the government to engage in inappropriate, Marxist-style reforms. An investigation of these reforms is unique to the present study and demonstrates that land reform replaced the traditional and locally efficient *mushā'* system by a considerably inferior system, in which plots were overconsolidated, and that further facilitated the transfer of land into Jewish hands. The parallel credit reform failed to replace the informal system of credit by a formal one. The key reason for high interest rates was the high risk from natural hazards and nationalist unrest and not, as British officials thought, the tendency of the *fallāḥīn* to "strategic default" and the exploitative practices of their moneylenders. The government also failed to "rationalize" tenancy agreements, and its reform increased the risk to landlords. In fact, no state intervention along Marxist lines was necessary or indeed effective in the conditions of Mandate Palestine.

In retrospect, the final balance sheet of British intervention was high expenditure for very limited returns. If the government had invested instead in a range of agricultural services and especially in agricultural infrastructure and irrigation, the *fallāḥīn* economy could have benefited significantly. The present study is a telling demonstration of how a single misleading concept can devastate progress. Such a fundamental mistake could have been overcome if British officials and policymakers had analyzed the *fallāḥīn* economy more thoroughly from within.

Finally, it was noted that the government put much effort into improving health conditions and rural education, especially after the Disturbances of 1929. These programs were not based on a paradigm of capitalist colonialism and initiated a steady improvement in "human development" in the villages.

Another aim of this study was to examine the microstructure of the *fallāḥīn* economy and the changes that occurred in it during the Mandate period. Five main features were identified: an increase in inequality; a production system that was largely based on labor-intensive methods; the use of very simple agricultural implements that were much cheaper than more modern equipment; a skillful recourse to various measures that reduced production and consumption costs and increased income; and the existence of traditional institutions that in no way hindered, and in some cases even assisted, sound economic functioning.

A major reason for increased inequality was the protracted unemployment and underemployment in *fallāḥīn* society until the prosperity years, and also—to some extent—the local manipulation of government assistance by a small number of typically well-off *fallāḥīn*. The entrenched labor-intensiveness of the Arab economy under the Mandate resulted from the comparatively cheap cost of labor in relation to the cost of modern equipment, a ratio that lasted throughout this period. Another reason was the lack of capital to purchase expensive equipment.

The *fallāḥīn* utilized a range of techniques and institutions to reduce production and consumption costs. The essence of their part-subsistence, part-surplus production system and barter trade was to reduce transaction costs in an impoverished economy. Thus they consumed mainly basic agricultural goods and avoided value-added products. Labor was managed efficiently and vigorously both on and off the farms in barter as well as money terms. Sharecropping was the preferred practice, since it did not reduce productivity, and—especially in the form of joint farming—enabled a better use of the combined factors of production of landlord and tenant. It also reduced risk for both parties, since, unlike wage labor, landlord and tenant were mutually responsible for both receiving some profit. We have also seen that, consistent with the theory of induced institutional innovation, dynamic changes in the institution of sharecropping occurred because of a shift in factor ratios. These changes were not related to government intervention. Finally, it was shown that the patrilineal structure of the *fallāḥīn* economy minimized risk and increased labor productivity.

This study leaves open some questions for further research. One of the most important is verifying growth in the Arab economy as a whole, especially in light of the new conclusion about growth and development in the Arab rural economy. More research is needed on: the use in the Arab sector of money from land sales to Jews; the reasons for the diversion of the *murabb'ah* tenancy agreement into "rent-sharing" agreements; the sources of money for moneylenders; and the effectiveness of the Department of Agriculture's activities from an agroscientific perspective. It is hoped that this book will encourage comparative research, especially on rural economies and colonial reforms.

The failure to establish a peaceful and sustainable colonial regime in Palestine was the major reason for the British departure from the country. Britain does not seem to regret this. The 1948 war occurred because of the immaturity of Arab and Jewish leaders, who were unable to reach agreement on the division of the country. Today, on the same land, Arab and Jewish leaders still suffer from immaturity. There is no hope either in colonialism or immaturity.

Bibliography

Archives

Israel State Archives, Jerusalem (ISA)
Public Record Office, London (PRO)
Barclays Bank Archives, Manchester (Barclays)
Central Zionist Archives, Jerusalem (CZA)
Hagana Archives, Tel Aviv (Hagana)
Rhodes House, Oxford (RHs)
Palestine Exploration Fund, London (PEF)

Newspapers

Al-'Itiḥād
Al-Difa
Al-karmil
Al-karmil al-jdīd
Haaretz

Books, Articles, and Unpublished Dissertations

Abboushi, Wasfi F. "The Road to Rebellion: Arab Palestine in the 1930s." *Journal of Palestine Studies,* 6, no. 3, Issue 23 (1977), pp. 23–46.

Abcarius, M. F. "Fiscal System." Sa'id B. Himadeh (ed.), *Economic Organization in Palestine* (Beirut, 1938), pp. 507–56.

Abū Naṣir, Sāliḥ Mas'ūd. *Jihād sha'b filastin khilal niṣf qarn*, 3rd ed. (Beirut, 1970).

Abū Rajīlī, Khalīl. "'Al-zirā'ah al-'arabiyyah fī filasṭīn qabl dawlah 'isrā'īl." *sh'ūn filasṭīniyyah*, 11 (1972), pp. 128–43.

Adams, J. Vassall. *The Ottoman Bank in the Middle East* (London, 1948).

"Ahl." *The Encyclopaedia of Islam.* (CD edition: Leiden, 1999, author not mentioned).

Allen, Harold Boughton. *Rural Education and Welfare in the Middle East: A Report to the Director General, Middle East Supply Centre, September 1944* (London, 1946).

'Allūsh, Nājī. *Al-ḥarakah al-filisṭiniyyah 'amām al-yahūd wa-alṣahaynah* (Beirut, 1974).

Antonius, George. *The Arab Awakening* (New York, 1965).

Arab Bank. *Twenty-five Years of Service to the Arab Economy, 1930–1955* (Amman, 1956).

'Araf, Shukrī. *Al-qaryah al-'arabiyyah al- filasṭīniyah: mabnī wa-'isti'imālāt 'arāḍī* (Tarshīḥā, 1996).

'Araf, Shukrī. *Maṣādir al-'iqtiṣād al-filasṭīnī: min 'qdam alfatarāt 'ilā 'ām 1948* (Tarshīḥā, 1997).

Arnon-Ohana, Yoval. *Falaḥiym ba-mered ha-'aravi be-'erez yishrael 1936–1939* (Tel Aviv, 1978).

Arnon-Ohana, Yoval. "Heybetim ḥevratiyim 7epoliṭiyim betno'at hamered ha'aravi, 1936–1939." Danin, 'Ezra (ed.), *Te'udot vedmoyot miginzei haknufiyot ha'arviyot beme'ora'ot 1936–1939* (Jerusalem, 1981), introductory pages, pp. 25–34.

Artan, Scott. "Hamula Organization and Masha' Tenure in Palestine." *MAN*, 21, no. 2 (1986), pp. 271–295.

Asad, Talal. "Class Transformation under the Mandate," *Middle East Research and Information Project*, no. 53 (1976), p. 3.

Askari, Hossein, Ahmad Mustafa, and John Thomas Cummings. "Islam and Modern Economic Change." John L. Esposito (ed.), *Islam and Development: Religion and Sociopolitical Change* (New York, 1980), pp. 25–47.

Atkinson, Dorothy. *The End of the Russian Land Commune 1905–1930* (Stanford, CA, 1983).

Austin, Gareth M., and Kaoru Sugihara (eds.). *Local Suppliers of Credit in the Third World, 1759–1969* (London, 1993).

Avineri, Shlomo. *Karl Marx on Colonialism and Modernization* (New York, 1969)

Avneri, Arieh. *The Claim of Dispossession: Jewish Land Settlement and the Arabs, 1878–1948* (Tel Aviv, 1980).

Avrahamoviz, Ze'ev, and Izḥaq Guelfat, *Hamesheq ha-'aravi* (Tel Aviv, 1944).

Ayalon, Ami. *Reading Palestine: Printing and Literacy 1900–1948* (Austin, TX, 2004).

Bachi, Roberto. *The Population of Israel* (Jerusalem, 1977).

Baer, Gabriel. *'arviyey hamizraḥ hatikhon* (Tel Aviv, 1960).

Baer, Gabriel. *Fellah and Townsman in the Middle East: Studies in Social History* (London, 1982).

Baer, Gabriel. *Mavo layaḥasim ha'agrariyim bamizraḥ hatikhon, 1800–1970* (Jerusalem, 1971).

Ball, Richard, and Laurie Pounder, "'Efficient but Poor' Revised," *Economic Development and Cultural Change,* 44, no. 4 (1996), pp. 735–60.

Barro, Robert J. "Economic Growth in a Cross-Section of Countries." *Quarterly Journal of Economics,* 106, no. 2 (1991), pp. 407–44.

Bauer, P. T. "The Economics of Resentment: Colonialism and Underdevelopment." *Journal of Contemporary History,* 4, no. 1 (1969), pp. 51–71.

Beeri, Eliezer. *Reshit haiḥsoḥ yishrael 'arav* (Tel Aviv, 1985).

Beiger, Gid'on. "Ha-mivneh ha-ta'ashiyati shel 'arey 'ereẓ yishra'el venafoteyha be-reshit tequfat ha-mandat." *Qatedra,* 29 (1983), pp. 79–112.

Ben-Arieh, Yehosua. "The Population of Large Towns in Palestine during the First Eighty Years of the Nineteenth Century according to Western Sources." Moshe Ma'oz (ed.), *Studies on Palestine during the Ottoman Period* (Jerusalem, 1975), pp. 49–69.

Berenstein, Deborah S. *Constructing Boundaries: Jewish and Arab Workers in Mandatory Palestine* (New York, 2000).

Bowden, Tom. "The Politics of the Arab Rebellion in Palestine 1936–39." *Middle Eastern Studies,* 11, no. 2 (1975), pp. 147–174.

Brewer, Anthony. *Marxist Theories of Imperialism: A Critical Survey* (London, 1990).

Brown, Montague. "Agriculture." Sa'id B. Himadeh (ed.), *Economic Organization in Palestine* (Beirut, 1938), pp. 111–211.

Buheiry, R. Marwan. "The Agriculture Exports of Southern Palestine, 1885–1915." *Journal of Palestine Studies,* 10, no. 4, issue 40 (1981), pp. 61–81.

Bunton, Martin. "Demarcating the British Colonial State: Land Settlement in the Palestine *Jiftlik* Villages of Sajad and Qazaza." Roger Owen (ed.), *New Perspectives on Property and Land in the Middle East* (Harvard, 2000), pp. 121–58.

Burckhardt, John Lewis. *Travelers in Syria and the Holy Land* (London, 1822).

Cohen, Amnon. *Economic Life in Ottoman Jerusalem* (Cambridge, 1989).

Cohen, Amnon. "*Ḥamūla.*" in *The Encyclopaedia of Islam* (CD Edition: Leiden, 1999).

Cohen, Amnon. "*Mīrī.*" *Encyclopaedia of Islam* (CD Edition: Leiden, 1999).

Crafts, N. F. R. "Economic Growth in East Asia and Western Europe since 1950: Implications for Living Standards." *National Institute Economic Review,* no. 162 (1997), pp. 75–84.

al-Dabāgh, Muṣṭafa. *Bilādnā filasṭin* (Kafar Kara', 1988).

Danin, 'Ezra (ed.). *Te'udot vedmoyot miginzei haknufiyot ha'arviyot beme'ora'ot 1936–1939* (Jerusalem, 1981).

Dasgupta, Partha, and Martin Weale. "On Measuring the Quality of Life." *World Development,* 20, no. 1 (1992), pp. 119–31.

Dequech, David. "Rationality and Irrationality." Phillip A. O'Hara (ed.), *Encyclopedia of Political Economy* (London, 1999), pp. 957–60.

Doukhan, J. Moses. "Land Tenure." Sa'id B. Himadeh (ed.), *Economic Organization in Palestine* (Beirut, 1938), pp. 75–107.

Doumani, B. Beshara. "Rediscovering Ottoman Palestine: Writing Palestinian into History." *Journal of Palestine Studies,* 21, no. 2, issue 82 (1992), pp. 5–28.

Doumani, Beshara. *Rediscovering Palestine: Merchants and Peasants in Jabal Nablus, 1700–1900* (Berkeley, CA, 1995).

Dowson, Ernest M. *Progress in Land Reforms, 1923–1930* (Kent, 1930).

El-Eini, Rosa I. M. "The Agricultural Mortgage Bank in Palestine: The Controversy over Its Establishment." *Middle Eastern Studies,* 33, no. 4 (1997), pp. 751–76.

El-Eini, Rosa I. M. "Government Fiscal Policy in Mandatory Palestine." *Middle Eastern Studies,* 33, no. 3 (1997), pp. 570–96.

El-Eini, Rosa I. M. "The Implementation of British Agricultural Policy in Palestine in the 1930s." *MES,* 32, no. 4 (1996), pp. 211–50.

El-Eini, Rosa I. M. "Rural Indebtedness and Agricultural Credit Supplies in Palestine in the 1930s." *Middle Eastern Studies,* 33, no. 2 (1997), pp. 313–37.

Eliashar, Eliahu. "Mifqad ha-ta'ashiya vehamelakha shel memshelet erez-ishrael 1928." *Riv'on le-kalkala,* 26, no. 101–02 (1979), pp. 248–56.

Elizur, Yuval. *Loḥama kalkalit: me'ah shnot 'imut kalkali byn yehudim le'aravim* (Jerusalem, 1997).

Ellis, Frank. *Peasant Economics: Farm Households and Agrarian Development,* 2nd ed. (Cambridge, 1993).

Fāhūm, Yūsif. *Al-falāḥūn fi-al'arḍ* (Nazereth, 1957).

Firestone, Ya'akov. "Cash-Sharing Economics in Mandatory Palestine." *Middle Eastern Studies,* 11, no. 1 (1975), pp. 3–23 and no. 2, pp. 175–94.

Firestone, Ya'akov. "The Land-Equalizing *Mushā'* Village: A Reassessment." Gad G. Gilbar (ed.), *Ottoman Palestine, 1800–1914* (London, 1990).

Firestone, Ya'akov. "Production and Trade in an Islamic Context: Sharika Contracts in the Transitional Economy of Northern Samaria, 1853–1943." *International Journal of Middle East Studies,* vol. 6, 1975, pp. 185–209.

Forman, Geremy. "Settlement of Title in the Galilee: Dowson's Colonial Guiding Principles." *Israel Studies,* 7, no. 3 (2002), pp. 61–83.

Gavish, Dov. *Qarqa vemapa: mehesder haqarqa'ot lemapat erez yishra'el* (Jerusalem, 1991).

Gellner, Ernest. *Le'umim vele'umiyut* (Tel Aviv, 1994).

Gerber, Haim. "A New Look at the *Tanzimat:* The Case of the Province of Jerusalem." David Kushner (ed.), *Palestine in the Late Ottoman Period: Political, Social and Economic Transformation* (Jerusalem, 1986), pp. 30–45.

Gerber, Haim. "*Mushā'*." *The Encyclopedia of Islam* (CD Edition: Leiden, 1999).

Gertz, Aaron. *Hahityashvut haḥakla'it ha'ivrit beerez ishrael: sefer yad statisti leḥaklaut* (Jerusalem, 1945).

Gertz, Aaron (ed.). *Statistical Handbook of Jewish Palestine* (Jerusalem: Jewish Agency for Palestine, Department of Statistics, 1947).

Gertz, Aaron, and David Gurevich. *Hahityashvut haḥakla'it ha'ivrit beerez ishrael: sqira klalit 7esikumim statistiyyim* (Jerusalem, 1938).

Gertz, Aaron, and David Gurevich. *Hityashvut ḥakla'it 'ivrit beerez ishrael: sqira klalit 7esikumey mifqadim* (Jerusalem, 1947).

Gilbar, Gad G. "The Growing Economic Involvement of Palestine with the West, 1865–1914." David Kushner (ed.), *Palestine in the Late Ottoman Period: Political, Social and Economic Transformation* (Jerusalem, 1986), pp. 188–210.

Gilbar, Gad G. *Kalkalat hamizraḥ hatikhon ba'et haḥadasha* (Tel Aviv, 1990).

Gilbar, Gad G. "Megamot bahitpatḥut hademografit shel hapalesṭinim, 1870–1987." *Sqirot,* 108 (1989), pp. 1–53.

Goldberg, Mūsah. *vehakeren 'odena qayemet: pirqey ziḥronot* (Merchavia, 1965).

Goren, Tamir. *'meḥorban lehit'osheshut: korot ha-'uḥlusiyah ha'aravit beḥaifa, 1947–1950* (M. Phil. thesis, University of Haifa, 1993).

Gottheil, Fred M. "Money and Product Flows in Mid-Nineteenth-Century Palestine: The Physiocratic Model Applied." David Kushner (ed.), *Palestine in the Late Ottoman Period: Political, Social and Economic Transformation* (Jerusalem, 1986), pp. 211–230.

Government of Egypt. Department of Statistics. *Al-'iḥṣa' al-sanawī al-'am lil-qūtr al-maṣri, 1925–1927* (Cairo, 1927).

Government of Palestine. *The Banking Situation in Palestine with a*

Commentary on the Co-operative Society Movement, by F. G. Horwill (Jerusalem, 1936).

Government of Palestine. *Blue Books* (Jerusalem, various years).

Government of Palestine. *Census 1922: Enumeration Book* (Jerusalem, 1922).

Government of Palestine. *Census of Palestine 1931: Population of Villages, Towns and Administrative Areas, by E. Mills* (Jerusalem, 1932).

Government of Palestine. *Census of Palestine 1931: Report by E. Mills, Assistant Chief Secretary* (Alexandria, 1933).

Government of Palestine. Commissioner for Lands and Surveys, *Annual Report* (Jerusalem, various years).

Government of Palestine. *Cooperative Societies in Palestine: Report by the Registrar of Cooperative Societies on Developments During the Years 1921–1937* (Jerusalem, 1938).

Government of Palestine. Department of Agriculture (Forests and Fisheries). *Annual Reports* (Jerusalem, various years).

Government of Palestine. Department of Agriculture and Fisheries, *Annual Reports* (Jerusalem, various years).

Government of Palestine. Department of Agriculture and Fisheries. *Important Factors Governing Vegetable Growing in Palestine* (Jerusalem, 1938).

Government of Palestine. Department of Agriculture and Fisheries. *A Review of the Agricultural Situation in Palestine, by E. S. Sawer, Director of Agriculture, Palestine* (Jerusalem, 1922).

Government of Palestine. Department of Agriculture and Fisheries. *Village Note Book* (undated blank books for the years 1935–38 and 1943–46).

Government of Palestine. Department of Agriculture and Forests. *Agricultural Leaflet*(s) (Jerusalem, various years).

Government of Palestine. Department of Commerce and Industry. "Special Supplement: Life in an Agricultural District in Palestine." *Commercial Bulletin* (1922), pp. 172–78.

Government of Palestine. Department of Customs, Excise, and Trade. *First Census of Industries, Taken in 1928 by the Trade Section of the Department of Customs, Excise and Trade* (Jerusalem, 1929).

Government of Palestine. Department of Customs, Excise, and Trade. *Statistics of Imports, Exports, and Shipping* (Alexandria, various years).

Government of Palestine. Department of Education. *Annual Report* (Jerusalem, various years).

Government of Palestine. Department of Land and Survey. *Annual Reports* (Jerusalem, various years).

Government of Palestine. Department of Statistics. "Enumeration of Livestock." *General Monthly Bulletin of Current Statistics* (August 1943), pp. 237–47.

Government of Palestine. Department of Statistics in collaboration with the Department of Customs Excise and Trade. *Statistics of Foreign Trade* (Jerusalem, various years).

Government of Palestine. Department of Statistics. *General Monthly Bulletin of Current Statistics* (various months).

Government of Palestine. Department of Statistics. *National Income of Palestine 1944, P. J. Loftus, Government Statistician* (Jerusalem, 1946).

Government of Palestine. Department of Statistics. *Statistical Abstract of Palestine* (Jerusalem, various years).

Government of Palestine. Department of Statistics. *Survey of Social and Economic Conditions in Arab Villages, 1944: Special Bulletin No. 21* (Jerusalem, 1948).

Government of Palestine. Department of Statistics. *Village Statistics, 1937* (data collected in 1935: Jerusalem, 1937).

Government of Palestine. Department of Statistics. *Village Statistics, 1945* (Jerusalem, 1945).

Government of Palestine. Department of Statistics. *Vital Statistics Tables* (Jerusalem, 1947).

Government of Palestine. Department of Statistics on Behalf of the Controller of Manpower. *Survey of Skilled Tradesmen 1943* (Jerusalem, 1945).

Government of Palestine. *Explanatory Note on Land Settlement* (Jerusalem, undated).

Government of Palestine. *Memorandum on the Water Resources of Palestine* (Jerusalem, 1947).

Government of Palestine. Office of Statistics. "Statistics of Wage Rates in Palestine 1927–1935." *Wage Rate Statistics Bulletin,* no. 1 (1937), pp. 1–16.

Government of Palestine. *Ordinances: Annual Volume* (Jerusalem, various years).

Government of Palestine. *Ordinances, Regulations, Rules, Orders, and Notices* (various years).

Government of Palestine. *Palestine Census 1931: Household Schedule* (Jerusalem, 1931).

Government of Palestine. *The Palestine Gazette* [and *Supplement to the Palestine Gazette*] (Jerusalem, various dates).

Government of Palestine. Palestine Development Department. *Agricultural Development and Land Settlement in Palestine (First and Supplementary Reports), by Lewis French, Director of Development* (Jerusalem, 1931).

Government of Palestine. *Proclamations, Regulations, Rules, Orders and Notices: Annual Volumes* (Jerusalem, various years).

Government of Palestine. *Report and General Abstracts of the Census of 1922: Taken on the 23rd of October 1922; by J. B. Barron* (Jerusalem, 1923).

Government of Palestine. *Report by Mr. C. F. Strickland of the Indian Civil Service on the Possibility of Introducing a System of Agricultural Co-operation in Palestine* (Jerusalem, 1930).

Government of Palestine. *Report of a Committee on the Economic Condition of Agriculturists in Palestine and the Fiscal Measures of Government in Relation Thereto, W. J. Johnson, R. E. H. Crosbie et al.* (Jerusalem, 1930).

Government of Palestine. *Report on the Accounts and Finances, 1946–47* (Jerusalem, 1948).

Government of Palestine. *Statistics of Foreign Trade for the Years Ended 31st December, 1942 and 1943: Compiled and Published by the Department of Statistics in Collaboration with the Department of Customs, Excise and Trade* (Jerusalem, 1946).

Government of Palestine. *Supplement to Survey of Palestine: Notes Complied for the Information of the United Nations Special Committee on Palestine* (Jerusalem, 1947), p. 88.

Government of Palestine. *A Survey of Palestine: Prepared in December 1945 and January 1946 for the Information of the Anglo-American Committee of Inquiry* (Jerusalem, 1946).

Government of Palestine. *Wholesale Price Bulletin* (Jerusalem, 1936–1939).

Graham-Brown, Sarah. "The Political Economy of the Jabal Nablus, 1920–48." Roger Owen (ed.), *Studies in the Economic and Social History of Palestine in the Nineteenth and Twentieth Centuries* (Oxford, 1982), pp. 88–176.

Granovsky, Avraham. *Land Policy in Palestine* (New York, 1940).

Grant, Elihu. *The People of Palestine* (Philadelphia, 1921, reprinted 1976).

Great Britain. *Palestine Royal Commission Report* (London, 1937).

Great Britain. Colonial Office. *Report on Immigration, Land Settlement* and *Development, by Sir John Hope Simpson* (London, 1930).

Gross, T. Nacum. "Hamediniyut hakalkalit shel memshelet erez ishrael betkofat hamandat." Nacum T. Gross (ed.), *lo 'al haroach levada* (Jerusalem, 1999), pp. 172–227.

Gross, T. Nacum. *Lo 'al haroach levada* (Jerusalem, 1999).

Grossman, David. *Hakfar ha'aravi 7e-bnota7: tahaliḥim bayeshuv ha'aravi be-'erez ishra'el batqufa ha'otmanit* (Jerusalem, 1994).

Hakim, George, and M. Y. El-Hussayni. "Monetary and Banking System." Sa'id B. Himadeh (ed.), *Economic Organisation in Palestine* (Beirut, 1938), pp. 443–504.

Hardi, Noah. *Education in Palestine* (Washington, DC: Zionist Organization of America, 1945).

Harik, Iliya. "The Impact of the domestic Market on Rural-Urban Relations in the Middle East." Richard Anton and Iliya Harik (eds.), *Rural Politics and Social Change in the Middle East* (London, 1972), pp. 323–56.

Haykal, Yūsif. *Al-qaḍīyah al- filasṭīniyah: taḥlīl wa-naqd* (Jaffa, 1937).

Himadeh, Sa'id B. (ed.). *Economic Organisation in Palestine* (Beirut, 1938).

Himadeh, Sa'id B. "Natural Resources." Sa'id B. Himadeh (ed.), *Economic Organization in Palestine* (Beirut, 1938), pp. 41–72.

al-Ḥizmāwī, Mohammad. *Milkiyah al-arāḍī fī filasṭīn 1918–1948* (Acre, 1998).

Hobsbawn, E. J. *Bandits,* 2nd ed. (New York, 1981).

Horowitz, David, and Rita Hindan. *Economic Survey of Palestine* (Tel Aviv, 1938).

Hulten, Charles R. "Total Factor Productivity: A Short Biography." [U.S.] National Bureau of Economic Research, Working Paper 7471, January 2000, pp. 1–75.

Hurwitz, Shmuel. *Ḥaqla'ut ba-mizraḥ ha-*'aravi (Tel Aviv, 1966).

al-Ḥusayni, Moḥamad Yūnīs. *Al-tatwūr al-'ijtimā'ī fi filasṭīn al-'arabiyyah* (Jerusalem, 1946).

Imtiaz, Diyab. *'iṭr madinah yafa* (Nazareth, 1991).

Jewish Agency for Palestine. Department of Statistics. *Report and General Abstract of the Censuses of Jewish Agriculture, Industry and Handicrafts, and Labour* (Jerusalem, 1931).

Jewish Agency for Palestine. Economic Research Institute. *Jewish Agriculture in Palestine: A Progressive Factor in Middle East Economy, by Dr. Ludwig Samuel* (Jerusalem, 1946).

Jewish Agency for Palestine. Institute of Agriculture and Natural History. *The Fellah's Farm by I. Elazari-Volcani, Director of Agricultural Experiement Station* (Tel Aviv, 1930).

Jewish Agency for Palestine. *The Influence of Jewish Colonisation on Arab Development in Palestine* (Jerusalem, 1947).

Jewish Agency for Palestine. *Land and Agricultural Development in Palestine* (London, 1930).

Jewish Agency for Palestine. *Land Settlement, Urban Development and Immigration: Memorandum Submitted to Sir John Hope Simpson, C.I.E., Special Commissioner of His Majesty's Government, July 1930* (London, 1930).

Jewish Agency for Palestine. "The Palestinian Arabs under the British Mandate." *Palestine Papers,* No. 4 (London, 1930).

Kadish, Alon. "Ovdey maḥanot hazava kemiqre boḥan be-ḥeqer ha-ḥevra ha-falesṭinit" (forthcoming).

Kahneman, Daniel. "Maps of Bounded Rationality: A Perspective on Intuitive Judgment and Choice." Tore Frangsmyr (ed.), *Les Prix Nobel 2002* (Stockholm, 2003), pp. 416–99.

Kamen, Charles S. *Little Common Ground: Arab Agriculture and Jewish Settlement in Palestine, 1920–1948* (Pittsburgh, 1991).

Kanafānī, Ghasān. "Thawra 1936–39 fī filisṭin: khalfiyat watafāīṣil wataḥlīl." *Shu'ūn filisṭiniyah,* 6 (1972), pp. 35–77.

Kark, Ruth, and Haim Gerber. "Land Registry Maps in Palestine during the Ottoman Period." *Cartographic Journal,* no. 21 (1984), pp. 30–32.

Katz, Yossi. *Beḥazit haqarqa': qeren kayemet leyisrael beterem hamedina* (Jerusalem, 2001).

Kayyali, Abdul-Wahhab (ed.). *Watha'iq al-muqāwamāt al-filisṭiniyyah al-'arabiyyah ḍid al-'ikhtilāl al-brīṭanī wa-alṣahaynah* (Beirut, 1968).

Kayyali, Abdul-Wahhab Said. *Palestine: A Modern History* (Beirut, 1978).

Keen, B. A. *The Agricultural Development of the Middle East: A Report to the Director General Middle East Supply Centre, May 1945* (London, 1946).

Khalaf, Issa. "The Effect of Socioeconomic Change on Arab Social Collapse in Mandate Palestine." *International Journal of Middle Eastern Studies,* 29, no. 1 (1997), pp. 93–112.

Khalaf, Issa. *Politics in Palestine: Arab Factionalism and Social Disintegration 1939–1948* (New York, 1991).

Khalidi, Walied. *All That Remains: The Palestinian Villages Occupied and Depopulated by Israel in 1948* (Washington, DC, 1992).

Khalidi, Walied (ed.). *From Haven to Conquest: Readings in Zionism and the Palestine Problem until 1948* (Washington, DC, 1987).

Khūri, 'Imil. *Filisṭin 'abr sitin 'āmān* (Beirut, 1972).

Kimmerling, Barauch. *Zionism and Economy* (Cambridge, 1983).

Kligler, I. J., and A. Geiger. "An Inquiry into the Diets of Various Sections of the Urban and Rural Population of Palestine." *Bulletin of the Palestine Economic Society,* 5, no. 3 (1931), pp. 1–72.

Kno, Jack. *Ba'ayat haqarqa' basikhsokh hale'umi beyn yehudim le'aravim 1917–1990* (Tel Aviv, 1992).

Kolinsky, Martin. *Law, Order and Riots in Mandatory Palestine, 1928–35* (London, 1993).

Latron, André. *La vie rurale en Syrie et au Liban: Etude d'économie sociale* (Beirut, 1936).

Law Report of Palestine. *Current Law Report; Law Report of Palestine; Selected Cases of the District Courts of Palestine;* and *Collection of Judgements* (Jerusalem, various years).

League of Nations. International Labour Office. *Year-Book of Labour Statistics* (Geneva, 1937).

Lewis, William Arthur. "Economic Development with Unlimited Supplies of Labour." *Manchester School,* 22 (May 1954), pp. 139–91.

Lewis, William Arthur. *The Theory of Economic Growth* (London, 1956).

Little, M. Ian. *Economic Development: Theory, Policy and International Relations* (New York, 1982).

Ludwig, Samuel. *Jewish Agriculture in Palestine* (Jerusalem, 1946).

Lurie, Yehoshua. *'Ako 'ir haḥumut* (Tel Aviv, 2000).

Ma'oz, Moshe. *Ottoman Reforms in Syria and Palestine, 1840–1861* (Oxford, 1968).

Marshall, Alfred. *Principles of Economics,* 7th ed. (London, 1916).

Marx, Karl. "The Future Results of British Rule in India." *New York Daily Tribune* 8 August 1853, Reprinted in Avineiry, pp. 132–39.

McCarthy, Justin. *The Population of Palestine: Population History and Statistics of the Late Ottoman Period and the Mandate* (New York, 1990).

Metzer, Jacob. *The Divided Economy of Mandatory Palestine* (Cambridge, 1998).

Metzer, Jacob. "Fiscal Incidence and Resource Transfer between Jews and Arabs in Mandatory Palestine." *Research in Economic History,* no. 7 (1982), pp. 87–132.

Metzer, Jacob, and Oded Kaplan. *Mesheq yehudi 7e-mesheq 'aravi beerez ishrael: tozar ta'asuqa 7ezmiḥah betqufat hamandat* (Jerusalem, 1991).

Migdal, S. Joel. *Palestinian Society and Politics* (Princeton, 1980).

Miller, Ylana N. *Government and Society in Rural Palestine, 1920–1948* (Austin, TX, 1985).

Mubarak, Ali, and Derek Byerlee. "Economic Efficiency of Small

Farmers in a Changing World: A Survey of Recent Evidence." *Journal of International Development,* 3, no. 1 (1991), pp. 1–27.

Mundy, Martha. "La propriété dite *musha'* en Syrie: une note analytique à propos des travaux de Ya'akov Firestone." *Revue du Monde Musulman et de la Méditerrannée,* 79–80, no. 1–2 (1996), pp. 273–87.

Mundy, Martha. "Qada' 'Ajlun in the Late Nineteenth Century: Interpreting a Region from the Ottoman Land Registry." *Levant* 28 (1986), pp. 77–95.

Mundy, Martha. "Village Land and Individual Title: *Musha'* and Ottoman Land Registration in the 'Ajlun District." Eugene L. Rogan and Tariq Tell (eds.), *Village, Steppe and State: The Social Origins of Modern Jordan* (London, 1994), pp. 58–79.

Nadan, Amos. *The Arab Rural Economy in Mandate Palestine, 1921–1947: Peasants under Colonial Rule,* Ph.D. thesis, London School of Economics and Political Science, 2002.

Nadan, Amos. "Colonial Misunderstanding of an Efficient Peasant Institution: Land Settlement and *Mushā' Tenure in Mandate Palestine,* 1921–47." *Journal of the Economic and Social History of the Orient,* 46, no. 3 (2003), pp. 320–54.

Nadan, Amos. "From the Arab Revolt to al-Aqsa Intifada: The Economic and Social Dimensions." Tamar Yegnes (ed.), *From Intifada to War: Milestones in the Palestinian National Experience,* in Hebrew (Tel Aviv, 2003), pp. 53–85.

Nadan, Amos. "Reconsidering the Arab Human Development Report 2002." Amnon Cohen and Elie Podeh (eds.), *Israel, the Middle East and Islam* (Truman Institute, 2004 forthcoming).

Nair, Kusum. *In Defense of the Irrational Peasant* (Chicago, 1979).

Naor, Mordechi. *Hah'apala: 1934–1948,* 4th ed. (Tel Aviv, 1988).

Nevo, Yosef. "Medinot 'arav vereshit me'oravotan beshe'elat ereẓ ishrael." Yosef Nedava (ed.), *Sugiyot baẓiyunot, 1918–1948* (Haifa, 1979), pp. 63–80.

North, Douglas C. *Institutions, Institutional Change and Economic Performance* (Cambridge, 1990).

North, Douglass C. "The New Institutional Economics and Third World Development." John Harriss, Janet Hunter, and Colin M.

Lewis (eds.), *The New Institutional Economics and Third World Development* (London, 1995), pp. 17–26.

Olson, Mancur. *The Logic of Collective Action* (London, 1971).

Olson, Mancur. "The Varieties of Eurosclerosis: The Rise and the Decline of Nations since 1982," *Jean Monnet Chair Papers* 32 (1995), pp. 1–37.

Owen, Roger. "Economic Development in Mandate Palestine: 1918–1948." George T. Abed (ed.), *The Palestinian Economy: Studies in Development under Prolonged Occupation* (London, 1988), pp. 15–38.

Owen, Roger. *The Middle East in the World Economy, 1800–1914,* 2nd ed. (London, 1993).

Owen, Roger (ed.). *Studies in the Economic and Social History of Palestine in the Nineteenth and Twentieth Centuries* (Oxford, 1982).

Owen, Roger, and Sevket Pamunk. *A History of Middle East Economies in the Twentieth Century* (London, 1998).

Palestine Liberation Organization. Research Center Palestine Liberation Organization. *Village Statistics 1945: A Classification of Land and Area Ownership in Palestine, with Explanatory Notes by Sami Hadawi Official Land Valuer and Inspector of Tax assessments of the Palestine Government* (Beirut, 1970).

Patai, Raphael. "Musha'a Tenure and Co-operation in Palestine." *American Antropologist,* 51, no. 3 (1949), pp. 436–445.

Peretz, Don. "Problems of Arab Refugee Compensation." *Middle East Journal,* no. 8 (1954), pp. 403–416.

Popkin, Samuel L. *The Rational Peasant: The Political Economy of Rural Society in Vietnam* (London, 1979).

Porath, Yehoshua. *Mehamehumot lameridah: hatnu'a ha'aravit hapalestinit, 1929–1939* (Tel Aviv, 1978).

Porath, Yehoshua. "Social Aspects of the Emergence of the Palestinian Arab National Movement." Menahem Milsom (ed.), *Society and Political Structure in the Arab World* (New York, 1973).

Quateat, Donald. "Rural Unrest in the Ottoman Empire." Farhad Kazemi and John Waterbury (eds.), *Peasants and Politics in the Modern Middle East* (Miami, 1991), pp. 38–49.

Rabinowitz, Dan. *Antropologiya vepalesṭinim* (Ra'anana, 1998).

Raichman, Shalom. *Mema'aḥaz le'ereẓ moshav: yeẓirat hamapa hahityashvotit Be'eretz Israel 1918–1948* (Jerusalem, 1978).

Ray, Debraj. *Development Economics* (Princeton, 1998).

Reilly, James. "The Peasantry of Late Ottoman Palestine." *Journal of Palestine Studies,* 10, no. 4, issue 40 (1981), pp. 82–97.

Repetto et al. *Wasting Assets: Natural Resources in the National Accounts* (Washington, 1980).

Roman-Munoz, Ramon. "Specialization in the International Market for Olive Oil Before World War II." Sevek Pamuk and Jeffrey G. Williamson (eds.), *The Mediterranean Response to Globalization before 1950* (London, 2000), pp. 159–98.

Romer, Paul M. "Endogenous Technological Change." *Journal of Political Economy,* 98, no. 5 (1990), pp. S71–S102.

Rostow, Walt W. *The Stages of Economic Growth: A Non-Communist Manifesto,* 2nd ed. (Cambridge, 1960).

Ruttan, Vernon W., and Yujiro Hayami. "Toward a Theory of Induced Institutional Innovation." *Journal of Development Studies,* 20, no. 4 (1984), pp. 203–23.

Said, Edward. *Orientalism* (London, 1978).

Sawwaf, Husni. "International Trade." Sa'id B. Himadeh (ed.), *Economic Organization of Palestine* (Beirut, 1938), pp. 387–441.

Sayigh, Rosemary. *Palestinians: From Peasants to Revolutionaries* (London, 1979).

Schaebler, Birgit. "Practicing *Musha':* Common Lands and the Common Good in Southern Syria under the Ottomans and the French." Roger Owen (ed.), *New Perspectives on Property and Land in the Middle East* (Harvard, 2000), pp. 241–307.

Schölch, Alexander. "European Penetration and the Economic Development of Palestine, 1856–82." Roger Owen (ed.), *Studies in the Economic and Social History of Palestine in the Nineteenth and Twentieth Centuries* (Oxford, 1982), pp. 10–87.

Schultz, Theodore W. *Transforming Traditional Agriculture* (London, 1964).

Scott, James C. *The Moral Economy of the Peasant: Rebellion and Subsistence in Southeast Asia* (London, 1976).

Sdomi, Isaac. *Shiyaḥ rishonim* (Rechovot, 1988).

Sela, Avraham. "*Kalkalat* haseqṭor ha'aravi be-'erez ishra'el betqufat hamandaṭ." Riv'on lekalkalah, no. 103 (1979), pp. 407–19; and no. 104, 1980, pp. 66–79.

Shepherd, Dawson. "Some Aspects of Irrigation in Palestine," *Palestine and Middle East Economic Magazine,* 8 (February 1933), pp. 63–65.

Shepherd, Naomi. *Ploughing Sand: British Rule in Palestine 1917–1948* (New Brunswick, 2000).

Singer, Amy. *Palestinian Peasants and Ottoman Officials: Rural Administration around Sixteenth-Century Jerusalem* (Cambridge, 1994).

Smelansky, M. "Jewish Colonisation and the Fellah." *Palestine and the Near East,* 5, no. 8 (May 1930), pp. 146–59.

Smith, Charles D. *Palestine and the Arab-Israeli Conflict* (New York, 1996).

Solow, Robert M. "A Contribution to the Theory of Economic Growth." *Quarterly Journal of Economics,* 70 (1956), pp. 65–94.

Spalding, William F. *Tate's Modern Cambist,* 29th ed., (New York, 1929).

State of Israel. Central Bureau of Statistics. "Jewish Agricultural Production by Branches (1936/37, 1943/44, 1947/48)." *Statistical Bulletin of Israel,* 1, no. 1 (July 1949), pp. 34–45.

Stein, Kenneth W. "Hitpatḥuyot bakalkalah hakafrit ha'aravit be'erez yishrael (1917–1939) vemashma'uteyhen haḥevratiyot vehapolitiyot." *Qathedra,* 41 (October 1986), pp. 133–54.

Stein, Kenneth W. "Palestine's Rural Economy, 1917–1939." *Studies in Zionism,* 8, no. 1 (Spring 1987), pp. 25–49.

Stein, Kenneth W. "The Intifada and the 1936–1939 Uprising: A Comparison." *Journal of Palestine Studies,* 19, no. 4, issue 76 (1990), pp. 65–85.

Stein, Kenneth W. *The Land Question in Palestine, 1917–1939,* 2nd ed. (London, 1985).

Stiglitz, Joseph E. "Incentives and Risk Sharing in Sharecropping." *Review of Economic Studies,* 42, no. 2 (1974), pp. 219–55.

Sussman, Zvi. "The Determination of Wages for Unskilled Labour in the Advanced Sector of the Dual Economy of Mandatory Palestine."

Economic Development and Cultural Change, 22, no. 1 (1993), pp. 95–113.

Swedenberg, Ted. "The Role of the Palestinian Peasantry in the Great Revolt (1936–39)." Ilan Pappe (ed.), *The Israel/Palestine Question* (London, 1999), pp. 129–67.

Šandūq al-'ummah al-'arabiyyah, taqrīr majlis al-aidārah al-mukarrim 'ila al-jam'iyyah al-'umūmiyyah al-'ādiyyah lil-'ai'ādah sanah 1945 (Jerusalem, 1946).

Taminian, Lucine. "Ain." Martha Mundy and Richard S. Smith (eds.), *Part-Time Farming: Agricultural Development in the Zarqa River Basin, Jordan* (Irbid, 1990), pp. 13–59.

Taqqu, Rachelle Leah. *Arab Labor in Mandatory Palestine, 1920–1948*. Ph.D. thesis, Columbia University, 1977.

Taqqu, Rachelle. "Internal Labor Migration and the Arab Village Community under the Mandate." Joel S. Migdal (ed.), *Palestinian Society and Politics* (Princeton, NJ, 1980), pp. 261–85.

Taysir, Nashif. "Palestinian Arab and the Jewish Leadership in the Mandate Period." *Journal of Palestine Studies,* 6, no. 4 (1977), pp. 113–21.

Tessler, Mark. *A History of the Israeli-Palestinian Conflict* (Indianapolis, 1994).

Todaro, P. Micheal. *Economic Development,* 6th ed. (New York, 1997).

Tyler, Warwick P. N. *State Lands and Rural Development in Mandatory Palestine, 1920–1948* (Brighton, 2001).

UNDP. *Human Development Report 1990* (Oxford: Oxford University Press, 1990).

UNDP. *Human Development Report 2002* (Oxford: Oxford University Press, 2002).

UNDP's website: http://www.undp.org.

Vashitz, Joseph. "Temurut ḥevratiyut bayeshuv ha'aravī shel ḥeyfah betqufat hamandaṭ habriṭī: soḥarīm ve-yazamīm aḥerīm." Avi Bareli and Nahum Karlinsky (eds.), *Khalkhala veḥevra betqufat hamandaṭ* (Jerusalem, 2003), pp. 393–38.

Warriner, Doreen. *Land and Poverty in the Middle East* (London, 1948).

Warriner, Doreen. "Land Tenure Problems in the Fertile Crescent in the Nineteenth and Twentieth Centuries." Charles Issawi (ed.), *The Economic History of the Middle East* (London, 1966), pp. 71–78.

Weinstock, Natan. "The Impact of Zionist Colonization on Palestinian Arab Society before 1948." *Journal of Palestine Studies,* 2, no. 2 (1973), pp. 49–63.

Wilmington, Martin W. *The Middle East Supply Centre* (London, 1971).

Wilson, Charles Thomas. *Peasant Life in the Holy Land* (London, 1906).

Wilson, Rodney. *Banking and Finance in the Arab Middle East* (New York, 1983).

Wolf, Eric R. *Peasants* (New Jersey, 1966).

Worthington, E. B. *Middle East Science, A Survey of Subjects Other Than Agriculture: A Report to the Director General, Middle East Centre* (Oxford, 1946).

Yāsin, Šubḥī. *Al-thawra al-'arabiyyah al-kubra' fī filisṭin 1936–1939* (Cairo, 1967).

Yazbaq, Mahmoud. *Hahagira ha'aravit leḥeyfa beyn hashanim 1933–1948.* Master's thesis, University of Haifa, 1986.

Yazbaq, Mahmoud. "Hahagira ha'aravit leḥeyfa 1933–1948: *Nituḥ 'al-pi meqorot 'arviyim.*" *Qatedra,* 45 (1987), pp. 131–46.

Zacharia, Shabtai. *Soḥarim veba'aley melakhah yehudiyim beyerushalayim ha'atikah ba'var* (Jerusalem, 2002).

al-Ẓāhir, 'Alī Nasūj. *Shajārah al-zaytūn: tārīkhhā zirā'thā, 'amrāḍihā, ṣinā'thā* (Amman, 1947).

Zinger, Avraham. *Gidul Ha-Zayit* (Tel Aviv, 1985).

Zu'bi, Nahla. "The Development of Capitalism in Palestine: The Expropriation of the Palestinian Direct Producers." *Journal of Palestine Studies,* 13, no. 4, issue 52 (1984), pp. 88–109.

Index